INNOVATION ECONOMICS

ROBERT D. ATKINSON AND STEPHEN J. EZELL

Innovation
Economics

THE RACE FOR
GLOBAL ADVANTAGE

Yale UNIVERSITY PRESS

NEW HAVEN AND LONDON

Published with assistance from the foundation established in memory of Philip Hamilton McMillan of the Class of 1894, Yale College.

Yale University Press books may be purchased in quantity for educational, business, or promotional use. For information, please e-mail sales.press@yale.edu (U.S. office) or sales@yaleup.co.uk (U.K. office).

Set in Scala type by Westchester Book Group
Printed in the United States of America

Library of Congress Cataloging-in-Publication Data

Atkinson, Robert D.
    Innovation economics : the race for global advantage /
Robert D. Atkinson and Stephen J. Ezell.
        p. cm.
    Includes bibliographical references and index.
    ISBN 978-0-300-16899-0 (cloth : alk. paper)
    1. Technological innovations—Economic aspects—United States.
    2. Technological innovations—Economic aspects.   3. Diffusion of
innovations—United States.   4. Industrial policy—United States.
    I. Ezell, Stephen J.   II. Title.
    HC110.T4 A8187 2012
    338'.0640973—dc23

                                                2012006642

A catalogue record for this book is available from the British Library.

This paper meets the requirements of ANSI/NISO Z39.48–1992
(Permanence of Paper).

10 9 8 7 6 5 4 3 2 1

As Winston Churchill wrote, "Writing a book is an adventure. To begin with, it is a toy and an amusement; then it becomes a mistress, and then it becomes a master, and then a tyrant." I want to extend my deepest appreciation to my wife Anne-Marie, son David, and daughter Claire, who were more than patient with me when I was struggling with my tyrant, instead of being the husband and Dad I would have liked to be.

—RDA

To my wife Lisa, for your enduring love, patience, and support; and to my parents, for a lifetime of inspiration.

—SJE

CONTENTS

The Race for Global
Innovation Advantage

T he so-called Great Recession that convulsed the U.S. economy
        from the end of 2007 to the middle of 2009 has been officially
        over for several years, but for most Americans it certainly doesn't
feel that way. The official unemployment rate still hovers around 8.5 percent, and if the part-time workers who would rather be working full-time
were included, the rate would be almost double.[1] In fact, the Congressional
Budget Office reported in February 2012 that after three years with unemployment topping 8 percent, the United States has seen the longest period
of high unemployment since the Great Depression, yet it still expects that
unemployment will remain above 8 percent through 2014.[2] Less than two-
thirds of adults are in the labor force, a twenty-five-year low.[3] Worse, from
2000 to 2010, the United States did not add a single net new job.[4] Both the
federal budget and trade deficits remain unsustainably high. U.S. companies are sitting on, rather than investing, close to $2 trillion in cash reserves.
And some regions remain mired in recession, with many cities, towns, and
even states on the brink of bankruptcy.

By most accounts, this is all the result of an uncommonly severe but ultimately survivable financial crisis, akin to the destruction wrought by a

category 5 hurricane—immense, more or less random, but with rebuilding and recovery largely assured. Economic pundits tell us that we can expect things to get back to "normal," eventually. Housing prices will go back up, unemployment will go down, and economic confidence will return, if slowly.

But neither the recession nor the slow recovery can be attributed simply to a random financial crisis caused by the burst housing bubble. Rather, we argue that a major contributing factor has been the United States falling behind in the race for global innovation advantage. Indeed, since the late 1990s especially, the United States has been losing out to other nations with respect to competitiveness and innovation, the result of too few resources going to wealth-creating investments like research and factories and too many resources going to a housing-market Ponzi scheme. America lost almost one-third of its manufacturing jobs from 2000 to 2011, while it ranked forty-third out of forty-four nations in the rate of progress in innovation-based competitiveness.[5] Until U.S. policymakers grasp and act on this fundamental reality, we can expect recovery to be anemic and the United States to continue to lose ground relative to most other nations. Recovery will depend on two mutually reinforcing factors: a faith that America will once again lead in the global innovation economy and sufficient private and public investments in research, plant and equipment, skills, and infrastructure to realize that vision.

It's not that America hasn't faced competition before. It has. But this time it's different. Since the mid-1990s, nations around the world have accelerated their efforts to lead in innovation-based economic development (e.g., by gaining jobs in key sectors like computers and software, aviation, pharmaceuticals and biotechnology, machine tools, medical devices, instruments, and clean energy). Ever since World War II (WWII), when America's arsenal of democracy helped defeat the Axis powers, high-tech sectors had been America's sweet spot. While America might lose textile jobs or call centers, it was still the dominant technology leader. Indeed, as late as the 1960s, U.S. government funding of research and development (R&D) exceeded that of all other nations' R&D funding—business and government—combined.

But starting in the 1980s and accelerating rapidly in the new century, that all began to change. While other nations were now setting their sights on winning the race for global innovation advantage, America was asleep, convinced of its own innate economic superiority and preoccupied by the challenge of the "War on Terror" and conflicts between "Red" and "Blue" states over a range of hot-button social issues. Losing this race will have profound implications for the future of the American economy and society. This book examines how America is losing the race for global innovation advantage and what it needs to do to come from behind and lead once again.

From Rust Belt to Rust Nation

To understand what's happened to the American economy, we need to look back forty years to the early 1970s. People were driving Gran Torinos, listening to eight-track tapes, and wearing long sideburns. But the United States was enjoying the fruits of a twenty-five-year postwar economic boom during which real per capita gross domestic product (GDP) exploded, jobs were plentiful, and tens of millions of American households were vaulted into the middle class. But starting with the recession of 1969 (the longest since 1949) and then the much longer and deeper recession of 1974 (the longest since the Great Depression), that robust economic performance began to falter, leading many to question if the good times were over.

For America as a whole, the answer was an emphatic no. Things did keep getting better. Indeed, growth even accelerated from 1975 to 1985. But underneath this apparently healthy national growth was a troubling phenomenon—the emergence of two quite different economies: a slower-growing industrial Midwest and Northeast and a faster-growing South and West. After WWII and until the end of the 1960s, these regions grew at about the same rate.[6] But starting in the 1970s and through the mid-1980s, the former areas downshifted into slow growth, with a struggling industrial belt from western Massachusetts to northern Wisconsin and down to St. Louis.[7] Portrayed in rock ballads like Billy Joel's "Allentown" or Bruce Springsteen's "My Hometown," places that had grown in the twentieth century to become industrial powerhouses, providing a path to the American Dream for millions of workers, now faced shuttered factories, boarded-up homes, and shattered lives. But while these areas struggled, regions like the Rocky Mountains and the West boomed, growing 37 percent and 27 percent faster than the nation, respectively.[8]

Cities that had once powered America's Industrial Revolution were now struggling for their economic lives. Take Buffalo, New York, for example. Buffeted by factories moving to the South and West, Buffalo's total income grew at less than half the rate of Brownsville, Texas, from 1969 to 1986. While Brownsville saw its jobs grow by 75 percent, Buffalo saw its jobs decline by 1 percent. Likewise, Syracuse, New York, home in the early twentieth century to companies that manufactured more diverse products than New York City, saw its income grow just 53 percent as fast as that of Santa Fe, New Mexico, with jobs growing just 28 percent compared to Santa Fe's 124 percent.

In short, entire regions never again experienced the robust growth rates they enjoyed in the century following the Civil War; they suffered deindustrialization, job loss, and fiscal crises. So if you were in Buffalo, Syracuse, or similar places, things probably weren't so good. But if you were in Brownsville, Santa Fe, or other growing places, things were likely good and getting better. Indeed, if the South had won the Civil War, economic historians might be writing about the economic decline of the United States after the 1960s and the boom of the Confederate States of America. Instead, they talk about overall modest U.S. growth.

There was a variety of reasons for the emergence of these two American economies, but a key one was that it *could* happen. With the completion of the Interstate Highway System in the 1970s, the emergence of jet travel, and nationwide electrification and telephone access, companies in traded sectors now had the freedom to locate almost anywhere in the United States. And they did so, with factories migrating away from the Northeast and Midwest to the South and the West. Combined with this was the emergence of new high-growth industries (e.g., electronics, aviation, and instruments) that didn't need to be located at the ports or rail spurs in the Midwest and East. Couple this with the high costs and lack of competitiveness of the "rust belt" region, and the implications were clear.

This process has played out once again in the 2000s, but on the global level. This time, it's the United States that has become the Great Lakes from a geoeconomic perspective. "Rust belt" is now "rust nation." Santa Fe has become the Syracuse of its day, with Shanghai the Santa Fe. Brownsville has become the Buffalo of its day and Bangalore, India, the Brownsville.

Places like North Carolina and Georgia, which benefited from the shift of manufacturing from the North from the 1940s to the 1970s, have seen their own textile, furniture, and other traditional factories move to lower-wage nations. Today, container ships, air freight, the development of the Internet, and undersea fiber-optic cables have linked together not just state economies but also national ones. In essence, what was once a set of separate national economies in the 1970s has evolved into a single integrated global economy in the twenty-first century. And other parts of the world are now the economic engines, growing much faster than the United States (or Europe or Japan).

When Northeast and Midwest states realized their factories could relocate anywhere in the country, they began to compete fiercely with each other to attract those "smokestacks." Emblematic of efforts of the day, a 1954 issue of *Fortune* magazine included a full-page ad from the state of Indiana that touted its benefits as a location of corporate investment, including attractors such as "no government debt," a labor force that was "97 percent native" (with the implication that native-born workers were less likely to strike than immigrants), low taxes, and ample supplies of raw materials, calling itself "the clay capital of the world." By the 1970s, virtually every state had established an economic development agency whose mission was to go out and compete with an arsenal of tools ranging from tax breaks, to free land, to workforce training programs.

In today's global economy, nations must compete fiercely to retain and attract mobile investment. But in contrast to states competing by "smokestack chasing" forty years ago, most nations now compete by "innovation chasing," trying to grow and attract the highest-value-added economic activity they can: the high-wage, knowledge-intensive manufacturing, research, software, information technology (IT), and services jobs that power today's global, innovation-based economy. Indiana is a case in point. It no longer touts its abundant clay, but now markets itself as a place "where innovation, discovery, and success are nurtured," and "that provides a pipeline of bright minds and new thinking."

It is this intense race for global innovation advantage that most clearly distinguishes today's global economy from the collection of regional and national economies that competed to attract "smokestacks" a generation ago. As a February 2012 *Washington Post* article noted, "Europe, as well as Asia and Latin America, is offering ever stronger competition to the United States, even in its strongest sectors, such as Internet technology, aerospace, and pharmaceuticals."[9] And it's not a competition for the faint of heart. In fact, it makes the World Cup look like a kids' playground game, for the struggle for innovation advantage is being fought with all the tools at a nation's disposal. Nations around the world are establishing national innovation strategies, restructuring their tax and regulatory systems to become more competitive, expanding support for science and technology, improving their education systems, spurring investments in broadband and other IT areas, and taking a myriad of other pro-innovation steps. But unlike the old competition between the U.S. states, where they generally played by national rules established in the Constitution, a new approach, "innovation mercantilism"—which can entail stealing intellectual property (IP), discriminating against foreign technology firms, requiring foreign firms to transfer technology for market access, or manipulating currency—has become a mainstay of many nations' game plans in the new global competition.

Yet, notwithstanding the intensity of this new competition, as recently as fifteen years ago, many nations did not even think they were competing. And if they did acknowledge a contest, they thought they were in last century's quest for smokestack industries like steel mills, shipbuilding, textiles, and other labor- and/or capital-intensive industries. Today, however, most nations recognize that they have to be intense competitors if they are to be successful, as more and more firms can now produce goods and services virtually anywhere on the globe. And most nations also realize that high-wage innovation- and knowledge-based industries play a key role in driving prosperity. There are now only a few nations still blind to these new realities, and unfortunately the United States is one. A bit like the old car rental commercial from the 1970s, the United States still thinks of itself as Hertz ("We're number one"), while most other nations think they are Avis, and as number two, they must try harder.

So where does this leave the United States and, for that matter, older industrial regions like Europe and Japan? Looking back to the United States of the mid-1970s, it's important to note that not all Northeast-Midwest regions were fated to relative decline. Some, in fact, transformed themselves and thrived. A case in point is Boston, which like Buffalo lost much of its industry to the South, especially textile and shoe firms in search of cheap labor. Boston looked like it was on the same path to decline as Buffalo. But unlike Buffalo, Boston reinvented itself. With the growth of the cold war and defense spending, Boston's early success in electronics (much of it a spin-off from the Massachusetts Institute of Technology) enabled a thriving tech industry. Its long-standing strength in financial services provided a base for expansion. But by the mid-1980s, Boston's future again looked troubled. Much of the region's computer industry had placed its bets on the minicomputer, and firms like Data General, Digital Equipment Corporation (DEC), and Wang all went into bankruptcy with the emergence of the California-based personal computer (PC) industry, centered in the more dynamic Silicon Valley. But Boston would rebound again around its three long-standing pillars: leading-edge research universities, a large number of talented and well-educated residents, and a venture capital industry willing to invest in the future. By the 2000s, the region's IT industry had reinvented itself. Boston also became one of the world's leading hubs of biotechnology. And it retained a strong financial services sector. Indeed, if Massachusetts were a nation, it would be the most innovative nation on earth, according to the Information Technology and Innovation Foundation's (ITIF's) *Atlantic Century II* report.

So if Boston could rebound to win the race, can the United States? Indeed, perhaps the single most important question confronting the United States (as well as Europe and Japan) is whether over the course of the next quarter century it will become Boston and rise from its decline through innovation and economic transformation, or Buffalo and sink further into relative economic decline.

"Becoming Boston" means moving aggressively into next-generation industries, including advanced IT, biotechnology, nanotechnology, robotics, and high-level business services, while at the same time maintaining a share of highly efficient and competitive traditional industries (such as autos, machine tools, chemicals, and so forth), and continually raising productivity in "nontraded" sectors such as retail and health care. "Becoming Buffalo" implies losing out in the competition for new, globally traded industries, continuing to lose shares in existing manufacturing industries, and experiencing slow productivity growth in nontraded sectors. Becoming Boston means putting in place an aggressive national innovation-based economic strategy, which includes both increased government investment in innovation and lower taxes on corporate investment in innovation. Becoming Buffalo implies doing what we've been doing: cutting government investment in innovation while seeing our overall corporate tax system become less competitive compared to other nations as each year goes by. Becoming Boston means waking up to the crisis, becoming full-throated advocates—indeed, zealots—for innovation, and embracing a new kind of economics ("innovation economics"), which puts advancing innovation and competitiveness at the forefront of economic policy. Becoming Buffalo means continuing in our somnolence about the nature of the global race for innovation, erecting barriers to innovation, and placing our faith in a neoclassical economics dogma that holds that countries don't compete, that innovation is "manna from heaven," and that government action to spur innovation only makes things worse. To be sure, Boston's academic infrastructure made the region ripe for innovation, but the fact remains that Boston and Buffalo took very different approaches and this has made all the difference. And the United States can do the same; or not.

Outline of the Book

This book takes up the central questions and critical issues of the new race for global innovation advantage: who is winning and why; who is losing and why; and what the United States, other nations, and indeed the world community need to do to maximize innovation and economic growth (see www.globalinnovationrace.com).

Because innovation is our theme, it's important to describe up front what we mean and do not mean by innovation. We are not just referring to some kind of esoteric activity to develop the latest electronic apparatus in a place like Silicon Valley. Innovation is that, of course, but it is much, much more. By innovation we mean the development and widespread adoption of new kinds of products, production processes, services, and business and organizational models. It is a new John Deere cotton harvester that is chock-full of computing power and a precision GPS location system that is accurate to several inches. It is a small factory that uses advanced computer-controlled machining cells that are twice as productive as the ones they replaced. It is the travel industry relying much more on the Internet and kiosks for self-service. In other words, innovation is bringing to production, to the market-place, and to society new products, processes, services, and functionalities that consumers and organizations find useful and valuable. It is this kind of innovation that is at the heart of national and global economic prosperity.

And it is in this kind of innovation that the United States is increasingly falling behind. As we document in chapter 2, after at least a fifty-year run, the United States is no longer the global innovation leader. Whether it's the rapid and precipitous decline of manufacturing, the more rapid growth of R&D overseas, or the relative decline in the number of scientists and engineers, the United States is getting left behind in the new race for global innovation advantage. And, as we describe, it's this lackluster performance, particularly since 2000, that led Wall Street—an industry stuck on an autopilot that refused to downsize, even when the need for its services had contracted—to think it could make money issuing mortgages to people who couldn't afford them, as "real" investment opportunities dried up. Wall Street's massive misallocation of investment capital was both a key contributing factor and cause as the United States experienced a relative decline during this period that only one other medium- to large-sized nation—Great Britain in the 1960s and 1970s—has ever before encountered in modern times.

As we discuss in chapter 3, America is not the first country to experience rapid industrial decline; the United Kingdom did so a generation ago. And the similarities in the nature and causes of the decline experienced by both the United States and the United Kingdom are truly striking. Both nations failed to enact the right innovation-supporting policies, and both have paid the price with industrial decline. Remarkably, virtually all the factors that historians and economists attribute to the causes of British industrial decline match the U.S. experience. Despite the fact that the two nations experienced decline in wholly different time periods, the same suite of twenty major causes operated in each case. This suggests that industrial decline (and industrial success) is perhaps not all that much of a mystery, a topic we readdress in chapter 8.

But while the evidence of relative industrial decline is crystal clear to anyone who chooses to look, most U.S. economic pundits, policymakers, and academic economists remain in denial. In chapter 4, we discuss the myths, nostrums, and dogmas that all too often pass for reasoned economic analysis, including the top eight reasons why the Alfred E. Neuman–like deniers say, "What, me worry?" and why in each case they are wrong. This speaks to a central challenge facing the United States and, for that matter, all nations: success for any organization, whether a company or a nation, depends first and foremost on an ability to challenge status quo thinking, for "groupthink" leads individuals to believe that they know what the problem is (or worse, that there is no problem in the first place). As Henry Ford once said, "Thinking is the hardest work there is, which is probably the reason why so few engage in it." For any nation to win in the race for innovation advantage, it has to start with thinking and, where necessary, challenging the prevailing thinking.

Challenging prevailing, out-of-date thinking is innovation in its own right, but innovation is more than that. Chapter 5 discusses and defines innovation, and how it has now become the key factor in determining most nations' economic success. While organizations (and entrepreneurial individuals) drive innovation, it is nations that enable, support, and spur it on, or restrict, hinder, and retard it. Because of that, innovation policy—the constellation of government policies from tax, to trade, to talent, to technology that support a nation's innovation ecosystem—has become the single most important factor nations need to get right if they are to thrive in the globally competitive economy. Thus, chapter 5 also defines and describes innovation policy, countering the conventional neoclassical economists who assert that "markets always get it right" by explaining the myriad ways that markets acting alone underproduce innovation and, by extension, economic welfare. Innovation is not producing "widgets" (what most economists study). It's vastly more complex and subject to such a large array of market failures that it makes more sense to talk about how policy can maximize the performance of innovation systems, rather than remedy an occasional "market failure." Chapter 6 follows on this discussion of the need for innovation policy by examining the innovation strategies that scores of countries have implemented to strengthen their nations' innovation ecosystems.

Given how important innovation policy is, it is perhaps surprising how many nations get it wrong. As nations struggle for innovation advantage, a growing number have adopted what we call "innovation mercantilism." These are zero-sum, beggar-thy-neighbor innovation policies that seek to attract or to grow high-wage industries and jobs at the expense of other nations and in violation of the spirit and/or letter of the law of the global trading system, thus making the global economy less prosperous and more fragile in the process. Whereas chapter 6 discusses the best examples from around the world of nations' constructive or "good" innovation policies, chapter 7 chronicles the worst "bad" innovation policies that an increasing number of nations, led by China, are relying on.

As the discussion of nations' good innovation policies in chapter 6 suggests, there are a number of innovation-supporting policies countries can implement. However, the United States has not been doing what it should. Based on these insights and on the particular challenges facing the United States, chapter 8 lays out a detailed innovation policy road map explaining how the United States can regain the lead in the race for global innovation advantage and, in so doing, turn around its economy both in the long term and the short term. This road map is based on what we term the eight "I's" of innovation policy: Inspiration, Intention, Insight, Incentives, Institutions, Investment, Information Technology, and International.

It's one thing to lay out a road map for renewal and recovery and quite another for the United States or any nation to follow it, for the political economy of innovation and innovation policy is a difficult one, chock-full of barriers, roadblocks, and pitfalls. Chapter 9 explores these challenges, and chapters 10 and 11, respectively, lay out a path forward, for nations and for the world as a whole. As chapter 9 explains, incumbents at risk of becoming tomorrow's "buggy whip" industries raise many of the obstacles to innovation and innovation policy. But in many nations these barriers also increasingly come from ideological resistors: "neo-Luddites" who fear change, prefer the stability of the past, and actively seek laws and regulations to impede innovation. This is a futile and counterproductive endeavor. As noted urbanist

Lewis Mumford once observed, "Traditionalists are pessimists about the future and optimists about the past."[10] Unfortunately, in too many nations, including the United States, the traditionalists have come to dominate.

And, of course, any discussion of innovation and innovation policy would not be complete without a discussion of economics and economists. More than any other intellectual force today, at least in the United States and most other Anglo-Saxon nations, conventional economists (known as neoclassical economists) remain the most powerful intellectual force working against robust innovation policies. Fundamentally, the neoclassical economics guild (and it is just that, for the majority of their claims are not science in the sense of physics or biology) neither understands nor appreciates innovation. To the extent that neoclassicists even consider innovation, most believe it is "manna from heaven" that government cannot influence.[11] But they go even further and argue that most government policy to get more innovation will likely do more harm than good by distorting "allocation efficiency" (the process by which markets use prices to efficiently allocate goods, services, labor, and other factors). This twentieth-century conceptualization of the economy has been overthrown in many nations by a new "innovation economics" that understands innovation and the role of organizations, including government, in spurring it and gets that letting market forces alone prevail will lead to innovation underperformance. Yet the economists who dominate economic policy thinking in Anglo-Saxon nations remain wedded to an old economy, not the new twenty-first-century one, and so cannot be relied upon to guide economic policy if the goal is to win the race for global innovation advantage and maximize economic growth. Finally, innovation policy is a subset of economic policy, and economic policy is made in the context of politics. At least in the United States, the politics of innovation policy are difficult, for one political party distrusts business and the other government, while both have vocal and powerful constituencies pressing for government to redistribute wealth rather than to grow it through innovation.

What then are the prospects for global innovation and the race for global innovation advantage for individual nations? Winning the race requires an entrepreneurial and competent business community willing to make investments in innovation that may not pay off in the next quarter or year. But it also requires a government willing to craft and implement effective innovation policies. As chapter 10 explains, for nations to succeed at innovation, they must master the "Innovation Triangle," which means getting the factors right to support a robust business environment, regulatory environment, and innovation policy environment. Some nations do well on one or even two of these factors, but no nation yet gets all three right.

And, ultimately, whether nations can engender a robust innovation economy or not hinges on whether they can balance the innovation "yin and yang" between: individual freedom versus collective action; the interests of the current generation versus those of the next; and the desire for stability and security versus the dynamic change that innovation brings. Nations that can find balance between these competing interests are likely to excel. But today neither of the two heavyweights on the global scene—the United States and China—get it right. For the United States, the pendulum has shifted dramatically to the individual freedom and current generation side. Indeed, as the United States has become a society focused on "Me, now!" crafting a politics of collective sacrifice for future innovation and competitiveness is exceedingly difficult, whether it's to drive down the value of the dollar, to reduce government spending, to raise personal taxes in order to lower corporate taxes, or to increase investment in science, technology, and infrastructure. This, more than any other factor, may be at the heart of America's economic failure. After all, the United States was able to dominate the world economically after WWII precisely because it had found a way to balance "me" and "us," and "today" and "the future."

China, in contrast, faces the opposite challenge. If it's to ultimately thrive in the global innovation economy, it must enable individual freedom, creativity, and entrepreneurship, and get out from under the yoke of overly centralized state direction. At the same time, it needs to focus more on the needs of the present generation, instead of depriving it as China does for the sake of some distant future generation. Running massive trade surpluses but failing to invest those surpluses in domestic innovation and more vibrant consumer markets ironically risks not only reducing China's long-term innovation but also its short-term prosperity. Given these factors, chapter 10 assesses the prospects for major regions of the world—North America, Europe, Japan, China, India, and Latin America—in the race for innovation advantage.

Finally, any race, whether in sports or economics, is more enjoyable to watch and participate in if there are rules that participants must abide by, in particular, rules that make contenders work harder and perform better. But as we argue in chapter 11, the rules guiding the global economy and the economic interactions between nations today are woefully outmoded, having been created for a postwar world of commodity trade, not a twenty-first-century world driven by the race for global innovation advantage. The leading international economic organizations established after WWII—the International Monetary Fund (IMF), the World Bank, and the World Trade Organization (WTO; previously the General Agreement on Tariffs and Trade)—have failed to create the conditions and frameworks needed to maximize global innovation and productivity. As a result, the outmoded and inadequate rules governing this competition put some nations, including the United States, at an unfair disadvantage, and constrain overall global innovation and productivity growth. Innovation is now too linked together globally for the world to approach it with national frameworks alone. If we are to maximize global prosperity and innovation, we will need to collectively develop and abide by a new global innovation framework that provides real incentives for nations to pursue win-win innovation strategies. To date, the major multilateral organizations have failed in the task.

At the end of the day, the new race for global innovation advantage is so different from past experience that it calls into question what passes for conventional wisdom on the economy and economic policy. This is particularly true for the United States, which still persists in seeing the world as if it is not in competition with other nations. The new race for global innovation advantage also calls into question traditional liberal and social democratic views that working-class prosperity and corporate profits are antithetical. For, unless nations design policies that make their economic environments conducive to investment in innovation by companies, and especially by multinational corporations, workers will be the ones who suffer because they are the ones who have a hard time moving. But it equally calls into question traditional conservative free market views that less government (as opposed to smarter, more strategic government) is the key to economic success. In the race for global innovation advantage, the key is for governments to be partners with their nations' business enterprises (especially its traded-sector business enterprises) in the sense of providing the right tax, regulatory, public investment, and trade policy environment for success.

Organizing to win the race—or at least to not fall farther behind—requires that nations take a number of difficult actions. They must have the right framework to think about winning, especially because the global race for innovation limits what nations can do if they want to be successful, forcing them to behave like organizations. And the success of organizations (whether for profit or nonprofit) depends on two factors: investing for the future and continually innovating. Nations that do not organize themselves to ensure that adequate societal resources go to investing in the future—in education and skills; infrastructure, both tangible and intangible; and knowledge and technology—will be left behind in the race. Likewise, nations that do not continually adapt by developing new policies, new kinds of institutions, and new approaches to governing and governance, even though this will lead to short-term disruption, will lag.

But for all the pressures involved in training for and competing in races, the race for global innovation advantage, if structured properly, can be a race in which all of humankind wins. Winning means not just that some nations will be more prosperous than others; it means robust global income growth and dramatic poverty reduction. We should strive for a world where, in thirty years, sub-Saharan Africa is at the economic level of Latin America today; Latin America and China are where Korea is today; and Korea is where the United States is today. And if the United States, Japan, and Europe can achieve 3 percent productivity growth for twenty-five years, they can double their real per capita incomes. We should envision a world in which many pressing challenges are solved, including those related to human health and the global environment. We can be well on the way to moving to a carbon-free energy system and to a world that has made sustained progress in the battle against cancer and other chronic diseases. The world of the future should be universally connected, with digital interoperability and high levels of digital literacy. To achieve this vision, nations need to put "good" innovation policies at the center of their own economic policies, and the world as a whole needs to restructure existing global economic institutions around support for innovation.

In 1946, as the cold war was just beginning to stir, George Kennan, deputy head of the U.S. mission in Moscow, wrote his now famous "long telegram" warning the United States of the growing Soviet threat and arguing that by taking up the mantle to respond to the challenge, America could become even more secure. America did accept those responsibilities and in so doing made the world freer, more democratic, and more prosperous than it otherwise would have been.

Today, America faces a similar challenge. But this time it is not from a totalitarian nation with imperialistic ambitions. Rather, the challenge we face is, on the one hand, our own shortsightedness and selfishness, and on the other, a global economic system in which too many nations have embraced a destructive innovation mercantilism. But Kennan's words fifty-five years ago are as apt today with regard to the new global innovation challenge: "We should experience a certain gratitude to a Providence, which by providing the American people with this implacable challenge, has made their entire security as a nation dependent on their pulling themselves together and accepting the responsibilities of moral and political leadership that history plainly intended them to bear." For there is no nation better positioned today to lead the world in innovation than the United States, both through reasserting its own innovation leadership and by leading the way toward a new global framework for innovation. But before America can do that, it will need to recognize that its leadership position has been lost, at least for the time being.

2

Explaining U.S. Economic Decline

I t will be many years before we truly understand the nature of the current economic downturn. Is it a typical but severe downturn caused by a financial crisis, the kind that the world has seen many times in many different nations?[1] Or should it be seen as more akin to the Great Depression, although moderated this time by better fiscal and monetary policy? Or might it be an inflection point in U.S. economic history? Looking back, will future generations point to this period and say, yes, this was when U.S. postwar economic dominance ended and the United States stood poised at the threshold of a decidedly less robust economic era?

We believe, and show in this chapter, that the latter is indeed the case—unless the United States takes dramatic steps to arrest and reverse its decline. But first, it is worth examining the nature and causes of the economic crisis more deeply. Why did the financial collapse happen? We believe that the conventional explanations (greed, incompetence, lack of regulation, and so forth) are not sufficient. Rather, a core contributing factor was the decline in the competitive performance of the U.S. economy, particularly after the mid-1990s.

Clearly, for the United States, Greece, Iceland, Ireland, Spain, and a number of other countries and regions, this has been a financially induced crisis, not a conventional economic downturn triggered by normal business cycle swings (for example, buildup of excess inventory or an overly restrictive monetary policy). The failure of assets (mostly housing mortgages) held by banks and other financial institutions was too much for them to absorb with their limited reserve requirements. The cascading effect of freezing credit markets, fear on the part of investors and businesses, reduced housing starts, and decreased consumer spending and business investment all led to a spectacular economic collapse. Between October 2007 and March 2009, U.S. real gross domestic product (GDP) fell by 4.7 percent and more than 5.7 million net jobs were lost.[2]

But why did this crisis occur when it did? Wall Street greed is usually trotted out as the explanation: greedy bankers who wanted too much too fast caused the whole house of cards to collapse. But there is nothing to suggest that Wall Street's motivations have changed in recent years. At least since the 1980s, if not before, Wall Street has focused on maximizing short-term profits, its excesses of greed well chronicled in Tom Wolfe's *The Bonfire of the Vanities*.

Others point to the rise of all sorts of complicated financial instruments—especially collateralized debt obligations (CDOs)—that made it hard for investors to understand what they were investing in. To be sure, CDOs were too complicated for many (even sophisticated) investors, who bought financial assets that were largely worthless from investment banks that were simultaneously shorting the investments they were selling. But CDOs and other instruments only made it easier for money from around the world to flow into underperforming and often fraudulent mortgage markets.

At the end of the day, the core cause of the financial collapse was the housing price collapse and the fact that so much money went into mortgages, particularly to people who couldn't or wouldn't pay their debts when prices collapsed. This elicits two main questions: (1) Why did so much money flow into mortgage markets, particularly into subprime mortgages with high risks of failure; and (2) Why did investors not realize sooner that these assets (and the housing they were based on) were dramatically overvalued?

To answer the first question, it's important to distinguish between capitalized consumption and investment. From an investor's perspective, and that of some economists, they are the same thing. In both cases, the investor either loans or invests money, enabling a borrower to buy something and hopefully to pay off the investment over its lifetime, ideally in excess of the costs in net present value terms.

But from a societal perspective, capitalized consumption and investment are fundamentally different. An investment is an expenditure that yields a future stream of societal returns greater than the cost of the initial investment. A classic example is investment in scientific research (for example, paying the salary of a scientist or buying research equipment). Such investment makes society poorer today (that is, able to consume less in the present) in the hope of becoming richer tomorrow. If that scientist is able to discover a cure for cancer or a way to produce energy without carbon emissions, the investment yields the future benefits of better human health or a cleaner environment.

In contrast, taking out a loan to buy capitalized consumption items— a new car, a new house, a backyard swimming pool—doesn't produce future economic value. Even if such loans are paid back with interest, the economy as a whole is not more productive or innovative because someone has a fancy car, a bigger house, or a pool to sit beside in the summer.

So from a societal standpoint, investments are critical as a nation's way of forgoing current consumption (on TVs, clothing, vacations, houses, cars, and so forth) to help ensure that the future economy can be more productive and innovative. If any society spent all its money on current consumption (including capitalized consumption) and none on investing in the future, its economy would not grow or become more innovative. Conversely, if society spent all of its resources on investments for the future, it could not meet basic human needs today (for food, clothing, and heat, among other things). As we discuss in chapter 10, getting the right balance between investment and consumption is key. Too little investment means that the future economy will be smaller and less innovative than it would be otherwise.

Returning to the financial crisis, the real question is why capital markets poured so much money into capitalized consumption—housing markets— especially in the six years before the collapse. In the last half of the 1990s, spending on U.S. housing averaged $360 billion per year. But in the first half of the 2000s, it increased by almost 50 percent, to an average of $538 billion annually. No wonder Wall Street cranked up the housing CDO market. Just as Willie Sutton said that he robbed banks because "that's where the money was," Wall Street invested in mortgages because that's where the profits were.[3]

But why was there so much money in the housing sector? The standard answer for most economists is that money was going into housing because that's where the largest societal returns were. How could it be otherwise, they argue, since markets acting independently of government allocate capital most efficiently? Most neoclassical economists view Wall Street (the nation's financial intermediation sector) as a highly rational system for transferring money from savers and investors to borrowers in a way that maximizes returns for all parties (savers, borrowers, financial intermediaries, and the economy as a whole).[4] But as we so painfully saw, this was not what happened with housing. Housing assets were not, it turned out, the best place to put investors' money.

Why did housing appear to be such an attractive investment? The short answer is because the demand for capital from the investment side of the economy shrank while the supply of capital (especially from China) surged. There was significantly reduced demand for capital to fund real wealth-creating activities in the United States—capital that would go to finance new mines, farms, factories, software and content firms, and the equipment needed to modernize and expand; money to finance new creative and fast-growing start-up companies; and money to finance research and development (R&D) to create the next generation of products and services. The entities that used to go to Wall Street for money to finance these kinds of wealth-creating activities were now doing it less frequently because the United States was losing the race for global innovation advantage.

The shortfall in demand for real investment capital in the United States was, in fact, quite significant. This can be seen by contrasting the demand for capital investment from 1995 to 2000 and from 2000 to 2005. Between 1995 and 2000, corporate investment in new capital equipment ("cap ex") exceeded spending on new housing by 173 percent. During these five years, annual corporate investment increased by $537 billion (73 percent), while

spending on housing increased by $147 billion (49 percent). This is gener-
ally consistent with the historic relationship between corporate expenditures
on capital and housing expenditures. However, from 2000 to 2005, corporate cap ex investment exceeded housing investments by only 112 percent.
More worryingly, corporate investment increased by just 17 percent ($192
billion), while spending on housing increased 82 percent. In other words,
U.S. capital expenditures by companies—a key source of productivity and
prosperity—began to stagnate and banks shifted capital into housing instead. We see the same trend when looking at bank balance sheets. When
examining the assets of commercial banks in the United States, the ratio of
industrial and commercial loans to real estate and consumer loans fell precipitously, from more than 80 percent in the early 1980s to around 52 percent at the end of the 1990s and then to just 28 percent five years later, as
figure 2.1 shows.[5] In other words, banks used to funnel capital to productive
investments; now they direct it to capitalized consumption (housing and
consumer loans).

Figure 2.1 Ratio of U.S. Banks' Industrial and Commercial Loans to Real Estate
and Consumer Loans, 1980 to 2011

This stagnation was actually an outright decline when it came to manu-facturing. Historically, manufacturing drove both demand for investment capital and the broader U.S. economy. But from 2000 to 2010, capital in-vestment within the United States by U.S. manufacturers declined more than 21 percent. These declines were even steeper for particular industries. Motor vehicles declined by 40 percent, paper by 44 percent, furniture by 53 percent, and apparel by 69 percent. Even sectors that the United States is supposed to lead in saw declines: capital investment in computers and elec-tronic products declined 49 percent, while investment in electrical equip-ment and appliances decreased 35 percent. In the two years following the 2001 recession, manufacturing cap ex fell 22 percent. In the five years follow-ing 2003, manufacturing cap ex increased by 34 percent before dropping by 25 percent in 2009. As of 2010, it was still only 79 percent of its year 2000 level. Some might argue that this was because of the high level of invest-ment in the boom year 2000. But between 1989 and 1998, manufacturing investment grew by 72 percent.[6] It wasn't that manufacturers weren't invest-ing, they were just doing it overseas. In 2000, U.S.-headquartered manufac-turing multinationals invested thirty-three cents overseas for every dollar invested domestically; in 2009, they invested seventy-one cents overseas for every dollar invested here, as figure 2.2 shows.[7] When looked at as a share of gross national product (GNP), manufacturing multinational corporations' overseas capital expenditure increased by 9 percent between 2000 and 2009, while their domestic expenditure decreased by nearly 50 percent.

Well, apologists will contend, manufacturing isn't today's economic en-gine anyway, for the United States specializes in innovation and in creating products and services on the front end, rather than production. But even here we see a similar picture of decline in demand for capital. While corpo-rate R&D as a share of GDP increased by just 3 percent in the United States from 1999 to 2006, it increased 11 percent in Germany, 27 percent in Japan, 28 percent in Finland, 58 percent in Korea, 66 percent in Spain, 90 percent in Hungary, and a stunning 187 percent in China.[8] As a result, the U.S. share of global R&D fell from 39 percent in 1999 to 34 percent in 2011, a period during which China's share increased fourfold.[9] Why did U.S. cor-porate R&D grow so slowly? For the same reason that manufacturing cap ex grew so slowly: U.S. multinationals were investing in R&D overseas.

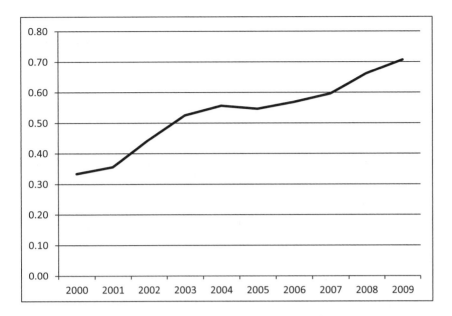

Figure 2.2 Ratio of U.S.-Headquartered Multinational Manufacturing
Corporations' Foreign Investment to Domestic Investment
Source: Based on statistics from the U.S. Bureau of Economic Analysis.

From 1998 to 2007, investment by U.S. corporations in R&D increased
more than two and a half times as fast overseas as all corporate investment
(by U.S. and foreign corporations investing in the United States) did domestically.[10] In fact, the share of R&D spending by U.S.-headquartered multinational corporations going to foreign subsidiaries rose from 9 percent in
1989 to 15.6 percent in 2009.[11]

Demand for capital to fund other investments that create real wealth also
shrank in the first half of the 2000s. From the second half of the 1990s to
the first half of the 2000s, corporate outward foreign direct investment (the
amount of money U.S. corporations invest in other nations) increased by
$29.2 billion, or 20 percent, while foreign corporations' inward direct in-
vestment to the United States decreased by $7.6 billion, or 4 percent. The
value of initial public offerings (the first time a company lists its stock on
an equities market) declined from $108.6 billion in 1999 to just $19.9 billion in 2009. Venture capital investments fell by 78 percent between 2000
and 2008. In short, the corporate engine of investment stalled in the 2000s

at home while it was revving up overseas, especially in China and India. Instead of investing in the United States and creating demand for U.S. investment bank services and capital, corporations invested overseas, in large part because other nations had much more attractive investment and innovation climates, including much better corporate tax systems.

But rather than downsizing in the face of declining demand for its services (e.g., investment capital) and seeing their profits, jobs, and bonuses shrink, Wall Street actually expanded, largely by increasing "investments" in mortgages for people with little income and even less credit, and by dramatically ratcheting up their casino-like trading functions. Indeed, by the 1990s, Wall Street had become a machine on autopilot, bringing in hefty returns for its investors and delivering big salaries and bonuses to partners and employees. Ever since most Wall Street investment banks went public (with the last major investment bank, Goldman Sachs, going public in 1999), they were essentially required by financial markets to keep generating high returns. Any manager who did not come through was at risk of losing his or her job. And the expected high returns depended on making deals. As John Cassidy writes in the *New Yorker*, "Think of all the profits produced by businesses operating in the U.S. as a cake. Twenty-five years ago, the slice taken by financial firms was about a seventh of the whole. . . . In 2006, at the peak of the boom, it was about a third. . . . From the end of the Second World War until 1980 or thereabouts, people working in finance earned about the same, on average and taking account of their qualifications, as people in other industries. By 2006, wages in the financial sector were about 60 percent higher than wages elsewhere."[12] By 2008, the assets of the six largest U.S. banks, taken together, equaled a stunning 60 percent of the United States' overall GDP, significantly more than before the great panic of 1929.[13]

In this environment, housing deals were as good as or better than corporate deals (such as mergers and acquisitions, IPOs, or corporate bond underwriting). If Wall Street couldn't make money from real wealth-creation efforts, it thought it could make money from capitalized consumption (e.g., housing), and it proceeded to try. Thus, given reduced demand for capital from corporate America, U.S. investment banks went looking for other deals to make up for the missing income and, in the process, figured out how to

transform the housing market into corporate finance. Or, as Richard Mc-
Cormack, editor of the newsletter *Manufacturing News* puts it, "the United
States replaced traditional engineering with financial engineering."[14] In
fact, as Ron Suskind notes in *Confidence Men*, even after the U.S. government's Troubled Asset Relief Program (TARP) would help bail out the U.S.
banks, "Investing in the U.S. manufacturing or industrial sectors, and even
in high tech, remained negligible, and there was no discernible bump in
credit. The banks and their financial subsidiaries went back to earning
money the way they had for much of the decade: through exotic, often computer driven, trading."[15]

In a way, Wall Street couldn't help itself. The machine was programmed
to generate deal flow, and if traditional societal wealth-enhancing deals were
lacking, capitalized consumption deals would suffice—both generated fat
bonuses. So the real question isn't why Wall Street did this, but instead:
Why did the U.S. economy evolve in such a way that the financial industry
got locked into a CDO corner? In other words, why did corporate wealth-
generating activities contract? The answer to that, as we describe below and
in chapter 3, was that the U.S. economy lost international competitiveness,
including on its longtime strength: technology and innovation.

But it wasn't enough that U.S. demand for capital was declining; the
supply of capital was expanding. While the sagging fortunes of the U.S.
economy in the first half of the 2000s led to a surfeit of good investment
opportunities, the exploding U.S. trade deficit ironically created a glut of
capital looking for a home. As other countries ramped up their mercantilist, export-oriented economic policies while limiting U.S. imports, the U.S.
trade deficit exploded from $120 billion a year in the early to mid-1990s to
around $600 billion a year by the mid-2000s. And this meant that large
amounts of capital now flowed back into U.S. financial markets.

Normal investors would not have been jamming all that money back into
the United States, where there were fewer good deals needing investment
capital. But these were not normal investors. These were national governments, particularly China and Japan (but also Korea, Malaysia, Singapore,
Taiwan, and others), desperate to keep their currencies from appreciating
as normal market forces would have effected. It's important to remember
that if these nations did not buy dollars (that is, invest in the United States)

their currencies would naturally rise relative to the dollar. Had this happened, the United States, in response, would have exported more and imported less, thereby reducing its trade deficit and creating millions of good-paying jobs. This not only would have created the demand for hundreds of billions of dollars worth of capital investments in wealth-creating activities but also would have increased wages for workers, enabling more to actually pay their mortgages, all the while reducing the flow of capital into mortgage markets and limiting the growth of the housing bubble.

All that foreign money seeking to keep the dollar high had to find a home, in this case, literally. And coupled with faulty policies from the Federal Reserve, which kept interest rates too low for too long (which it felt was necessary because the underlying U.S. economic engine was sputtering precisely because of faltering U.S. competitiveness), investors saw subprime mortgages as now worth the risk. With few good deals in the real economy, money now flowed into the Ponzi economy of housing. As *Businessweek* reported, "Overbuilding isn't the culprit in this bust. An oversupply of money is what pushed commercial real estate over the edge."[16] In fact, while there was a modest correlation of 0.35 between growth in spending on housing and growth in the trade deficit between 1996 and 2000, there was an almost one-to-one correlation (0.94) during the period from 2001 to 2005. In other words, expansion of the trade deficit almost perfectly matched expansion in spending on housing. Americans who were no longer working in high-wage manufacturing jobs (or jobs supplying manufacturers) were now buying DVD players, clothes, and cars made in China, Germany, Japan, or elsewhere and then borrowing money from Chinese, German, and Japanese workers (through Wall Street financial intermediaries) to buy houses they couldn't afford. But since capitalized consumption doesn't create wealth, these "investments" were only valuable if the next "sucker" kept buying, the essential feature of a Ponzi scheme. Eventually, the next sucker didn't buy, and the entire rotten edifice came tumbling down.

It should thus be clear that the financial crisis was not an isolated situation caused by greed, a lack of financial regulation, or any other single issue. This is not to say that a more regulated, transparent, ethical, and astute Wall Street would not have reduced the flow of money into the housing

Ponzi bubble. But at the end of the day, the key problem was the decline of demand for real wealth-creating investments in the United States and the expansion of foreign capital coming into America to keep the U.S. currency uncompetitive.

That was a problem Wall Street couldn't solve. Although it would be nice to think Wall Street would have lobbied for U.S. innovation and competitiveness policies, but they didn't. Wall Street's job is to channel savings into wealth-creating investments, not to ensure that there are enough of those investments to generate sustainable prosperity. Nor is it a problem that "Main Street" could solve either, if by Main Street we mean the millions of small and midsized businesses providing goods and services largely to local customers. Main Street is almost completely dependent for its economic vitality on "Manufacturing Street," "Research Park Street," and "Office Complex Street" (in other words, manufacturing, technology, and advanced office functions like corporate headquarters, globally traded engineering services, and so on). Nor is it a problem that Manufacturing Street, Research Park Street, or Office Complex Street could solve on their own. While some parts of Manufacturing Street were poorly managed (think General Motors), many U.S. companies are highly competitive internationally (think Boeing, Intel, and Microsoft). Thus, the problem has not been Manufacturing Street, Research Park Street, or Office Complex Street; the problem is that, in recent years, the United States has not been as attractive a place in which to make investments in innovation and productivity as other nations.

As such it was society's job, in particular the federal government's job, to create the conditions for sustainable prosperity. And, as we demonstrate, it's a job at which the federal government has failed. This has happened not because the federal government is incompetent or incapable, but because American voters and their elected representatives have not made it a priority for the federal government to take the steps needed to ensure that the United States remains the leader in the global innovation economy.

Finally, it's one thing to show that the fundamental building blocks of innovation and economic prosperity are not as strong as they used to be. But the real question is why didn't Wall Street (and so many economic leaders such as Alan Greenspan and Ben Bernanke) see that investing in capitalized consumption was creating an unsustainable housing bubble? Even though Wall Street managers are focused on short-term returns and maximizing their own end-of-year bonuses, almost none of them would have done what they did if they thought their investments would collapse less than a year later, regardless of how big their bonus was. As Michael Lewis notes in his masterful analysis of the process of collapse, *The Big Short*, they did what they did because most of them believed these were good investments.

Certainly, evidence to the contrary existed. Wall Street has access to more and better financial data than any place on the planet. New York Federal Reserve Bank economists Himmelberg, Mayer, and Sinai wrote in their 2005 article "Assessing High House Prices: Bubbles, Fundamentals, and Misperceptions": "Between 1975 and 1995, real single-family house prices in the United States increased an average of 0.5 percent per year, or 10 percent over the course of two decades. By contrast, from 1995 to 2004, national real house prices grew 3.6 percent per year (40 percent for the decade), a more than seven-fold increase in the annual rate of real appreciation. In some individual cities, such as San Francisco and Boston, real home prices grew about 75 percent from 1995 to 2004."[17] Since housing does not produce wealth (in fact, real housing, as opposed to land, prices should fall because of depreciation), this means that home buyers had to devote 40 percent more of their resources to housing at a time when median household incomes were increasing at just 0.9 percent per year from 1995 to 2004.[18]

As figure 2.3 shows, housing prices from 1987 to around 2000 were actually fairly stable and on track.[19] But after 2001, prices accelerated—and continued to do so for another year after the Federal Reserve economists published their study.

Although such data painted a stark picture of an expanding bubble that would likely pop, few in government or the financial industry were willing to entertain the thought that this was a bubble (Nouriel Roubini, an economics professor at New York University's Stern School of Business, was a notable exception). In 2005, Ben Bernanke, current chairman of

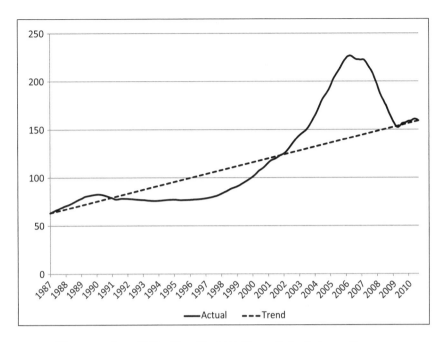

Figure 2.3 Case-Shiller Ten-City U.S. Home Price Index, 1987–2010

the Federal Reserve and then head of President Bush's Council of Economic Advisors, stated that rising home prices "largely reflect strong economic fundamentals," although the fundamentals were, in fact, anything but strong.[20] Likewise, then Federal Reserve chairman Alan Greenspan stated, "It doesn't appear likely that a national housing bubble, which could pop and send prices tumbling, will develop."[21] Amazingly, he said this when the ten-city-composite Standard & Poor's (S&P) Case-Shiller Housing Price Index was twice as high as it had been in 2000. Wall Street was equally oblivious. Unfortunately, the authors of the above-noted Federal Reserve Bank article—who were paid by taxpayers to advise the Federal Reserve Bank and others in the financial market to make better decisions— were also completely wrong. Even as they documented unprecedented increases in housing prices, they wrote: "As of the end of 2004, our analysis reveals little evidence of a housing bubble. In high-appreciation markets like San Francisco, Boston, and New York . . . recent price growth is supported by basic economic factors such as low real, long-term interest rates, high income growth, and housing price levels that had fallen to unusually low levels during the mid-1990s."[22]

They did give themselves an out, however, if things really turned south for their assessment: "Our evidence does not suggest that house prices cannot fall in the future if fundamental factors change. An unexpected rise in real interest rates that raises housing costs, or a negative shock to a local economy, would lower housing demand, slowing the growth of house prices, and possibly even lead to a house price decline."[23] But between 2004 and 2007, mortgage interest rates did not appreciably rise. And while some economies may have had local difficulties, the overall U.S economy grew at 8 percent in real terms. Yet notwithstanding these favorable conditions, housing prices collapsed, falling approximately 40 percent from their peak, and thus drove the economy over the cliff.

To be fair, it wasn't only the Ph.D. economists paid to assess the housing market who failed. The companies who still issued mortgages and bought and sold mortgage-backed securities at the height of the boom failed as well, and their mistakes directly cost society trillions of dollars. The fundamental mistake was that economists, bankers, and policymakers did not believe housing prices would go down. As *Businessweek* stated, "loans were made based on an unshakeable belief that the market would never go down."[24] Indeed, some investment banks like UBS bought the lion's share of their underperforming CDOs just months before the collapse.[25]

Why was there such misplaced, almost childlike trust in housing markets? The easy answer is that since housing prices hadn't gone down before, at least on a nationwide basis, the possibility that they would go down now was a "black swan" (although, as they say, past performance is not a guarantee of future performance). But the real answer is that virtually all economists and financial industry analysts subscribed to the theory that in an efficient market, all the information that would allow an investor to predict the next price move is already reflected in the current price. In other words, under efficient-market theory, the price of an asset accurately reflects its value. As Yves Smith documents, many of the players drank the Kool-Aid that markets always get it right.[26] Indeed, neoclassical economists and their fellow travelers in finance refused to acknowledge the reality that markets might misprice assets.

On average, and over the long term, efficient-market theory is valid. But its claim that all assets are perfectly, accurately priced at any given point in time is unrealistic. How can efficient-market theory explain dramatic swings in market prices, like the precipitous 508-point fall of the stock market on Black Monday, October 19, 1987? What piece of information presented that morning could have clued investors that all the assets they owned were over-valued by 22.6 percent? The answer is, of course, none.

As many of the advocates of what has become known as behavioral economics know, efficient-market theory is fundamentally flawed. But economists, investors, and regulators who rely on neoclassical-economics thinking bought into it and largely still do. If the market says that something is priced at a dollar, it's worth a dollar. If housing prices increase 40 percent in just a few years, then their actual worth increased 40 percent. If this is not true, it shakes the entire foundation of economics. A bit like the reaction of someone being told that the laws of gravity only work at certain times of the day, failure to believe the doctrine of efficient-market theory upsets an entire comforting way of looking at the economic universe. Because of this, believers in efficient-market theory will contort any analysis of data (even data showing that the real, inflation-adjusted price of housing grew seven times faster than before) to come up with the conclusion that the laws of gravity (efficient-market theory) still apply.

In summary, the U.S. financial crisis brought into sharp relief two major problems going forward. And unless both are solved, the long-term prospects for the U.S. economy are troubling. First, the fundamental investment environment in the United States is not good compared to that in other nations. Other nations have put in place the tax, trade, talent, and technology policies both to draw in and to grow innovation and productivity-enhancing investment. The United States has performed relatively poorly in these areas. Second, those in charge of guiding U.S. economic policy are caught up in a failed economic doctrine—neoclassical economics. They resist admitting that there is a problem (just as they resisted admitting that a housing bubble was forming), and worse, they believe that much-needed government action to solve it will just make things more difficult. We might as well ask Newtonian physicists to design microchips.

A deeper look into the nature of U.S. economic decline can help put these critical issues into perspective.

America's Long-Term Structural Economic Decline

Since the Great Recession was clearly a financially induced crisis, many believe that once bad mortgage loans and other troubled assets are worked out of the financial system and the banks stabilized, the U.S. economy will return to a course of revitalized and sustained growth, just as it has for almost 250 years. But while the U.S. economy retains many strengths, what contributed to the Great Recession, and what the Great Recession itself has since masked—and further amplified—is a deeper and more serious problem: an unprecedented long-term structural decline of U.S. economic competitiveness. To paraphrase Rogoff and Reinhart (authors of the 2009 book *This Time It's Different: Eight Centuries of Financial Folly*), "this time it really is different."

This decline has two underlying causes. The first is the deterioration domestically of fundamental sources of U.S. competitiveness, from decaying industries and infrastructure to an erosion of U.S. innovation capacity reflected by a weakened innovation ecosystem, a faltering education system, and a relatively poor environment for innovation and investment. The second cause is that foreign countries are competing more fiercely and strategically than ever to attain the standards of living and wealth that American citizens have come to take for granted. They want what Americans have. This is not simply the rebalancing of global economic activity to a more even distribution as seen in the decades after World War II (WWII), as the U.S. share of global GDP slid from 46 percent in 1946 to 24 percent in 2009.[27] Such a rebalancing can happen without the United States losing millions of high-paying jobs in manufacturing and technology and without U.S. growth rates being anemic. Rather, this is about the United States losing its presumptive leadership in many of the highest-value-added, often technology-based sectors of economic activity. It's a competition for the future, particularly for the kinds of jobs capable of sustaining the standards of living to which American citizens have grown accustomed.

Evidence of America's long-term structural economic decline abounds. It is apparent with regard to the current state of the U.S. economy—for example, in the across-the-board decline in U.S. manufacturing industries, whether in low-value-added industries such as textiles and furniture, medium-value-added industries such as automobiles or consumer electronics, or high-value-added industries such as advanced displays or printed circuit boards. It is seen in the nation's worsening trade balances, high unemployment rate, stagnant wages and slipping median incomes, and unsustainable debt loads.

Given the erosion of the country's underlying innovation capacity, America's ability to compete for the future is in doubt. The deterioration of U.S. innovation capacity is evidenced by underinvestment in R&D; an underperforming education system, particularly in science, technology, engineering, and math (STEM) fields; a decaying physical infrastructure; and an increasingly middling (by global standards) digital infrastructure—all within a public policy framework that does not comprehend the essential role of innovation and innovation policy in driving economic growth. The net result is that the United States has already lost a range of high-tech industries, from desktop and notebook PCs to liquid crystal displays (LCDs), advanced batteries, and compact fluorescent lightbulbs (CFLs). Moreover, U.S. leadership in the industries that will define the future—including high-performance computing, artificial intelligence, biotechnology, nanotechnology, robotics, energy storage, and clean energy production—is by no means assured.

Most, however, believe the financial crisis that sparked the Great Recession is a separate phenomenon from long-term U.S. structural economic decline. A case in point is the 2010 update of an original 2005 report issued by the National Academies of Science, *Rising Above the Gathering Storm, Revisited: Rapidly Approaching Category 5*, which states: "While the *Gathering Storm* report warned of an impending financial crisis, it was not addressing the type of crisis that subsequently occurred. It appears that the latter was relatively unique—triggered by government policy that encouraged excessive mortgage borrowing; poor judgment in assessing risk on the parts of both borrowers and lenders; overly aggressive practices by investment banks when creating new financial instruments; and a lack of diligence on the part of regulators. This produced what has been a severe downturn. But it is not the long-term crisis of which the *Gathering Storm* committee sought to warn and avert."[28] They see the Great Recession as "not rooted in the same fundamental causes" of long-term economic decline.[29] But, as stated above, we argue that the Great Recession in fact did result in large part from a fundamental deterioration of U.S. innovation capacity that led to "investing" in consumption rather than wealth-creating innovation. In other words, the Great Recession was but the first wave in the gathering storm of U.S. economic decline.

So what is the evidence for and what are the causes of long-term structural U.S. economic decline and erosion of U.S. innovation capacity?

Decimation of U.S. Manufacturing

Perhaps the most apparent sign of U.S. economic decline has been the decimation of the country's manufacturing base. In the 1980s and 1990s, many saw this as a "rust belt" phenomena with old, dirty factories in places like Akron, Ohio, and Pittsburgh, Pennsylvania, being closed down to make way for shiny new tech complexes in places like Austin, Texas, and Portland, Oregon. But overall manufacturing was expected to continue to be pretty stable. In 1996, in its ten-year forecast of jobs, the federal Bureau of Labor Statistics (BLS) estimated that by 2006, U.S. manufacturing would lose only about 350,000 jobs.[30] In fact, the U.S. economy lost 3.1 million manufacturing jobs from 1996 to 2006—and another 2.4 million from 2007 to 2011—for a loss of 5.5 million manufacturing jobs since 1996, or about one-third of the U.S. manufacturing workforce, as figure 2.4 shows.[31] Figure 2.5 shows annual job gains and losses in U.S. manufacturing industries from 1992 to 2010, vividly illustrating how U.S. manufacturing firms have lost far more jobs than they've created in almost every year since 1998.[32]

However, as figures 2.4 and 2.5 graphically illustrate, it was really in the 2000s that U.S. manufacturing jobs collapsed, as more than 54,000 U.S.

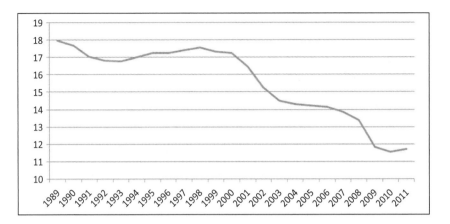

Figure 2.4 Decline in U.S. Manufacturing Employment (millions), 1989–2011
Source: Based on statistics from the U.S. Bureau of Labor Statistics.

factories closed. In fact, of the ten nations the BLS tracks, only the United Kingdom lost a greater share of its manufacturing jobs than the United States between 1997 and 2010 (see figure 2.6).[33] This is not a "rust belt" phenomenon, it's a "rust nation" debacle, with every single state except Alaska losing manufacturing jobs in the 2000s. What's more, in no previous decade has the United States ever lost such a large share of its manufacturing jobs. Even with the destruction of the Great Depression in the 1930s, the rate of manufacturing job loss was less than it was in the 2000s.[34] How could this devastation not have a broader effect on the macroeconomy?

As a result, in 2011, there were more unemployed Americans (15.7 million) than worked in manufacturing (just under 12 million). The last time fewer Americans worked in manufacturing was before WWII.[35] Capacity utilization in America's factories is nearly as low as it has been in any period since WWII.[36] And, in early 2011, the United States ceded its title as the world's leading manufacturer—a position it has held for the last 111 years, since 1900—to China.[37]

Nevertheless, many continue to argue that there's little cause for concern over the state of U.S. manufacturing because, after all, the United States is still one of the world's largest manufacturers and because output and productivity growth in manufacturing supposedly remains strong. As the

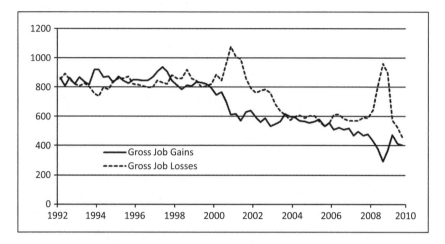

Figure 2.5 Job Gains and Losses in U.S. Manufacturing (thousands), 1992–2010
Source: Based on statistics from Stone and Associates and the Center for
Regional Economic Competitiveness.

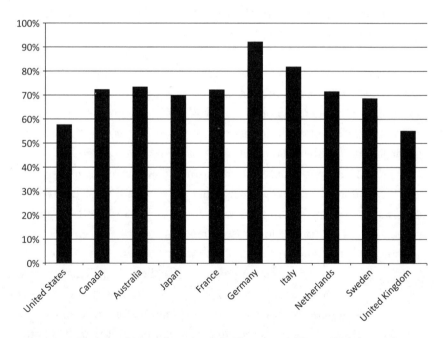

Figure 2.6 Manufacturing Job Change as a Share of Adult
Population Growth, 1997 to 2010
Source: Based on statistics from the U.S. Bureau of Labor Statistics.

Economist writes, "For all the bellyaching about the 'decline of American manufacturing' and the shifting of production en masse to China, real output has been growing at an annual pace of almost 4 percent since 1991 [to 2005], faster than overall GDP growth." They continue, "Since, contrary to conventional wisdom, manufacturing output has been growing strongly, not declining, the fall in [manufacturing] employment in America and elsewhere should be seen as a good thing."[38] Kevin Williamson, deputy managing editor of *National Review*, also points to productivity growth in U.S. manufacturing to allay concern, maintaining that "the real productivity of U.S. businesses overall grew at an average rate of 1.5 percent per year from 1973 to 1995, which is a really robust number. But the productivity of U.S. manufacturing businesses grew by 3.5 percent in those same years, which is enormous."[39]

The largely consensus view among U.S. economic elites is that the massive U.S. job loss in manufacturing is simply a reflection of manufacturing doing well: using technology to automate work and to become more efficient. It's the agriculture story they tell us. The United States produces more food than ever, but because farming has gotten so efficient, it requires very few farmworkers to produce this output. So while manufacturing productivity may be tough on workers, the consensus goes, it's not a sign of U.S. economic decline, it's a sign of strength. "So," they ask, "what's the problem?" Other than the recession, U.S. manufacturing appears quite healthy.

There are two big problems with this view. The first is that it's not supported by the official government data. In fact, U.S. manufacturing lost jobs much faster in the 2000s than in the 1990s, even though productivity growth was similar during the two decades. In the 1990s, U.S. manufacturing employment fell 1 percent, while productivity increased 56 percent. Yet, in the 2000s, manufacturing employment fell 32 percent while productivity increased only slightly faster, 61 percent. So, clearly, higher productivity was not the main cause of the manufacturing employment collapse.

But there is an even deeper problem. The official government measurement of manufacturing output, the very data so many analysts cite for their rosy views, vastly overstates the output of a key manufacturing sector—NAICS (North American Industry Classification System) 334, the computers and electronics industry. To see how, consider that the federal government classifies manufacturing into two major groups: durable goods (industries like automobiles, machines, and computers) and nondurables (industries like food, chemicals, apparel, and petroleum products). From 1987 to 2010, increases in the output of nondurables added just 1.96 percent to overall GDP growth. This is just over half of the approximately 3.73 percent they should have added to GDP had they contributed their "fair share" (that is, if they had grown at the same rate as the overall economy). Durables, in contrast, added 81 percent more than their fair share. However, a closer look reveals that every durable goods industry grew more slowly in output than GDP except one: computers/electronics which grew a whopping 720 percent faster than GDP. In fact, close to 8 percent of total U.S. GDP growth came from this one sector, which accounted for less than 1.6 percent of GDP. Does anyone really believe that the computers and electronics industry in America is actually 5,734 percent larger than it was in 1990? To put this in perspective, this one sector accounted for 113 percent of U.S. manufacturing output growth in the 2000s, even though, in 1997, it accounted for just 12 percent of manufacturing output.

What's going on? In part, the answer is the rapid technological improvement that is inherent in the computer and electronics industry. In a sense, Moore's Law (the prediction that the price of computing power falls by half and doubles in power every twenty-four months) makes it look like the industry is producing much more output than it really is. This poses a problem for output and productivity statistics because, although the rapid quality improvement may indeed accurately represent the increased computing value experienced by consumers, from an industry perspective it falsely implies a rapidly expanding industry.

When we look at durables minus computers and electronics, we see that they performed even worse than nondurables. In fact, when we look at manufacturing trends since 2000, the picture is much worse, one not just of slow growth, but actual decline. Between 2001 and 2010, the sum of yearly changes in GDP was 15.8 percent (in other words, if GDP grew 2 percent in one year and 3 percent the next, the sum would be 5 percent).[40] Manufacturing accounted for about 12 percent of the U.S. economy, on average, over this time period. Had manufacturing contributed its fair share to

GDP growth, it would have added a sum of changes of 1.91 percent (12 percent of 15.8 percent). In fact, it contributed 1.86 percent. But when we take out the inflated output of computers, the expected contribution to growth is 1.7 percentage points, but manufacturing minus computers actually subtracted 0.5 percentage points from GDP. This is because, during 2001–2010, manufacturing minus computers actually lost 6 percent of its value-added. Output of the electrical equipment and wood products industries declined by 7 percent, plastics by 8 percent, fabricated metals by 10 percent, printing by 12 percent, furniture by 19 percent, nonmetallic minerals and primary metals and paper by 31 percent, apparel by 34 percent, and textiles and motor vehicles by 39 percent. In other words, thirteen manufacturing sectors that made up 58 percent of U.S. manufacturing employment all produced less in 2010 than in 2001, all at a time when the overall economy grew 15.8 percent.[41]

Yet the government tells us that computers and electronics increased its output by 419 percent, even though the number of workers in the industry declined from 1.75 million to 1.09 million. In their study, "Offshoring and the State of American Manufacturing," economists Susan Houseman and colleagues report similar findings, with overall manufacturing output growing 1.18 percent per year from 1997 to 2007, but just 0.46 percent per year once computers are removed.[42] The failure of the Department of Commerce to accurately measure manufacturing output, and the fact that economists do not drill down into the data more carefully to tell the real story of what has happened is a breakdown of significant proportions since it has allowed policymakers to believe that all is well with U.S. manufacturing.

So where was all the growth in the U.S. economy if manufacturing was declining? Many conservatives will assert that it must have been in government. But, in fact, from 1987 to 2010, federal government output grew at just 11 percent the rate of growth in GDP, while state and local government grew just 57 percent as fast. (Growth in entitlements is not counted as government output since entitlements are a transfer payment.) Well, surely given the increased litigiousness of America, the legal industry must have exploded. In fact, legal services grew at just 36 percent the rate of overall GDP growth.

What industries, then, did assume a bigger share of the economy? Some of the expanders added real value to the economy. Computer systems services grew seventeen times faster than the rate of GDP growth. Information processing grew twelve times faster. But other fast-growing sectors arguably contributed less real value to the economy. Wholesale trade almost doubled, warehousing outpaced GDP by 175 percent, and water transportation increased twelve times faster, in part to handle the massive increase in manufacturing imports. And, of course, health care grew 63 percent faster than its share as the population aged. But the big growth was in financial services. The securities industry added over eleven times more to GDP than it would have if it grew at the national average. Funds, trusts, and other financial vehicles—think of your 401(k) plan—grew almost six times faster. In fact, while the ratio of banking profits to manufacturing profits was generally about 20 percent for most of the postwar period until the late 1970s, after that it grew rapidly to around 60 percent in the 1990s, reaching an astounding 317 percent in 2002. In other words, in 2002, the banking sector made more than three times the profits of manufacturing. And while the ratio went down during the financial crisis, it rebounded to 145 percent in 2010.[43]

Both a cause and an effect of this decline can be seen in trends in capital investment; that is, the amount invested every year in new plant and equipment. Unless the amount of new machines, equipment, and buildings put in place each year exceeds the amount of depreciation on existing machines, equipment, and buildings, overall capital stock (the aggregate value of the plant and equipment) will decline. Since WWII and through the 1970s, manufacturing capital stock increased at a robust pace as companies built new factories and added new machines in America. But since about 1980, a different picture has emerged. Table 2.1 shows the years in which the overall capital stock peaked in various industries, and the change from that peak year to 2009. For example, the capital stock of the primary metals industry (that is, the steel and aluminum industries) peaked long ago, in 1981, and has fallen by 27 percent since. Other industries peaked later, but in some cases saw a similarly steep fall in capital stock. For example, in just eight years, the value of buildings, machines, and equipment in the apparel industry fell by 21 percent. Contrast that to some other industries, such as

Table 2.1. Year of Peak Capital Stock by Manufacturing Industry
and Level of Decline to 2009

Industry	Year of peak capital stock	Decline to 2009
Primary metals	1981	–27%
Paper products	1996	–19%
Textile mills and textile product mills	1997	–29%
Wood products	2000	–6%
Food, beverage, and tobacco products	2000	–2%
Apparel and leather and allied products	2001	–21%
Computer and electronic products	2001	–1%
Electrical equipment, appliances, and components	2002	–5%
Plastics and rubber products	2002	–3%
Motor vehicles, bodies and trailers, and parts	2003	–7%
Furniture and related products	2007	–4%
Nonmetallic mineral products	2007	–2%
Printing and related support activities	2007	–2%
Wholesale trade	2008	–3%
Miscellaneous manufacturing	2008	–1%
Retail trade	2008	–1%
Chemical products	2008	0%
Fabricated metal products	2008	0%
Ambulatory health-care services	2009	0%
Funds, trusts, and other financial vehicles	2009	0%
Machinery	2009	0%
Other transportation equipment	2009	0%
Petroleum and coal products	2009	0%
Real estate	2009	0%
Securities, commodity contracts, and investments	2009	0%

Source: Bureau of Economic Analysis, Fixed Assets Accounts Tables (Table 3.2ES; chain-type quantity indexes for net stock of private fixed assets by industry), http://www.bea.gov /national/FA2004/index.asp (accessed February 11, 2011).

the securities and health-care industries, which have more capital stock than ever in their history.

Another way to view this is to look at the rate of change of fixed assets (equipment, software, and buildings) by industry and by decade, as table 2.2 does. In the 1960s and 1970s, manufacturers expanded their capital stock by 59 and 55 percent, respectively. In other words, in the 1960s, American manufacturers expanded their buildings and machines by close to 60 percent and almost did it again in the 1970s. In the 1980s, in part due to the severe recession at the start of the decade and the emergence of tough international competition, the growth of manufacturing capital stock fixed assets slowed to 23 percent, but picked up to 36 percent in the 1990s. However, from 1999 to 2009, manufacturing fixed assets actually fell by 1.2 percent, the first time they declined since the Great Depression.

But some sectors were booming. While the 2000s saw a decline in manufacturing capital stock, there were at least two industries where the 2000s marked the fastest growth: funds and trusts, and performing arts and spectator sports. More than 8 percent of Americans may not have jobs, but at least they can watch what retirement savings they have grow (hopefully) while watching the football game at the expensive new stadium built with taxpayer funds.

Indeed, the reality is that the United States has seen its global share of manufacturing production eviscerated. While the decimation of America's manufacturing base has occurred over several phases, the common theme has been that the industries lost are in ever higher value-added sectors, as foreign competitors move up the value chain and increasingly pick off high-technology manufacturing sectors from the United States.

Of course, it all began with the well-documented offshoring of low-technology, low-value-added, labor-intensive manufacturing industries such as textiles, apparel, and luggage to East Asian and Latin American countries starting in the mid-1970s. For example, today American producers account for just 1 percent of the U.S. luggage market and 1.7 percent of the outerwear apparel market. And the trend has continued. Between 2000 and 2008, the U.S. furniture industry has also been gutted, with the closure of 270 major factories. Imports of wood furniture accounted for 68 percent of the U.S. market in 2008, up from 38 percent in 2000.[44]

Table 2.2. Rate of Change of Fixed Assets by Industry and by Decade

	1959–1969	1969–1979	1979–1989	1989–1999	1999–2009
Total private fixed assets	69%	69%	39%	54%	38%
Manufacturing	59%	55%	23%	36%	–1%
Funds, trusts, and other financial vehicles	160%	82%	95%	164%	357%
Performing arts and spectator sports	64%	62%	–26%	69%	97%

Source: Bureau of Economic Analysis, Fixed Assets Accounts Tables (Table 3.2ES; chain-type quantity indexes for net stock of private fixed assets by industry), http://www.bea.gov/national /FA2004/index.asp (accessed February 11, 2011).

It would have been one thing if the United States was only losing employment in such labor-intensive, low-tech manufacturing industries (the kind people would see in movies like *Norma Rae*), for that could have represented a restructuring of U.S. manufacturing toward more high-tech, high-value-added manufacturing. This is essentially the story of German manufacturing, which lost some low-tech industries but more than made up for them with increased higher-tech production in industries like solar panels, machine tools, and autos. But the U.S. manufacturing sector was not restructuring, it was declining.

Throughout the 1980s, manufacturing of consumer electronic products left the United States almost entirely, as Asian players came to dominate production of personal cassette players, stereos, video recorders, TVs, digital cameras, and the like. Next, the United States started losing market share in capital goods industries. After WWII, with America being the arsenal of democracy, the United States became the world's leader in machine tools, the backbone of an industrial economy and the means by which all other products are manufactured. But by 2008, the U.S. share of global machine tool production had fallen to 5 percent, as China's rose to 35 percent. From 2005 to 2008, 80 percent of five-axis machine tools (the most sophisticated) sold in the United States were imported, with Japanese and German products comprising the vast majority of models.[45]

Meanwhile, since the mid-1970s, the U.S. share of domestic passenger vehicle production has been declining. The U.S. share of global passenger vehicle production fell by almost half from 1999 to 2008 (from 14.5 percent to 7.5 percent), as the Chinese share rocketed from 1.5 percent to 12.7 percent. China is now the world's largest passenger vehicle manufacturer (in addition to now having the world's largest passenger vehicle market). The bankruptcies of General Motors (GM) and Chrysler were clearly emblematic of this ongoing loss of U.S. manufacturing competitiveness.

Then, in the 2000s, the United States began losing out in the development and manufacturing of the next generation of high-technology products. Without a printed circuit board (PCB) industry, a country cannot expect to have an industrial foundation for high-tech innovation. But whereas the United States claimed 29 percent of global printed circuit board production in 1998, by 2009, that share had plummeted to 8 percent. Meanwhile, China's market share of global PCB production has been the exact inverse, growing from 7 percent in 1999 to more than 31 percent in 2008.[46] In fact, Asian countries now control 84 percent of the global production of PCBs. Similarly, in 2007, 40 percent of the semiconductor fabrication plants under construction in the world were located in China, with just 8 percent being built in the United States. Table 2.3 shows the nearly perfectly inverse relationship between the decline in U.S. and corresponding increase in Chinese manufacturing for several industries between the late 1990s and 2008.

The same story holds for the next generation of clean/green energy products. In an industry America pioneered, the U.S. share of global photovoltaics (solar panels) production cratered from more than 40 percent in 1995 to 7 percent in 2011. High-profile bankruptcies in 2011 and 2012 of solar panel companies like Evergreen Solar (which first moved to China before going bankrupt), Solyndra (which received a loan of $535 million from the federal government that became controversial after its bankruptcy), SpectraWatt, and Energy Conversion Devices, are indicative of the decline. Meanwhile, China's share of the photovoltaics market grew from 5 percent in the mid-2000s to more than 50 percent in 2011, largely due to massive subsidies to the industry, including no-interest loans, free electricity, free land for facto-

Table 2.3. U.S. Decline and Chinese Rise in Global Manufacturing

Industry	U.S. share global manufacturing		Chinese share global manufacturing	
	Late 1990s	2008	Late 1990s	2008
Printed circuit boards	29% (1998)	8%	7% (1998)	31.4%
Semiconductor plants under construction		8% (2007)		40% (2007)
Photovoltaics	30% (1999)	5.6%	1% (1999)	32%
Passenger vehicles	14.5% (1999)	7.5%	1.5% (1999)	12.7%
Machine tools		5.1%		35%

ries, and other incentives. In fact, China became the world's leading producer of solar panels in 2009, the leading producer of wind turbines in 2010, and intends to become the world's largest manufacturer of lithium ion (Li-ion) batteries sometime between 2015 and 2020.

Meanwhile, investment in these technologies continues to flow into Asia, not the United States. In fact, ITIF estimates that over the years 2009 to 2013, the governments of Asia's "clean technology tigers"—China, Japan, and Korea—will invest three times more than the United States in clean technology, with those nations investing a total of $509 billion, while the United States invests $172 billion.[47] This became clear as early as March 2010, when a U.S. company, Applied Materials, opened the world's largest private solar research and development facility—but in Xian, China. Likewise, in November 2010, General Electric (GE) made a $2 billion investment in clean technologies in China, expanding its R&D and customer support capabilities in the field of low-carbon technologies, particularly in smart grid and rail infrastructure. GE will spend $500 million on customer innovation centers in six Chinese cities, and within two years its investment will add one thousand jobs in the country.[48]

The story is the same for the next generation of advanced vehicles. A single Japanese automobile, the Toyota Prius, constitutes about half of the U.S. hybrid market, and a single Japanese company produces more than 75 percent of the world's nickel-metal hydride batteries used in vehicles.[49] GM's all-electric Volt has been much touted as the leading-edge of next-generation

U.S. advanced vehicle development, but the rechargeable lithium-ion batteries at its heart were designed and manufactured in Korea.

Chapters 3 and 4 explore in fuller depth the causes of the decline of U.S.
manufacturing industries since the early 1980s, including how the loss of
one high-tech manufactured product industry sows the loss of future industries in subsequent technology life cycles. For the moment, suffice it to say
that the primary causes have been a combination of misguided economic
beliefs in the United States and the intentional result of foreign countries'
strategies, legitimate and illegitimate, to relocate R&D and manufacturing
activity from the United States to their nations. Regardless of why, the loss of
U.S. manufacturing industries has been a critical factor contributing not
just to the financial crisis but also to the anemic U.S. jobs recovery through
2011. This is in part because manufacturing jobs have the highest employment multiplier of any sector, meaning that the loss of 5.7 million manufacturing jobs led to significant job loss in the rest of the economy, with
the result being no net job creation in the United States from 2000 to
2011.[50]

Deteriorating Trade Balances

A large share of the decline of U.S. manufacturing jobs and output has
stemmed from the increase in the U.S. trade deficit. While the United
States has been running a trade deficit in manufacturing for more than
three decades, it grew considerably worse after 2000. During the ensuing
decade, the United States accumulated an astounding aggregate negative
$5.5 trillion trade balance in goods and services with the rest of the world.[51]
In no year in the 2000s did the United States have a negative global trade
balance of better than negative $360 billion; and in five of those years, the
annual trade deficit topped $600 billion. To put this in perspective, during
each of those five years, on average, each American household imported
$5,450 in goods and services that was not matched by equivalent exports. In
just five years, every American household got the equivalent of a new BMW
essentially on credit, since we were not exporting an equivalent amount. At
5 percent of U.S. GDP in 2010, the current account deficit remains at extremely high levels.

But the story has been even worse with regard to the balance of trade in goods: from 2006 to 2008, the United States accrued a trade deficit in goods of at least $823 billion annually. The goods trade balance for the 2000s decade was negative $7 trillion.[52] Thanks to this, since 2000, the U.S. share of world exports has declined from 17 percent to 11 percent, even as the European Union's share held steady at 17 percent over that time period.[53] In fact, between 1999 and 2009, America's share of world exports fell in almost every industry: by thirty-six percentage points in aerospace, nine in information technology (IT), eight in communications equipment, and three in cars.[54]

Many Americans comfort themselves by thinking that the vast majority of the U.S. trade deficit in goods is comprised of oil; cheap, low-value items, such as clothes, toys, or knickknacks; or the mass-market consumer electronics we've gotten used to importing from Asia. Surely, the United States must have a positive trade balance in advanced technology products from industries such as life sciences, medical devices, optoelectronics, information technology, aerospace, and nuclear power. But no, as figure 2.7 illustrates, the United States has run a deficit in advanced technology products since 2001. In fact, in the ten-year period from the beginning of 2002 to the end of 2011, the United States ran a trade deficit in advanced technology products every year, tallying a $526 billion deficit in advanced technology products over that time period.[55] And over that period the trend worsened virtually every year; indeed, the United States ran an $81 billion trade deficit in advanced technology products in 2010 and a $99 billion deficit in 2011.[56]

Even in industries where one might expect the United States to surely run a trade surplus, such as renewable energy products, the country runs a trade deficit. In fact, from 2004 to 2008, the U.S. trade deficit in renewable energy products increased by 1,400 percent, to nearly $5.7 billion.[57] And in a number of the advanced technology sectors, such as medical devices, where the United States still runs a trade surplus, that surplus is shrinking. Overall, from 2005 to 2010, the U.S. share of global high-tech exports dropped from 21 percent to 14 percent, while China's share grew from 7 percent to 20 percent.[58] China has now replaced the United States as the world's number one high-technology exporter.

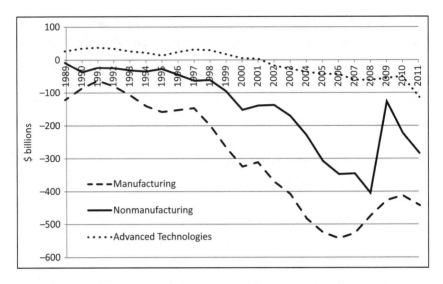

Figure 2.7 U.S. Trade Balances for Manufactured, Nonmanufactured,
and Advanced Technology Products, 1989–2011
Source: Based on statistics from the U.S. Census Bureau.

So just what does the United States manufacture and export these days?
It turns out that its two largest exports (by value) via ocean container are
wastepaper and scrap metal. Moreover, the largest U.S. exporter via ocean
container in 2007 was not even an American company, but Chinese: American Chung Nam, which exported 211,300 containers of wastepaper to its
Chinese sister company, Nine Dragons Paper. By comparison, in 2007,
Walmart imported 720,000 containers of sophisticated manufactured
products from overseas factories into the United States, followed by Target
(435,000 containers), Home Depot (365,300 containers), and Sears, which
owns Kmart (248,600 containers).[59]

These figures recall Winwood Reade's 1872 book *The Martyrdom of Man*,
which chronicled the economy of ancient Rome: "By day the Ostia road
was crowded with carts and muleteers, carrying to the great city the silks
and spices of the East, the marble of Asia Minor, the timber of the Atlas,
the grain of Africa and Egypt; and the carts brought nothing out but loads
of dung. That was their return cargo."[60] Dung for the Romans; scrap metal
and wastepaper for the United States.

To be sure, semiconductors remain the largest U.S. export industry by absolute value, accounting for $48 billion in exports from 2005 to 2009, $10 billion ahead of automobiles, in second place.[61] And despite the declines in its share of the global market, aerospace also remains a strong export industry for the United States. But having just a few strong export industries has not been enough to offset the massive trade deficits the United States has generated over the past decade. And while the United States has had a positive trade balance in services over the past decade, services trade is still much smaller than manufactured goods trade, and therefore the U.S. trade deficit will not diminish absent a significant increase in domestic manufacturing. Unfortunately, every year America runs a trade deficit, it passes on debt to the next generation of Americans. While this generation has been enjoying its BMWs that it didn't work for, the next generation will be stuck with the bill—in other words, stuck having to produce more than it consumes and shipping the rest to other nations.

Erosion of U.S. Innovation Capacity

Some who acknowledge that America is losing manufacturing will counter with the claim that the United States is still strong in innovation and that this will power its future competitiveness. For more than fifty years after WWII, the United States was the undisputed global innovation leader. America's global leadership in technology innovation was taken as a given. Research from U.S. corporate and government laboratories spawned a string of transformative innovations, everything from transistors, mobile phones, and personal computers to lasers, graphical user interfaces, search engines, the Internet, and genetic sequencing. However, the United States has lost its innovation lead and its rank appears to be rapidly slipping.

In 2011, the Information Technology and Innovation Foundation (ITIF) released a report, *The Atlantic Century II*, which benchmarked forty-four nations and regions on sixteen core indicators of innovation-based capacity (using mostly 2009 data).[62] In addition to the United States, countries assessed included twenty-five European Union nations along with Brazil, Canada, Chile, and Mexico, and leading Asian economies including Australia, China, Japan, Korea, and Singapore. Among the indicators evaluated were higher-education attainment, researchers per capita, levels of government and corporate R&D, entrepreneurship (new firms and venture capital), corporate tax levels, and ease of doing business as well as innovation outputs, such as levels of per capita GDP growth, foreign direct investment (FDI), productivity, and trade balances.

The report found that a coterie of hard-charging Asian and Western European countries, headlined by Singapore and Korea from Asia, which placed first and fifth, respectively, as well as Finland and Sweden from Europe, which ranked second and third, is pacing the world in the race for global innovation advantage. The United States ranked fourth.[63] The United Kingdom, Canada, Denmark, Holland, and Japan rounded out the top ten countries.

Many will say, "Well the United States still ranks close to the top, in fourth place; that's close enough, so what's the big cause for concern?" The first cause is that when one benchmarks these forty-four countries on the same sixteen indicators using 1999 data, the United States stands out as the clear leader, far ahead of then number two Sweden. But in ten short years, the United States lost its top perch, slipping to number four behind Singapore, Finland, and Sweden. Nor is ITIF alone in finding that the United States has lost its world-leading position in innovation: a March 2009 Boston Consulting Group study ranked the United States eighth out of 110 countries in innovation capacity.

But while that's concerning enough, *The Atlantic Century II* report found a far more disturbing trend. When assessing rates of change in innovation capacity during 2000–2009 (that is, the rate of improvement on these sixteen indicators), the United States ranked second to last, ahead of only Italy.[64] China ranked number one. But other advanced nations like Australia, Austria, Japan, and the United Kingdom also significantly outpaced the United States. In other words, forty-two nations or regions made faster progress than the United States did at bolstering their innovation competitiveness.

In fact, the United States placed near the bottom for rates of change at enhancing its levels of higher-education attainment, number of scientific researchers per capita, and number of scientific publications per capita, while also scoring poorly at increasing its levels of corporate R&D, increasing broadband Internet and e-government usage and penetration, and improving its trade balances. The report should be seen as both a backward- and forward-looking indicator. That is, it clearly shows a dramatic erosion of U.S. innovation capacity during the 2000s. But as the report includes a number of inputs to the innovation process—levels of government and corporate R&D investment, higher educational attainment, levels of venture capital, and so forth—it also suggests weakened U.S. innovation competitiveness continuing into the future.

We see signs of U.S. innovation decline particularly in four categories: R&D intensity; shares of scientific publications and scientific researchers; patenting activity; and numbers of bachelors, graduates, and doctorates in STEM fields. In total, these trends reinforce the reality that the United States is not as attractive a location for investment as it used to be or as other nations increasingly are.

A nation's investments in R&D are vital to its ability to develop the next-generation technologies, products, and services that keep a country and its firms competitive in global markets. A nation's R&D intensity measures its aggregate investments in R&D as a share of its total GDP, enabling comparisons to other countries. While the United States still leads the world in aggregate R&D dollars invested, on a per capita basis it is falling behind. The United States ranks just eighth among Organization for Economic Co-operation and Development (OECD) countries in the percentage of GDP devoted to R&D expenditures (2.8 percent), behind Israel (4.3 percent), Finland (4.0 percent), Sweden (3.6 percent), Korea (3.4 percent), Japan (3.3 percent), Denmark (3.0 percent), and Switzerland (3.0 percent), with Germany and Austria both less than .04 percent behind the United States.[65] Worse, the United States is one of the few nations where total investment in R&D as a share of GDP fell from 1990 to 2005, largely because of a decline in public R&D support over that time frame. And in 2008, for the first time, Asian nations as a group surpassed the United States in R&D investment, investing $387 billion to the United States' $384 billion.[66]

The Great Recession has further eroded U.S. corporate R&D activity. According to the European Commission's 2010 *EU Industrial R&D Investment Scoreboard*, R&D by top U.S. companies fell by 5.1 percent compared to the year prior, a decline twice as sharp as EU corporations experienced.[67] In contrast, major companies headquartered in Asian countries continued their high R&D growth rates, with Chinese firms increasing their R&D investment activity by 40 percent, Indian firms by 27.3 percent, and those in Hong Kong and Korea by 14.8 percent and 9.1 percent, respectively. Japanese corporations maintained their R&D investment levels. While American firms have had to cut back on R&D into the technologies and products of the future, Asian firms are using the opportunity to put themselves on a stronger competitive footing for the future.

As another example, business R&D expenditures by U.S. IT manufacturing and IT services industries as a share of GDP fell substantially compared to twenty-one other OECD peer countries between 1997 and 2005. While at first glance the United States appears to score fairly well on these measures—fifth in business R&D expenditures in IT manufacturing and sixth in IT services—the data reveal a striking decrease of almost 50 percent in the amount of U.S. IT manufacturing industry R&D as a percentage of GDP from 1997 to 2005.[68] Moreover, during this time, businesses in IT manufacturing and services industries in countries such as Finland, Korea, Denmark, Ireland, and the Czech Republic substantially increased their IT R&D investment as a percentage of their countries' GDP. Finland and Korea increased their business R&D expenditures in IT manufacturing by 67 percent and 73 percent, respectively, and businesses in Denmark's IT services industries increased theirs by 189 percent.[69]

The United States has also slipped in the number of scientific publications per capita and global share of scientific publications. As a November 2010 Thomson Reuters Global Research Report concludes, "The United States is no longer the Colossus of Science, dominating the research landscape in its production of scientific papers, that it was 30 years ago. It now shares this realm, on an increasingly equal basis, with the EU-27 and Asia-Pacific."[70] The U.S. share of scientific papers in journals indexed by Thomson Reuters has fallen from 40 percent in 1980 to 29 percent in 2008. Moreover, Asian nations have surpassed the United States in share of annual total output of journal papers, with China now the second-largest single-producer nation behind the United States. The United States ranks just fourteenth among countries for which the National Science Foundation (NSF) tracks the number of science and engineering articles per million inhabitants. Sweden and Switzerland produce over 60 percent more science and engineering articles in relation to the size of their populations than does the United States.[71]

While the United States continues to lead in patents, other nations have encroached on the U.S. lead. In 2009, 51 percent of patents issued in the United States were awarded to non-U.S. companies. Only four of the top ten companies receiving U.S. patents in 2009 were based in the United States. In fact, nearly 60 percent of the patents filed with the U.S. Patent and Trademark Office (PTO) in the field of information technology now originate in Asia.[72] At the same time, the increase in patent litigation in the United States (120 percent between 1990 and 2005) imposes a significant tax on the U.S. innovation system.[73] In total, U.S. firms spend more than twice as much on patent and other litigation as they do on R&D.[74]

One of the most worrying signs of deteriorating U.S. innovation competitiveness has been the steep decline in American college graduate, master's, and doctoral students earning science and technology degrees. The United States ranks just twenty-seventh among developed nations in the proportion of college students receiving undergraduate degrees in science or engineering.[75] And although Americans (citizens and permanent residents) are getting graduate degrees at an all-time high rate, the increase in graduate degrees in natural science, technology, engineering, and math fields has been minimal since the early 1990s. According to the Department of Education, only 41 percent of students who enter STEM majors in higher education end up obtaining a STEM degree of some kind (certificate, associate's, or bachelor's) after six years.[76] In 2009, U.S. colleges awarded more undergraduate sports-exercise majors than electrical engineering majors.[77] At the same time, an increasing number of master's and Ph.D. recipients in STEM fields from U.S. universities are foreign-born. For example, almost three-quarters of electrical engineering and two-thirds of industrial engineering doctorates are awarded to foreign students.[78] Of course, these students are increasingly returning home after they graduate, either to capitalize on opportunities there or because U.S. immigration policies make it difficult for them to stay in the United States.

Of course, challenges with the U.S. educational system go far beyond STEM fields; they are seen broadly across secondary and tertiary education.

Thirty percent of Americans do not hold high school diplomas. In fact, the United States ranks just twentieth in high school completion rates among industrialized nations and sixteenth in college completion rates.[79] Even worse, literacy among those college graduates is quite low.[80] Among second semester seniors at four-year U.S. colleges, just 34, 38, and 40 percent were proficient in quantitative, document, and prose literacy, respectively.[81] In other words, 60 percent of students who have spent more than three years in college (hopefully taking some time away from partying to study) were not fully literate.

Overall, we should be deeply concerned that America's educational system is not adequately preparing the next generation with the skills it will need to be competitive in the globalized economy of tomorrow. As the authors of the *Rising Above the Gathering Storm* report concluded, the U.S. K–12 education system is on average "a laggard among industrial economies—while costing more per student than any other OECD country."[82] As we explore in chapter 8, a large part of the problem is that we have not brought sufficient innovation to the U.S. education system.

But even if the overall U.S. innovation ecosystem is sputtering, one would expect that Silicon Valley surely continues to do well and pace the world in innovation. Actually, as Russell Hancock, chief executive of the Joint Venture Silicon Valley Network, which has indexed the region's business climate each year since 1995, argues in the organization's 2010 report, "I'm not telling you the sky is falling, but I have a duty to report that some of the indicators are not good."[83]

Taken together—whether it's R&D intensity, scientific publications, patenting activity, higher education attainment, or a variety of other indicators—it's clear that there has been a stark erosion of U.S. innovation capacity, particularly since 2000. And it's no surprise that the erosion of U.S. innovation leadership has gone hand in hand with U.S. structural economic decline.

Losing the Race and Stagnating Incomes

It should be clear that a large part of the explanation for the loss of U.S. manufacturing jobs lies in increased global competition and the loss of not just low-value-added but also high-value-added manufacturing and R&D

activities to foreign countries. Likewise, we have not been able to fully offset these losses with higher-wage jobs in other sectors and functions related to technology and innovation. And so the United States' loss of global competitive advantage has led not just to job loss and slow GDP growth but also to income stagnation. We were already seeing evidence of this even before the Great Recession. A June 2009 study by the Bureau of Labor Statistics found that the average wage increase for all U.S. workers from 2000 to 2007 was eleven cents an hour. However, the average wage that companies paid their workers actually increased by twenty-two cents an hour during that time frame, meaning that there was an eleven-cent reduction in U.S. wages through occupational shift.[84] In other words, if the United States had the same composition of jobs in 2007 as in 2000, the average wages paid to U.S. workers would have increased twenty-two cents an hour, whereas on average U.S. workers only realized one-half that increase, because a larger share of workers in 2007 were in lower-paying occupations. To risk being flippant, the American workforce has increasingly moved from manufacturing high-technology products to manufacturing hamburgers. This is in part why the median annual income in the United States grew by an anemic 2 percent between 1990 and 2010.[85]

This is one reason why, according to the 2010 *Prosperity Index* published by the Legatum Institute, a London-based research firm, the United States ranked only the tenth most prosperous country in the world, continuing its downward slide from its ninth-place rank in 2009, fifth in 2008, and third in 2007, the initial year of the report. Likewise, the International Monetary Fund has assessed growth in GDP per capita (at purchasing power parity) for twenty-one of the world's largest (mostly OECD) economies since 1980.[86] Among these nations, the United States ranked eighth in growth in GDP per capita from 1980 to 1990. From 1990 to 2000, it slipped to eleventh. From 2000–2010, U.S. per capita GDP growth fell to seventeenth. At this rate, by 2020, it will be last.

It should be no mystery as to the relative decline. Relative incomes can and do shift across national economies in response to changes in competitive advantage for technological advantage. As Nobel Laureate Paul Samuelson puts it, "Invention abroad that gives to [other countries] some of the comparative advantage that had belonged to the United States can induce for the United States permanent lost per-capita real income."[87] Or as Greg Tassey, senior economist at the National Institute of Standards and Technology (NIST), explains, "Technological change can not only shift comparative advantage through trade but also lower real incomes in the economies that do not develop and use new technologies to a sufficient degree."[88] When an economy loses such a large number of "traded jobs," the impact on the overall economy will be nothing less than severe.[89] The message is clear: relative American prosperity is waning.

But the United States is not the first country to experience such stunningly rapid industrial decline; the British economy charted that path from the 1950s to the 1970s. As we discuss in chapter 3, dreadfully poor economic policymaking largely begat both collapses.

3

Learning from the Wrong Master

LESSONS FROM U.K. INDUSTRIAL DECLINE

A fter being the global economic leader for more than a century, the experience of relative economic decline is new for the United States, a bit like waking up one morning to find that your mansion has termites and your Cadillac is leaking oil. This is not to say that some U.S. regions, particularly in the Northeast and Midwest, haven't had termites and leaking oil for some time. Places like western Pennsylvania saw their economies go into relative decline in the 1950s and 1960s. But for most of America, until fairly recently, the economic foundations were termite-free and the economic engine roared like new. And even though America faced increased international economic competition in the 1980s and 1990s— particularly from Japan and Germany, who took a large bite out of U.S. leadership in sectors such as steel, automobiles, and machine tools—the economy came surging back in the 1990s, powered by the information technology (IT) revolution. It has only been since the late 1990s that the United States as a whole began to experience what places like western Pennsylvania have long endured, and to see tangible ways in which it is losing ground to other nations, particularly in its ability to field a globally competitive, high-wage export sector.

So with the termites now eating the foundation and the oil puddle forming on the garage floor, how should America respond? One answer is to
pretend the termites are not there and to put a mat on the garage floor to
soak up the oil. Indeed, the dominant view of U.S. elites has been to deny
that there is a problem. If you repeat "we live in a new mansion and drive a
new Cadillac" often enough (or in the case of the economy, "America is still
the most innovative, competitive economy with the American worker able
to outcompete anyone"), then it must be true. Moreover, too many elites,
particularly economists, believe that nations don't really decline or even
compete, especially the United States, which is more market-oriented than
many nations and therefore, by definition, can't decline.

But nations do decline relative to others if they do the wrong things long
enough and fail to do the right things. An instructive case in point is the
United Kingdom, whose industrial decline from the 1950s to the early
1970s looks troublingly similar to America's present decline. As late as the
1880s, the United Kingdom led the world in industrial might. And while
Britain did lose ground before World War II (WWII), as Aaron Freidberg
documents in his book *The Weary Titan: Britain and the Experience of Relative Decline, 1895–1905*, even as late as the late 1940s, it was second only to
the United States. But within thirty years, the United Kingdom lost much of
its industrial base and economic leadership, just as the United States is now
doing. Although Britain was "the world's workshop" throughout the 1800s
and into the early 1900s, in the forty years after WWII, that workshop closed
and moved to other nations. Between 1973 and 1992, U.K. manufacturing output increased just 1.3 percent, compared to 32 percent in Germany, 55
percent in the United States, and 69 percent in Japan.[1]

To be sure, the United Kingdom and the United States are different, and
not all of their experiences are transferable. But when one studies the
causes of U.K. industrial decline, what quickly emerges is an eerie feeling
of déjà vu. In area after area, America is making the very same mistakes
that Britain did. In fact, if one substituted a "S" for the "K" in "U.K.," many
of the explanations given by experts for U.K. decline would seem as if they
were written today about the United States. The United Kingdom, however, had no one to learn from in averting its decline, making it more difficult for British leaders to stop what was avoidable. The United Kingdom

could have killed the termites and fixed the oil leak. Instead, it fed the termites and exacerbated the leak. The United States is luckier. We aren't the first nation to decline. We can remember the past if we choose to, learning from and avoiding the mistakes the United Kingdom made. But as Spanish philosopher George Santayana said, "Those who cannot remember the past are condemned to repeat it." The question is whether America will pretend that the past is not prologue and go merrily on its way, making the same mistakes its British cousins made before it, or learn from Britain's troubled industrial past. To answer that, it is useful to first examine the experience and causes of the U.K. decline.

At the end of the day, the United Kingdom's experience from the mid-1950s to the late 1970s suggests that industrial decline is perhaps not very complicated after all. The recipe for decline is actually pretty straightforward: ignore the industrial sector in favor of finance; keep currency values high relative to other currencies; pretend that you are not in global competition; oppose the introduction of new technological innovations; skimp on investments in the future; focus on macroeconomic stabilization at the expense of microeconomic policies to spur investment and innovation; fight over the slices of the pie rather than making a bigger pie; and so forth. The British did all this and more, and in hindsight the results were sadly predictable: a dramatic loss of industrial leadership over the course of just two decades. While the British have since suffered four decades of slower economic growth because of this, perhaps their failure can have a purpose: educating other nations about what not to do.

By economic decline, we do not mean an absolute decline in living standards. Indeed, the average per capita income in the United Kingdom is higher today than it was in the 1970s, just as U.S income today is higher than in 1990. Rather, we mean a decline in real manufacturing output as a share of gross domestic product (GDP), the development of chronic foreign trade deficits, and slower per capita economic growth than most peer nations over a sustained period of time.

By these measures, both the United Kingdom (in the postwar period) and more recently the United States can be said to be suffering from economic decline. Like America, Britain was once the world's dominant economy. Even after WWII when the United States had overtaken it, both in absolute and per capita output, the United Kingdom led all other nations. But within a span of two decades, the wheels came off the U.K. economy as it lost industry after industry to foreign competition. As Sydney Pollard wrote in 1982, "How does Britain fare in such comparisons? The statistics confirm the national consciousness of a staggering relative decline, such as would have been considered utterly unbelievable only a little over thirty years ago." Pollard went on to note, "After having led the world for two hundred years, Britain is no longer counted among the economically most advanced nations of the world. A wide gap separates her from the rest of industrialized Europe. The difference as measured in national product per head between Britain and, say, Germany, is now as wide as the difference between Britain and the continent of Africa. One short generation has squandered the inheritance of centuries. . . . There is no record of any other economic power falling behind at such startling speed."[2] To be sure, the United States has not fallen that far and that fast, yet. But it certainly has fallen relatively far since the late 1990s.

As both the United Kingdom and the United States fell behind on manufacturing investment, both nations became increasingly dependent on imported goods, with resulting increases in their trade deficits. As Ajit Singh noted in 1977, "The U.K. therefore seems to be becoming increasingly unable to pay for its current import requirements by means of exports of goods and services and property income from abroad."[3] Likewise, Rex Pope observed, "Overall, manufacturing declined sharply in relative importance. The sector had provided 28 percent of GDP in 1972; this fell to 21 percent by 1983. . . . A consequence of this process, as domestic consumption of manufactures rose by nearly a third from 1979–89, sucking in imports, was that the traditional trade surplus in manufactured goods had become a £16.1 billion deficit (3.1 percent of GDP) by 1989."[4] Comparatively, U.S. performance has been, in fact, significantly worse. The United States has been running an overall trade deficit since 1976, and since 2000, exports generally have not even matched 75 percent of imports, as figure 3.1 shows.[5]

These losses in relative industrial leadership occurred quite suddenly. As Nick Crafts writes, "The main losses in the British share of manufactured trade came in the 1950s and 1960s."[6] In the United States, the crisis devel-

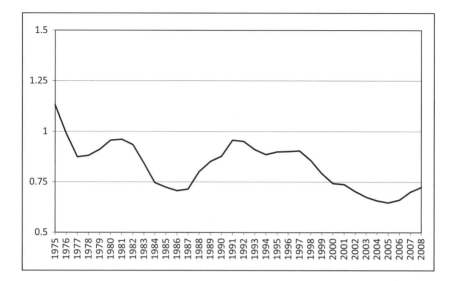

Figure 3.1 Ratio of U.S. Exports to Imports, 1975–2008
Source: Based on statistics and information from the Bureau of Economic Analysis.

oped toward the end of the 1990s, as the country lost one-third of its manufacturing employment. In the case of the United Kingdom, it was the rise of
continental European manufacturing that hurt it the most. As Crafts notes,
"The European overtaking of the U.K. is revealed as a new phenomenon of
the 1960s and 1970s."[7] In America's case, it was Southeast Asia in general,
and China in particular.

The risk is that once a nation gets into this cycle of decline it is very hard
to get out of it. As Singh explains, "Once the economy is in long-run dis-
equilibrium, for whatever reason, continued participation in international
economic relations on the same terms as before may produce a vicious cir-
cle of causation. As a consequence, a country in a weak competitive position
may have balance-of-payments difficulties, which lead the country to have a
lower level of demand, which leads to lower investment and hence lower
growth of productivity and continuing balance-of-payment difficulties.
There may be no automatic market mechanism to correct the disequilib-
rium."[8] As the United Kingdom has now experienced for thirty years, this
has largely been true. The U.K. economy recently has gained from some
foreign direct investment in manufacturing, largely because both relative

wages and the value of the pound fell, making it cheaper to produce in Britain. But it wasn't enough to offset the prior losses. And while the losses were somewhat masked in the late 1990s and the 2000s by the expansion of the financial sector, the global financial crisis swept away much of that growth.

In the case of the United States, it's too early to tell whether decline can be replaced by renewal: whether we can tear down the rotting house and build a new one, scrap the Cadillac and buy a Tesla Roadster. But what the experience of the United Kingdom demonstrates all too well is that nations can lose innovation leadership. If the United States hopes to avoid the United Kingdom's fate it will need to do what Britain did not: recognize the gravity of the situation and act decisively and boldly before it's too late.

There is actually no secret to global economic success (and decline). Success comes when nations combine the ingredients needed to build vibrant, healthy business establishments in globally traded sectors. Decline comes when they do not. Traded-sector success requires business leaders willing to take risks and invest in research and development (R&D), engineering, and new plants and equipment (including computers and software), especially when these investments may not immediately pay off. It requires a workforce that supports the introduction of those technologies and associated changes in work organization.

But private-sector action alone is not enough. Success also requires government policies that actively support enterprises investing in the future. At the macro level, this means trade and currency policies that enable businesses to be internationally competitive, and fiscal and monetary policies that encourage them to invest. At the micro level, it means an innovation policy focused on supporting industrially relevant R&D; efficient transfer of technology from universities, federal labs, and other intermediary research organizations to industry; and technical assistance for small- and midsized manufacturers. It also means support for key input factors, including a skilled workforce and the right infrastructures, including digital infrastructure (such as wireless and wireline broadband and the smart electric grid). Two key political economy factors make it more likely that a government will take these steps: The first is the presence of an economics profession that sees loss of industrial market share not as evidence of markets working, but of their failure, and one that also believes government action is needed to support industrial competitiveness. The second is an understanding on the part of elites that maintaining a relatively high standard of living requires industrial competitiveness.

Traded-sector decline comes when businesses, labor, governments, economists, and political elites fail to support innovation policy, or support it to a lesser extent than a nation's competitors. The United Kingdom generally did the opposite of what was needed to thrive economically and it paid a heavy price. The United States has followed a similar path for at least a quarter century, and it has also paid a price. And if Britain is any guide, America will continue to decline unless it changes course.

Before discussing the causes of industrial decline, it's important to note what we mean by industrial "establishments." Many companies and all large ones are multiestablishment enterprises, an establishment being the factory, office, or other facility of a business enterprise. In other words, General Motors (GM) is an enterprise, but it has hundreds of establishments, such as car assembly factories, throughout the nation. Even in an uncompetitive economy, a nation's multinational enterprises may be highly competitive, but enterprises in globally traded industries locate many of their establishments, especially ones engaged in high-value-added production, in other nations. In contrast, an economy packed with highly productive and innovative establishments at home will be successful. We also use the word "industrial" specifically to mean an economy's traded sectors that are subject to international competition. This includes some of the extraction sectors (mining, lumber, farming, and so forth), most of manufacturing, and some services (such as software, entertainment content like movies, consulting, and engineering services). National industrial success does not require success in all sectors, but the larger the nation, the broader the success must be in order to avoid chronic trade deficits and relatively slower income growth.

Comparing U.K. and U.S. Factors of Industrial Decline

Because the United Kingdom's decline occurred more than forty years ago, there is an array of scholarly articles and books analyzing it. Reviewing this literature, the commonalities between U.S. and U.K. industrial decline are remarkably striking. While it is not possible to construct a "scientific" comparison of factors of decline, at least twenty factors appear remarkably similar.

Factor 1: Uneven Management Quality

Much has been written about the failure of U.K. industries. Just say "British Leyland" (the ill-fated move to consolidate British automaking), and industrial decline springs to mind. But why did British companies fail to meet the challenge of international competition when companies in other nations did? Some blame the widespread failure of managers. Crafts cites an array of studies to make his argument that "the chief of these persistent weaknesses relative to other leading economies lay in poor quality of management."[9] While U.S. management appears to be better on the whole, certainly poor management has been at the heart of the decline of some key U.S. sectors, such as automobiles.[10]

Factor 2: Corporate Investment Cuts

Without constantly investing to refresh the drivers of innovation in establishments—R&D, new plant and equipment, and a skilled workforce—sustained industrial success is impossible. Yet, firms in both nations cut back on these building blocks in favor of short-term profits and overseas expansion. As Crafts notes, R&D played a role "in explaining weak British trade performance in manufacturing . . . the share of U.K. GDP spent on R&D remained at the same level while for the average of the other countries there was a rise of 0.43 percentage points."[11] In the United States, corporate R&D as a share of GDP increased by just 3 percent from 1999 to 2008, while it increased in China (187 percent), Korea (58 percent), and Japan (27 percent), as well as the European nations of Hungary (90 percent), Spain (66 percent), Finland (28 percent), and Germany (11 percent). Crafts attributes the United Kingdom's decline in part to "weak research and development by the business sector and inadequate training of workers."[12] Likewise, American firms have cut back on both. From 1999 to 2007, investments by U.S. business in workforce training declined by 45 percent (as a share of GDP), while corporations struggled to maintain R&D investment (which declined by 0.03 percent as a share of GDP) after increasing it for decades.[13]

Manufacturing firms in both nations also curtailed investment in plant and equipment. As Singh writes, "Whatever index is used, the United Kingdom's investment record in recent years has been disappointing. . . . Whereas between 1954–56 and 1963–65 manufacturing investment at constant prices grew by 39 percent, between 1963–65 and 1972–74 it grew only by 19 percent. Further, over the period 1964–72, manufacturing investment as a proportion of GDP was on average lower in the United Kingdom than in most competitor countries."[14] Change the years and substitute "U.S." for "U.K." and the story is even worse: "Whereas between 1989 and 1998 the stock of U.S. manufacturing plant and equipment at constant prices grew by 36 percent, between 1999 and 2009 it declined by 1 percent, while fixed assets overall (including housing) increased by 38 percent."[15] Further, during the period 2000 to 2008, manufacturing investment as a proportion of GDP was, on average, lower in the United States than in most competitor countries.

Factor 3: A Focus on Overseas, Rather Than Domestic, Investment

While foreign investment can help enterprises, if it comes at the expense of domestic investment, it can hurt domestic establishments. This happened in both nations. As Kitson and Michie note, there was "continued overseas orientation of . . . [U.K.] multinational corporations."[16] Crafts writes that "relative to large firms elsewhere, large U.K. manufacturing firms may be investing more abroad than at home."[17] We see the same pattern in the United States, where, when examined as a share of gross national product (GNP), the overseas capital expenditures of U.S.-headquartered, manufacturing multinational corporations increased by 9 percent between 2000 and 2009, while their domestic expenditure decreased by nearly 50 percent.[18] In essence, factors 2 and 3 indicate that

U.S. enterprises have been investing less, especially compared to other nations.

Factor 4: Focus on Short-Term Returns, Dividend Payments, and Rate of Return Ratios

Companies in both nations focused more on financial engineering and short-term calculus than on investing for the long term. As Kitson and Michie write, in the United Kingdom, there was a focus on "growth in companies by acquisition and financial engineering rather than through organic development and building on products and markets . . . with an emphasis on comparisons of near-term financial results on judging our companies."[19] The same was true in the United States. In a 2004 survey of more than four hundred U.S. executives, 80 percent indicated that they would decrease discretionary spending on areas such as R&D, advertising, maintenance, and hiring in order to meet short-term earnings targets, and more than 50 percent said they would delay new projects, even if it meant sacrifices in value creation.[20]

These pressures from financial markets for immediate returns meant, as Kitson and Michie write with regard to the United Kingdom, "that increased profits went disproportionately into dividend payments rather than investment."[21] This has happened with U.S. manufacturers, with the ratio of dividends paid to the amount they invested in capital equipment increasing from the low 20 percent range in the late 1970s and early 1980s, to around 40 percent to 50 percent in the early 1990s, to above 60 percent in the 2000s.[22] In other words, rather than reinvesting in capital equipment in U.S. establishments, market pressures have forced companies to keep share prices high by paying greater dividends. Significantly, dividend payments increased substantially after Congress slashed the tax rate individuals paid on corporate dividends in 2003, exactly as predicted by financial experts like Aswath Damodaran, professor of business at the Stern School of Business at New York University (NYU). Damodaran predicted that tax cuts on dividend income would lead to "a dramatic surge both in the number of companies that pay dividends and in how much they pay and a cut-back on larger investments that take longer to receive a payback." He went on to portend: "If the desire to pay dividends causes firms to shift funds from good investments to dividends, these firms and society will pay a price in the form of less real investment and lower growth."[23] And this is exactly what happened.

In this sense, the neoclassical economics view that high rates of hostile takeovers and short-term financial pressures lead to superior performance is wrong. As Crafts writes, "The British arrangements might be thought more likely to correct managerial failure, but . . . in practice, the effectiveness of German banks as monitors of firm performance and the ineffectiveness of the British takeover mechanism in singling out poor performance and leading to efficiency gains post-merger may make the German arrangements unambiguously superior."[24]

In the United States, too, this pressure to achieve short-term profits all too often has meant sacrificing long-term investment. As the Business Roundtable, the leading trade association for large American businesses, reported, "The obsession with short-term results by investors, asset management firms, and corporate managers collectively leads to the unintended consequences of destroying long-term value, decreasing market efficiency, reducing investment returns, and impeding efforts to strengthen corporate governance."[25]

Such financial pressures have forced many U.S. firms not only to cut back on the growth of their research budgets but also to reallocate their research portfolios more toward product development efforts and away from longer-term and more speculative basic and applied research. As figure 3.2 illustrates, from 1991 to 2008, basic research as a share of corporate R&D conducted in the United States fell by 3.6 percent, while applied research fell by roughly the same amount, 3.5 percent. In contrast, development's share increased by 7.1 percent.[26]

Harvard Business School's Clayton Christensen raises a related concern: that the aggressive pursuit of short-term profitability—which is taught in American business schools mostly as profitability understood in percentage rates of return (because evaluating rates of return in percentages allows easy comparisons with other investment alternatives)—is actually killing

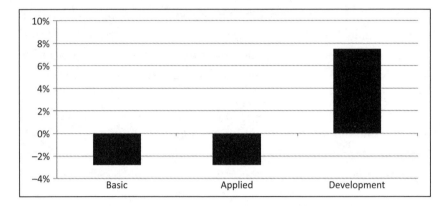

Figure 3.2 Change in Allocation of Corporate R&D, 1991–2008
Source: Based on statistics from the National Science Board.

American innovation. As Christensen notes, many American firms focus on a measure called RONA, Return on Net Assets, as a key measure of performance, but this often leads them to focus on reducing the denominator, assets, as many U.S. companies did in outsourcing much of their manufacturing plant to Asia. Another example, as Steve Denning notes, is firms' "pernicious methodology for calculating the internal rate of return (IRR) on an investment. It causes you to focus on smaller and smaller wins. Because if you ever use your money for something that doesn't pay off for years, the IRR is so crummy that people who focus on IRR focus their capital on shorter and shorter-term wins."[27] Christensen excoriates mainstream thinking about profitability in U.S. business schools and on Wall Street, "We measure profitability by these ratios. Why do we do it? The finance people have preached this almost like a gospel to the rest of us that if you describe profitability by a ratio you can compare profitability in different industries. This 'neutralizes' the measures so that you can apply them across sectors to every firm."[28] Christensen notes that Asian enterprises explicitly reject this type of thinking and are much more focused on accumulating assets that can build future wealth, and he argues that the outsourcing that has occurred in many U.S. manufacturing industries—from autos and steel to semiconductors and pharmaceuticals—has been driven in part by this overzealous and misguided focus on profitability measures like RONA.

Factor 5: Businesses That Reject Government's Role in Industrial Development

National industrial success depends on the acumen of business, but government can help or hurt business efforts. Finding the right balance is at the heart of any successful political economy, but if business leaders reject government assistance as an inappropriate intrusion into the marketplace, government is likely to stay on the sidelines. After all, why go where you are not wanted? In the United Kingdom, industrial leaders "were deeply suspicious of anything which smacked of state socialism" and that included efforts to develop a private sector supporting national industrial strategy.[29] Many U.S. businesses and the organizations representing them have exactly the same view. With respect to the twenty million jobs America needs, the U.S. Chamber of Commerce asserts that "only American free enterprise is capable of meeting this challenge."[30] When the head of the National Federation of Independent Businesses announced opposition to efforts by the Obama administration to spur job creation, he stated that government help wasn't wanted because jobs will be created by "the hard working small business men and women when these entrepreneurs have taken enough calculated risks needed to expand their businesses."[31] Funny how they didn't take the calculated risks on their own to keep the economy out of a deep recession with no net job creation in more than a decade. When your nation's leading business organizations are telling government, "stay out, we don't want or need your help," you can bet that government will do just that. But the result is tantamount to removing a leg from a three-legged stool.

Factor 6: Unions' Push for Excessive Compensation

While business decisions ultimately determine a nation's industrial advance or decline, workers play an important role. Workers certainly have rights to decent wages, benefits, and working conditions, but in the United Kingdom and the United States unions often failed to see their obligations to their members' employers or became stakeholders in their long-term health only too late. While they can do little to turn shortsighted, timid industrial managers into farsighted, risk-taking leaders, unions can thwart the efforts of the latter. And in both nations, unionized workers did that all too often, seeking wage and benefit packages that firms ultimately could not support and remain competitive. As Pollard writes, "In many branches of [U.K.] industry the employees reached the view that since there was no natural growth, they should take as much as possible out of their firm."[32] Likewise, in some U.S. unionized industries like autos and steel, union wage and benefit demands exceeded the ability of the companies to pay them and still be competitive. Moreover, management gave in to the demands, ignoring the competition on the horizon. And one result, among others, was the bankruptcy of GM and Chrysler. Or, as legendary U.S. labor leader Samuel Gompers was once asked: What, exactly, was organized labor after? What was the endgame? How much would be enough? Gompers answered "more," explaining that "when it becomes more, we shall still want more. And we shall never cease to demand more until we have received the results of our labor."[33]

Factor 7: Union Opposition to New Technology

Unions actively negotiated with firms in both nations to slow down the introduction of new technology that would have helped firms in their battle for international innovation advantage. As Crafts writes, "Bargaining practices in the United Kingdom tended in the 1970s to retard and dilute the gains from the introduction of new technology."[34] In the United States, many industrial unions have seen new technology as a threat. In the early part of the 2000s, for example, the United Auto Workers (UAW) special bargaining convention set an agenda that called for income protections, including from layoffs associated with new technology or productivity improvements. A few short years later, many got laid off—not from productivity improvements, but from a lack of them. To be fair, in contrast to most industrialized countries, the United States has a weaker safety net and one that is still significantly tied to jobs, making union demands for job security more likely than what unions in nations like Sweden might bargain for.

Factor 8: Adversarial Labor Relations

Unions (and managers) in both nations often saw industrial relations as zero-sum. Unions didn't try to increase the size of the pie and then ensure that workers got their fair share; instead, they focused on getting a bigger share of the pie, regardless of whether it was growing. As Pollard writes, "Even if the future should show that new technology means better jobs rather than unemployment, this will still be a long way from the widespread conviction which is familiar in other countries, but very rare here, that improvements in pay, except of the most limited and temporary kind, can come only from greater productivity. We are even further away from a positive interest by unions themselves in the productivity of their members."[35] Another U.K. observer, Peter Jenkins, contends, "[But] the approach so successful wherever it has been tried will not be allowed to be tried here. The trade unions will see to that. . . . Their commitment to competitive collective bargaining, their vested interests in declining industries and over-manned plant, and their inability to reform themselves or effectively lead their members are seemingly insuperable barriers to the adoption of a wealth-creating Social Democratic approach."[36] In the United States, industrial unions all too often played the same role, believing it their job to oppose managerial efforts to boost productivity and to innovate.

Factor 9: Union Focus on Short-Term Gains

Industrial unions in both nations acted in ways that jeopardized their long-term interests for the same reasons corporate managers did: all their incentives were to maximize short-term gain at the expense of long-term stability. Even if unions realized they were harming the firm, all too often they couldn't stop themselves. As Pollard concludes, "What occurred in industry after industry in the U.K. was a Greek tragedy. . . . Somehow workers in some sectors have found themselves destroying their firm, fully aware of what they were doing, yet unable to stop. They found themselves answering strike calls . . . in the full awareness that . . . the result could only be ruin for all concerned."[37] The description bears a striking resemblance to what occurred in many unionized U.S. industries. We asked a former United Auto

Workers union leader: If the UAW knew then what it knows now about the decline of the Big Three (Ford, General Motors, and Chrysler), would it have done things differently? His response was "no." While he acknowledged that UAW actions hurt the Big Three, he believed that union leadership could have acted no differently. If it did, he said, workers would have voted UAW leadership out and installed leaders who would "stand up for the interests of workers now."

Factor 10: *Governments Saw Their Main Role as Preserving Macroeconomic Stability*

The list of errors made by the U.K. and U.S. governments is extensive, but perhaps the most fundamental was that they let economic policy be run by their respective Treasury Departments. While other ministries/departments have an interest in the economy, in both nations, they were shunted to the sidelines as secondary players. This would be okay if it was not for the fact that Treasury officials ignored industrial competitiveness. In reviewing why the U.K. government not only failed to act time after time to address industrial decline, but actually took actions that made things worse, Pollard writes:

> We are looking for a body of ideas and of principles strong and pervasive enough to make governments continue with their policies even though they have led over a period of three decades . . . to the most devastating economic failure recorded in modern history and do not even make sense in their own terms. . . . Moreover, we are looking for principles held by British governments and policymakers but not by others—except those, like the United States in recent years, that have shown equally dismal economic results. . . . There is one and only one principle which will fit the bill: it is the principle of concentrating first and foremost on symbolic figures and quantities, like prices, exchange rates, and balances of payments, to the neglect of real quantities, like goods and services produced and traded. In particular, the subordination of one to the other is such that whenever there is a clash of interests, the real must be sacrificed to the symbolic.[38]

It is no different in the United States, where policymakers at the Treasury (but also at the Office of Management and Budget and the President's

Council of Economic Advisors) spend much of their time focused on issues related to interest rates, inflation, savings rates, tax simplification, and other monetary factors. For them, the actual industrial composition of an economy is irrelevant, for in the words of Michael Boskin, head of former president George H. W. Bush's Council of Economic Advisors: "Potato chips, computer chips, what's the difference?" For policymakers at these agencies, any kind of manufacturing strategy is seen as inappropriate "industrial policy" that distorts the natural allocation of resources in the economy.

Factor 11: Policymakers Abdicated Any Role in Reversing Industrial Decline

Even in the rare cases where businesses in both nations asked government for help, government's response was more often than not, "We're not going to give it to you, because helping you would be bad for the economy. After all, you are just another rent seeker coming for your government handout." As Pollard explains, U.K. officials believed that "government has no role or function in the productive sphere of the economy as such. Its task is to set the scene, to provide the best possible conditions by demand management, by a favourable fiscal and financial system and by general legislation, and let business . . . flourish within them." He goes on to note, "the whole of post-war policy has been built on the assumption that whatever else can be manipulated or changed, actual production and investment cannot be and must be left to industry, and that the most the government can do is to set the scene which therefore receives top priority—at the expense of damaging the production and the investment."[39]

This is, of course, exactly what most U.S. economic policymakers believe, whether Democrat or Republican. It has become almost a requirement that any government report on economic policy start with the disclaimer that the job of government is merely to set the stage and to create the climate in which companies can create wealth and jobs. The next statement is normally something right from the Chamber of Commerce Web site, such as "the government does not create jobs."[40] When the prevailing view is that civilized governments do not help ensure industrial competitiveness, governments do not. This high-minded stance reminds one of then secretary of state Henry Stimson's old-school assertion (when shutting down the State Department's Intelligence Office in the 1920s) that "gentlemen do not open other gentlemen's mail." Fortunately, Stimson changed his view when serving as secretary of war during WWII.

Factor 12: Policies That Deter Investment

Investment is the most important factor determining industrial success or decline. And government plays a key role in investment, both through the investments it makes directly (for example, funding scientific research) and through policies it implements (or does not) to encourage private-sector investment. In the United Kingdom, a particularly damaging government role was its on-again, off-again fiscal policy. Because the government was so concerned with maintaining the value of its currency and avoiding a balance-of-payments crisis, it put the brakes on growth whenever excess demand threatened to run up the trade deficit, making it difficult for business to invest. As Pollard writes, "In our search for a cause of the British failure to invest we have come upon one single overwhelmingly important answer: investment in Britain was low because the whole panoply of government power, as exercised above all by the Treasury, was designed to keep it so." As one government official put it, "It was a good thing that businesses were investing less . . . as this helped exports and the balance of payments."[41] Of course, by investing less, industry became even less competitive and the balance-of-payments problem became even worse.

There is no direct analogue in the United States, where economic policymakers have been blasé at best about massive trade deficits. However, since the late 1970s, federal policy—particularly Federal Reserve Bank policy—has focused more on keeping inflation in check than on keeping unemployment low, with the result being reduced demand and industrial investment. Case in point, the Federal Reserve under the leadership of Paul Volker in the 1970s pursued aggressive anti-inflation policies to limit investment and, in so doing, spurred a deep recession, all in an effort to address what was likely a temporary blip of inflation from the 1979 Organization of Petroleum Exporting Countries (OPEC) oil embargo.

Policymakers in both nations also shared the same view toward public investment and tax incentives for investment. U.K. policymakers were quick to cut investment tax credits for industry, especially in times of tight budgets. In the United States, because of the views of neoclassical economists, particularly at the Treasury, policymakers eliminated tax incentives for investment in plants and equipment in the 1986 U.S. Tax Reform Act. With the exception of a few temporary incentives put in place during recessions, the tax code has not favored capital investment since (with the exception of housing). In addition, despite having the twenty-sixth weakest R&D tax credit in the world as of 2011, almost all attempts to expand the R&D credit have been sacrificed on the altar of budget balancing. More recently, there was resistance from conservative and liberal neoclassical economists alike to President Obama's proposal to let companies (big and small) expense the full cost of their equipment purchases made in late 2010 and 2011.[42] Yet, allowing accelerated depreciation of capital equipment purchases is exactly the type of policy the United States needs to counter the slow growth of capital equipment investment by companies in the United States, particularly manufacturers; the noncompetitiveness of the U.S. corporate tax code; and the dramatic decline in U.S. manufacturing output and jobs.

Factor 13: Governments Don't Distinguish between Spending and Investment

For the U.K. Exchequer and U.S. Office of Management and Budget (OMB), spending and investment are the same: they both cost the government money and both are on the chopping block when it comes time to wield the budget ax. At times, investments were actually singled out for special cuts. As Pollard states, "To cut investment was the easy touch."[43] He goes on to note that "in times of stress they were treated as equally worthy of cuts—indeed, capital expenditure was generally treated as more easily dispensable, since it offered fewer toes to be trodden on."[44] One U.K. prime minister agreed: "So far as possible, the necessary cuts will be made at the expense of longer-term projects, because the constituency for spending was much stronger than the constituency for investment, which by definition costs money now to produce benefits in the future."[45]

The same can be said for the OMB, which is as likely to cut budget requests from the National Institute of Standards and Technology (NIST) for R&D funding as requests for wasteful farm subsidies from the Department of Agriculture. In the face of growing budget deficits, U.S. policymakers have largely refused to cut spending (either direct spending on entitlements or indirect spending in the form of tax cuts to individuals), but have been more than willing to cut investment (for example, in science, technology, transportation, workforce training, and education).

In both nations, budget agencies saw their role as limiting spending rather than ensuring adequate resources for investments to maintain their respective nation's industrial leadership. As Pollard writes, "It is to be found in the traditional job of the Treasury, which is to keep down the expenditure of the other government departments. Expenditure is therefore traditionally seen as the enemy, the evil to be kept down; the actual efficiency of the expenditure in terms of the social or economic good it might do, or the comparative efficiency of two competing claims, are completely outside the Treasury's traditional range."[46] The same statement applies equally well to the United States' OMB, where all agency budgets are viewed with suspicion.

Factor 14: A Focus on Military Spending

Budget agencies did, however, stand up for one kind of spending: military spending. In explaining why the United Kingdom cut key public investments, particularly support for civilian R&D, Pope writes: "One important reason for this was the substantial diversion of resources into an international military role that was beyond the country's means."[47] Pollard notes that "while we built tanks and planes, they [Germany and Japan] built the machinery with which to achieve their later successes."[48]

The same is true for the United States, where military budgets have been sacrosanct with support for commercial R&D taking a backseat to military R&D. For example, 51.4 percent of the U.S. federal R&D budget is devoted to defense-oriented R&D, almost triple the U.K. share of expenditure (18.3 percent). In contrast, non-U.S. Organization for Economic Cooperation and Development (OECD) countries, on average, allocate 3.9 percent of their federal R&D budgets to defense-oriented activities. And whereas just 5 percent of the U.S. federal R&D budget is dedicated explicitly toward economic growth, the OECD average is three times greater, and much more in countries such as Finland and Korea, which allocate 40 percent and 44 percent, respectively, of their federal R&D budgets toward broader economic growth.[49] The responsibilities of superpower status carry a high price, but the policies of the United Kingdom and the United States to favor military over civilian spending, instead of supporting both, could have an even higher price.

Factor 15: Policymakers Support a Strong Currency

When industries lose international market share and the nation starts running a trade deficit, currency markets should lower the value of the nation's currency so that companies can regain price competitiveness. But because of their financial as opposed to industrial orientation, policymakers in both countries ignored this simple lesson and instead defended their currency. In the United Kingdom, policymakers were obsessed with preserving the value of the pound sterling. As Kitson and Michie write, "macroeconomic policy for the past 30 years has resulted repeatedly in an overvalued exchange rate."[50] As Pollard explains, the reason was clear: "The sterling was still a world currency used by many of the oil producers, among others, and in order not to let them down or disappoint those who used the City of London as their banking centre, devaluation was ruled out repeatedly and much more harmful measures to the economy preferred instead."[51]

A half century later, the dollar is the reserve currency and economic policymakers concerned more with helping Wall Street than "Industrial Street" seek to keep its value high. Otherwise, in the face of massive trade deficits and soaring unemployment, how can President Obama's Treasury secretary, Timothy Geithner, proclaim that "we will never weaken our currency"?[52] Perhaps he can say this because he does not see a "contradiction between the U.S.'s policy of bolstering its exports and its strong-dollar policy."[53] But Geithner is not an anomaly. Since the mid-1970s, a strong dollar has been the stated policy of every administration, Republican or Democrat. In mid-2008, as the economy could begin to hear the roar of the financial crisis waterfall in the distance, President Bush made it clear: "We're strong dollar people in this administration, and have always been for a strong dollar."[54] In the rare instance where a Washington official did not support the Washington strong dollar consensus, the pressure was on. As former Bush administration Treasury secretary Paul O'Neill stated, "When I was Secretary of the Treasury I was not supposed to say anything but 'strong dollar, strong dollar.' I argued then and would argue now that the idea of a strong dollar policy is a vacuous notion."[55] For these and other heretical views, O'Neill was replaced by someone who knew the right tune. Interestingly, unlike most recent Treasury secretaries who either came from Wall Street (for example, Nicholas Brady, Robert Rubin, Henry Paulson, and Tim Geithner) or were financial economists (Larry Summers), O'Neill came from industry, having served as CEO of Alcoa, a metals firm. As such, he knew firsthand the negative effect of an overly strong dollar on industrial competitiveness. To be sure, a stronger dollar means consumers pay less for imports, but that is a bit akin to saying that consumers are better off when they don't pay their monthly credit card bills in full. They are better off in the short term, but at some point, the day of reckoning arrives when the full bill must be paid.

Factor 16: Neoclassical Economists Call the Shots

While economics is far from a science, and is characterized by competing doctrines or worldviews, the dominant one in both nations is "neoclassical economics." Neoclassical economists focus principally on price-mediated transactions in marketplaces, which they believe produce the most efficient allocation of goods and services.[56] Since, by definition, markets are efficient, the natural role of government is limited.

No other nations have ceded economic policymaking to neoclassical economists to the degree that the United Kingdom and the United States have. As Pollard observes, "It may well be that the very quality of post-war economics, the greater sophistication of its theoretical constructions, its much refined statistical and econometric methods, have put it out of touch with real economic situations. Economic theory, as it has developed in the Anglo-Saxon world, turns out to have been a handicap rather than an aid to good policy." He goes on to argue that "neoclassical economic theory, the kind taught in recent decades, may therefore be an excellent training of the mind, but it is among the worst possible preparations for giving advice on practical economic policy decisions. It was precisely that training in which Britain excelled."[57] Unfortunately, the dominance of neoclassical economics is, if anything, even stronger in the United States, where all major (and almost all of the minor) university economic departments teach it, and virtually all economists in important positions in the federal government are trained in and subscribe to it.[58]

The problem with neoclassical economics is that not only do its devotees lecture policymakers that there is little they can do to spur industrial development, but they also warn that any efforts to examine individual sectors with an eye to helping only makes things worse by preventing the market from efficiently allocating resources. As Pollard notes with regard to the United Kingdom, "It is highly significant that nowadays economists specify carefully that they are considering the 'real economy' on the rare occasions when they do so, instead of the world of symbols in which they usually move." Asking them to understand actual industries and design policies to spur industrial competitiveness would be akin to asking a theoretical physicist to design a bridge. The result is that U.K. and U.S. neoclassical economists look with disdain on "real world" economics. As Pollard comments in reference to the attitude of British economists toward French policies in the 1960s to steer investment to key sectors such as iron, steel, and transport, "such a plan would have been much beneath the dignity of British economists, trained to think in macrofigures: they would have left such tasks to hacks and to East Europeans."[59]

In the United States, the neoclassical straitjacket is even more constricting. Before one can advocate for even the most modest government action to spur innovation, one must prove "market failure." If someone has the temerity to assert that U.S. manufacturing has declined, the response is "the market produced this result, so it is beneficial, and by the way, manufacturing is no more important than any other industry." If that person then proposes a solution—like a national manufacturing renewal strategy—the neoclassicists rise as one with a cry of "show us the market failure!" The de facto assumption is that the market is working, and it is the responsibility of the supplicant to prevail before the tribunal as to why individuals and organizations don't automatically act in their own interest; why that action doesn't produce a Pollyannaish public interest; and why government action doesn't make things worse.

But the neoclassical guild employs completely circular logic. Unless there is evidence of monopoly or government barriers, market outcomes are, by definition, the right outcomes. Thus, virtually any outcome is, by definition, the right outcome. The fact that when measured properly U.S. manufacturing output declined by over 10 percent in the last decade means not that there is a crisis in need of action, but rather that market forces are working. Like Voltaire's Dr. Pangloss, who proclaimed, "Tis demonstrated . . . the things cannot be otherwise; for, since everything is made for an end, everything is necessarily for the best end," the British and American Panglossian economists agree, virtually everything that happens in the market is for the best.

Needless to say, this is a formidable obstacle for the relatively small collection of business leaders, advocates, and scholars who call for a national innovation and competitiveness policy. On top of that, challenging the neoclassical canon is not without its risks. As Pollard argues, "It is true that anyone offering a solution out of line with the thoughts of mainstream economics runs the risk of being dubbed a crank."[60] It's no different in the United States, where the apostates risk a taunt from the neoclassicists: "It's clear that you just don't understand economics. Do you actually have a degree?"—by which they mean, "Do you have a degree in *neoclassical* economics?"

Factor 17: The Political System Ignored the Most Important Economic Issues

Businesses, unions, policymakers, and economists were all complicit in the industrial decline of the United Kingdom and the United States. But these issues all play out in a political system. And in both countries the political system largely ignored the problem, choosing instead to debate economic issues that were largely irrelevant to the challenge at hand. In the

United Kingdom, "the issues on which party debates did take place, such as nationalization, tax incentives, the social services, or the Common Market, were all issues with only marginal connections or none at all with the issues of growth and decline."[61] In the United States, the issues that have been at the heart of U.S. economic policy debates—such as the appropriate marginal tax rates for individuals, whether to sign a few more free trade agreements, whether to cut the budget deficit, or whether to simplify (as opposed to cut) corporate taxes—are also issues with only marginal connection to the issue of industrial renewal. Broader discussions about forward-looking innovation policy; the imperative to do more than tinker with the education and training system; and a frank call for patience, sacrifice, and hard work by workers, investors, and taxpayers have been absent from the political debate for years.

Factor 18: A Political System Focused on Redistribution

In both countries, the energies of the political system have been tied up in issues of distribution rather than growth. Referring to the inability of U.K. policymakers to grasp the importance of an overall growth strategy, Pollard observes: "This blindness contributed to, as it was certainly made worse by, the British political tradition of fighting over the share out of the cake rather than considering ways of increasing its size. While such emphasis on distribution is not unknown elsewhere, the consciousness that all might gain by enlarging the cake is far more firmly rooted abroad."[62] In the United States, likewise, as we discuss in chapter 9, both parties spend much of their energies fighting for a share of the pie for their respective constituencies. When tough choices have to be made between promoting innovation and supporting redistribution, the choice is usually the latter. For example, rather than fund the America COMPETES Act in 2007, which authorized increased funding for science and science education, Congress increased funding for programs like farm subsidies, income security, and health care. American voters and interest groups are determined to ensure their particular ox doesn't get gored—even if the government supplied the ox.

Factor 19: A Belief That a Healthy Manufacturing Sector Is Not Required for Economic Success

While manufacturing is not the only sector that contributes to a nation's international competitiveness, it is impossible for large economies like the United Kingdom or United States to be competitive without a viable manufacturing sector. Yet, in both nations, many elites believed that manufacturing was unimportant (a theory we debunk in chapter 4). As Kitson and Michie write, the view that the "economy can flourish internationally in the future, in the absence of a strong manufacturing sector" was widespread in the United Kingdom.[63] In the United States, statements like Kevin Hassett's, a scholar at the conservative American Enterprise Institute, that "manufacturing has been on a more-or-less-steady decline as a share of national output for decades, part of the natural evolution of the U.S. economy," or Lawrence Summers's comment that "America's role is to feed a global economy that's increasingly based on knowledge and services rather than on making stuff" have become part of the Washington economic consensus.[64] Inside the closed world of the Washington economic consensus there is no way to justify a manufacturing strategy: If manufacturing has declined, the market has deemed it is no longer important. If manufacturing hasn't declined, then there is no need for a strategy. And besides, manufacturing is no different than massage therapy; they both employ people and produce economic output, the Washington economic consensus claims.

Factor 20: Reluctance by Elites to Admit Relative Decline

Finally, in both nations, a distorted view of past advantage made it difficult for elites to admit decline. As Eatwell observes, a problem was that the United Kingdom was "unable, or unwilling, to adapt to a competitive world in which its pre-eminence could no longer be taken for granted."[65] Likewise, the consensus view among most U.S. elites is that America has been number one, is number one, and will continue to be number one. In short, America is exceptional. From Tocqueville to the present day, there is a long strand of thinking that holds that America is qualitatively different from other nations and, for many, this means qualitatively better. To acknowledge that the U.S. economy is no longer the innovation leader directly challenges this ideology. Presenting evidence from the *Atlantic Century* report that the U.S. rank in global innovation-based competitiveness has fallen has elicited responses ranging from "we are still the biggest innovator" to "we may be losing this round, but we will out-innovate them in the next round" to "other nations may be the assemblers, but we will be the orchestrators." Indeed, President Obama's patriotism and fitness to govern came under attack when he offered a thoughtful reflection that past greatness is not a guarantee of tomorrow's success.

Some argue that the reason for denial is like the proverbial frog in the frying pan—the heat of economic decline has been increasing too gradually to notice. These advocates invoke the need for a "Sputnik moment" that will wake America up. When the Russians launched a satellite that orbited our skies, it was clear that the United States had been trumped. But another Sputnik moment for competitiveness is unlikely, and if we can only act with one, we won't act. (We don't even notice them anymore when they do occur, such as China's announcement in 2011 that it had built the world's fastest supercomputer, taking that crown from the United States.)[66] Moreover, when President Obama invoked the Sputnik challenge in his January 2011 State of the Union address to argue for increased investments in science and education, the response was muted at best, dismissive at worst.

As Pollard notes, "There are some who hope for the power of the trauma: the trouble with Britain, they argue, is that at no point have her misfortunes been severe enough to force upon her a fundamental reappraisal. If only we sink far enough, and disaster strikes hard enough, wide-spread changes in outlook will follow. . . . At the same time, there must be some doubt whether this sort of brinkmanship will really work as a method of concentrating the mind."[67] The same is true for the United States. The investment in denial remains strong. If the 2008–2010 economic near-death experience was the Sputnik moment that we needed, our political system seems to have missed it. For accepting that there is a crisis means accepting that what America has been doing and believing in is no longer working and that new ways of doing and believing are needed. It is easier to just deny the existence of the problem. As T. S. Eliot wrote, "Humankind cannot bear very much reality." And if the reality in the United Kingdom was bad, it's potentially as bad in the United States, especially in the absence of action.

One would assume that after the U.K. industrial sector sank as far as it did, elites would have woken up and sounded the clarion call for action. But even today it is not widely accepted that the United Kingdom suffered a serious decline. Even some who have studied the issue remain in denial. After all, they assert, Britain is still richer today than some other nations. Rex Pope, author of *The British Economy since 1914: A Study in Decline?* reflects this view when he states, "However we measure U.K. economic condition and well-being in relation to the G7 nations or the other members of the European Commission, we should remember that these are clubs containing the richest of the world's states. The gap between the U.K. and those within these groups with stronger economies is much less than that between the U.K. and the great majority of the world's nations."[68] Should the United States fail to turn around its economic ship of state, such sentiments will likely be standard fare in the 2020s. You can almost hear the neoclassical economist–inspired *New York Times* editorial board stating: "Even though we no longer have much manufacturing and even though our per capita income growth has slowed to a crawl, we are still richer than the Zimbabweans."

These views—excuses, really—are all too prevalent today in America and are a central barrier to action. For, just as Alcoholics Anonymous famously states that the first step to overcoming alcoholism is to admit being an alcoholic, the first step to reversing America's slide in the race for global innovation advantage is to admit that our nation is slipping.

4

Why Do So Many Refuse to See U.S. Structural Economic Decline?

Given how clear it is that the United States is losing the race for global innovation advantage, why isn't this regularly the subject of op-eds, conferences, and congressional hearings? The simple answer is that notwithstanding the occasional report or op-ed,[1] most U.S. pundits, policymakers, and economists have steadfastly refused to heed the abundant warning signs of long-term structural U.S. economic and competitive decline. For example, in a 2008 report prepared for the Bush administration, the RAND Corporation reviewed key indicators to evaluate the current state of U.S. science and technology (S&T) competitiveness.[2] The report contended that the "clarion call" of concern about threats to the state of U.S. S&T competitiveness was alarmist and overblown, despite the fact that many of the indicators they presented actually did suggest significant decline in the U.S. position. But, as we have seen, there is ample room for concern about the current state of the U.S. economy, its S&T enterprise, and the country's future ability to compete.

Excuses for Ignoring Competitiveness Decline

Whether it comes to individuals, organizations, or nations, admitting defeat or decline is difficult. It's much easier and more comforting to profess that all is well. As we discuss in chapter 3, that's what much of the U.K. elite did for decades. In both the United Kingdom and the United States, "apostles of denial" emerged to preach a comforting—but ultimately counterproductive—gospel of good news.[3] There are at least eleven major reasons why the United States has been so slow to recognize its structural economic decline. The first six relate to a denial of the problem, the last five to the belief that we are doing better than we really are.

Excuse 1: The United States Always Has Led in Innovation, and Always Will

There's no question that in the half century after World War II (WWII), the United States boasted the world's leading economy and dominated the innovation landscape. Indeed, in the decades following WWII, an ingrained attitude developed that the U.S. economy was so superior that no other country could conceivably match it. President Harry Truman boasted that "American industry dominates world markets and our workmen no longer need fear the competition of foreign workers."[4] In 1953, the President's Advisory Board for Mutual Security called for the unilateral elimination of U.S. tariffs on automobiles and consumer electronics imports because "U.S. producers are so advanced no one can touch them." Secretary of State John Foster Dulles advised the Japanese to concentrate on exporting to Southeast Asia and forget about the U.S. market because "Japan could not make anything Americans would be interested in buying." The chief U.S. negotiator with Japan from 1954 to 1955, C. Thayer White, even emphasized that it would be stupid for Japan to build an auto industry and that it should instead import cars from America. Clyde Prestowitz notes that State Department attitudes in the 1950s were well captured by one official who stated that "the U.S. trade surplus is a serious problem and we must become really import-minded."[5] The State Department even took the extraordinary step of instructing its officers abroad to promote foreign exports to the U.S. market (but not for automobiles, of course, since others could never make them as well as we did). While American officials were looking down on Japanese economic capabilities, they were at the same time encouraging them to export to America so as to help their economy and thereby keep Japan from "going Red."[6]

The default view that the United States must by right continue to lead the world in innovation persists to this day. Economist Irwin Stelzer forthrightly declares: "America remains the source of most of the world's innovations and the home of most of its great entrepreneurs."[7] RAND confidently affirmed that "despite perceptions that the nation is losing its competitive edge, the United States remains the dominant leader in science and technology worldwide."[8] A U.S. senator reflected this prevailing wisdom in a May 2010 Senate Energy Subcommittee hearing, proclaiming: "We know that America is second to none in innovation."[9]

Most commentators assume as a matter of faith that the United States leads in research and innovation prima facie and will continue to do so indefinitely. *New York Times* columnist David Brooks asserts that if you're a member of the global creative class, whether in 2010, 2025, or 2050, you'll want to come to America "because American universities lead the world in research and draw many of the best minds from all corners of the earth."[10] Indeed, there is a widely held view that the United States must certainly lead in terms of university-based research, given our institutions such as MIT, Stanford, and the California Institute of Technology. But in fact, America ranks just twenty-second out of thirty major nations in university research and development (R&D) funding as a share of gross domestic product (GDP).[11] Even the Council on Competitiveness, the organization that presumably should be at the forefront in sounding the alarm, does the opposite, telling us that "America is better positioned than perhaps any other country to benefit from the forces that are reshaping the global economy."[12]

In his book *The Post-American World*, Fareed Zakaria asserts that the United States is not even really in direct competition with other nations because America's true economic power exists at different levels of the global supply chain. He argues that whereas Chinese manufacturers and Indian software technicians can take market share in the production phase of the supply chain, at the R&D back end and the commercialization front end—where the money is—the United States has irrefutable market dominance. Zakaria dismisses Asia, saying its countries cannot compete with the U.S. education system, and Europe, in part because its population is aging too quickly. And he asserts that no other country comes close to the United States when it comes to tomorrow's big innovations in emerging technologies like nanotechnology or biotechnology. While the United States certainly has strengths in these areas, as Greg Tassey of the National Institute of Standards and Technology (NIST) observes, "The growing global capability to innovate is casting doubt that past U.S. first-mover advantages will continue to be realized in the future. As a result of global convergence, nanotechnology will be the first emerging technology for which multiple economies are competing on equal footing to be first movers."[13] Moreover, as we see from *The Atlantic Century II* report, the United States is rapidly losing ground in innovation-based competitiveness.[14]

In short, during the past half century, the United States has developed an attitude that we always have led in innovation and always will. This has fostered an entitlement mentality which assumes that policies that were good enough to assure U.S. innovation leadership in the past will be sufficient in the future. And, even worse, this mentality believes that we can afford to abandon the successful policies of the past, such as robust funding for government R&D or the R&D tax credit. But the United States cannot simply leave its science, technology, and innovation enterprise on autopilot and expect it to continue to deliver the same level of success it produced in the past.

Excuse 2: We're Not Really Behind; The Data's the Problem

Some skeptics insist that the United States is not really lagging in innovation competitiveness, contending that some reports show America still maintaining an innovation lead, that the data or methodology used in the Information Technology and Innovation Foundation's (ITIF's) *Atlantic Century* reports (or similar ones) are faulty, or that the countries cited as innovation leaders don't count because they are smaller or have different political structures.

For example, skeptics cite reports like the World Economic Forum's (WEF's) *2009–2010 Global Competitiveness Report* or the *2008–2009 Global Innovation Index*, released by INSEAD and the Confederation of Indian Industry, which both rank the United States as first in innovation, as proof that the United States is doing just fine.[15] However, what's interesting is that the 2011 updates of both of these reports also show the United States' rank in innovation falling, from first to fourth in the WEF *Global Competitiveness Report* and from first to seventh in the *Global Innovation Index*.[16]

But, in reality, it is the methodology behind these reports that is seriously flawed, because more than two-thirds of the *Global Competitiveness Report* indicators are derived from opinion surveys. These ask business leaders questions such as "How would you rate the protection of property rights, including financial assets, in your country?" For the report's innovation subsection, only one of the indicators—patents per million citizens—is based on hard data. As another example, the 2010 WEF report ranked the United States first in venture capital and third for corporate investments in R&D out of 133 countries, based solely on executive opinion. However, among just thirty-seven nations, the actual data showed that the United States ranked fifth in both venture capital and corporate R&D.[17]

To their credit, some commentators have recognized the discrepancy between reputation and fact. For example, in response to an ITIF critique of *The Post-American World*, *Newsweek* columnist Fareed Zakaria acknowledged:

> I'd always viewed the rankings that routinely show America on top [in innovation] as authoritative. But they may be misleading. Most traditional competitiveness studies use polls—of CEOs, scientists, investors—as a key part of their measurements. For example, The World Economic Forum report relies upon surveys for almost two thirds of its data. But two studies of global innovation [the aforementioned ITIF and Boston Consulting Group studies] have been released this year, both comprehensive, and both relying entirely on government statistics and other hard data. In both, the United States does considerably worse, coming in eighth in the BCG study and sixth in ITIF's. Like a star that still looks bright in the farthest reaches of the universe but has burned out at the core, America's reputation is stronger than the hard data warrant.[18]

Some skeptics object that the nations identified as innovation leaders aren't really comparable to the United States. For example, skeptics argue that four of the top five nations in the first *Atlantic Century* report—Singapore, Sweden, Luxembourg, and Denmark—don't really count because of their small size and less complex government structures. They argue that the United States can be compared only to countries of comparable size. For example, in *The Post-American World*, Zakaria argues that Northern Europe is too small to compete and is of no consequence to American economic leadership.[19] He considers the United States' slipping somewhat in competitiveness compared to "small northern European countries like Sweden, Denmark, and Finland (whose collective population is twenty million, less than that of Texas)" of little concern. But U.S. competitiveness with these economies matters because countries around the world are intensely competing for the highest-value-added sectors of economic activity: those that generate the highest-paying jobs and the greatest economic wealth. So when Denmark gains global leadership in wind power, Singapore in life sciences, Sweden in health information technology (IT), or Finland in mobile technologies, the United States risks losing industries, companies, and ultimately employment in these leading sectors. In other words, these countries matter because they are in competition for the kinds of high-technology, high-value-added, high-paying jobs that Americans desire. The other problem with dismissing the innovative potential of small- and mid-sized nations is that, when taken together, emerging innovative nations such as the Nordic and Baltic countries, Korea, Singapore, Taiwan, and others may create a critical mass that can rival the United States in international competitiveness.[20]

Others claim that the United States isn't losing its lead because U.S. businesses are still at the technological frontier. Robert Shapiro, chair of the Washington, D.C., think tank New Democratic Network's Globalization Initiative, argues: "The data do not show that the United States is losing its technological edge, but rather that its technology companies are fully globalized."[21] Shapiro points out that U.S. companies' share of the global technology market has increased compared to those of Europe and Japan. But this is not the point. While it's certainly good that U.S. companies are not losing their global technological leadership, it's also important where that activity takes place. The key to winning the race for global innovation advantage is for a country to have a significant share of innovation-based establishments (that is, the factories, laboratories, and offices of enterprises), not just enterprises. It doesn't do as much for American workers if U.S. companies are producing high-value-added goods and services at overseas establishments (and exporting some of them to the United States) as it does if those activities are occurring at establishments inside the United States. When countries like India and China give generous subsidies or low tax rates to U.S. companies to build high-tech factories or research labs in their nations, it helps the competitiveness of U.S. companies, but it hurts the U.S. economy.

To the extent that analysts like Shapiro even admit a problem, it's that not everyone is benefiting from U.S. economic strength. As he states, "For all its strengths and successes, America's new, idea-based economy does not benefit all Americans."[22] In other words, the U.S. innovation engine is fundamentally healthy, and the only problem is that the distribution of those benefits is skewed. If that's the diagnosis, there's no need for a more competitive tax code, increased government R&D investments, and other competitiveness policies. Just provide more generous unemployment insurance benefits for the millions of Americans losing their jobs when the establishments they work for shut down or downsize.

Excuse 3: Countries Don't Compete; Only Companies Do

When young boys find themselves losing a race with their buddies, they will often stop and yell, "I'm not racing!" American elites are doing much the same thing. Better to simply pretend that you aren't racing than to lose. And a central challenge for the United States is that many of its elites, particularly those who dispense economic "wisdom," do not believe that America is in global economic—and innovation—competition with other nations. In large part, this perspective results from fundamentally flawed advice from the dominant neoclassical economists who are on record as counseling that countries do not compete, only companies do. Indeed, economist Paul Krugman made the astounding—but quite conventional (at least among neoclassical economists)—contention that "the notion that nations compete is incorrect . . . countries are not to any important degree in competition with each other."[23] Likewise, the lead economist at the Congressional Research Service has gone so far as to claim that international [economic] competitiveness is a "term without rigorous meaning."[24] As conservative economist Kevin Hassett claimed with all-too-typical economist conceit, "Non-economists regularly appeal to competitiveness when motivating a wide array of policies, while economists protest or look the other way."[25]

Since the notion that "countries don't compete, only companies do" has come to inform so much of U.S. economic and trade policy, it's important to explore the two arguments underlying Krugman's assertion. First, Krugman argues that because about 80 percent of the U.S. economy consists of nontraded goods and services intended for domestic use, the growth rate of U.S. living standards essentially equals the growth rate of domestic productivity, not U.S. productivity relative to competitors. He maintains that since the domestic, nontraded sectors of an economy really drive its productivity and growth, countries are not competing against one another for economic preeminence.

While Krugman is correct in stating that raising productivity in nontraded sectors (e.g., grocery stores, insurance companies, trucking companies, and so forth) is vitally important to a country's growth, the flaw with his first argument is that it vastly underestimates how important a nation's traded sector is to its terms of trade and to the health of its nontraded sectors. For example, there are considerable spillover effects from a healthy, high-value-added export sector because it leads to growth in domestically traded sectors. Moreover, the growth of high-value-added sectors—a predominant share of which are technology or IT jobs traded in international competition—changes the mix of sectors in an economy toward more high-value-added ones, leading to higher productivity, wages, and standards of living.

The second argument underpinning Krugman's assertion is not just partially flawed, it's fundamentally wrong. Krugman reasons that while companies do sell products that compete with each other, the companies and consumers in these nations are also simultaneously each other's main export markets and suppliers of useful imports. Since (in Krugman's view) international trade is not a zero-sum game, even if European or Asian countries gain a larger share of global high-value-added production, this benefits the United States by providing it with larger export markets and access to superior goods at a lower price. In other words, he argues, since trade is inherently win-win in nature, even if the United States lost most of its high-value-added traded sectors (imagine Apple, Boeing, Cisco, Eli Lilly, Ford, General Motors, IBM, Intel, Merck, Microsoft, and other similar companies laying off the majority of their U.S. workforce), America would still benefit from trade because at least it would receive cheaper imports and have access to larger export markets.

But the reality is that if Boeing, Ford, or the other companies mentioned here were to lay off most of their U.S. workers, America will be worse off, not better. The fact that one even has to state this is amazing since to the average "noneconomist," it's obvious and right. And here noneconomists are right. While some of those laid-off workers might find jobs with equal wages and value added, the majority would not and would ultimately end up with lower-wage, lower-value-added jobs. How could they then afford to buy those goods and services now produced overseas, other than to do what the United States has been doing for a generation: borrowing the money from overseas creditors who want us to keep importing? As chapter 7 explores, many countries intentionally seek to move their economies up the value chain to higher-value-added sectors by unfairly manipulating international trade flows. Thus, Krugman's second argument is fundamentally flawed because it drastically underestimates the impact that countries' strategies—whether fair and consistent with global trade rules or not—can have in shifting comparative advantage in critical technology-based sectors their way. It's almost as if neoclassical economists like Krugman tautologically believe that countries don't compete simply because this is stipulated in the ground rules of neoclassical economics (since countries are not supposed to have any explicit policies that drive productivity or innovation), even as stark evidence that they do compete stands in plain sight.

Returning to the flaw in Krugman's first argument, one reason so many pundits undervalue or even ignore the importance of an economy's traded sectors is that they are regurgitating the conventional neoclassical economic wisdom that what a country makes does not matter. As Michael Boskin memorably quipped, "Potato chips, computer chips, what's the difference? A hundred dollars of one or a hundred dollars of the other is still a hundred dollars."[26] But there is a difference, and it is profound. First, some industries, such as semiconductor microprocessors (computer chips) can experience very rapid growth and reductions in cost, spark the development of related industries, and increase the productivity of other sectors of the economy. In essence, spillover effects from computer chips make potato chip manufacturers more efficient. But the converse is not true. Cheaper potato chips don't make Intel more productive, they just make us fat. Second, jobs producing computer chips require a higher skill level and thus pay more than jobs producing potato chips. Third, if a country loses the computer chip industry to foreign competitors, that value similarly disappears as the industry's supply chains and industrial commons are hollowed out; the neoclassical assumption that residual assets will be redeployed to high-value-added sectors is not necessarily the case. More likely than not, many of the laid-off computer chip workers would end up working in lower-paying sectors. In fact, among the U.S. workers laid off between 2007 and 2009, about 75 percent are employed after three years, and of them, approximately 17 percent report earnings of 20 percent or more higher than their previous wages, while approximately 30 percent report earnings of 20 percent or more below their previous wages.[27]

To be generous, this conventional view that America is not in competition may have accurately described a country's economy before the emergence of the globalization era prior to the late 1970s. But today, it clearly no longer does. During the prior national economy era, if firms could not compete and went out of business, the only issue was making sure that their assets, including employees, were quickly redeployed to other companies that could compete successfully. And they almost always were deployed to firms in the same nation, so while individual workers and sometimes communities like Buffalo or Cleveland could be hurt, the nation as a whole only had to pay the transition costs (e.g., lost output while the worker was unemployed). When a high-wage, high-value-added steel mill closed in Buffalo but opened in Birmingham, Alabama, that production stayed in America. The new mill may have even used some of the same equipment that was moved from Buffalo. Buffalo may have been hurt, but Birmingham was helped. In today's economy, however, knowledge is increasingly the major factor of production and production itself is global. Today, when a software establishment closes or loses market share in America, the establishment that ends up taking that share is often located overseas. And all too often those assets, particularly knowledge, cannot be redeployed at home because they are too specialized. In other words, countries lose not only jobs but also knowledge to foreign competitors. When this happens, nations can become relatively poorer than what they would have been otherwise.

In contrast to the dominant neoclassical view, knowledge is not a free-flowing commodity held solely by individuals and traded in markets like cabbage at the grocery store. It is embedded in organizations and if organizations die, so too does a significant amount of knowledge. Moreover, there are significant spillover effects from firm activities and significant first-mover advantages, including learning effects that enable firms' early leads to translate into dominant positions. There are also significant network effects, which mean that advancement in one industry (e.g., broadband telecommunications) can lead to advancement in a host of others (e.g., Internet video). As a result, for many parts of the U.S. economy exposed to international competition, if you lose it, you can't easily reuse it. In these cases, foreign high-value imports often end up substituting for the defunct domestic product.

This alternative framework—what some have termed a neo-Schumpeterian framework (after noted economist Joseph Schumpeter)—better describes a growing share of countries' economies, particularly those sectors focused on technology- and knowledge-based production, than does the neoclassical commodity adjustment model. This means that losing international competitions in knowledge-based industries means losing much more than just the firms and their output. It means losing much of the value now dispersed among unemployed workers and underutilized suppliers. As innovation economist Greg Tassey argues, "The central failure of current economic growth models is the assumption that shifts in relative prices will automatically elicit a Schumpeterian-type efficient reaction from domestic private markets—namely an adjustment involving development/assimilations of new technologies to replace offshored ones."[28]

Take the example of advanced aerospace. Today it is a complex technology- and knowledge-based industrial ecosystem. In the United States, it involves original equipment makers (such as Boeing) manufacturing some of the most technologically complex products in history; a network of tens of thousands of specialized parts and component suppliers, including advanced jet engine makers; providers of specialized business services; educational institutions producing skilled workers, knowledge, and discoveries; and testing labs, standards, and other innovation infrastructures, all knit together by a complex system of interactions and relationships among the players. While Boeing is clearly the hub of this system, its health cannot be divorced from the health of the system.

If, however, innovation leadership is lost, it would be difficult and almost impossible to regain without dramatic, market-altering intervention. In the case of Boeing, Europe has long targeted U.S. leadership in commercial aircraft by funneling massive, World Trade Organization (WTO)–illegal subsidies to its champion, Airbus. This is coupled with significant European airline preferences for buying Airbus jets (as chapter 7 describes). On the other side of the world, China is seeking to build its own commercial airline industry, partly by copying, but ramping up, illegal European subsidies, but also by playing Boeing and Airbus against each other by tying the purchase of jets to the willingness of the winner to shift technology and production to China (also illegal under the WTO). And you can be sure that once China has extorted the technology it needs to gain competency in producing major passenger jets, it will not only stop buying foreign jets for its own market, but also will start massively subsidizing domestic jet sales to other nations, as it is currently doing for components of long-haul passenger jets.

The problem is that these subsidies distort global competition and represent a vast waste of global resources. Moreover, let us suppose that the worst were to occur, with Boeing going bankrupt because of these mercantilist practices. If this were to occur, the United States could not rely on market forces, including a steep drop in the value of the dollar, to later recreate a domestic civilian aviation industry. To do so would require not only creating a new aircraft firm from scratch but also the complex web of suppliers, professional associations, university programs in aviation engineering, and other knowledge-sharing organizations. With fewer aviation jobs, fewer students would become aeronautical engineers, making it difficult to rebuild capacity. If a country loses the intangible knowledge about how to build an airplane, it cannot reconstitute it without massive government subsidies and almost complete domestic purchase requirements.

But most neoclassical economists would argue that Boeing going out of business would be no big deal as long as the U.S. economy maintains its historic flexibility and doesn't restrict Boeing's assets from flowing to more productive uses. If the "market" dictates that the United States should not produce passenger jets (or even any manufacturing at all), then they would maintain it's better to redeploy these assets to more productive uses. Their assumption is that anyone smart enough to be an aeronautical engineer is smart enough to find another high-skill, high-wage job. But there are several glaring problems with this view. First, it would not be the "market" but mercantilist nations dictating the change. If anything, Boeing's global market share (and aviation jobs in America) would be significantly larger in the absence of other countries' mercantilist policies.

Second, let's suppose that somehow these assets—the workers, machinery, and financial capital—did get redeployed. Certainly, much of Boeing's tangible assets, its physical plant, would likely be redeployed. Someone (probably in China) would buy the advanced dies and other machinery Boeing uses to produce planes. (In fact, a multibillion-dollar industry has emerged in the United States that strips parts such as machinery, generators, tools, and dies from defunct American manufacturing plants and ships them to developing countries to be rebuilt, recycled, and reused.)[29] Amazon.com might buy the massive hangars where Boeing makes the planes to use for an e-commerce fulfillment center to sell Stephen King books and Lady Gaga videos.

But an increasing share of a nation's capital resides in intangible capital— the talent of its workers and the knowledge embedded in its organizations and industrial commons—and this is not easily reallocated. As Jon Clark, publisher of *Plant Closing News*, a newsletter that documents the 150 or more closures of American manufacturing plants each month, ruefully says about the resale business of parts from shuttered plants: "The only thing that doesn't get recycled or reused is the people."[30] To return to the Boeing example, the value-added per worker in the aerospace industry (that is, the amount of value that each worker adds to the materials and parts they get) is among the highest of any industry, at $133,000 per year. In contrast, the value-added per the average U.S. job is $103,000 per year.[31] But the highly trained scientific workers and technicians that Boeing employs cannot easily go to another firm and put their knowledge and skills to immediate work. Imagine the introduction: "I'd like to apply for the hedge fund trading position; I'm an aeronautical engineer specializing in carbon-fiber wing design." The newly unemployed Boeing engineer would more likely apply for a midlevel technician job at a warehouse, and make half of what he or she did before. So even if every Boeing worker and every worker at its suppliers got a new job, most of them would see a big cut in their wages and the nation would be poorer. Moreover, the closure would represent a big contractionary force in the overall economy as unemployed workers take time to get reemployed and as their spending cutbacks ripple through the economy leading to other jobs being lost.

This in a nutshell explains the race for global innovation advantage. It also explains the decline of the U.S. "rust belt," especially as the once-dominant, high-wage auto manufacturers have lost market share to global competitors. For example, whereas the Big Three (General Motors, Ford, and Chrysler) accounted for 92 percent of cars sold in the United States in the 1960s (with a large share produced in the "rust belt"), that share fell to 74 percent in 1980 and then plummeted to 44 percent by 2009.[32] With Michigan's second-largest industry now tourism, much of which employs people in lower-paying jobs, Michiganders no longer enjoy the above-average standard of living they did as recently as 1994; it's now 87 percent of the national average.[33] And it's unlikely to get back to average for the foreseeable future.

The final major flaw with the neoclassical view of economic competition is that it underestimates the beneficial impact government intervention can have. In the twenty-first-century global economy, nations can no longer be indifferent to the industrial and value-added mix of their economies. With the sole exception of the United States, virtually all nations have consciously adopted national policies to "intervene in the market" so it is easier for corporations to invest in higher-value-added activities that create higher-wage jobs at home. This brings us to perhaps the most insidious effect of the "countries don't compete, only companies do" canard: the prevailing U.S.

view that any government engagement in the market must be inherently pernicious has blinded U.S. policymakers to the fact that other countries reject this belief, precisely because they see themselves in explicit competition with the United States and other nations.

These countries are not content to sit idly by to observe how the market will allocate global production, for they know that the market could very well allocate to them low-wage T-shirt factories and call centers (or even worse, nothing at all, with the resulting massive trade deficits) instead of semiconductor factories and software companies. In essence, these nations recognize that while markets can create prosperity, they don't always do so at home. The next thousand high-value-added jobs could just as easily be created or located in another nation. Recognizing the need to go beyond letting firms alone determine the location of high-value-added economic activities, they "intervene" in their economies with policies such as implementing national innovation strategies, funding basic and applied research, providing R&D tax credits, and so forth.

Moreover, these nations are not blinded by the neoclassical economics dogma that any government engagement in markets is distorting and growth-reducing. They look to support their domestic companies and industries by facilitating government-industry-university partnerships, by developing strategic technology industry road maps and allocating scarce R&D resources accordingly, and by partnering with industry in technology deployment. Accordingly, as Tassey notes, a key "underlying problem is that U.S. manufacturing firms are attempting to compete largely as independent entities against a growing number of national economies in Europe and Asia in which government, industry, and a broad infrastructure (technical, education, economic, and information) are evolving into increasingly effective technology-based ecosystems."[34] Or as Wayne Johnson, Hewlett Packard's director of worldwide strategic university customer relations, observes, "We in the United States find ourselves in competition not only with individuals, companies, and private institutions, but also with governments and mixed government-private collaborations."[35]

Put simply, competition among governments has become a critical factor in determining global market share among nations. As chapters 6 and

7 explore, the measures countries take to win the race for global innovation advantage can be either constructive or destructive to both themselves and to the global economy, depending on how they implement those policies. For the moment, however, the key point is to understand that the globalization of innovation production and consumption has forced formerly dominant nations like the United States to move from being "price makers" to "price takers" in international markets. In other words, enterprises now shop the globe to find the countries with the most attractive markets—based on effective corporate tax rates, R&D tax credit generosity, workforce talent, availability of state-of-the-art digital and physical infrastructure, and the presence of technology clusters, among other factors—in which to locate their establishments performing R&D, design, production, and management activities.

For example, Intel, like virtually all multinational enterprises, shops the world to find the optimal locations for its R&D and production activities. Intel's recent decision to locate a semiconductor manufacturing plant in China instead of the United States was driven in part by the recognition that it can cost $1 billion more to build, equip, and operate a factory in America than it does elsewhere, with 70 percent of the cost difference accounted for by lower taxes, and 90 percent of the cost difference explained by factors other than wages. The decision was also informed by Intel's recognition that access to science and engineering talent in China is as good as or better than in the United States.

For the U.S. economy, the implication is that the United States has become a large state—in the sense that a large share of its economy is now traded—and it competes against other nations the way U.S. states have had to compete for investment since WWII. Indeed, as we discuss subsequently, both Republican and Democratic state governors have long supported state "industrial policies." It's only Washington that persists in seeing the world through the rose-colored glasses of "countries don't compete." But if it is left to the results of market competition alone, the United States will continue to lose out in global competitions for high-value-added technology and knowledge-intensive production. In fact, a January 2012 *Harvard Business Review* survey of alumni from its business school found that when the firms they worked for had to decide whether to locate an activity (such as

R&D, production, customer service, or back-office operations) in America or elsewhere, America lost two times of three.[36]

Excuse 4: We've Been Challenged Before and It All Worked Out

Many skeptics argue that concern about the state of U.S. competitiveness is just another case of alarmists "crying wolf." After all, the United States appeared to come through competitive clashes with the Soviet Union in the 1950s and 1960s and with Japan and Germany in the late 1970s and early 1980s just fine. They maintain, therefore, that since previous warnings that U.S. competitiveness was under threat turned out to be false alarms, current warnings are the same. In October 2009, Larry Summers, then director of President Obama's National Economic Council, reassured us that "predictions of America's decline are as old as the republic," comforting that "when the Soviet Union collapsed, the *Harvard Business Review* of 1990 proclaimed in every issue—every issue—in one way or another that the Cold War was over, and that Germany and Japan had won. . . . Now we are hearing the same thing with respect to China."[37] On the Right, as well, many voices have long argued that fears about U.S. competitiveness are overwrought. Take, for example, Neal McCluskey, a policy analyst at the conservative Cato Institute: "Using the threat of international economic competition to bolster federal control is nothing new. It happened in 1983, after the federally commissioned report *A Nation at Risk* admonished that, 'our once unchallenged preeminence in commerce, industry, science, and technological innovation is being overtaken by competitors throughout the world' as well as in the early 1990s, when George Bush the elder called for national academic standards in order to better compete with Japan."[38] Likewise, regarding the offshoring of jobs in the new century, Morgan Stanley's Stephen Roach argues that "this is exactly the same type of challenge farmers went through in the late 1800s, sweatshop workers went through in the early 1900s, and manufacturing workers in the first half of the 1980s."[39] Journalist Robert Samuelson agrees: "Ever since Sputnik (1957) and the 'missile gap' (1960), we've been warned that we're being overtaken technologically."[40]

In other words, since it is claimed that the United States retained its lead in commerce, science, and technology through past challenges of competitiveness, calls for concern are unfounded now, just as they were then. We'll prevail because market-oriented systems always prevail. But this rosy assessment ignores three key facts. First, policymakers from both sides of the aisle in the early to mid-1980s took competitive threats seriously and responded by instituting a comprehensive set of policy measures that were instrumental in strengthening U.S. competitiveness. Imagine if the response to Sputnik had been, "Well, we handled the British threat in the 1880s and the German challenge in the 1920s, so we'll just sit back and see what happens." Luckily, wiser heads prevailed and America responded.

The United States made a number of institutional changes to support the U.S. innovation ecosystem, including passing the Stevenson-Wydler Technology Innovation Act; launching the Advanced Technology Program (ATP) and Manufacturing Extension Program (MEP); establishing the Malcolm Baldridge National Quality Award; and creating new National Science Foundation programs to link industry and academic research, such as the Engineering Research Centers and Industry/University Cooperative Research Centers. Congress also passed the Bayh-Dole Act, which transformed the relationship among federal research funders, academic institutions and their researchers, and the commercial marketplace. And we shouldn't forget the states; all fifty of them established technology-based economic development policies in the 1980s.

The United States also made changes to its tax and regulatory systems. In 1981, it became the first country to introduce a research and development tax credit to spark corporate R&D activity. Laws regarding the "prudent man" rule governing institutional investors were relaxed, spurring an explosion in venture capital activity. Legal changes enacted in the 1984 National Cooperative Research Act led to an explosion of consortium-based research activity by removing a defect of antitrust law which suggested that collaborative joint research efforts among corporations were potentially collusive.[41]

In fact, no less a skeptic of government intervention than President Ronald Reagan adopted "a robust industrial policy aimed at competing head-on with both the Soviet Union and Japan."[42] President Reagan supported vital U.S. industries including semiconductors, machine tools, and automobiles, and made investments of billions into future U.S. technological capability. He supported the establishment of the Semiconductor Manufacturing Technology (SEMATECH) consortium, a partnership between major semiconductor companies and the Department of Defense, which started with a focus on actually making chips but then shifted to a role of fostering the entire semiconductor supply chain. Even though he was a staunch free-trade advocate, Reagan supported a five-year Voluntary Restraint Agreement with Japan and Taiwan on imports of machine tools based on grounds of national security, arguing that the machine tools industry was "a vital component of the U.S. defense base." He also supported the creation of the National Center for Manufacturing Sciences to foster the development of an advanced machine tool and automation industry. And the Department of Defense created the Defense Manufacturing Board as a permanent entity to provide visibility to manufacturing and industrial base issues.

The second flaw in the naysayers' argument that we don't need to worry about competitiveness challenges is their suggestion that the United States emerged unscathed and largely victorious from its competitive scraps with Germany and Japan in the 1970s and 1980s. The fact of the matter is that those countries gained substantial market share from the United States in a number of high-value-added industries, including semiconductors, steel, consumer electronics, automobiles, and machine tools. While the U.S. economy was bolstered by a new engine of growth in the IT revolution beginning in the early 1990s, the reality is that the United States never recovered the market share it lost in those key sectors. Moreover, as the effects of the adrenaline shot of low interest rates and abundant capital that fueled the asset bubbles that drove much of the U.S. economy in the 2000s subsided, this revealed the actual underlying weakness of many traded sectors of the U.S. economy.

The third flaw with this argument is that it ignores the fact that the threat is now different—and much bigger. It was one thing to compete against Germany and Japan, which have a combined population of two hundred million and wage levels near or even above American wages. It's quite another to compete with China and India, which have a combined population of more than 2.5 billion people and wage levels less than 10 percent of U.S.

levels, and which, especially in the case of China, practice innovation mercantilism on an unprecedented scale.

Excuse 5: Geopolitical Aims Are More Important than Economic Competitiveness, So We Can Make Trade-offs

When you consider your economic prowess to be unassailable, you can
afford to be magnanimous. And particularly since the advent of the cold
war, the United States has made trade-offs that subordinated its trade and
economic interests in pursuit of its geopolitical and national security objectives. The United States has cut favorable trade deals with countries we
wanted as allies, provided them foreign aid and technology transfers, reduced
tariffs on goods exported to America, and even encouraged U.S. companies
to locate activity there, all in the great geopolitical struggle against the Soviet
red menace.

For example, in the 1950s, through the U.S. Agency for International
Development (U.S. AID), the United States assisted Taiwan in launching
the China Productivity Center, which helped its manufacturers become
more productive (and compete better with U.S. manufacturers).[43] Likewise,
a 1969 U.S. AID report, *Expanding Exports: A Case Study of the Korean Experience*, documents how U.S. AID assisted Korea in developing its export
program and was instrumental in helping Korea launch the Korean Productivity Center and the Korean Industrial Research Institute.[44] In one instance, the report describes how "U.S. AID brought in a full-time quality
control advisor, Mr. John Jacobsen, who visited hundreds of Korean companies to advise them on methods. He was instrumental in organizing a quality control association, which sponsored a major public showing of quality
control methods that was partially financed by AID. . . . He also organized
seminars and study groups throughout the country."[45]

In essence, assistance from U.S. taxpayers helped Taiwan and Korea develop their technology-oriented export machines. Of course, the United
States never anticipated it was helping a competitor; all it cared about was
keeping Taiwan and Korea from going Red. However, as early as 1971, the
U.S. Commission on Trade and Investment Policy warned that Washington was overemphasizing geopolitical considerations at the expense of

U.S. economic interests.[46] Even then, the commission warned that the U.S. manufacturing base was declining as a result of the industry-targeting policies of other countries—and U.S. complicity with those policies. However, even today, the United States Agency for International Development continues to fund programs that train foreign workers with skills that position them to take away U.S. jobs. For example, in January 2012, U.S. AID helped fund a $5 million grant to establish the Higher Engineering Education Alliance Program (HEEAP), which will provide a model for advancing engineering education to prepare Vietnamese engineers to work in the high-tech industry.[47]

Perhaps the archetypal example of the United States favoring its geopolitical interests over its economic interests comes out of the trade conflicts with Japan in the late 1970s and 1980s, as Japan pursued a mercantilist, export-led economic growth strategy (just as China does today). Japan had implemented a number of policies designed to skew trade in their favor and to limit U.S. companies' access to Japanese markets, including placing high tariffs, import quotas, and onerous regulations, inspections, and standards requirements on U.S. products; limiting U.S. ownership of Japanese enterprises; manipulating the yen's value; and shutting U.S. companies almost entirely out of strategic markets, including autos, semiconductors, and mainframe computers, all while dumping their products on U.S. markets. For example, by 1984, Japanese companies had captured 60 percent of the U.S. semiconductor chip market.

Pressure mounted from business, labor, and Congress for the White House to file unfair trade complaints under the General Agreement on Tariffs and Trade and to declare Japan an unfair trader under then existing U.S. law. However, the U.S. policy community was torn about how much to pressure Japan, with the national security agencies (State, Defense, and the National Security Council) and neoclassical economist agencies (Treasury and the Council of Economic Advisors [CEA]) on one side, and the more pragmatic economic agencies (Commerce and the United States Trade Representative's Office [USTR]) on the other. The attitude of diplomats and military leaders was that "Japan was our unsinkable aircraft carrier" and that U.S. trade and economic interests should take a backseat to geopolitical concerns. As Assistant National Security Advisor Gaston Sigur insisted at the time, "We must have those bases. Now that's the bottom line."[48] The economists piled on. As Alonzo McDonald, a Carter administration trade negotiator, complained about resistance from the neoclassical economists at the CEA and the Treasury for a more activist policy against Japan (exactly what they continue to do today), economists had "lost all touch with reality; it's heart surgery handled by a biologist."[49]

As Clyde Prestowitz concludes, "Although negotiations [which resulted in the previously mentioned Reagan-supported voluntary import restraints on Japan] were declared a great success, most of the issues were left unresolved. Eventually a number of U.S. chip makers closed up shop, and more than one hundred thousand Silicon Valley workers lost their jobs. Even more important, the United States lost technological leadership in production of several important kinds of semiconductors."[50]

With the denouement of the cold war, the Clinton administration signaled a new strategic approach that would elevate economic concerns to stand alongside geopolitical and national security concerns. Clinton secretary of state Warren Christopher told the Senate Foreign Relations Committee that "among the three pillars of the new administration's approach to foreign policy, economic growth ranked first." As Andrew Bacevich observes in *American Empire*, in the new conventional wisdom emerging in the post–cold war era, "national economic interests would not be considered 'secondary' or subordinated to national security interests." "Broadly construed" national security would henceforth include "both economic and geopolitical concerns."[51] President Clinton created the National Economic Council (NEC) as a counterpart to the National Security Council to facilitate this reordering of priorities, and Robert Rubin, the NEC's first chair before becoming Clinton's Treasury secretary, observed that "the big change" with Clinton's approach was that "the economic component of any problem gets on the table at the same time as other issues." Or, as Mickey Kantor, Clinton's chief trade negotiator put it, "Trade and international economics have joined the foreign policy table." As Bacevich writes, "Traditional distinctions between the nation's physical security and its economic well-being were among the barriers that globalization swept aside."[52]

But the temporary economic boom of the second half of the 1990s put these concerns on the back burner. And September 11, 2001, firmly elevated geopolitical and national security concerns back to the top of the agenda, and once again the United States retuned to emphasizing geopolitical and national security concerns at the expense of economic ones. In his autobiography, *Decision Points*, former president George W. Bush writes that preventing another terrorist attack was his chief concern. Yet when Bush asked China's president Hu Jintao what kept him up at night, Jintao replied, "Creating 25 million new jobs a year."[53] While countries such as China place laserlike focus on economic growth, the United States continues to place primary focus on geopolitical and national security concerns. And while some of these goals are certainly inviolable, such as preventing another 9/11, others are elective, like focusing on human rights issues in China more than on U.S. economic concerns with China. In fact, the number one item President Obama spoke about with Chinese president Hu Jintao when Jintao visited the United States in January 2011 was Chinese human rights. In essence, President Obama was more concerned about securing human rights for Chinese citizens than he was about using his scarce political capital to press the Chinese on their rampant mercantilist practices that harm the economic rights of U.S. workers. The visit was declared a success, though: Jintao promised that he would try to get his own government agencies to quit using pirated U.S. software.[54] Yet, by the end of 2011, the Chinese government had made no progress on this issue.

Another example comes from President Obama's November 2009 visit in China with President Jintao, during which President Obama pledged closer technical collaboration and accelerated safety approval of China's planned ARJ21 commuter jet.[55] It's not clear why the president promised to help China develop commercial jetliners—one of the few high-value-added manufacturing industries in which the United States retains a strong trade surplus. But the most likely reason is that he extended this as a concession to secure China's assistance in negotiating with the recalcitrant North Korean and Iranian regimes, or perhaps to soften the blow of recent U.S. arms sales to Taiwan. But while the United States makes such deals with geopolitical concerns top of mind, the focus of China and other nations is squarely on gaining economic advantage, which they parlay into military advantage. Indeed, months before the United States agreed to provide China technical assistance in developing a commercial jetliner, in a speech entitled "Let the

Large Aircraft of China Fly in the Blue Sky," Chinese prime minister Win Jinbao had articulated a Chinese vision for developing and producing its own commercial jets in direct competition with Boeing, even though China could readily afford to buy all the Boeing jets it needs and more from its $200 billion annual trade surplus.[56]

After fifty years, it's still the same story. All too often, U.S. policymakers continue to trade U.S. economic interest for global foreign policy concerns because, just like the rich person who can afford to be altruistic, the U.S. establishment thinks its economic position is so secure that it can afford to make concession after concession. The cumulative effect of so often trading economic interests for geopolitical ones has only further contributed to long-term structural U.S. economic decline, which ironically over time will only weaken our relative military security.

Excuse 6: The Massive U.S. Trade Deficit Is Our Own Fault; We Don't Save Enough

One key indicator of America's competitiveness challenge is its chronic trade deficit. As noted, during 2000–2010, the United States accumulated an astounding $5.5 trillion negative trade balance in goods and services. Yet, the story told by most conventional (that is, neoclassical) economists is that the trade deficit is a simple accounting function: low U.S. savings requires overseas borrowing, which by definition requires running a trade deficit. Former George W. Bush economist Greg Mankiw reflects this conventional view when he writes: "My view is that the trade deficit is not a problem in itself but is a symptom of a problem. The problem is low national saving."[57] The Council on Competitiveness agrees, stating: "These threats [e.g., the trade deficit] stem from global financial imbalances rather than from the inability of American companies or American workers to compete in global marketplaces."[58]

The United States has among the highest corporate tax rate in the world, fails to match many foreign nations in investment in research, and has deteriorating infrastructure. But, by definition, these factors can have no effect on the ability of business establishments in the United States to thrive in international markets because that is determined solely by our savings rate. By this definition, there is no trade deficit of any size that can be evidence of competitiveness failure.

But as non-neoclassical economist Robert Blecker states, "This identity does not prove causality, and is consistent with other causal stories about the trade deficit."[59] In other words, what the conventional story fails to recognize is that savings is a function of national competitiveness. If, for example, the Chinese stopped manipulating their currency, the U.S. trade deficit would fall and the Chinese would buy less of our government debt. The result would be a rise in both U.S. exports and interest rates. And both would spur more savings. Higher interest rates would lead more Americans to save. More exports (and relatively fewer imports) would boost U.S. corporate savings. And more jobs and higher wages through exports (exporting firms pay 9.1 percent more than jobs in firms that export less)[60] would boost individual savings and reduce the budget deficit.

Excuse 7: We're Doing Well on Some Things, So Don't Worry about Competitiveness

One reason it's difficult to have a national dialogue about U.S. innovation competitiveness is because parts of the U.S. economy are in fact doing well, and the apostles of denial point to these to support their claim that all is fine. As discussed previously, an economy can be divided into its traded and nontraded sectors. The United States has very innovative and productive nontraded sectors and some still-competitive traded sectors such as software, biotechnology, pharmaceuticals, aviation, medical devices, movies, video games, and instruments. But to argue that strength in these sectors alone will be enough to sustain a vibrant U.S. economy is akin to a coach saying his team is doing great and the players don't need extra practice or new plays because they win more than half of their games. If the United States is to win the race for global innovation advantage, it can't be content with a record slightly over .500; it needs to win most of the time, in most traded and nontraded sectors.

A representative example of this type of thinking comes from Adam Segal, a senior fellow at the Council on Foreign Relations. In his book *Advantage: How American Innovation Can Overcome the Asian Challenge*, Segal argues that Asia's science and technology sectors, principally in China and India, will probably catch up to and overtake the United States in what he calls the "hardware" of innovation—quantifiable factors such as the number of Ph.D.s awarded, investments in product innovation, number of patents obtained, facilities, and so forth.[61] However, he believes that the United States will continue to maintain a competitive advantage in innovation due to American advantage in the "software" of innovation, pertaining to the political, social, and institutional factors that move ideas from the lab to the marketplace. He argues that America's cultural values of individualism, social mobility, entrepreneurship, and limited barriers to market access will provide such a significant advantage as to make up for the United States falling behind on the "hardware" of innovation. Segal goes so far as to state that U.S. inability to compete in hardware innovation is actually a positive that could fuel U.S. growth.

While the "software" of innovation certainly is important, and the United States does have advantages there, to say that U.S. decline in the "hardware" of innovation is actually good requires a particular take on reality. For one, America's past world leadership in innovation has rested on both U.S. advantages in the "hardware" and "software" of innovation. Moreover, as the United States sees other countries catch up to and surpass it in leadership in the "hardware" of innovation, nothing in this should suggest to us that these countries won't also catch up in the "software" of innovation, or that America is somehow special and destined to lead in innovation "software." America needs both.

This is not to diminish the strengths America retains. Productivity growth in the nontraded sectors has been high compared to that of many developed nations. ITIF's *Atlantic Century* report finds that the United States boasts the second-highest rate of corporate investment in IT as a percentage of GDP in the world.[62] In fact, the superior use of IT by U.S. firms and industries has been found to directly explain differences in productivity levels between the United States and Japan and many European Union (EU) economies.[63] And America is actually pretty good in sectors like retail, hotels, insurance, and logistics. The problem is that these sectors, by and large, aren't traded.

And while the United States has lost competitive advantage in many traded industries, it still leads in some, such as life sciences and biotechnology. From 1995 to 2007, the U.S. share of global life sciences value-added increased 6 percent, while Europe's stayed flat and Japan's decreased by almost 15 percent. During that time frame, the life sciences share of U.S. exports increased by 5 percent, while the electronics share dropped by 10 percent. Seventeen percent of U.S. R&D is conducted in the life sciences field, double the percentage in Germany or Japan.[64] And the U.S. life sciences industry has produced a number of breakthrough products, from personalized gene therapies to synthetic skin to cures for certain types of cancer. (Much of the U.S. strength in life sciences has resulted from the American government providing more R&D funding, through the National Institutes of Health, to this sector than any other in the economy.)

Nevertheless, U.S. strength in some sectors has given rise to "tastes great/less filling" thinking and debates, with each side tending to take all-or-nothing propositions. Some agree with Steve Rose, who insists in his book *Rebound: Why America Will Emerge Stronger from the Financial Crisis* that the United States is doing great. Others argue, like Earl Fry in his book *Lament for America: Decline of the Superpower, Plan for Renewal*, that the United States is in very rough straits. To effectively manage the challenges of the present and future, policymakers and pundits need to recognize that America has two economies: a nontraded economy that by international standards is fairly productive and innovative and a traded sector that, with the exception of some key strengths, faces major competitive challenges. Without strength in both parts, no economy can reach its full potential.

Excuse 8: We Are the Innovators, They Are Copiers

Part of America's challenge is that for so many years after WWII it didn't have any serious competition, so it adopted a "shining city on the hill" attitude, captured brilliantly in Truman's proclamation that U.S. workers would never again need fear foreign competition. The United States would be the exemplar and eventually others would learn from us and emulate our sterling ways. So what if other countries began to aggressively pursue mercantilist, beggar-thy-neighbor policies designed to gain unfair advantage in international markets? We didn't care; in fact, there was an attitude that whatever we do, let's not get down in the mud to fight them. This notion of American exceptionalism—or as a July 2010 article in the *Economist* put it, the sense that "greatness is part of America's birthright and lexicon"—is still a powerful legacy that keeps us from competing.[65] Besides, if we keep to our lofty principles, eventually these wayward mercantilists will see the error of their ways and become like us.

Moreover, when it comes to innovation, the notion of American exceptionalism manifests itself in the mythology that we are a nation of tinkerers, inventors, and innovators, while others are just imitators or copiers. While this belief has played an important role in America's history, it becomes self-destructive if it blinds us to the very real innovation capabilities of foreign competitors, whose workforces and enterprises, as we have seen, are increasingly highly skilled and innovative.

However, where this claim might have had some merit—in the past—was in the 1960s and 1970s, when East Asian countries did pursue an "imitative catch-up" strategy designed specifically to catch up with Western economies. Japan and Korea implemented policies targeting specific industries—notably automobiles, steel, shipbuilding, and consumer electronics—through which they sought to reach technological parity and then comparative advantage over Western countries. Justin Lin and Celestin Monga of the World Bank note that Korea is a particularly good exemplar of a country that looked to achieve "industrial upgrading" through its "imitative catch-up" strategy. They observe that "in electronics, Korea's focus was initially on household appliances, such as TVs, washing machines, and refrigerators, and then moved to memory chips, the least technologically complex segment of the information industry" and then further "upgraded into such industries as automobiles and semiconductors."[66]

Of course, a number of high-tech consumer electronics and IT products—including compact disc players, high-definition television (HDTV), dynamic random access memory (DRAM) chips, and other products—were originally conceived, researched, and developed in the laboratories of U.S. universities and corporations. But then, in each case, Asian companies and countries took the underlying technology and developed and refined it into mass-

manufactured, exportable products. More recently, the technological discoveries behind lithium-ion batteries, compact fluorescent lightbulbs, and
solar panels were pioneered in the United States, after which scaled manufacturing of these products was taken over predominantly by Korean, Chinese, and Japanese companies. This would seem to reinforce the stereotype
that we are the innovators and they are the copiers.

But the first problem with that perspective is that winning the race for
global innovation advantage means producing—not just innovating—
advanced products, and the United States has been outperformed by Asian
competitors on that score. While innovation is important, it is not enough
for a nation like the United States to be able to balance its trade on the exports of knowledge alone. The greater fallacy is that the countries America
competes against today have moved far beyond the imitative stage. They
are innovating too, making new scientific discoveries and their own technical innovations outright. Japan has moved ahead of the United States in
crystalline and polycrystalline silicon solar cells, inverters, and power semiconductors for solar panels. While the United States is still in the game for
next-generation thin-film solar cells, it is at best on an even footing with
Asian countries for the next generation of photovoltaics. Asian and European countries are competing on an equal footing with the United States
for leadership in nanotechnology, and in fact there's evidence that China
has taken a lead over the United States in nanotechnology research (at least
as measured by the number of scientific publications on the subject).[67]
Taiwan, Korea, and Japan lead in electrophoretic displays for e-readers and
next-generation "electronic paper" displays for portable devices such as
e-readers, retail signs, and advertising displays. And East Asian countries
increasingly lead in production of advanced ceramics and composites and
are at the technological frontier in developing the next generation of carbon composite components for aerospace and wind energy applications.[68]

In fact, these countries are even pioneering new forms of innovation. In
India and China, companies utilize an approach called "reverse innovation," which strips down full-featured products originally designed for developed economies to their core features and functions. They then tweak
them to meet the needs of citizens in emerging market economies and sell
them at much lower price points (often to mass markets). For example, the

nonprofit organization Embrace, whose mission is to help the millions of vulnerable babies born every year in developing countries, has designed critical-care infant incubators for neonates that cost $200 instead of the typical $20,000.

And, in an interesting turn of "double-reverse innovation," Western companies are increasingly recognizing that de-featured products designed to meet the needs of emerging markets often meet the core requirements of customers in developed countries, presenting enormous market opportunities at home. For example, in the early 2000s, General Electric (GE) served the Chinese ultrasound market with conventional ultrasound machines developed in the United States that cost $100,000 or more, but the bulky, expensive devices sold poorly in China and India.[69] So a local GE team in China developed a portable ultrasound machine (using a laptop computer enhanced with a probe and sophisticated software) that cost just $15,000 but had the essential functionality needed for use in rural Chinese clinics. Recognizing that such a mobile ultrasound product could be used by ambulances and emergency rooms everywhere, GE took the product back to the developed world and, in the process, created a global portable ultrasound marketplace that grew from $4 million to $278 million between 2002 and 2008. Other "reverse innovations" that began in China or India and have since migrated back to developed markets include handheld electrocardiogram devices and scaled-down automobiles such as the Smart Car, whose template was the Tata Motors Nano.

It's also worth noting that the notion of a distinct American culture of invention ignores that many technologies were developed roughly contemporaneously by inventors around the world. While Alexander Graham Bell received the patent for the telephone over Elisha Gray in 1876, Italians Antonio Meucci and Innocenzo Manzetti, German Philipp Reiss, and Frenchman Charles Boursel were demonstrating working prototypes of telephones, or "speaking telegraphs," as early as 1864. While most people credit the Wright brothers with the first manned flight, in Brazil and France, Alberto Santos-Dumont is still considered the inventor of the airplane for test flights he took from 1898 to 1905. Even Orville Wright, in *How We Invented the Airplane*, credits a number of other American and foreign inventors as instrumental to the brothers' success, including: Leonardo, Cayley, Maxim,

Bell, Lilienthal, Langley, and Chanute. Indeed, throughout history, the same innovation often has been introduced nearly simultaneously by separate individuals in different countries (think of Newton and Liebniz's near-simultaneous discovery of calculus), in large part because virtually all innovations build upon the same infrastructure of knowledge and prior innovation.[70] So while the United States surely has a storied legacy of innovation and invention of which it should be most proud, we should not assume there is something innate to Americans that endows them with preternaturally superior innovation capacity.

Related to the myth that we in the United States will be the innovators is the notion that we also will be the managers. As one prominent Silicon Valley venture capitalist told us, "We don't worry about U.S. competitiveness, because America is incredibly innovative. Our firm finds start-ups in which to invest in the United States, and those firms outsource everything—R&D, design, manufacturing, and even marketing—to lower cost locations overseas. So you see, we are incredibly innovative. And the firms we invest in will do just fine." The small number of U.S. owners and managers of these firms may do well, but what about the thousands or tens of thousands of workers they didn't hire in the United States?

Excuse 9: The United States Will Be Okay If It Loses Manufacturing Because It Can Migrate Up the Value Chain to Services Sectors

Perhaps no canard has been more damaging to U.S. competitiveness than the notion that the United States will be okay if it gives up its manufacturing industries because it can seamlessly "migrate up the value chain" to knowledge-based services industries. While services industries do account for the majority of most developed countries' economic activity and are important components of a nation's competitiveness, this does not mean that a large country's economy can thrive without globally competitive manufacturing sectors.

Yet many economic pundits have long contended that America does not really have to have an industrial base. Kenneth Green, a resident scholar at the conservative American Enterprise Institute (AEI), has written: "As long as China is selling us the products we need, the location of manufacturing isn't really that critical for the economy."[71] When asked how much manufacturing the United States could really lose and still be economically healthy, the head of one Washington, D.C.–based international economics think tank replied: "Really? Really we could lose it all and be fine." Columbia University's Jagdish Bhagwati goes so far as to dismiss anyone who says manufacturing is important as suffering from a "manufacturing fetish."[72] Christina Romer, former head of the Council of Economic Advisors for President Obama, dismissed the president's very own manufacturing policy (after she left the White House) claiming that manufacturers didn't need "special treatment," that there is no convincing rationale to treat manufacturing any different than services like haircuts, and that any claim as to why manufacturing is different is based on "sentiment."[73] These pundits make such claims because, like the "potato chips-computer chips" view, they believe in the "car manufacturing-car rental, what's the difference?" view. It's hard to succeed in a global economy exporting haircuts. But as we saw earlier, these neoclassical economists don't even care about the trade deficit or competitiveness, so how can they think manufacturing (and traded-sector industries generally) is any different than barber shops (or other nontraded sectors).

They also assume that the United States can effortlessly move up the value chain from manufacturing to services-oriented activities and sectors because the United States supposedly has a natural comparative advantage at more knowledge-intensive activities (such as R&D, product design, marketing, and finance). For example, economists Jonathan Eaton and Samuel Kortum have argued that because the United States has a comparative advantage over foreign countries in the performance of R&D, the globalization of innovation activity will actually be good for America and lead to more R&D activity here, as research activity naturally concentrates in the country that performs it best.[74] As AEI economist Kevin Hassett argues, "Any economist can tell you that this decline (in manufacturing) is not necessarily a cause for concern. . . . We have become an ideas economy."[75] In other words, the United States should feel fine about losing manufacturing because the R&D, design, headquarters, and financing functions will stay here.

Likewise, Harvard Business School's David Yoffe counsels perspective and the preeminence of services, maintaining: "The loss of some manufacturing in a high-cost country such as the United States is inevitable and need not lead to a decline in competitiveness. Indeed, the future of U.S. competitiveness in high-tech industries such as computers, software, communications, and electronics may depend more on the transition to services than on trying to retain the country's manufacturing base."[76] Yoffe's argument reflects the dominant logic of original equipment manufacturers (OEMs) of IT products (such as computers, telephones, and semiconductors) in the United States in the 1980s, as they began to outsource the manufacture and assembly of printed circuit boards (PCBs) to specialist contractors in Korea, China, and Taiwan. U.S. OEMs did so because the contractors offered significant cost savings, partly because they were located in low-wage countries and partly because of the economies of scale the contractors achieved by serving many OEMs. At the time, the OEMs did not see the move as risky because they retained the critical intellectual property (IP) and design skills and because manufacturing PCBs wasn't a source of competitive advantage for them.

But as competition intensified among the Asian contractors and they sought to improve upon razor-thin margins, they began to move up the value chain, seeking higher-value-added work from the OEMs. First, they persuaded the American OEMs to allow them to assemble a greater share of the overall product, then they took over complete product assembly, ultimately assuming supply-chain management responsibilities from the OEMs, a logical step given that many of the component parts were sourced from Asian suppliers anyway.[77] But as Harvard's Willy Shih and Gary Pisano recount in "Restoring American Competitiveness," the contractors quickly began to take over high-value-added design functions as well: "Then came design. Initially, these firms took over design-engineering tasks on a contract basis. The OEM typically would provide the high-level conceptual design and specifications, contracting with the Asian supplier to do the detailed engineering. Eventually, though, the suppliers took over these activities as well for products like notebooks, which require designers to interact frequently with manufacturing. The result: These 'original design manufacturers,' as they describe themselves, ended up designing and manufacturing virtually all Windows notebook PCs."[78]

Just like that, the United States lost global comparative advantage in the service-based activity of designing notebook computers, and soon for designing desktop computers, cellular phones, tablet computers, and e-readers. This, then, is the fundamental flaw in the belief that the United States can give away the manufacturing but keep the high-value-added services: The notion that we can separate out the design and R&D value-add components from the manufacturing of a technology-based product is fundamentally wrong. In reality, as Shih and Pisano point out, "The outsourcing did not stop with low-value tasks like simple assembly or circuit-board stuffing. Sophisticated engineering and manufacturing capabilities that underpin innovation in a wide range of products have been rapidly leaving too."[79]

Greg Tassey likewise excoriates the received wisdom that the United States can outsource manufacturing but keep the higher-value-added service activities at home, observing that this view fundamentally misunderstands the nature of technology development, especially across current and subsequent technology life cycles:

> When technological advances take place in the foreign industry, manufacturing is frequently located in that country to be near the source of the R&D. The issue of co-location of R&D and manufacturing is especially important because it means the value-added from both R&D and manufacturing will accrue to the innovating economy, at least when the technology is in its formative stages. Thus, an economy that initially controls both R&D and manufacturing can lose the value-added first from manufacturing and then R&D in the current technology life cycle—and then first R&D followed by manufacturing in the subsequent technology life cycle. This is the economics of decline.[80]

In fact, examples abound of the United States losing technology leadership in one product life cycle with the result that it falls behind in subsequent technology life cycles. America lost leadership in rechargeable battery manufacturing technology years ago, largely because most innovation in batteries in recent decades has been driven by increasing demands in consumer electronics for ever more power in smaller packages.[81] When U.S. companies largely abandoned the "mature" consumer electronics business, the locus of R&D manufacturing—not just for the laptops and cell phones but also their batteries—shifted to Asia. And lo and behold, as U.S. and global attention has turned toward developing energy-efficient vehicles using advanced electric batteries, Japan's and Korea's strong battery and car industries have given them an advantage over U.S. companies in developing electric and hybrid vehicles. Hence, GM has had to source the advanced battery for its Chevy Volt from a Korean supplier. Likewise, the migration of semiconductor foundries to Asia has caused a sharp decline in silicon processing and thin film deposition capabilities in the United States. But now that thin film deposition turns out to be a critical process in manufacturing photovoltaic solar cells, the United States increasingly risks falling behind in the manufacture and development of solar cells.

Another complication is that, before the emergence of a globalized economy with increasingly sophisticated competitors, shifts in technology life cycles were less likely to shift global competitive advantage between countries. For example, when the United States was the dominant technology-based economy, both the old and new industries were likely domestic; U.S. semiconductor firms replaced U.S. vacuum tube firms, or emerging U.S. biopharmaceutical firms took market share from the dominant U.S. pharmaceutical firms. But in an integrated world with increased global trade, domestic transfers of market leadership are increasingly less likely to occur. More global players mean that more potential first movers will come from an increasingly large pool of technology-based economies. Thus, shifts in the locus of global competitive advantage across technology life cycles will occur with increasing frequency.[82]

A related failure in this regard is an assumption by neoclassical economists that, as current technologies age, most products devolve into pure commodities whose production should be offshored to other nations. Princeton University economist Alan Blinder recently wrote: "The TV manufacturing industry really started here, and at one point employed many workers. But as TV sets became 'just a commodity' their production moved offshore to locations with much lower wages. And nowadays the number of television sets manufactured in the United States is zero. A failure? No, a success."[83] Losing an industry is a success? Blinder was right that the old black-and-white and then color cathode-ray tube television sets had become commodities where competition was based largely on production cost, but this assumption of "technological stasis" betrays a stunning inability to understand dynamic technologies and how product life cycles regularly renew themselves. Once the United States took the neoclassical economists' advice and allowed the TV industry to disappear, it lost out entirely as televisions evolved from cathode-ray tubes to high-definition, flat-screen TVs— first using liquid crystal display (LCDs) and then light-emitting diode (LED) displays—and as these technologies have been deployed across a wide range of products, from digital advertising signage systems to large-scale video displays. Or do we really still think that American workers are better off not manufacturing the multimillion-dollar, jumbo-screen displays found in ballparks across the country, or the thousand-dollar Asian-manufactured high-definition televisions (HDTVs) found in living rooms from coast to coast (which are increasingly coming to market as converged devices with computing and connectivity features, 3-D capabilities, and soon ultra-HD resolution)?

In summary, as George W. Bush's President's Council of Advisors on Science and Technology (PCAST) has written, "The proximity of research, development, and manufacturing is very important to leading-edge manufacturers."[84] Or as Susan Houseman of the Institute for Employment Research states, "The big debate is whether we can continue to be competitive in R&D when we are not making the stuff that we innovate. I think not; the two cannot be separated."[85] Put simply, the continuing shift of manufacturing outside the United States is beginning to also pull high-end design and R&D capabilities out of the country. In fact, 90 percent of all electronics R&D now takes place in Asia, in part because firms need volume production to be able to afford general R&D.[86] This shift is also evident in the fact that from 1998–2008, U.S. corporate R&D expanded 2.7 times faster overseas than all corporate R&D in the United States.[87] And it's evident in Georgia Tech's *2008 High-Tech Indicators* study, which found that China improved its technological standing by nine points (on a scale of one hundred), moving the nation ahead of the United States in technological capability for the first time.[88] Likewise, a survey of scientific researchers in thirty-eight countries conducted by *R&D Magazine* for the

"2011 Global R&D Funding Forecast" finds the researchers believing that China will lead the world in technical strength by 2015, with the United States slipping to third, behind both China and Japan.[89] Nevertheless, many continue to discount China's growing technological prowess. As Michael Levi, senior fellow for Energy and the Environment at the Council on Foreign Relations, argued in December 2010, "The reality is that China still tends to take the expensive stuff from elsewhere and adds a little value to it before stamping "Made in China" on the product."[90] While this may have been the case in the past, it's getting increasingly difficult to dismiss China's ability to develop cutting-edge, high-tech products with a simple wave of the hand.

The net effect is the deepening erosion of the U.S. industrial base, the hollowing out of advanced production supply chains, and the loss, for many U.S. industries, of their "industrial commons"—the R&D know-how, advanced process development, engineering skills, and manufacturing competencies related to a specific technology. As Pisano and Shih conclude, "decades of outsourcing manufacturing have left U.S. industry without the means to invent the next generation of high-tech products that are crucial to rebuilding its economy."[91] This message was forcefully driven home when we recently spoke with the CEO of a leading U.S. high-tech company about a major new product line it was introducing. When we asked where the very advanced display that was being incorporated in the device was sourced, his response was: "We looked long and hard around the United States to see if we could source it here. But we couldn't find any company with the capability of producing here, so we ended up sourcing it in Taiwan" (where, it should be noted, the Taiwanese government funded R&D programs designed precisely around supporting this capability).

Excuse 10: Manufacturing Losses Are a Sign of Strength, Not Weakness

Without a manufacturing sector, it's flat-out impossible for most nations, unless they are endowed with oil or other natural resources, to balance their trade. The United States' current trade performance, with about a $646 billion goods deficit and scant $146 billion services surplus in 2010, is not tenable going forward.

Yet, many continue to believe that the migration of mature manufacturing industries away from developed countries like the United States is just part of a healthy, natural process of economic evolution that allows resources to be redeployed to new, higher-potential businesses. As Harvard's Yoffe argues, "Maybe the most important point to make is that the United States has been moving towards a service economy for the last 100 years."[92] Harvard sociologist Daniel Bell's 1976 book, *The Coming of Post-Industrial Society*, outlines a new kind of society that would be information-led and service-oriented and that would replace the economics of goods that had previously existed.[93] *The Economist* writes: "Deindustrialization—the shrinkage of industrial jobs—is wrongly perceived as a symptom of economic decline, when it is really a stage of economic development, because as a country gets richer, it is inevitable that a smaller proportion of workers will be needed in manufacturing." This is a bit like saying that a digestive disease that leads someone to lose weight to the point of anorexia is a sign of health. As we demonstrate in chapter 2, the loss of U.S. manufacturing jobs has not been just a story of high productivity leading to fewer jobs—as was the case with U.S. agriculture over the last century (a clear case of success). Nor is it a story of the "natural" growth in services as countries get rich. In fact, in constant dollars, the consumption of manufacturing products (not output) as a ratio of consumption of services has been unchanged since the early 1970s. Rather, it's also been a story of decline in output and competitiveness, with U.S. manufacturing producing 11 percent less than it did in 2000, while the overall economy grew around 16 percent.

Even if apologists admit that U.S. manufacturing is suffering, they assert that the situation is no different elsewhere. For example, as Larry Summers argued in December 2010, "We are moving towards a knowledge and service economy. You don't succeed by producing exactly the same thing that other people are producing in the same way just at a lower cost. . . . There is no going back to the past. Technology is accelerating productivity in mass production to the point where even China has seen manufacturing employment decline by more than ten million jobs over the most recent decade for which data is available."[94] As Senator Pat Moynihan used to be fond of saying, you are welcome to your own opinions but not your own facts. And Summers's facts are flat-out wrong. China's manufacturing employment actually rose by an astounding 11 million workers between 2002 and 2006, creating as many manufacturing jobs in four short years as exist in the United States.[95]

Moreover, during the last decade, many nations, including ones with higher manufacturing wages than the United States, have seen either stable or increasing manufacturing output as a share of GDP. For example, during the 2000s, Austria, Germany, the Netherlands, and Norway all have seen stable manufacturing shares, while other nations actually have seen their manufacturing sectors grow as a share of their economy, by 5 percent in Switzerland, 13 percent in Finland, 39 percent in Korea, and 68 percent in the Slovak Republic.[96] America's loss of manufacturing output and competitiveness is not a reflection of some iron law of development and is certainly not progressive.

Figure 4.1 graphically illustrates the U.S. fall and corresponding, almost equivalent, Chinese rise in share of world manufacturing output from 1970 to 2008.[97] (The U.S. share declined by 12 percent, from 28.6 to 17.9 percent, while China's share rose 13 percent, from 3.8 to 17.2 percent.) But the U.S. fall was not inevitable. Japan and Germany have maintained their global manufacturing share (despite ups and downs and despite having a slower-growing population and workforce) over this period, avoiding the precipitous decline the United States experienced. Thus, deindustrialization of high-wage economies is not preordained; something happened differently in the United States than in Germany and Japan to explain its decline.

In conclusion, it's worth noting that the neoclassical dogma "we don't need manufacturing" is so strong that the United States has even tried to get other nations to follow our folly and favor services industries at the expense of manufacturing. A May 2009 *Financial Times* editorial advised Japan to follow the U.S.-U.K. strategy of largely giving up on manufacturing in the interest of "supporting high-paying research and management jobs" in the domestic economy.[98] This is great advice to give other nations if we want to win the race for global innovation advantage, as long as we ignore it and they don't. Finally, to be clear, this is not about choosing old-line manufacturing over new-era innovation jobs. Much of manufacturing is at

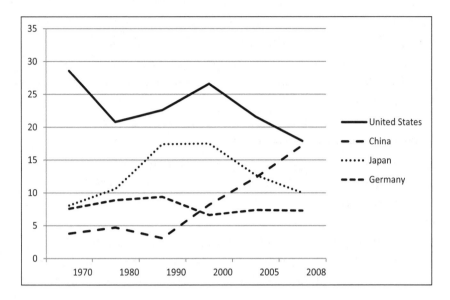

Figure 4.1 Country Share of World Manufacturing Output, 1970–2008
Source: Based on information and statistics from the United Nations Conference
on Trade and Development.

the cutting edge of technology. Moreover, the United States needs to further build on its strengths in design, research, intellectual property, and marketing. But these strengths, as important as they are, are not enough.

Excuse 11: Cleantech Will Save Us

In the last half of the 2000s, "cleantech" (clean technology) became the great green hope, particularly among the Left. This was seen as the sector that will put America back in the race, creating millions of jobs and reindustrializing economically devastated regions. David Fenton, writing in *The Nation*, claimed that "clean energy transformation is the best—perhaps the only—path to economic and job growth, including rebuilding our industrial base and competitiveness."[99] The liberal Center for American Progress wrote: "The transformation of our antiquated energy infrastructure can be the great engine for American innovation, productivity growth, and job creation in the coming decades."[100] Both urged Obama administration officials and fellow clean energy advocates to come out swinging for the cause.

Many advocates have touted overly optimistic figures for potential job growth from cleantech as a driver of American economic transformation, including the cleantech advocacy group Apollo Alliance, which promised that cleantech will create five million green jobs. David Foster, executive director of the BlueGreen Alliance, has written: "For years, the U.S. pursued a trade policy that resulted in the loss of millions of jobs and decimated the manufacturing base in this country. Now we have an opportunity to rebuild that base and create good jobs in all sectors of the American economy."[101] *New York Times* columnist and author Thomas Friedman made the well-known prediction that clean energy could be the next "industrial revolution" and has drawn comparisons between clean energy and the IT revolution.[102]

One reason for this enthusiasm, beyond the Left's inclination to only like "good" industries like cleantech, is that the clean energy sector has exhibited growth during the past several years. In fact, according to the Brookings Institution, the cleantech economy—including firms in photovoltaic, wind, fuel cell, smart grid, and biofuel industries developing new technologies to solve energy-related challenges—grew at 8.3 percent annually from 2003 to 2010 and accounted for three hundred thousand U.S. jobs in 2010.[103] However, assumptions about the long-term potential of the clean energy sector also must be tempered due to cold hard reality: even if we properly structure our domestic energy innovation policies and perfect our ability to invent, develop, and support radical new energy technologies, the clean energy sector—while vitally important—won't be enough by itself to counteract job losses from other sectors and act as the single engine propelling the American economy forward.

The problem is that green energy-producing jobs will mostly just displace ones in dirty industries such as oil, gas, and coal. Energy is a commodity: substituting electrons generated by coal with electrons generated by solar power is inherently meaningless in terms of the work performed because electrons are electrons. Moreover, clean energy does not inherently make the work it performs more productive. Because energy expenditures as a share of the overall economy have tended to remain flat—and because carbon-emitting energy sources must be reduced in the long run—we would expect clean energy to supplant the current energy system, not augment it. This means that most future clean energy jobs will be created in lieu of, or in replacement of, fossil fuel jobs, not in addition to them. Like-wise, capital that perhaps would have gone toward fossil fuel investment will instead go toward clean energy investment. This is a story about asset redirection, not expansion.

Exports of clean energy products do hold the potential to boost U.S. employment and competitiveness, but here too aspirations run against logic and facts. First, why would we automatically expect that America can win in this industry when it's losing in so many others? No doubt, world energy demand will see massive growth in the coming decades, but much of this growth will occur in non–Organization for Economic Cooperation and Development (OECD) nations, where the United States tends to be at a disadvantage in terms of cost to manufacture energy technology. Second, as we note in chapter 2, the United States is already experiencing a trade deficit in renewable energy technologies. Moreover, none of our overseas com-petitors are likely to cede any ground to a reawakened cleantech industrial behemoth. According to a report from Harvard's Belfer Center, China's in-vestment in energy R&D stood at $11.8 billion in 2008, while six up-and-coming nations—China, India, Brazil, Russia, South Africa, and Mexico—are out-investing the major economic powers in energy research.[104] Moreover, as ITIF explained in its report with the Breakthrough Institute, *Rising Tigers, Sleeping Giant,* Asia's rising clean energy tigers—China, Japan, and Korea—have already surpassed the United States in the production of virtually all clean energy technologies (save carbon storage and sequestration), and from 2008–2012, the governments of these nations are expected to out-invest the United States three to one in these sectors, by $509 billion to $172 billion. This public investment gap will allow Asian nations to attract a significant share of private investment that will total into the trillions. And as we pointed out previously, the significant high-profile bankruptcies or downsizing of U.S. solar firms in the face of Chinese competition does not bode well for future trade dominance. At this moment, the jobs, tax revenues, and other benefits of clean energy are positioned to overwhelmingly accrue to Asia's cleantech tigers, not to the United States.[105]

While cleantech is not the salvation to America's competitiveness woes, one area where it could provide real opportunity to boost U.S. employment is if the United States can displace foreign imports of oil with clean alternatives, such as biofuels or electric vehicles (or, more likely, a mix of the two). Imports of foreign crude and other petroleum products account for roughly half of our international trade deficit, and replacing this through domestic suppliers would boost American jobs and reduce the massive transfer of wealth driven by the oil trade.

5

What Are Innovation and Innovation Policy and Why Are They Important?

I nnovation has become the central driver of national economic well-being and competitiveness—and this is why so many nations are engaged in the race for global innovation advantage. But what actually is innovation? Most believe innovation is only technological in nature, resulting in shiny new products like Apple's iPad or Boeing's 787 Dreamliner. Others believe it pertains only to the research and development (R&D) activity going on at universities, national laboratories, and corporations.

While that is all true, it is much too limiting; innovation is about much more. The Organization for Economic Cooperation and Development (OECD) defines innovation as "the implementation of a new or significantly improved product (that is, a physical good or service), process, a new marketing method, or a new organizational method in business practices, workplace organization, or external relations."[1] Innovations can arise at many different points in the innovation process, including conception or ideation, R&D, transfer (the shift of the "technology" to the production organization), production and deployment, or marketplace usage.

Innovation Defined

By definition, all innovations must contain a degree of novelty, whether that novelty is new to the firm, to the market, or to the world. It's also important to remember that an innovation is not just anything new; it must also constitute a viable business concept.

General Electric (GE) offers a useful definition for innovation, contending that "to innovate . . . is to challenge and change the status quo to enhance the customer's experience and bring new forms of value to them." Two attributes are attractive in GE's definition. First, it places focus on challenging the status quo and upsetting the established order, evoking Joseph Schumpeter's dictum that "every piece of business strategy must be understood against the perennial gale of creative destruction."[2] Second, it reminds us that organizations ultimately innovate in service of their customers and that genuine innovation must create real value for them, even if it's an innovation they never see, such as new kinds of machines to produce a product at a lower price. Another useful, aspirational definition of innovation comes from author John Kao, who describes innovation as "the transformation of existing conditions into preferred ones."[3]

Innovation traditionally has been understood in an engineering context, entailing either the creation of new or improved consumer-product goods, such as the original iPod and its brethren, or enhanced machines and devices, such as lasers and the computer-controlled machine tools by which products are manufactured. But innovation in services has become increasingly important, as services industries now account for more than 80 percent of the U.S. economy and 75 percent or more of most European ones.[4] Thus, the understanding of innovation has broadened from a purely scientific and technical focus to include the application and use of information technologies, evolution of new business models, and creation of new customer experience or service delivery approaches. These have the potential to transform virtually all service sectors, from retail, logistics, and hospitality to health care, professional services, and financial services.

Why Innovation Is Important

However defined, innovation is vitally important because it drives economic, employment, and income growth; quality of life improvements; and the competitiveness of nations. As OECD secretary-general Angel Gurría commented at the release of the OECD's Innovation Strategy in March 2010, "Countries need to harness innovation and entrepreneurship to boost growth and employment, for innovation is the key to a sustainable rise in living standards."[5]

In recent years, a small but growing number of economists have come to see that it is not so much the accumulation of more savings or capital that is the key to improving standards of living. Rather, it is innovation that drives a country's long-run economic growth.[6] For example, two-thirds of U.K. private-sector productivity growth between 2000 and 2007 was a result of innovation.[7] And when Klenow and Rodriguez-Clare decomposed the cross-country differences in income per worker into shares that could be attributed to physical capital, human capital, and total factor productivity, they found that more than 90 percent of the variation in the growth of income per worker was a result of how effectively capital is used (that is, innovation), with differences in the actual amount of human and financial capital accounting for just 9 percent.[8] Moreover, technological innovation in particular delivers substantial economic returns. For example, a study of a sample of fourteen research projects funded by the U.S. Department of Commerce showed a median rate of return to society of 144 percent, far higher than their cost of capital.[9] And economist Edwin Mansfield found the social rate of return from investment in academic research (in terms of its impact on product and process development in U.S. firms) to be at least 40 percent.[10]

Innovation—the wellspring of that "gale of creative destruction" of which Schumpeter wrote—achieves its outsize economic impact through two principal channels: empowering productivity improvements and spurring the dynamic creation of new firms or activities that create new value. With regard to the former, during the 2000s, in industry after industry, firms have adopted computers, telecommunications, and software to streamline operations and boost efficiency. As a result, the production and innovative use of information technology (IT) has been responsible for at least 50 percent of the acceleration in the growth in U.S. total factor productivity between 1995 and 2008, contributing to a U.S. economy that is approximately $2 trillion larger in terms of annual gross domestic product (GDP) than it would be otherwise.[11]

In addition to enabling productivity improvements within existing firms, innovation empowers the creation of new (and often more productive and competitive) firms—and industries. And these innovative firms and industries tend to pay higher wages. In the United States, average compensation per employee in innovation-intensive sectors increased 50 percent between 1990 and 2007—nearly two and a half times the national average.[12] This is a major reason why so many nations are competing so fiercely in the race for global innovation advantage; they want to be the home to the next thousand high-paying innovation jobs.

Innovation, however, is not just about the creation of new value but also the replacement of old firms and activities. Indeed, this turbulent, dynamic process of firm churn and turnover is a vital source of renewal and growth in the economy. (If innovation were a coin, the other side of that coin would certainly be change, for the two are inextricably linked.) Innovation's demand for constant renewal holds true at both the firm and economy levels. At the firm level, research by Carl Franklin and Larry Keeley suggests that firms not replacing at least 10 percent of their revenue stream annually with new products or services are likely to be out of business within five years.[13] The information technology revolution has only accelerated this dynamic, across both the IT production and consumer industries. As Massachusetts Institute of Technology (MIT) economist Eric Brynjolfsson writes, "We see much greater turbulence and volatility in the information industries, reflecting the gale of creative destruction that inevitably accompanies disruptive innovation."[14] In fact, this has contributed to a dramatic widening since the mid-1990s in the disparity in profits between the leading firms in industries that use technology intensively. Today, the leaders truly benefit from innovation while the innovation laggards pay a stiff price, and sometimes the ultimate one—bankruptcy and dissolution.

Just as businesses must constantly renew themselves through innovation, so must economies. For example, within U.S. manufacturing, the reallocation of production from less productive to more productive firms accounted for significantly more than half the growth in manufacturing productivity between 1976 and 1996.[15] Firms either innovated and became more productive, or they lost market share and jobs. Innovation likewise accelerates the pace of turnover of firms in an economy. Whereas, at the beginning of the last century, the average life span of a S&P 500 company was greater than sixty years, today the average life span is just twenty years. Ninety-eight percent of American companies disappear within eleven years.[16] The average life span of a company in Japan and Europe is twelve and a half years. Despite sounding regressive, this process of churn is actually vitally important to a nation's economic health. In fact, before the Great Recession, approximately 750,000 new establishments opened in the United States each year—500,000 of which were new start-up companies— creating more than seven million new jobs. At the same time, nearly 700,000 establishments closed each year, destroying more than six million jobs in the process.[17] In a study of twenty-three OECD countries, Audretsch et al. found that such sustained rates of entrepreneurship are essential for economic growth.[18] As the Kaufman Foundation's Robert Litan notes, if just sixty of these new start-up companies were to grow up to be $1 billion companies (and, in so doing, create new markets), then the United States could add one additional percentage point to its annual economic growth, and U.S. GDP would double in size six years earlier than it otherwise would (eighteen years versus twenty-four years).[19] Countries in which either firm creation or dissolution is impaired constrain the dynamic effects that innovation brings to an economy.

Thus, the ability to innovate is inextricably linked to the competitiveness of both individual firms and entire economies—and the impact on both from failing to innovate is greater than ever before. In both organizations and nations, before the emergence of the race for global innovation advantage since about 1995, failure to innovate usually just meant slower growth, much as overeating and lack of exercise result in people becoming tired "couch potatoes." But today the failure to innovate, particularly for developed nations, leads to failed companies, loss of national export competitiveness, and ultimately structural economic crises. Today, failure to innovate fast and effectively enough leads to the economic equivalent of a heart attack. As Schumpeter elaborated, "In capitalist reality, as distinguished from its textbook picture, it is not [price] competition which counts but the competition from the new commodity, the new technology . . . which strikes not at the margins of the profits of the existing firms but at their very lives."[20] Today, it is this competition for innovation advantage that strikes at the very economic lives of firms and national economies.

Now, more than ever, nations need innovation to remain globally competitive. This is especially true for developed nations, which without innovation have a hard time competing with low-income, low-wage nations. Especially critical is their ability to lead in process innovation (to automate production and produce more with fewer workers) and to move up the value chain to develop higher-value-added products and services that less-developed nations simply can't make, at least not as well for the near and medium term. Moreover, for large nations like the United States to succeed, they must innovate not just in new high-growth start-ups—the focus of much of U.S. innovation policy—but also in a wide array of midsized and large firms and establishments. Doing this will enable America to reduce its trade deficit while creating higher-wage jobs. And it's much easier to create jobs in an economy not running large sustained trade deficits because, at least in the United States, a dollar of exports produces twice as much employment as a dollar of domestic consumption.[21] Finally, a healthy traded sector enables economies to avoid high trade debts that will ultimately have to be paid off by future generations consuming less of what they produce.

What Is Innovation Policy?

Since the late 1990s, dozens of countries—small and large, rich and poor, North and South—have created and implemented national innovation strategies designed to boost the potential of their economies to produce a stream of commercially successful innovations. These countries recognize that innovation drives economic growth and that losing the race for innovation advantage can result in a relatively lower standard of living as nations lose higher-value-added sectors. They know that success in the competition to develop globally competitive domestic companies and industries, to attract internationally mobile innovation-based economic activities, and thus to achieve high and sustainable levels of economic and employment growth increasingly depends on the strength of their innovation ecosystems. The more advanced countries also realize that innovation-based economic activity is not just about moving up the value chain to higher-value-added activities in traded sectors, but also about boosting the productivity of sectors across the board and developing new capabilities and functionalities in their economies. All of these nations have come to understand that relying on markets shaped by price signals alone will not usually be as effective as smart public-private partnerships in spurring higher productivity and greater innovation. They understand that government can—and must—play a constructive role in helping the private sector compete. Therefore, they see the promotion of innovation as a focal point of their economic growth and competitiveness strategies.

Just as we defined innovation as more than the development of shiny new widgets, we define innovation policy as more than just science policy. Innovation policy involves the same set of policy issues that countries deal with all the time, but focuses on how countries can address those issues with a view toward maximizing innovation and productivity. For example, countries can operate their government procurement practices the same way they always have, or they can reorganize their practices in a manner specifically designed to promote innovation. Likewise, countries can organize their corporate tax systems simply to raise revenues, or to raise revenues in ways that also drive innovation and traded-sector competitiveness.[22] They can set up their science policies just to support science, or organize their investments in scientific research in ways that also support technology commercialization and the innovation needs of industry.

The most sophisticated countries recognize this. Their innovation strategies constitute a coherent approach that seeks to coordinate disparate policies toward scientific research, technology commercialization, IT investments, education and skills development, tax, trade, intellectual property (IP), government procurement, and regulatory policies in an integrated fashion that drives economic growth by fostering innovation. As Finland's National Innovation Strategy argues, it is vital that a nation's innovation strategy comprehensively addresses a broad set of policy issues because "piecemeal policy measures will not suffice in ensuring a nation's pioneering position in innovation activity, and thus growth in national productivity and competitive ability."[23]

Ultimately, a country's innovation policy aims to explicitly link science, technology, and innovation with economic and employment growth, effectively creating a game plan to compete and win in innovation-based economic activity. That's why Finland placed its national agency charged with spurring innovation, Tekes, within its Ministry of Economy and Employment: to make explicit the linkage between innovation and economic and employment growth. As Annabelle Malins, a British consul general to the United States, explained Britain's decision to develop a national innovation strategy, "The United Kingdom has made a conscientious decision to place innovation at the center of our nation's economic growth strategy."[24] If countries want to succeed in the race for global innovation advantage, they need a well-articulated, generously funded, and effectively implemented innovation strategy. But not everything that passes as an innovation policy is effective. Chapters 6 and 7 explore how countries can implement their innovation strategies in ways that are effective (win-win) for the country and the world, in ways that benefit the country at the expense of others, or in ways that are outright ineffective.

Is Innovation Policy Just Another Name for Industrial Policy?

Just what is the appropriate role of government in facilitating innovation, boosting productivity, and driving traded-sector competitiveness? Is growth best left to markets and private enterprise alone, as many free-market conservatives stubbornly believe, or does government play a role? In his seminal book *The Wealth of Nations*, released in 1776, Adam Smith observed that debate about the appropriate role of the state in technology development and in fostering economic growth had already raged for more than two hundred years.[25] Clearly, the debate has not abated in the centuries since, perhaps even picking up steam during the recent economic downturn as countries have increasingly intervened in their economies to support faltering corporations or to restore growth.[26]

In the United States and most British Commonwealth countries, many scholars, policy analysts, and policymakers interested in these questions subscribe to the neoclassical economics view that most innovations come from the private sector acting alone and that government's role in supporting innovation should be strictly limited. As a result, they restrict their recommendations regarding government's role to at most supporting "innovation environment" measures—ensuring a good business climate and backing basic science research and education—that will enable the private sector to have the inputs it needs to innovate on its own. They believe that the vitality of economies rests almost exclusively on the private sector acting on its own volition with no guidance or influence from the public sector. As such, for them, a too-active government innovation policy amounts to "industrial policy"—a shorthand pejorative for inappropriate intervention into markets that either hinders private firms from developing innovative technologies and/or distorts the supposedly efficient market-based allocation of resources. In fact, according to this view, many policy efforts to help firms become more innovative or productive only make matters worse, for the worst possible sin in the eyes of neoclassical economists is to "pick winners and losers." Substituting for the wisdom of the market can only lead to a worse, not better, allocation of resources, they opine. For such individuals, innovation policy is simply a more politically correct term for "industrial policy," a distinction without a difference.

For example, the August 2010 *Economist* article "Picking Winners, Saving Losers" assails industrial policy, painting an insidious picture of governments' increasing intervention in market economies, arguing that the hideous Leviathan of the state was gobbling up one sector after another and warning that "picking industrial winners nearly always fails."[27] As the article asserts, "Industrial policy may be designed to support or restructure old struggling sectors, such as steel or textiles, or to try to construct new industries, such as robotics or nanotechnology. Neither track has met with much success. Governments rarely evaluate the costs and benefits properly."[28] But there are three problems with the *Economist*'s argument. First, it is flat wrong in its contention that such activities "nearly always fail." Second, it's not as if governments evaluate the costs and benefits of neoclassical recommendations, such as instituting a flat tax. But that doesn't stop them from advocating for them. Third, the *Economist* (reflecting the general neoclassical view regarding government's role in fostering economic growth) bandies indiscriminately about a number of terms—"industrial policy," "innovation policy," "picking winners"—without adequately distinguishing between them. And it brands them all as inappropriate manifestations of government economic intervention, all the while making claims with the flimsiest of evidence—usually a few often-misinterpreted anecdotes.

Notwithstanding the efforts of free-market ideologues to blur the differences, distinctions between "innovation policy" and "industrial policy" are, in fact, real and important. To illustrate this, it is useful to envision a continuum of government-market engagement, increasing from left to right in four steps: from (1) a "laissez-faire, leave it to the market" approach, to (2) "supporting factor conditions for innovation," going further by (3) "supporting key broad technologies/industries" and, at the most extreme, (4) "picking specific technologies/firms," which is tantamount to industrial policy, as shown in figure 5.1.

The debate in the United States (and most Commonwealth nations) is usually framed in terms of two choices: either leave economic growth principally to the market (position 1), or engage in industrial policy to pick specific technologies and/or specific firms (position 4). For example, one high-ranking Obama administration economic official told us that the United States won't win the race for global innovation against China if we become like China. For him and many others, there are only two choices: American laissez-faire capitalism or some kind of foreign-inspired, heavy-handed

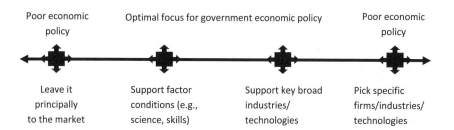

Figure 5.1 The Innovation Policy Continuum

industrial policy that is just one short step away from nationalized industries and state socialism.

Clearly, the market view is against innovation policy in principle, holding that policies should not be designed particularly to spur innovation or
address the different challenges facing different industries. Government
should just go about its business, raising revenues, regulating what it
needs to (which is not much), managing macroeconomic policy (preferably
through monetary policy only), and enforcing the rule of law, all ideally as
lightly and unobtrusively as possible. Leave it to entrepreneurs motivated
by making a profit (ideally with no capital gains tax) and all will be well.

The industrial policy view is also clear. Industrial policy is designed to
intervene in an economy to support, favor, or restructure specific businesses, such as particular automobile or steel companies, or narrowly defined technologies (e.g., lithium-ion batteries). Industrial policies often seek
to pick specific national champion companies or technologies. For example,
France's investment of 56 billion francs ($11.4 billion) between 1976 and
1996 in Minitel, a monochrome teletext phone system, is a classic case of a
country trying to pick a national champion,[29] as is Groupe Bull, France's
state-sponsored computer giant.[30] French president Jacques Chirac's ill-fated
gambit to introduce the French-backed search engine Quaero "as the next
Google-killer" was also a clear manifestation of industrial policy.[31] No wonder industrial policy has gotten a bad name with ill-advised policies like this.

The practices of Japan and Korea after World War II (WWII), in which
specific companies or networks of companies (the chaebol in Korea and the
zaibatsu in Japan) were selected as national champions to lead certain industries such as automobiles, electronics, concrete, or shipbuilding, also qualify
as industrial policy. The Synthetic Fuels Corporation, a U.S. government–
funded corporation established in 1980 to create a financial bridge for the
development and construction of commercial synthetic fuel manufacturing
plants (such as coal gasification), was industrial policy aimed at producing
alternatives to imported fossil fuels (and would probably have worked if oil
prices had stayed high). The U.S. government's action in 2009 to bail out
General Motors and Chrysler—an intervention in the economy to assist two
very specific firms—was industrial policy, albeit done in the context of business cycle policy.

The choice, however, should not be between the extremes of laissez-faire and industrial policy. There is a range of activities between these two poles that governments can and should take to spur innovation. Governments support economic growth best by engaging at points 2 and 3 on the spectrum depicted in figure 5.1: supporting factor conditions (including tax policy designed to encourage innovation and designing incentives to spur institutional innovations like better technology transfer from universities) and placing strategic bets to support potentially breakthrough nascent technologies (such as the Internet, nanotechnology, human genome mapping, robotics, or advanced batteries) and industries rather than specific firms (such as broadband telecommunications, life sciences, software, and clean energy), all the while enabling competitive markets and a beneficial business climate.

Engaging between the extremes requires thoughtful policies to support innovation, including strategic investments to spur emerging technologies with the potential to form the basis for the industries, companies, and jobs of the future. But smart policy can do this successfully. In fact, U.S. government support has a long and distinguished history of playing a fundamental role in bringing to realization an extensive and compelling list of technologies. These include: interchangeable parts, the manufacturing assembly line, the microwave, the calculator, the transistor and semiconductor, the relational database, the laser, jet propulsion, nuclear energy, the Internet, the graphical user interface, and the global positioning system (GPS), among many others. Research supported by the National Institutes of Health practically created the U.S. biotechnology industry. And yes, even Google, the Web search darling, isn't a purebred creature of the free market; the search algorithm it uses was developed as part of the National Science Foundation (NSF)–funded Digital Library Initiative. Google got off the ground, in part, through a portion of a $4.5 million digital libraries research grant from the NSF to Stanford University, which sought to better understand, sort, and find information using the World Wide Web—and has since transformed from a two-person start-up to a global company that employs twenty-five thousand Americans and boasts a market value greater than $200 billion.

Neoclassical economists will certainly object, "But isn't this an industrial policy process of picking winners?" It is, insofar as it means government identifying industries and technologies broadly where the country needs to be more innovative and productive and then developing and implementing policies to work with the private sector to ensure that result. But this is not the derided "industrial policy" in which the government selects specific firms or extremely narrow technologies, nationalizes industries, or impedes beneficial market forces.[32]

In contrast, innovation policy is concerned with enhancing the strength of a nation's innovation ecosystem. Innovation policy recognizes that businesses innovate with the help of many other institutions and that public policies can either spur or retard the innovation activities of companies. It further recognizes that technological progress depends on certain tangible and intangible infrastructure investments and on specific innovations that are too risky, complex, or interdependent with other breakthroughs for private firms to risk the substantial investments that are needed.[33] Indeed, government funding beyond support for basic research and procurement has played a key role in the technological advances that have sustained U.S. industry's global predominance since WWII. Likewise, the government's role in coordinating collaborations between private industry and publicly funded research in university and government laboratories has spilled far beyond the defense sector to include large parts of the civilian economy.[34]

A current example is the U.S. government's support for battery technology. Advanced batteries will be key to the clean economy of the future and without government support for battery research, innovation will lag behind what is societally optimal. This is in part because the spillovers—or benefits that accrue to society and not the innovating firm—from battery research are huge. It would be industrial policy if the U.S. government picked a particular national battery champion (e.g., Duracell) or a specific technology that government planners thought was the best (e.g., lithium-ion). But it is innovation policy when the government, as it does through the Department of Energy's Advanced Research Projects Agency-Energy (ARPA-E) agency, supports a wide range of firms (including start-ups) and technologies (such as lithium-ion, lithium-air, Zinc-air, all electron, metal-molten salt, or magnesium-ion), recognizing that while it needs to support the private sector in its efforts to spur battery innovation, neither it nor the private sector can adequately predict which firms and technologies will ultimately win.

Economist Dani Rodrik paints a helpful picture of the appropriate relationship between government and business with respect to innovation policy when he describes "an interactive process of strategic cooperation between the public and private sectors which, on the one hand, serves to elicit information on business opportunities and constraints and, on the other hand, generates policy initiatives in response."[35] As the Obama administration's September 2009 "Strategy for American Innovation" wisely argued, "The true choice in innovation is not between government and no government, but about the right type of government involvement in support of innovation."[36] In summary, innovation policy recognizes that while the private sector should lead innovation, in an era of globalized innovation and intensely competitive markets, governments can and should play an important enabling role in supporting private-sector innovation efforts at both the firm and industry level.

But still, free-market advocates will contend that markets generally get it right and will provide what the market needs (one definition of innovation) if they are just left to their own devices and the motivation to make a profit. "We don't need no innovation policy!" they insist. But as we describe next, unlike the production of commodity-type widgets, innovation is subject to a vast array of "market failures," such that in the absence of effective innovation policies, markets will underproduce innovation and economies will suffer.

Why Do Nations Need an Innovation Policy?

It's one thing to want more innovation; it's quite another to take the next step and say that an innovation policy is needed to maximize innovation. But nations with innovation policies understand—in contrast to what the conventional neoclassical economic doctrine holds—that while markets acting on their own might produce societally optimal numbers of commodity-based widgets, they will produce suboptimal levels of innovation, for there are a significant number of systemic market failures around innovation, including externalities, network failures, system interdependencies, and the public-goods nature of technology platforms. Moreover, even if these failures did not exist, most nations recognize that they need an innovation policy because the stakes have been raised as innovation competition intensifies among nations. Nations without innovation policies are like soccer teams taking to the field without coaches, trainers, or a game plan; they're just a collection of players (businesses) running around, competing against other players (businesses in nations with effective innovation policies) that are well equipped, well coached, and running specific, well-designed plays.

Finally, even if there weren't systemic market failures or tough new competition, smart countries would still want innovation policies, if for no other reason than because addressing complex and systemic challenges—such as providing universal and much less costly health care to growing and aging populations, combating climate change and environmental degradation, achieving sustainable energy production, and deploying complex digital infrastructures—requires coordinated strategies that leverage the limited resources of a nation's businesses, academic institutions, and government agencies.

How the Free Market Acting Alone Fails Innovation

It's bad enough that conventional economists give short shrift to innovation; worse, they give little consideration to the role of government in spurring innovation. Endlessly repeating the mantra "markets are best at allocating resources," most conventional economists see government intervention as likely to hurt innovation and growth because, by definition, it distorts market-based allocation. For them, there is little risk of market failure, but a high risk of government failure. As a result, in order to justify any government action to stimulate innovation, advocates must come before the high court of neoclassical economics and present in chapter and verse why what they are proposing responds effectively to an actual "market failure," and why the risk of government failure is low. Ninety-nine times out of a hundred, the verdict is "guilty: no market failure here, go back to leaving it to the wisdom of the market." And it's not as if the rejection is based on any kind of objective analysis (academic research is neither consulted nor rejected)—it's ideological in nature, pure and simple. While this might be a reasonable way to look at markets for commodities like barley or wheat, it's a completely inappropriate concept for looking at innovation systems.

As Douglas North argued in his 1993 Nobel Prize lecture, neoclassical economic theory is an inappropriate tool for analyzing the processes of economic development and innovation.[37] Or, as British economist John Barber elaborates, the standard neoclassical model "has become increasingly unsatisfactory as research into innovation and analysis of innovation policy measures means that the list of identified market failures has become longer and longer so that the standard neoclassical model becomes modified to a degree which undermines its validity."[38] When it comes to innovation systems, the very concept of market failures is a faulty one in the first place, for it assumes that markets for innovation work most of the time and, at worst, suffer from occasional minor failures. A better frame is the notion of maximizing the potential of complex national innovation systems, which absent a facilitating innovation policy will underperform. But, because the neoclassical "high court" demands proof of "market failure" before they even consider blessing any government action, we present ten leading market failures that cause markets to innovate suboptimally:

1. Because Individual Firms and Entrepreneurs Cannot Capture All the Benefits of Their Own Innovative Activity, They Will Produce Less Innovation Activity than Society Needs

When Steve Jobs launched the Apple iPad—a novel innovation that combined new capabilities in hardware, software, and communications—in April 2010, he rightly intended for Apple to make money. And while Apple has clearly profited from its innovation, there are now dozens of other companies selling similar tablet computers in competition with the iPad (in fact, the 2011 Consumer Electronics Show in Las Vegas saw eighty new tablet computers introduced by a variety of vendors),[39] suggesting that Apple was not able to capture anywhere near all the returns from its innovation. This is an example of the first market failure from innovation: the inability to appropriate full benefit from one's own innovative activity.

The knowledge needed to create new products, processes, and organizational forms cannot be contained completely within an individual firm, even when the firm patents its discoveries. It inevitably spills over to other firms and individuals, who can use it without paying the costs of creating it. For example: an entrepreneur like Michael Dell develops a new business model for building and selling computers that others copy; a university transfers discoveries from the lab to the marketplace; or a company makes a breakthrough that forms the basis of innovations that other companies can use. Such spillovers are rampant in innovation, arising from product R&D, process R&D, technology adoption (particularly IT adoption), and the development of new business and organizational models.

A plethora of studies have found that the rate of return to society from corporate R&D and innovation activities is at least twice the estimated returns that the company itself receives.[40] For example, Tewksbury, Crandall, and Crane examined the rate of return from twenty prominent innovations and found a median private rate of return of 27 percent but a median social rate of return of a whopping 99 percent, almost four times higher.[41] Yale economist William Nordhaus estimates that inventors capture just 4 percent of the total social gains from their innovations; the rest spill over to other companies and to society as a whole.[42]

And these spillovers are not confined to breakthrough products like the iPad. There are also significant spillovers from process R&D (that is, the R&D conducted to help organizations produce things better). Hitt and Tambe find that spillovers from firms' investments in IT are "significant and almost as large in size as the effects of their own IT investment."[43] On average, firms capture only about half the total societal benefits from their investments in computers, software, and telecommunications, suggesting that current levels of IT investment are significantly less than societally optimal. Ornaghi also finds "statistically significant knowledge spillover associations for process and product innovation."[44] He asserts that these "knowledge spillovers play an important role in improving the quality of products, and to a lesser extent, in increasing the productivity of the firm."[45] At least one study finds that firms invest more in product R&D when they invest more in process R&D, meaning that spurring process R&D also stimulates product R&D.[46] Cefis, Rosenkranz, and Weitzel observe that positive externalities in process R&D indicate relatively high technological spillovers in this type of innovation.[47]

The problem with standard neoclassical economic theory is its insistence that firms should keep investing only until their net present value rate of return equals their cost of capital. But if the actual rate of return to society is much greater than to the firm, firms will stop investing long before the societal rate of return equals the cost of capital. In other words, the inability of firms to capture all the benefits of their own innovative activity means that, left on their own, they will invest less in innovation-spurring activities than is optimal for society. This is the key rationale for policies such as the R&D tax credit, which is designed to stimulate additional private R&D activity by increasing the private rate of return from R&D closer to the public rate of return. Neoclassical defenders will argue that patents, copyright, and other means by which companies can protect their discoveries from being used by others solve the appropriability problem and obviate the need for government innovation policies like the R&D tax credit, but the reality is that not everything can be protected, and even if it could be, there are still significant spillovers that keep firms from appropriating all the benefits from their innovations.

2. High Levels of Risk, Expense, and Differing Time Horizons Stifle the Development of Complex New Technology Platforms

Even "rational" companies are reluctant to invest in next-generation technologies, especially when it involves high levels of risk and exceedingly lengthy R&D time frames. This is the principal reason it was the U.S. government's Defense Advanced Research Projects Agency (DARPA) that supported the initial development of the Internet (then the ARPANET) and not private communications or computer companies. At its beginning, the private sector was reticent to invest in the "Internet" because the sums required were significant and the nascent technology was so far from potential commercialization that companies were unable to foresee how they could monetize potential investments. Accordingly, the government stepped in and provided initial R&D funding; helped coordinate research among the military, universities, and industry; and created interoperable standards, thus seeding development of a breakthrough digital infrastructure platform, making the Internet a reality decades before the free market would have (if ever) left to its own devices. In fact, the Defense Department has played this role with regard to multiple technologies that have become critical to U.S. innovation leadership.[48]

Yet even if defenders of neoclassical economics acknowledged this point, they would contend that government is most likely to invest in unwise, money-losing projects; in other words, that government is a dumb investor. The market shows itself to be the wise investor by staying on the sidelines. But leaving aside the fact that the market was an incredibly dumb investor during the U.S. housing bubble, the market only invests, at least in theory, in activities where the private rate of return is above the cost of capital. But as noted above there are many, many innovation investments where the return to society is much, much higher. Without innovation policy, the market won't invest in these innovations, because the market is completely indifferent to societal rates of return.

Take the Internet, where the return on investment has been astronomical. In fact, the commercial Internet adds at least $1.5 trillion to the global economy each year, vastly more money than DARPA ever invested in it, even in net present value terms.[49] It wasn't the lack of an opportunity to realize potentially high investment returns that kept the market from investing in the Internet initially; rather, it was the vast level of uncertainty involved and the inability of industry players to capture all the benefits of their investment. Moreover, when the market did invest in early stage computer networks, it came up with uncompelling, noninteroperable systems like CompuServe, Prodigy, and MCI Mail, where it was only possible to exchange e-mail if both the sender and receiver used the same service provider, obviating the scale and network effects that the fully interoperable TCP/IP-based World Wide Web ultimately delivered.

This same corporate reticence to invest on the risky future evident in the Internet's development pertains today to a range of emerging infrastructure-based technologies including biotechnology, nanotechnology, and robotics. At the same time, as Tassey notes, a related challenge is that "the complex multidisciplinary basis for new technologies demands the availability of technology platforms before efficient applied R&D leading to commercial innovation can occur."[50] In other words, the levels of investment required to research and to develop emerging technologies are so great that in many instances the private sector cannot support the effort alone, and therefore "government must increasingly assume the role of partner with industry in managing technology research projects."[51]

Moreover, to innovate successfully, businesses rely on much more than their own efforts, or even those of the suppliers they contract with. They increasingly rely on ubiquitous "shared infratechnologies" including measurement methods, process-control techniques, and science and engineering data. These infratechnologies, which make no sense for individual firms to develop on their own, deliver substantial economic benefits. For example, a National Institute of Standards and Technology (NIST) study estimated that the U.S. semiconductor industry has invested more than $1 billion (with government assistance) to improve its measurement capabilities. The study found that these improvements generated $17 billion in economic benefits. Yet, because the public goods characteristic of technology infrastructure precludes firms from capturing all the benefits of their investments (that is, once developed, all firms who need it can benefit from it) and because they have limited funds, industry has substantially underinvests in infratechnologies, despite the fact that the societal economic benefits from such investments are substantial, as a NIST study of the biopharmaceutical industry demonstrated.[52] For the United States to overcome this market failure, it must discard its "black box model" of innovation, which views industrial technologies as homogenous private goods, and move toward a more accurate conceptual framework in which technology is understood as having both public and private components.[53]

Japan is particularly strong at facilitating cooperation between competing firms and the government in developing and deploying new technologies. Okimoto describes the importance of the Japanese government's focus on working with companies on consensus building and articulating a long-term vision in the development of new technologies.[54] The Japanese government views its role as helping firms overcome the downfalls of "bounded vision," meaning that different kinds of organizations receive various types of information as the result of their primary activities and are limited in what they search for and "see" by the overall objectives of the organization. Japan believes that the limitations in the visions of for-profit firms and of the government can be overcome by bringing the two together.[55]

3. Capital Market Failures Have Caused Private Financing of R&D to Shift Away from Innovation-Based and Entrepreneurial Efforts

The neoclassical model holds as a matter of faith that investors as a group accurately scan the market and the array of technology opportunities available and invest in the ones with rates of return above the cost of capital. Even more remarkable, their faith appears to be as rock solid even after the financial industry dumped trillions into subprime mortgages and other failed housing investments. But as we tragically saw with the housing bubble, private-sector investment is often misallocated, with grievous results. One reason, as we note in chapter 2, is that investors wrongly bought into efficient market theory. But another is that while investors may be able to deal with risk, they don't deal well with uncertainty where it's difficult if not impossible to model expected outcomes. As with the initial development of the Internet, these capital market failures occur when unfamiliar investments such as those involving new companies, novel technologies, or innovative business models appear too uncertain for investors to undertake in relation to the anticipated returns.

One manifestation of this is that private financing of R&D in the United States has shifted away from more entrepreneurial and early stage research efforts, largely because of decision makers' shorter time horizons.[56] The idea that investors make the same kinds of rational decisions with respect to investment opportunities over time is simply not true, as the history of the last thirty years shows. Before the 1980s, many U.S. corporations made investment decisions on the basis of expectations of long-term returns. But changes in the institutional system of U.S. investing and management beginning in the 1980s under the rubric of the "shareholder value movement" changed all that.

You would think that for-profit corporations should always invest to maximize shareholder value. But the real question is: which shareholders—the ones (including senior managers) currently holding stocks who want to sell in a year, six months, or six weeks, or the "widows and orphans" who are holding on for the long term? Maximizing net present value for the first set of shareholders—what the shareholder value movement meant—can lead to significantly different outcomes than maximizing net present value for the second. But how investment funds were structured and their managers rewarded meant that funds moved money around in search of the quickest return, regardless of where long-term value was. How managers were compensated—increasingly with stock options that were not related to actual managerial performance—reflected this new view that a manager's job was to maximize value for the first set of shareholders. And because managers themselves became key short-term stockholders (through the significant growth of stock options), they made even more efforts to boost the welfare of short-term stockholders, including by boosting dividends and stock buybacks instead of reinvesting in plant and equipment. And because the short-termers were more likely to be insiders with access to better information than the long-termers, pressure from short-term investors for high short-term returns meant that companies acted differently. But this was not rational in the sense of maximizing returns for society, or even for companies (if returns are defined as maximizing the net present value of all future profits). As former General Electric CEO Jack Welch (one of the founders of the shareholder value movement) said in 2009, "On the face of it, shareholder value is the dumbest idea in the world. Shareholder value is a result, not a strategy . . . your main constituencies are your employees, your customers, and your products."[57]

As we note in chapter 3, starting in the 1980s, companies began paying out more in dividends and engaging in stock buybacks as a way to boost stock prices for short-term investors, even though this meant relatively less investment in activities that would boost long-term innovation and productivity. Similar changes have occurred in the U.S. venture capital market. Venture capitalists have found it more profitable to invest in larger deals and less risky later-stage deals at the expense of smaller, riskier, early stage efforts in basic and applied research. In fact, while total venture capital funding for zero- and first-stage deals increased from 1996 to 2008, the share of total venture capital going to these kinds of deals actually declined from 35 percent to 24 percent over the same time period.[58] Likewise, average deal size in inflation-adjusted dollars has doubled, meaning that smaller deals are harder to get funded.[59] Also, as noted previously, corporate-funded R&D is increasingly less focused on earlier stage research and more on later stage, development-related activities. While generic technology developed from earlier stage research can produce robust returns, it can take considerable time to show payoffs for the bottom line. In contrast, development can show quick, albeit lower, returns. As economist William Lazonick notes, today "a combination of innovation, redistribution, and speculation drives the stock market," with maximizing innovation often playing second fiddle.[60]

4. Coordination Failures Undermine the Innovation Process

Because of the complexity of the innovation process, especially today, firms cannot maximize innovation by working in isolation. Adam Brandenburger and Barry Nalebuff describe this new world as "co-opetition," where competitors are competing and cooperating.[61] To do so, they need to interact with organizations such as suppliers, customers, competitors, universities, research institutes, investment banks, and government entities to gain various kinds of technology, knowledge, information, and market access. Such interactions take time, effort, and resources, and in a fast-moving world, the pattern of cooperation between firms and other agents is far from optimal, not least because of a lack of information about possible useful partners.[62] For example, multiple actors often work on similar research problems. They could share information to everyone's benefit, but they usually don't if left on their own. Such coordination failures are one reason why government agencies like DARPA have filled such a valuable niche. Perhaps more important than its role in funding actual research, DARPA orchestrates the involvement of established companies with start-ups and academic experts, supports knowledge sharing between industry competitors through invitation-only workshops, provides third-party validation of new technology directions, and supports technology platform development.[63] Without programs like DARPA; Advanced Research Projects Agency-Energy (ARPA-E), which plays a similar role for energy innovation; and NIST's Technology Innovation Program, which supports high-risk, high-reward research in areas of critical national need, the private marketplace would undersupply this coordination.

For example, DARPA played an instrumental role in identifying emerging directions in the research community, coordinating star scientists, and seed-funding initial research into materials technology for silicon-geranium (Si-Ge) semiconductors that was crucial in the late 1980s to perpetuating

Moore's Law. DARPA's program manager realized through his connections with the research community that three different research teams (unbeknownst to each other) at IBM, UCLA, and start-up Amberwave were independently considering exploring Si-Ge technology. As a central node to which information from the research community flowed, DARPA's program manager was able to recognize the potential of Si-Ge technology, provide funding, and coordinate research activities, thus helping to launch a research effort that led to fundamental semiconductor breakthroughs, and therefore extend Moore's Law.[64]

A related challenge pertains to the fact that, while successful technological innovation increasingly depends on collaboration between firms and universities, the interests of these collaborators are not well aligned. As we have seen, short-term competitive pressures make it difficult for even the largest firms to support applied research, much less basic research. As a result, firms are relying more on university-based research and industry-university collaborations. Yet the divergent needs of firms and universities can hinder the coordination of R&D between these two types of institutions. University researchers are not necessarily motivated to work on problems that are relevant to commercial needs. They are rewarded for things like how many peer-reviewed publications they author. Likewise, university technology-transfer offices do not always promote the licensing of university intellectual property to firms, or they do so on terms that maximize revenue but not licensing. Conversely, individual businesses sometimes want to "rent" universities' research capabilities and appropriate the resulting discoveries for themselves. All of these factors can impede the generation and transfer of knowledge that contributes to innovation.[65]

5. "Chicken-or-Egg" Challenges Inhibit Development of Technology Platforms

If innovation involved no more than a company or an entrepreneur inventing and selling something, it would be a lot easier and much more prevalent. But all too often, successful innovation depends on others. When Steve Jobs developed the iPod, he needed customers to have broadband Internet access and he needed to have music available for purchase online. Without either, the iPod would have gone the way of the Newton (an earlier, failed Apple attempt at creating a PDA). Luckily, he was able to coordinate music licensing, and broadband Internet had been deployed in the prior few years to most households. Moreover, broadband demand increased after this, in part because of applications like the Apple iTunes store itself, and music firms put even more content online because people had devices like iPods.

But this coordination isn't always easy. In fact, another market failure that afflicts innovation in complex ecosystems stems from the fact that markets tend to be poor at coordinating action when multiple parties need to act together synergistically and simultaneously. Chicken-or-egg challenges must be overcome for innovation to occur around technology platforms such as near field communications (NFC)–enabled contactless mobile payments, intelligent transportation systems (ITS), health IT platforms, digital signatures and electronic IDs, and the smart electric grid. This can be daunting, particularly if government doesn't play a facilitating role.

Take the case of NFC-enabled mobile phones. These devices empower consumers to use their cell phones as electronic wallets, allowing individuals to make payments at subway stations, vending machines, taxis, retailers' point-of-sale (POS) devices, and many other venues simply by waving their cell phone in front of a payment terminal. But mobile payments are significantly different from the classic "widget" industry in which a company need only acquire the requisite inputs to manufacture its products and sell them on the open market. Contactless mobile payments are stymied by a classic chicken-or-egg problem, which is why there are almost none in the United States. For consumers to demand mobile phones with embedded electronic wallets—and thus, critically, for mobile network operators to require this feature from the handset manufacturers—they must be certain that a sufficiently deployed mobile payments infrastructure exists at merchants' POS terminals, at fare readers in metro subways and buses, at airports, in parking garages, in automated devices like vending machines and parking meters, and in other places where they can use the device. Merchants, for their part, are not likely to deploy NFC-enabled payment terminals until a critical mass of users gives them confidence that their investments in such technology will be repaid. Thus, the market is still-born unless and until, as happened in Japan and Korea, a wide range of actors, including the mobile network operators, handset manufacturers, financial institutions including major banks and credit card issuers, commercial retailers, merchant stores, public transit authorities, and government agencies act simultaneously to develop the market.[66]

As the Information Technology and Innovation Foundation (ITIF) has documented in reports explaining why certain countries lead the world in digital technology platforms—including contactless mobile payments, ITS, health IT, and electronic IDs—in markets stymied by chicken-or-egg conundrums, governments can play important roles in facilitating development of these ecosystems and funding infrastructure deployment so that once the platform is deployed, the private sector can innovate on top of it.[67]

6. Many Industries and Firms Lag in Adopting Proven Technologies

Neoclassical economists simply assume that all industries are using and developing as much innovation as makes economic sense. We guess they have not recently bought a new house. Not only do the contractors use largely mid- to late twentieth-century tools to build the house,[68] but their productivity is lower than it was twenty years ago. And the realtors selling it actively oppose the introduction of new Internet-empowered business models.[69] In other words, it's a market failure when some industries and firms lag behind in technology adoption (thus impeding faster productivity growth in these sectors of the economy) for reasons generally unrelated to the chicken-or-egg challenges described above. With the exception of relatively new, science-based industries such as IT and biotechnology, many industries delay in adopting readily available, more productive technologies. Besides construction, the most significant is probably health care, which has lagged in adoption of available technologies that could boost productivity and health-care quality.[70]

There are actually two different problems at play here, depending on the industry and process in question: a principal-agent problem and a market fragmentation problem. The principal-agent problem arises where innovation may hurt its own implementers. Such industries have two attributes in common. First, they are usually characterized by professions where innovation represents a direct threat to the professionals themselves because the worker and the manager is essentially the same individual. For example, while Ford and Toyota managers might be loath to adopt managerial automation, they have strong incentives to adopt production automation because the shop floor workers don't control the means of production and consumers benefit. But in the legal, accounting, health-care, real estate, optometry, pharmacy, education, and many other industries, professional workers largely control or influence the means of production, so innovation can and often does mean cannibalizing their own jobs. Why would real estate agents embrace more efficient e-realty systems that would put many of them out of work and reduce commission rates for the rest due to increased agent productivity? Why should the legal industry not put up barriers to more efficient online provision of legal services?[71] But this is not enough to limit innovation. Even here, we would expect some intrepid entrepreneurs who are not fixated on protecting existing professionals to enter the market. This leads to the second characteristic of industries affected by the principal-agent problem: control over the marketplace. Through legal codes, required certifications, control over information platforms, monopolistic access to customers, and sometimes government rules they use their power to get enacted, these industries are able to keep innovators out. For example, in the case of realtors, the industry's professionals control the key technology platform, the Multiple Listing Service (MLS), and so they have designed the rules governing its use in ways to thwart more efficient e-realtor entrants.[72] And because the MLS is a natural monopoly, it would make no economic sense for start-up competitors to create their own, even if they had deep pockets.

There is a second problem limiting adoption of proven technologies that afflicts industries such as construction and health care, which have fragmented or atomistic structures. The extreme fragmentation of these industries, with many smaller players operating relatively inefficiently, hinders productivity growth and technology adoption in their sectors of the economy. For example, the construction industry is one of the least IT-intensive sectors of the U.S. economy, with one of the lowest rates of productivity growth. Why doesn't the market address this fragmentation? As industry expert Barry LePatner explains in his book, *Broken Buildings, Busted Budgets*, the reason for the industry's market fragmentation is that the buyers aren't very sophisticated, usually buying construction services only occa-sionally.[73] As a result, they have limited ability to demand quality and price efficiency. Likewise, in the case of health care, fragmentation arises be-cause an underdeveloped and not fully competitive marketplace results in inadequate price and quality signals for buyers. In both cases, the natural forces of innovation—market pressures leading to consolidation and scale, with more sophisticated suppliers adopting more technology—are under-developed. In these cases, the marketplace alone will underperform un-less government intelligently intervenes to spur competition, to be a smart buyer, or to support the development and adoption of shared technology platforms.

7. The Innovation-Producing Benefits of Industry Clusters Are Under-Realized

Imagine if the entire U.S. economy operated like California's Silicon Val-ley, where a large agglomeration of high-tech firms, research universities such as Stanford, technical colleges to train high-tech workers, venture capitalists, and other supporting institutions created the world's most vi-brant technology region. In other words, imagine if the U.S. economy were characterized by regions where firms interacted in a rich environment of cooperation and learning that enabled them to crank out innovations faster than firms located out in the hinterlands on their own. In fact, both the creation and the diffusion of innovation often occur in geographic clusters like Silicon Valley. Such industry clustering enables firms to take advantage of common resources (e.g., technical institutes, a workforce trained in par-ticular skills, or a common supplier base), which facilitates better labor-market matching and knowledge sharing. This process may be particularly relevant in industries that rely more on the creation or the use of new knowledge, as clustering appears to spur knowledge transfers.[74] In fact, evi-dence suggests that industry clustering has become even more important for productivity growth since the 1980s: the extent to which an industry is geographically concentrated has been increasingly associated with subse-quent productivity growth during the last three business cycles.[75]

Just as each additional broadband user makes the Internet more valuable to existing users, each firm in a cluster makes the cluster more valuable to other firms. As such, because the benefits of geographic clustering spill over beyond the boundaries of the firm, market forces produce less geographic clustering than society needs. Each firm in a cluster confers benefits on other firms in the cluster, but no individual firm takes the "external" benefits it produces into account when making its own location decisions. In addition, the firms in a cluster usually have common needs (e.g., for worker training or infrastructure) that they have a harder time meeting on their own. Clustered firms, therefore, usually require external coordination (from governments or industry associations) to effectively meet these needs. But because no individual firm can capture all the benefits, it's rational for firms to let others in the cluster bear the costs of coordination, which leads to free-rider problems. Failure to meet these common needs makes clusters smaller and less productive than they would be otherwise. If the benefits from clustering to all firms in economies were considered and the common needs of all firms in each cluster met, there would be more clustering and thus more innovation and higher productivity.

8. There Is More than One Equilibrium at Which Economies Can Settle, and by Definition, One of Them Is Worse from a Societal Perspective

If you remember your freshman year microeconomics class, you'll probably recall graphs of supply and demand curves intersecting. Usually, it was a picture showing something like the price at which farmers would sell their wheat and the price that buyers would be willing to pay. In this ideal universe visualized by neoclassical economists, there is only one point at which supply and demand are in equilibrium, and the job of government is to not get in the way of the market attaining it. At any particular time in this idyllic world, there should be only one price of wheat such that the market "clears," meaning that all who want to buy and sell at that price are able to do so. If government subsidizes or taxes wheat, the market will not efficiently allocate wheat production.

But, in fact, when we move to the economy-wide level, there can be multiple equilibriums in an economy, with some better than others. And markets acting on their own may actually pick the inferior one, with society suffering as a result. Research by economist Elvio Accinelli has shown that there is strategic complementarity between the percentage of high-skill workers and high-value-added, innovative firms in an economy. He finds that economies can be in perfect neoclassical equilibrium at either a high level of innovation and high skills or in a "poverty trap" of low skills and underinvestment in innovation. In other words, if there are not enough skilled workers, firms will not adopt advanced technology leading to higher productivity since their workers don't have the needed skills, and if firms don't adopt advanced technologies, workers won't seek out the skills needed to use these technologies. Hence, economies can settle into a "poverty trap." This trap can be avoided if the number of innovative firms in an economy exceeds a threshold level while the number of skilled workers also increases. As such, innovation policy can help move economies to this higher level equilibrium if it spurs workers to get more skills and firms to use more skills by investing in advanced technologies and high-performance work organizations.[76]

9. The Interests of Geographically Mobile Firms in Locating Innovative Activity May Diverge from Those of a Nation's Residents

Another failure has emerged that, while not a market failure as defined by economists, is in fact a failure as defined by the average citizen or elected official. This is the potential divergence between the interests of geographically mobile firms and those of the residents of a country.[77] The decisions that firms make about where to locate innovative activity are rightly based on their own interests, but these may or may not coincide with the interests of local residents. For this reason, many countries, just like most U.S. states after WWII, "intervene" in their economies with robust innovation and economic development policies designed to tilt the choice of businesses to invest in their location. These countries are not content to let the "market" determine how many and what kinds of jobs are created; rather, they work to ensure that they gain more high-paying, high-productivity jobs. Neoclassical economists might bemoan this reality, but it exists, and the responsibility of elected officials in any nation is to maximize the real economic welfare of their citizens, not some theoretical, textbook global market allocation. And if neoclassical economists were being forthright, they would admit that their economic prescriptions don't work for any one country if other nations have put in place economic development policies—especially ones that intentionally distort global markets.

10. There Can Be a Market Failure from Growth Itself

As Harvard economist Benjamin Friedman has shown, innovation and growth don't just provide narrow monetary benefits of the kind economists count.[78] Growth or its lack, according to Friedman, produces positive or negative externalities. Growth leads to more tolerant societies, improves civic discourse, and generally leads to societies that are more humane. Economic decline or stagnation leads to the opposite, as we saw in 2011 in societies like Egypt and Tunisia, where neither the market (nor failed economic policies) produced enough growth. To use Friedman's example, it was a lack of growth that paved the way for the Nazis to take power in Germany in the 1930s, a development that imposed untoward human and financial costs on humankind. Surely, investing a few billion dollars on proactive growth policies in the late 1920s and early 1930s to avoid the Great Depression and the subsequent rise of Hitler would have produced vast benefits and avoided the enormous costs the human race ultimately paid for Nazi depravity.

These multiple and systemic failures in the process of innovation should make it clear that, left to themselves, markets will produce significantly less innovation, productivity, and competitiveness than nations need. As discussed above, however, this is not a call for some kind of twenty-first-century state socialism or heavy-handed regulatory state, for that would produce the same, if not worse, result. In a globally competitive world, the cost of indulging in either free-market or state-directed ideology is something that countries can ill afford. This is why a growing number of nations have put in place robust and strategic innovation policies that balance market and state.

However, nations not only want to foster more innovation than the market alone will produce but they also want to win, or at least not lose, the race for global innovation advantage. Indeed, even if there were no market failures, countries would need an innovation policy because the stakes have been raised. To return to our soccer analogy, when one team gets a head coach, trainers, and a game plan, your team better do so as well, or it's going to find itself at the bottom of the rankings.

Why It Matters to Get Innovation Policy Right

As modern technologies have brought countries increasingly closer together, global economic competition has become more intense than ever. Companies now face many more competitors from around the globe; and, at the same time, they now enjoy the opportunity to invest in many more places. As IBM chairman Sam Palmisano framed it, the last decade has seen the rise of the globally integrated enterprise. As a result, government officials in many countries now wake up every morning asking how they can do whatever it takes to win in the global competition to achieve innovation-based economic growth and to attract foreign investment and talent across their borders. These governments scratch and claw to win every last business deal and to create every last job they can in their countries, even by taking steps that clearly violate the spirit and the letter of World Trade Organization (WTO) law. In contrast, the unquestioned position of the United States as the world's leading economy over the past half century has led too many U.S. policymakers to falsely believe that America is immune from such ferocious global competition.

So while almost all other countries believe that they are competing in the "World Cup" of innovation, to borrow a popular sporting metaphor, the United States, uniquely, doesn't even think it's in a competition because "countries don't compete." Perhaps America just thinks it's a soccer practice, or perhaps a "friendly" without any permanent consequences. But the reality is that most countries understand they are in international economic competition and have developed strategies to compete, as figure 5.2 shows. However, just as in a soccer match, there must be rules about what constitutes fair and unfair competition.

To be sure, there is nothing sinister about countries engaging in fierce innovation and economic competition and there is nothing wrong with them competing to win—as long as they are playing by the international rules of commerce established by the global community. Indeed, as we've explained, competition among governments has become a critical factor in

Figure 5.2 Countries' Perception of International Competition
and How They Compete

determining which economies win and which lose in the race for global innovation advantage.

Thus, when a country intensely competes to win, within the rules of the system, doing so benefits both itself and the world. This is because fair competition forces countries to put in place the right policies on science and technology transfer, R&D tax credits, lower corporate tax rates, education policies, and so forth. In other words, competition forces countries to ratchet up their games, and to enact an array of "good" innovation policies. And if all countries are in the position that they have to raise their game through good innovation policies, the end result is that the world is much better off. In fact, it's only when one country decides that it doesn't need to raise its game because it thinks it's not in a competition (e.g., the United States) or when countries cheat and engage in mercantilist, negative-sum policies, that the world fails to realize these benefits, and actually ends up worse off. Put in terms of our soccer analogy, the world is better off when competition forces each country's soccer team to become better. Even if it hurts the United States or other countries when Spain's soccer team gets stronger, Spain's quality forces other teams to get better. The same dynamic holds with the quality of countries' innovation policies in fostering their global economic competitiveness, and that of the rest of the world.

Thus, when America invents the R&D tax credit, or France trumps the United States by offering an R&D tax credit six times more generous, or Denmark creates innovation vouchers for small businesses, or the Netherlands and Switzerland offer dramatically lower taxes on the profits generated from a newly patented product, or a country can lower its corporate tax rates because its public sector operates so efficiently, this is all tough, fair competition, like playing a hard-fought World Cup match. Countries' constructive innovation policies spur other countries to emulate or improve on them, and everyone wins. The following chapter explores these types of "good" innovation policies that scores of countries have put in place.

The problem comes when countries start to cheat and contravene the international economy's established rules (as if they were bribing the referees or using studded cleats in soccer). These practices—the mercantilist ones we describe in chapter 7—can indeed help countries win the game. But while these practices can work, using them is akin to cheating or rigging the game. And the problem is that not only do these policies harm other countries, they then encourage other countries to cheat, ultimately undermining the utility of the international trading system and causing the global economy to suffer, as we have seen recently with the global financial crisis. This is why, as we describe in chapter 11, it's critically important for countries to compete intensely but fairly. It's also why interested observers must be able to distinguish between the kinds and effects of policies that countries are putting in place—only then can they nurture the ones that are positive-sum while contesting those that are negative-sum and try to move them into the win-win category. The next two chapters provide a guide for how to do so.

6

Crafting Innovation Policy to
Win the Race

C ountries that want to lead the pack in the race for global innovation advantage must craft and implement a range of constructive
policies to support the innovative capacity of their economies. To
that end, some three dozen countries have created formal national innovation strategies and at least two dozen have established national innovation
agencies, actions that have only further intensified the global competition
for innovation leadership. These countries are not content to let their government policies and actions influence innovation in a haphazard and un-
coordinated way. They seek to develop mechanisms to assess their nation's
strengths and weaknesses, to examine other nations' policies in order to
learn from them, and to assess and revise their own policies in a broad array of areas that could influence their innovation and competitiveness.

The countries leading the world in developing innovation policy have
followed a three-step process. First, they recognized the need to approach
innovation systematically. Second, they effectively brought attention to the
need for innovation to the body politic, putting forth an inspirational vision
and strategy for action, replete with clearly articulated goals and ambitions.
These goals and a game plan for achieving them are clearly set forth in their

national innovation strategies. Finally, these countries made the tough decisions necessary to not only implement institutional reforms to drive their innovation strategies but also to adequately fund them (including providing tax incentives), even at the expense of other government spending or lower taxes for individuals.

The Innovation Policy "I's"

Rather than offer a laundry list of programs and policies that countries are implementing to support innovation, we instead present seven broad areas that a national innovation policy effort must get right. We call these the seven "I's" of innovation policy: Inspiration, Intention, Insight, Incentives, Institutions, Investment, and IT (information technology).[1]

Inspiration: Setting Ambitious Goals

Holders of free-market ideology will claim that nations should not set goals for their economies because, by definition, whatever economy the market produces is the right one and superior to any economy dictated by goals, whether they are "Stalinist" five-year plans or the most market-friendly innovation policies. This is one reason why the United States has generally not set innovation goals, other than recently with respect to broadband and clean energy. But as we discuss in chapter 5, markets acting alone will underperform when it comes to innovation, and that's why at least thirty-five nations have implemented national innovation strategies. As part of these strategies, many countries unabashedly state their intention to lead the world in certain industries, technologies, or application areas, and they commit to supporting these goals with the necessary resources. These countries believe that without ambitious goals to work toward, the private, nonprofit, and government sectors will not be adequately motivated to take the needed steps.

Perhaps the best example of a nation that sets ambitious goals is Singapore. In the late 1990s, the country set a goal to drive its economy through and to become a world leader in innovation. Singapore openly declared that it sought world leadership in the life sciences, digital media, and water/environment industries. Ten years later, Singapore has succeeded. As the Information Technology and Innovation Foundation (ITIF's) *Atlantic Century* report found, in 2009, Singapore ranked first among forty nations or regions in innovation-based competitiveness, making the second-fastest progress of any of these nations from 1999 to 2009 (with only China showing faster progress). Singapore also placed first when ITIF released *The Atlantic Century II* report in July 2011. Singapore clearly followed through on its goals with innovation policies: In 2003, the country launched Biopolis, a two-million-square-foot biomedical research center to support its goal of becoming a world leader in life sciences. Biopolis has attracted almost seven thousand Ph.D. graduates in the life sciences, including many of the world's preeminent biomedical researchers. To put this in perspective, the United States has about ten thousand life sciences Ph.D.s. Thus, as Azeem Ibrahim, a research fellow at Harvard's Kennedy School, puts it, "a country with roughly the same population as Alabama can now compete with the U.S. as a whole."[2] Near Biopolis, Singapore's Fusionopolis houses six thousand scientists in fields such as materials science, clean technology, and digital media.

Likewise, China has signaled its clear intention to move to the front of the pack in the race for global innovation advantage. In January 2006, China initiated a fifteen-year "Medium- to Long-term Plan for the Development of Science and Technology." The plan aims for China to become an "innovation-oriented society" by 2020, to develop indigenous innovation capabilities, to leapfrog into leading positions in new science-based industries, to increase research and development (R&D) expenditures to 2.5 percent of gross domestic product (GDP) by 2020, to increase the contribution to economic growth from technological advances to 60 percent, to limit dependence on imported technology to 30 percent, and to become one of the top five countries in the world in the number of patents granted.[3] On February 9, 2011, China announced its updated "China Innovation 2020" goals. The country plans to invest $1.5 trillion on seven "strategic emerging industries":—(1) energy saving and environmental protection; (2) new generation of information technology; (3) biotechnology; (4) high-end equipment manufacturing; (5) new energy; (6) new materials; and (7) new energy vehicles.[4] To get a sense of the level of this investment, for the

United States to match this on a per-GDP basis it would have to pass an American Recovery and Reinvestment Act (the 2008 "stimulus bill" that appropriated over $800 billion) every year for the next five years and have all the funds go to making U.S. industries more competitive.

Other nations also focus on technology areas or broad industries they seek to lead. For example, Australia, Canada, Denmark, Finland, Ireland, Japan, Korea, the Netherlands, Singapore, and Sweden have openly declared an aspirational goal to lead the world in transitioning to a digital economy. Leadership in the digital economy entails ensuring that almost all citizens have access to high-speed broadband connections; that the population is digitally literate; that government puts all services online; and that information technologies suffuse transportation, energy, and health networks as well as business enterprises. Savvy countries recognize that digital infrastructure applications—such as mobile- and wired-broadband, the smart electric grid, health IT, intelligent transportation systems, mobile payments, digital signatures, e-government, and kiosks and other self-service technologies—can transform their economies.

The Japanese government has identified advanced battery technology as a key driving force behind its competitiveness, and views battery technology as an issue of "national survival."[5] As a result, it committed more than ¥25 billion ($275 million) in funding for lithium-ion battery research over the five-year period from 2007 to 2012, and has committed to a twenty-year advanced battery research program. Likewise, China has targeted a number of clean energy sectors, including wind energy, solar power, rail, carbon capture and sequestration, and clean nuclear power as sectors in which it seeks technological leadership.[6]

Many nations identify a range of core industries they seek leadership in. For example, Finland's National Innovation Strategy identifies six industries central to its economy for which it seeks global leadership: forestry products, information and communications technology, health care, energy and the environment, construction, and mechanical engineering.[7] For each of these industries, Finland has created a Strategic Center for Science, Technology, and Innovation, partnerships in which companies, universities, and research institutes agree on a joint strategic technology research road map for the industry. Such "road mapping" exercises identify technology challenges and key areas of need over the next decade, providing a road map for technology development and subsequent rounds of research funding. More broadly, Finland's National Agency for Technology and Innovation, Tekes, has identified twenty-two key technology and application areas—such as nano-sensors, wireless technologies, broadband, advanced machining, lean manufacturing, and services innovation—in which it seeks cutting-edge advantage for its companies and industries and funds research accordingly. The Netherlands has targeted innovation leadership in the creative and financial services, retirement and pensions, logistics, and supply chain management sectors. And Denmark has targeted the IT services, retail, pension management, and transportaton sectors.

Other nations have set specific goals, akin to a football team's goal of being in the top five teams in scoring. For example, in 1997, Korea set a goal to raise R&D as a share of the government budget from 3.6 to 5 percent and almost got there, moving it to 4.7 percent. Turkey set a goal of raising R&D from 1.7 percent of GDP to 2.5 percent. Since 1999, China has increased its R&D expenditures by 21 percent a year, and the country seeks to increase its R&D intensity by 50 percent by 2020.[8]

While setting an ambitious goal is useful, sometimes the goals set by nations or regions are unrealistic. A case in point is Europe. In 2001, the European Union (EU) articulated its so-called Lisbon Strategy, which set a goal for Europe to become "the most competitive and dynamic knowledge-based economy in the world by 2010." This was never realistic and needless to say, Europe failed, if for no other reason than because it did not invest the funds to make that a reality and in part because, as chapter 10 describes, it isn't really sure if it wants more innovation, at least of the kind that leads to "creative destruction." But still, the agenda did help provide support for policymakers who wanted to make innovation more of a priority.

Intention: Making Innovation-Based Competitiveness a National Priority

It's one thing to set a goal; it's another thing to make the invariably tough choices needed to achieve it. As we have seen, Europe's Lisbon Strategy set an ambitious goal, but it lacked intention and follow-through. One nation that didn't lack resolve was Finland. When the Soviet Union broke up in 1991, the collapse sent Finland, its largest trading partner, into an economic tailspin. GDP plummeted 9 percent in two years, unemployment rocketed to 20 percent, and exports fell by 13 percent in 1991 alone. (By comparison, in the 2008–2009 recession, U.S. GDP shrank by 2.6 percent and unemployment peaked at 10 percent.) What did Finland do? Did it hunker down and try to ride out the storm by cutting investment in innovation, as the United Kingdom is doing and many in the United States advocate, in an effort to balance the budget? To the contrary, while slashing overall government spending, the Finnish government significantly expanded its support for R&D, in part through boosting funding for its national innovation agency, Tekes, and in part by putting in place innovation-based tax incentives for businesses. Finland increased its R&D intensity from less than 3 percent in the 1990s to nearly 4 percent by 2008.[9] On top of those measures, the Finnish government slashed the corporate income tax rate from 33 percent to 25 percent in 1990 and lowered it to 19 percent in 1992, all while staring in the face of huge budget deficits.[10] In other words, in the midst of an economic disaster of the first order, Finland went all out to make a massive bet on competitiveness, innovation, and productivity, while at the same time cutting spending that did not contribute to that goal.

And the bet paid off. Finland diversified its economy. Nokia, once a manufacturer of rubber boots and paper products, transformed itself into a cellular phone company that, at least until the emergence of smart phones, was a world leader. The country turned a budget deficit into a surplus. From 1993 to 1997, the Finnish government's budget deficit averaged −5.2 percent of GDP. But starting in 1998, the string of deficits turned into a string of surpluses, which averaged 3.8 percent of GDP from 1998 to 2002 and reached 5.2 percent of GDP by 2007.[11] From 1993 to 2009, Finland's GDP per capita (at purchasing power parity [PPP]) grew 50.2 percent while America's grew 28.4 percent.[12] During that same period, the dollar value of Finland's high-tech exports (in current $US) increased almost eightfold, while the dollar value of U.S. high-tech exports barely doubled. Today, Finland is widely recognized as one of the most innovative countries in the world and has, as one commentator put it, "as well-designed an innovation ecosystem as exists on the planet."[13] Likewise, Switzerland's response to

nomic crisis of 2009 was to expand the country's investments in
e, technology, and innovation, as the Swiss parliament increased
funding levels and launched an innovation voucher program to sup-
pu: innovation in small businesses.

A number of other countries, including Ireland, Korea, and Singapore,
have also developed national innovation strategies and institutions as a response to severe economic crises. They followed the logic of Mancur Ol-
sen's 1982 book *The Rise and Decline of Nations*, which argued that countries
whose economic foundations have suddenly been shaken tend to grow and
innovate faster than more stable nations, as dramatic change becomes an
issue of national survival. Certainly the Great Recession has likewise
shaken America's economic foundation. The question is: Will it be able to
emulate the paths of these countries and make the tough decisions needed
to strengthen its innovation-based competitiveness or will it get locked in
an interest-group and partisan stalemate?

Insight: Improving Understanding of Innovation Performance

Once nations set a goal to lead in innovation and develop the will to act,
the next step is to acquire the insight to do the right thing, not just anything. At least thirty nations have done the right thing, as evidenced by
their national innovation strategies.

A core component of these strategies is analysis and insight gathering.
This can take several forms. Many nations undertake a comprehensive
analysis of their competitiveness and benchmark it against other nations
at both broad economic and major industry levels. Among other things,
they assess the national tax, trade, and regulatory climate for the competitiveness of their traded sectors and how their science and technology (S&T)
and education and training policies affect competitiveness at the sector
level. These nations further identify critical emerging technology areas,
chart research road maps needed to keep their companies at the cutting
edge of these emerging technologies, look to identify gaps or shortfalls in
investments or technology competencies, and attempt to bridge those gaps.
The innovation strategies of many countries also support the coordination
of technology development within industry across a vertically fragmented

industrial ecosystem in order to align with larger commercial, societal, or security goals.[14] For example, Germany's *High-Tech Strategy for Germany*, released in 2006, identified seventeen advanced cross-cutting technologies (ranging from biotechnology, nanotechnology, and microsystems technology to optical, materials, production, and information and communications technologies) that are critical to the ability of German industries and its broader economy to compete. For each technology, the strategy undertakes a SWOT (strengths, weaknesses, opportunities, and threats) assessment of where Germany (that is, its enterprises, universities, and research institutions) stands with regard to the development and deployment of the technologies. The strategy helps to identify gaps and to coordinate the limited resources of Germany's government, enterprises, and universities toward charting technology road maps (and making the requisite investments) to ensure German leadership in these technologies.[15] The 2010 update of the *High-Tech Strategy* noted that the "German Federal Government's innovation policies are geared towards five fields of action: climate/energy, health/nutrition, mobility, security, and communication," and charted "forward-looking projects and R&D programs" in each field of action.[16]

To this end, most innovation agencies—including Finland's Tekes and Sweden's VINNOVA—operate a number of overseas technology liaison offices that conduct "technology scanning," seeking out emerging technologies bearing on the competitiveness of domestic industries, and sponsoring outreach efforts to help their domestic companies partner with foreign businesses and researchers. The mission of these technology liaison offices is to assure that their countries stay on top of the latest developments in cutting-edge technologies and to give their countries' businesses exposure to new technologies and business practices emerging in other parts of the world.

Creating new knowledge is a central goal of many countries' innovation strategies. This involves not only providing financial support to research universities but also creating new knowledge about innovation processes, methods, techniques, measurement, and how best to diffuse innovation throughout an economy. For example, through its *Technology Review* series, Finland's Tekes has a long history of funding research that seeks to create new knowledge about innovation. For example, "Tekes Technology Review

eizing the White Space: Innovative Service Concepts in the United
" surveyed innovative business models in U.S. financial services, pro-
nal services, logistics, and retail trade industries and explained how
Finnish small and medium-sized enterprises (SMEs) could adapt those
models.[17]

In the United States, the National Science Foundation (NSF) has launched
the Science of Science & Innovation Policy (SciSIP) program to support
interdisciplinary and multidisciplinary research aimed at developing theoretical models and empirical evidence to advance understanding of scientific, research, and innovation processes. The objective is to provide a
scientifically rigorous, quantitative basis upon which policymakers can
assess the impacts and dynamics of the scientific and engineering enterprise and improve outcomes.[18] One goal of SciSIP will be to help policymakers understand how the United States can enhance its R&D efficiency,
or return on invested R&D dollar, an objective shared by almost all nations.
Likewise, the United Kingdom has invested heavily to understand the role
of "service design" in innovation, while Norway has sponsored a large research program into "value-driven service innovation."

General Electric's (GE's) Jack Welsh famously said, "You can't manage
what you can't measure." But because innovation is such an intangible
concept—it can't be measured as easily as barrels of oil or counted like cars
coming off the assembly line—and because it includes difficult-to-quantify
activities such as changes in business and organizational models, developing accurate measures and metrics for innovation has been a challenging
task for many countries (and companies) and is a common focus of many
nations' innovation strategies. The United Kingdom's NESTA (National
Endowment for Science, Technology, and the Arts) has been at the forefront of this effort. Its 2008 report *Measuring Innovation* argued that "existing innovation metrics bear little relation to the innovation that is most
relevant to the modern U.K. economy."[19] NESTA points out that traditional
innovation measurements, based around S&T policy and the manufacturing economy, emphasize quantifiable activities—such as number of patents
granted, number of scientific publications, or amount of money invested—
but that these traditional metrics fail to adequately capture "hidden innovation" in services industries, creative industries, and the public sector, or

to recognize new methods of open and user-led innovation. Since December 2008, the United Kingdom has issued annual innovation progress reports that score the country on implementation of its national innovation strategy.[20]

Incentives: Encouraging Innovation, Production, and Jobs

Many countries that have come to recognize incentives as indispensible tools in building global competitiveness provide rewards ranging from grants and tax breaks for specific corporate projects and desired behavior (e.g., performing R&D or investing in new equipment) to general reductions in corporate taxes. Whether it's China providing tax holidays to attract a high-tech factory, France offering generous R&D tax credits, or Ireland providing one of the lowest corporate tax rates (10 percent), many nations actively encourage innovation and domestic investment. Indeed, as competition for internationally mobile investment has increased over the last quarter century, most nations have established more competitive corporate tax codes. Deveraux, Lockwood, and Redoano find that corporate tax rates for Organization for Economic Cooperation and Development (OECD) nations declined from nearly 50 percent in the early 1980s to less than 35 percent in 2001, and that international tax competition was the principal driver of those reductions.[21] By 2009, the non-U.S. OECD rate had declined even more, to just below 30 percent (while the combined state-federal U.S. rate remained at 39 percent).

Recognizing that incentives are an important driver of innovative behavior, a number of countries have begun to offer generous (and stable) R&D tax credits both to encourage existing companies to expand R&D activity and to attract globally mobile R&D activity. For instance, India and France now offer the world's most generous R&D tax credits, almost six times higher than that of the United States.[22] (In part because of aggressive reforms, corporate taxes as a share of French GDP are now lower than the European average and even lower than Ireland's.) Israel's R&D credit is four times greater than that of the United States. Despite the fact that the United States invented the R&D tax credit in 1981, and long offered the world's most generous credit, U.S. R&D tax credit generosity has slipped markedly.

In fact, America ranks twenty-first of twenty-four OECD countries assessed for rate of change in tax credit generosity between 1999 and 2008. By 2012, the United States ranked just twenty-seventh out of forty-one countries in R&D tax credit generosity, and had even fallen behind the non-OECD nations of Brazil, China, and India in R&D tax credit generosity.

Not only have other nations put in place more generous research incentives, they also have been more innovative in using novel incentives to spur research and innovation. For example, some countries—including Denmark, the Netherlands, and Norway—have begun to extend R&D tax credits to cover process R&D activities, effectively extending the R&D tax credit from goods to services industries as well. Other nations have more generous credits for companies cofunding research at national laboratories or universities. For example, in France, companies funding research at national laboratories and universities receive a 60 percent credit on every dollar invested. Denmark, Hungary, Japan, Norway, Spain, and the United Kingdom provide firms more generous tax incentives for collaborative R&D undertaken with public research institutions (than for R&D activity undertaken independently).[23]

Several countries have recently adopted or expanded tax incentives designed to spur the commercialization of R&D. These incentives, or "patent boxes" (so-called because there is a box to tick on the tax form), allow corporate income from the sale of patented products (or in some cases from innovation-based products) to be taxed at a lower rate than other income.[24] For example, Ireland does not tax income received from patents, and Belgium taxes such income at a rate not greater than 6.8 percent. Switzerland has reduced corporate taxes on income from all intellectual property to between 1 and 12 percent. In 2010, the Netherlands expanded this incentive such that income derived from patents or R&D is taxed at just 10 percent, instead of its normal 25 percent rate.[25] China, France, Luxembourg, and Spain also tax income from patents at reduced rates. In fact, China's patent box also goes beyond patents by providing the lower patent box rate to firms that spend at least 3 to 6 percent of gross revenue on R&D (depending on firm size), have 60 percent of firm revenue from core intellectual property (IP; defined as inventions, utility model patents, software, copyrights, proprietary layout designs, and new plant varieties), have 30 percent of their workforce with a college degree, or have 10 percent of their workforce employed in R&D or high-tech occupations.[26]

A number of countries also have implemented innovative tax policies offering preferential tax treatment to small businesses, especially those engaged in innovative activities. For example, France's Jeunes Enterprises Innovantes (JEI) program targets young companies that are less than eight years old, have fewer than 250 employees and less than €50 million in turnover, devote at least 15 percent of their expenditures to R&D, and are independent and not listed on a stock exchange. Another innovative tax technique France uses to support entrepreneurs is giving wealthy individuals the opportunity to invest in start-ups in lieu of paying a wealth tax.

Australia, Canada, France, Norway, and the United Kingdom also offer young innovative firms refundable R&D tax credits in lieu of using carry-forward or carry-backward provisions on business losses. Within the EU, governments also can give extra incentives to firms less than six years old that invest more than 15 percent of their total revenues on R&D across all regions and sectors without breaking EU state aid rules.[27]

Other nations offer very generous investment credits to encourage companies to invest in new capital equipment and other growth-producing investments. For example, Taiwan's Statute for Upgrading Industries, established in 1991, provides a package of corporate tax incentives, including accelerated depreciation and tax credits for investments in R&D, automation, worker training, pollution controls, and investments in newly emerging important and strategic industries. Thus, a company may take a credit of up to 20 percent for funds invested in hardware, software, or technology that can promote an enterprise's "digital information efficiency."

Such nations understand the importance of productivity to being internationally competitive. In one description of Taiwan's program to provide tax credits for companies to adopt automation, Wen-Jung Lien et al. note: "Companies are encouraged to adopt automation instead of the conventional labor-intensive production method so they can be less dependent on labor and less concerned about industrial hollowing-out."[28] And, in fact, one study found that the tax credit actually reduced unemployment by a small amount (0.06 percent). Lien et al. also find the Taiwanese R&D tax credit more than pays for itself, costing the government NT$10.4 billion

($358 million), but increasing tax revenue by NT$22.8 billion ($785 million).[29] They find the same result for a tax credit for investing in automation, a cost of NT$7.8 billion ($268 million) that led to an increase in overall tax revenues of NT$13.3 billion ($458 million). These incentives account for about 0.3 percent of Taiwanese GDP. To match these incentives as a share of GDP, the United States would have to offer tax incentives of $42 billion, far in excess of the $8 billion it offers in the R&D credit.[30]

Many other nations have corporate tax incentives for investment. Companies in Malaysia can depreciate general plant and equipment over six years, with heavy machinery over four years, and computer and IT equipment even faster.[31] In the United Kingdom, firms can expense investments for plant and machinery up to £100,000 ($156,000) in the first year. Singapore allows firms to expense in the first year all computer and prescribed automation equipment, robots, and energy-efficient equipment.[32] In Canada, purchases of computers are eligible for a 55 percent declining-balance capital cost allocation rate in the first year. Manufacturing equipment is also eligible for accelerated depreciation.[33] It should be noted that all of the incentives described here are not targeted at particular firms, but rather are open to all firms in all industries that make growth- and innovation-inducing investments.

Many nations also offer large incentives to multinational technology-based companies to move operations to their borders. Intel's experiences provide a good example. Of the $7.3 billion Intel has invested in Israel, $1.2 billion was subsidized by the Israeli government.[34] In India, Intel can take advantage of a ten-year tax deduction that is available for 100 percent of profits derived by exports of certain products from free-trade zones. In addition to tax breaks, as part of its "semiconductor policy" India offers interest-free loans amounting to 20 percent of capital expenditures for projects in special economic zones (and 25 percent in selected other locales) for investments of greater than $570 million.[35] India put these policies in place in 2007 after it lost out to Vietnam on a $1 billion Intel assembly and test facility, which Vietnam lured to Ho Chi Minh City thanks to its own generous incentives and tax breaks. For the Vietnam facility, Intel will not pay corporate taxes for the first four years of operation and will enjoy a 50 percent tax break the following nine years, after which

Intel will pay only 10 percent in taxes, compared with the normal 28 percent corporate rate.[36] (Such incentives are offered to all businesses that invest in the Ho Chi Minh City high-tech economic zone.) It is a bit ironic that a country with a city named after the iconic Communist leader Ho Chi Minh is better at attracting global capital investments than the United States. China offers similar tax breaks. It costs Intel $1 billion less to build a factory in China than in the United States—and the cost difference is only slightly attributable to cheap labor. Ninety percent of the difference comes from the Chinese government providing Intel with capital grants, equipment grants, tax holidays, and incentives.[37] Likewise, Korea offers its major high-tech companies virtually tax-free status, and interest-free loans to keep their investments in country.

As Intel CEO Paul Otellini explains, like it or not, offering incentives as part of the global competition to attract mobile high-tech investment is here to stay: "We're building factories in Ireland, Israel, China, or Malaysia and you get an incentive package that [includes] an end-of-the-year tax holiday or equipment credits or something like that worth several hundreds of millions of dollars because people want companies like ours to invest there and to hire their folks. What's different about Mississippi versus Malaysia? You're not taking anything away from the tax rolls that is there on the day you give the grant."[38] Intel's still investing in the United States (75 percent of its factories remain in America, though it sells 75 percent of its product overseas), but it's telling that Intel is one of the only semiconductor companies to open a new plant in the United States in the past half decade, with almost all others being offshored. The United States is going to have to get used to competing for globally mobile high-tech investments. But unlike virtually every other advanced country, it lacks any kind of coordinated federal capability to do so, has among the highest effective corporate tax rates, and has minimal investment tax incentives.

Many countries are also experimenting with measures to increase their R&D efficiency by using existing funding for scientific research to incent universities to focus more on technology commercialization. For example, in Sweden, 10 percent of regular research funds allocated by the national government to universities are now distributed using performance indicators. Half of these funds are allocated based on the amount of external funding the institutions have been able to attract, with the other half based on the quality of scientific articles published by each institution (as determined through bibliometric measures such as the number of citations).[39] Finland also has started to base its university budgets on performance—25 percent of the research and research training budgets of Finnish universities are based on "quality and efficacy," including the quality of scientific and international publications and the university's ability to attract research investment from businesses.[40] In other words, without increasing government budgets, these nations are using existing funds to provide a strong incentive for universities to be greater engines of national innovation.

In addition to incenting innovation, it's also important that countries remove impediments to innovation, such as the needlessly complex process of starting a business or inefficient regulations. For example, it takes forty-seven days to start a business in Indonesia or Spain—and an astounding average of 120 days to start a business in Brazil.[41] Yet the evidence clearly shows that delays caused by entry regulations are associated with lower rates of firm entry.[42] Some countries have streamlined their new business registration procedures, often with dramatic results. Portugal's "On the Spot Firm" initiative enables new businesses to register with the government online in just forty-five minutes, and has been so successful that sixty thousand new firms formed that way in just two years.

Smart governments also systematically review their regulatory regimes to remove regulatory barriers that hinder innovation. For example, Britain's Web site businesslink.gov.uk empowers businesses to directly influence how the regulations that affect them are devised and delivered.[43] Businesses may submit proposals on the Web site, outlining how specific regulations can be improved, such as ideas about how to reduce the amount of time it takes to complete forms or about how regulations that overlap or contradict can be rationalized.

Institutional Innovation

Technological innovation is not enough; nations need to drive institutional innovation as well. In other words, nations need to redesign a wide array of institutions to work more effectively, and not just science and technology institutions (although that's a good place to start). One way nations have done this is to create national innovation agencies. Recognizing that neither traditional science support agencies nor large, inflexible economic ministries can adequately support innovation, more than two dozen nations have created national innovation foundations, many just since the year 2000 (a selected list of nations is shown in table 6.1).

In 2000, India launched its National Innovation Foundation; Sweden created VINNOVA in 2001; Portugal introduced its Agência de Inovação in 2003; in 2004, Norway created Innovasjon Norge and the Netherlands launched Senter Novem; in 2006, Denmark created the Danish Agency for Science, Technology, and Innovation and South Africa launched its National Advisory Council on Innovation; and Uruguay launched its National Research and Innovation Agency in 2008. In June 2009, the United Kingdom reorganized several cabinet-level agencies to create the Department of Business, Innovation, and Skills and announced the creation of a $230 million fund to invest in technology-based U.K. businesses with high growth potential. Thus, while some countries do boast innovation agencies with a longer pedigree—Taiwan's Industrial Research Technology Institute (ITRI) dates back to 1973; Finland's National Agency for Technology and Innovation, Tekes, to 1983; and Ireland's Forfas to 1994—the past decade has seen a multitude of nations becoming serious about innovation-based competition and developing the institutional capacity to support it.

In addition, Australia, Austria, Chile, France, Germany, Iceland, Italy, Malaysia, New Zealand, Spain, and Switzerland also have dedicated innovation-promotion agencies.[44] And it's not just developed countries that have created innovation agencies and strategies. Uruguay has a staff of thirty at its National Research and Innovation Agency in Montevideo charged with driving innovation throughout the Uruguayan economy. Even tiny Ghana and Rwanda have articulated innovation strategies, while Ghana is in the process of launching its own national innovation agency. Nigeria launched a science, innovation, and technology policy in February 2012.

All these countries have agencies similar to America's National Science Foundation, which largely fund research at universities and national laboratories. But these countries realized that if they wanted to prosper in the

Table 6.1. Selected Countries with a National Innovation Strategy or Agency

Country	Has articulated a national innovation strategy	National innovation agency/foundation	Year agency introduced
Brazil	Yes	Brazil Innovation Agency	1967
China	Yes	Ministry of Science and Technology	1998
Denmark	Yes	Danish Agency for Science, Technology, and Innovation	2006
Finland	Yes	Tekes	1983
France	Yes	OSEO	2005
India	Yes	National Innovation Foundation	2000
Ireland	Yes	Forfas	1994
Italy	Yes	ENEA (National Agency for New Technologies, Energy and the Environment)	1999
Japan	Yes	New Energy and Industrial Technology Development Organization (NEDO)	1980
Korea	Yes	Korea Industrial Technology Foundation	2001
The Netherlands	Yes	Senter Novem	2004
Norway	Yes	Innovasjon Norge	2004
Portugal	Yes	Agência de Inovação	2003
South Africa	Yes	National Advisory Council on Innovation	2006
Sweden	Yes	VINNOVA	2001
Taiwan	Yes	Industrial Technology Research Institute	1973
Thailand	Yes	National Innovation Agency	2003
United Kingdom	Yes	Department of Business, Innovation, and Skills	2009
United States	Yes	N/A	N/A
Uruguay	Yes	National Research and Innovation Agency (ANII)	2008

competitive, technology-driven global economy, they needed an institution whose mission was specifically to promote technological innovation, particularly in small and midsized companies and in partnership with universities.

Foreign agencies that promote innovation are today a far cry from the strongly directive Japanese Ministry of International Trade and Industry (MITI) of the 1980s. While such agencies do seek to identify industries and technologies that their countries are well positioned to compete in and make research investments accordingly, they do not "pick winners and losers" in the sense of picking individual firms to champion. As Philip Rycroft, director general, innovation and enterprise at the U.K. Department of Business, Innovation, and Skills, who has overseen development of Britain's innovation policy, explains: "We're determined not to second-guess the future by trying to pick winners and losers. But we do think government can create the conditions so that new industries can rise more easily."[45] Agencies that promote innovation in their countries do not try to decide the path of business innovation and then induce firms to follow that path. Instead, they exemplify the cooperative, facilitative government role that is needed to address the market failures that hamper the innovation process, including coinvesting in key technology areas. And they seek to better align what government already does to ensure that it best supports innovation and competitiveness.

Another area of institutional innovation that countries are increasingly focusing on is reforming their education systems. These countries recognize that talent is an important source of competitive advantage and thus have made education and training a core component of their innovation strategies. For example, Finland has set a goal that all its young citizens will have the technical, analytic, and communications skills required for them to be competitive in a global economy the day they graduate from high school. Finland's *Oivallus* (*Insight*), a national educational foresight project, interviews corporations worldwide to understand what skills will be required by businesses in the years 2020 to 2030. It then advises how the Finnish education system needs to reform now so that students graduating in the future will be prepared to compete.[46] Sweden introduced universal school vouchers that can be used at any accredited private, nonprofi or public school in a sweeping reform to enhance the competitiveness of its secondary education system. Finland consolidated three of its institutes of higher learning—the Helsinki School of Economics, the University of Art and Design Helsinki, and the Helsinki University of Technology—into a single institution, Aalto University. Finland intends for it to become one of the world's leading academic institutions at combining business, technology, and design by 2020. Likewise, Denmark, desiring to create four very strong, globally competitive universities, merged eight universities into four.

Many nations also are reshaping how their governments buy goods and services in order to drive innovation through "intelligent demand." In most countries, public consumption accounts for approximately 20 percent of total domestic demand, so designed properly, government procurement policies can be an effective tool for fostering innovation.[47] Rothwell finds that, over longer time periods, government procurement policies triggered greater innovation impulses in more areas than did R&D subsidies, and they did so without any "buy domestic" requirements.[48] The United Kingdom, which spent £175 billion ($282 billion) on procurement in 2009, has made innovation a clear goal of its procurement process for years.[49] All British government departments are required to establish and develop an Innovation Procurement Plan and agencies at all levels of government must consider innovation when awarding government contracts. The Office of Government Procurement, the British government's procurement agency, and the Department of Business, Innovation, and Skills provide practical advice to procurers on how to ensure that innovation is incorporated into procurement practices.[50] Finland includes "innovativeness" among the criteria for public procurement decisions and reserves a percentage of appropriations granted to administration agencies to go toward innovation and development activities.[51] While these countries recognize that innovation should be a key element of government procurement, according to a report by the EU, "the United States has a strategic orientation in their public procurement as well, but not primarily connected to innovation."[52]

Government itself is the one area where needed institutional innovation is most lagging. In many nations, public-sector unions have become a heavy anchor on innovation, both in terms of the amounts of public monies they siphon off (largely for overgenerous pensions and overstaffing) that could be used for making investments in public-sector innovation and, more important, in terms of their own often deep resistance to institutional innovation. In the United States, for example, teachers' unions are the biggest barrier to real education reform, but at all levels of government public-sector unions have been a barrier to reinventing and automating government. In many nations, public-sector unions fight automation and institutional innovation, not to mention just simple downsizing to remove "dead wood" staff. Even in Scandinavia, a region where unions are relatively enlightened, public-sector unions limit innovation, particularly in health care. Perhaps one exception is Denmark, where the government funds pilot programs to demonstrate how technology can automate and actually eliminate government jobs without sacrificing high-quality services. This is possibly one reason why each Danish tax collection employee collects double the taxes that each Japanese employee does.

Investment: Increased Public Funding for Innovation

Many countries invest substantially in innovation on a per capita basis, and many have increased those investments since the late 1990s. While U.S. R&D intensity (R&D as a share of GDP) increased by a paltry 10.4 percent from 1995 to 2008, it increased substantially more in most other nations, including Germany (20.5 percent), Japan (26.2 percent), Korea (42.2 percent), Taiwan (61 percent), Finland (65 percent), Singapore (135.1 percent), and China (170.2 percent).[53]

Other countries also outstrip the United States in direct funding of efforts to promote innovation. In 2009, Finland invested €590 million ($801 million) in Tekes. Sweden's VINNOVA invests €220 million ($300 million) annually to promote growth in Sweden by funding needs-driven research and the development of effective innovation systems (this amount is effectively doubled to €440 million annually, since VINNOVA requires equal cofinancing of all projects).[54] Sweden invests 0.07 percent of GDP, Japan 0.04 percent, and Korea 0.03 percent in their agencies promoting innovation. In contrast, in fiscal year 2006, the U.S. government invested just $2.7 billion or 0.02 percent of GDP on its innovation programs, 28 percent less than in 1998. If the federal government were to invest the same share of GDP in these programs as many other nations have done, it would have to invest considerably more. For example, to match Finland's outlays per dollar of GDP, the United States would have to invest $34 billion per year.[55]

Many governments also directly support applied research activities, sector-based research, and industry-university research partnerships in their efforts to directly facilitate technology development and commercialization. For example, many countries offer competitive grants to national industry consortia for sector-specific research at universities and other research institutions, effectively bringing together researchers in the private, nonprofit, and public sectors. Such programs bridge the gap between basic research at universities and the introduction of new products and processes by industry.

Case in point is Germany's Fraunhofer Institutes, which undertake applied research of direct utility to private and public enterprise and of wide benefit to society. Whereas Germany's Max-Planck Institutes (like U.S. national laboratories) perform basic research wholly funded by government, Germany's fifty-nine Fraunhofer Institutes—funded 70 percent by industry and 30 percent by state and federal government—perform applied research that translates technologies into commercializable products.[56] The Fraunhofer Institutes, with an annual research budget of $2.35 billion, conduct industrially relevant cutting-edge research into a wide variety of sectors and technology platforms, including advanced machining, optics, robotics, microelectromechanical systems, nanotechnology, wireless technologies, and many others.[57] All firms in the country can avail themselves of these shared ecosystem support networks, participating in research programs to develop their capabilities and expertise in these functions and sectors. The German government also sponsors seventeen projects in industries including environmental technologies, medical technology, life sciences, information and communications technology (ICT), and transportation in collaboration with international partners to develop new research clusters in Germany. In addition, Germany's government is providing a total of €1.1 billion ($1.4 billion) over ten years to applied research on automotive electronics, lithium-ion batteries, lightweight construction, and other automotive applications.[58]

This is one reason why Germany still runs a manufacturing trade surplus, even though compensation for German manufacturing workers is almost 40 percent higher than for American manufacturing workers. Moreover, when the governments of Germany, Japan, and Korea are directly supporting their automotive sectors (and other industries) with hundreds of millions in research funding for the development of cutting-edge technologies like advanced batteries, it's increasingly difficult for American firms, not receiving such coordinated support, to simply "go out in the market" alone and compete against foreign rivals. While neoclassical economists persist in romanticizing a stylized view that companies compete as individual profit maximizing actors in international markets, the reality is that U.S. firms are increasingly running up against companies from other countries that are the beneficiaries of thoughtful and strategic government-funded advanced research programs into critical technologies that help their private sectors compete more effectively.

Like Germany, Finland, and others, the U.K. Technology Strategy Board's Innovation Platforms program has identified key sectors of technology development for the U.K. economy, including intelligent transportation systems, network security, low-carbon vehicles, assisted living, and low-environmental-impact buildings.[59] In addition to high-tech and engineering sectors, the Technology Strategy Board also targets knowledge-intensive industries such as the creative and financial service sectors as key pillars of the British economy.

Supporting the innovation capabilities of their SMEs, especially in manufacturing, is a core component of most countries' innovation strategies. At least a dozen countries operate extension services whose goal is to boost the productivity, innovation, and export capacity of their SME manufacturers.[60] For example, Canada's Industrial Research Assistance Program (IRAP), Japan's Kohsetsushi Centers, the United States' Manufacturing Extension Partnership (MEP), and the United Kingdom's Manufacturing Advisory Service (MAS) teach SME manufacturers lean manufacturing, Six Sigma, and quality techniques, as well as innovation and new product development skills, while also encouraging private-sector technology adoption. In several countries, including Austria, Australia, Canada,

;ermany, similar programs also provide direct funding support for innovation, and new product development activities. However, other countries more aggressively fund these programs than the United States: Japan's Kohsetsushi Centers receive a share of GDP thirty times larger than what the U.S. MEP program receives, while Canada's IRAP program receives ten times more as a share of GDP than the U.S. program.[61]

Several countries, including Austria, Canada, Belgium, Denmark, Germany, the Netherlands, Ireland, and Sweden, have begun using Innovation Vouchers to support SMEs. These vouchers, usually ranging in value from $5,000 to $30,000, enable SMEs to "buy" expertise from universities, national laboratories, or public research institutes. The intent is to provide incentives for research institutes to be responsive to the needs of SMEs and to stimulate knowledge transfer, whether assisting SMEs with particular technical research challenges or helping them implement improved innovation systems. For example, Austria's *Innovationsscheck* (Innovation Voucher) is designed to help SMEs start with continuous research and innovation activities. SMEs receive a $7,000 voucher for a cooperation project with a research institution for preparatory studies, analysis of technology transfer, or analysis of the innovation potential of a new technology. Holland's innovation agency, Senter Novem, has found that the program substantially stimulates innovation—eight out of ten vouchers issued resulted in an innovation that otherwise would not have come to fruition and 80 percent of new R&D jobs created in Holland since 2005 are attributable to the vouchers.[62] Likewise, a 2011 review of the Austrian *Innovationsscheck* found it to be "a very useful program" that engendered positive networking effects between SMEs and research institutions and through which approximately five hundred SMEs had started an R&D effort.[63]

Information Technology

From iPads to search engines to e-commerce, IT is the principal source of innovation today. But IT also plays an increasingly vital role in driving productivity and facilitating the innovation process. For instance, 32 percent of EU companies report having innovated, with IT enabling half of the product innovations and 75 percent of the process innovations.[64]

Recognizing that smart IT policies can spur the digital transformation of their economies and societies, many countries have implemented specific IT policies. For example, Japan's New IT Reform Strategy, launched in January 2006, set a goal of making Japan "the front-runner in the world's IT revolution" and sought "to complete the IT reformation by 2010 before other countries and to create a society in which all people feel the benefits of IT." This New IT Reform Strategy focused on the application of IT to key sectors, including medical services, the environment, safety and security, transportation (intelligent transportation systems [ITS]), and e-government. In July 2009, Japan announced its successor i-Japan 2015 strategy, which seeks to make Japan "a smart ubiquitous network society by 2015." I-Japan keeps the focus on sectorial transformation through IT (particularly in e-government, health care, and education), but also sets a goal of "establishing broadband infrastructure with 1 gigabit per second (Gbps) for fixed and over 100 megabytes per second (Mbps) for mobile." According to Japan's Ministry of Internal Affairs and Communications, Japan's IT industry contributed 34 percent of the country's economic growth during 2006–2010.[65]

In 2004, Korea launched its IT 8.3.9 Information Technology Development strategy, which identified eight key services areas, three telecommunications infrastructures (ubiquitous next-generation wired and wireless broadband networks, ubiquitous sensor networks, and implementation of the IPv6 next-generation Internet protocol), and nine IT product areas in which Korea sought world leadership. Korea has since articulated a "Ubiquitous Society" vision that will allow citizens to use computers or mobile devices anytime, anywhere. The nation has invested heavily in this area, by one estimate $1 billion in e-government alone between 2003 and 2007, directly saving more than $1 billion and increasing economic activity by $16 billion through more efficient government procurement, trade, and construction.[66] Further, Korea has enacted policies to spur upgrade of its broadband networks to 1 Gbps. Korea also has implemented policies to support deployment of an Ultra-broadband Smart Network and a Ubiquitous Sensor Network (IP-USN).[67]

Likewise, Singapore has implemented a national IT strategy. Intelligent Nation 2015 (iN2015) is Singapore's ten-year IT master plan, led by the

Infocomm Development Authority of Singapore and designed to help the country maximize the potential of IT. Following the country's previous IT master plans, including InfoComm 21 (2000 to 2003) and Connected Singapore (2003 to 2006), iN2015 contemplates national strategies for the deployment of critical digital infrastructure platforms, including ITS, contactless mobile payments for both smart cards and mobile phones, health IT, and digital signatures.[68] It also includes a substantial investment in high-speed networks, including the all-fiber Next Gen Nationwide Broadband Network (NGNBN) with speeds of 1 Gbps and a ubiquitous wireless network, Wireless@SG.[69] Singapore expects coverage of the fiber-based NGNBN to reach 95 percent nationwide by mid-2012.[70]

In the United Kingdom, the "Digital Britain" initiative, crafted in January 2009, called for upgrades to wired and wireless networks and communication infrastructure; universal broadband coverage; promoting investments and innovation in digital content, applications, and services; and developing the nation's digital skills. It also reaffirmed the United Kingdom's commitment to protecting IP, noting the importance of this to domestic creative-content industries. To support digital innovation, the United Kingdom plans to invest more than £120 million ($162 million) over three years in its digital economy research programs.[71]

In March 2010, the United States finally got in the game, releasing its National Broadband Plan. It represents "a plan for use of broadband infrastructure and services in advancing consumer welfare, civic participation, public safety and homeland security, community development, health care delivery, energy independence and efficiency, education, worker training, private-sector investment, entrepreneurial activity, job creation and economic growth, and other national purposes."[72] The 2009 U.S. economic stimulus package allocated $7.2 billion for expansion of broadband access. But compare that amount to other countries, such as Sweden, which provided more than $800 million, including tax incentives, to spur broadband deployment, particularly in rural areas. For the U.S. government to match this investment at the same share of GDP, it would need to invest more than $30 billion.[73]

Many countries leverage IT to drive innovation in specific segments of their economies, such as health care. Denmark, for example, has shown early and continuous efforts in developing and revising its national health

IT strategy.[74] Denmark's first national e-health plan began in 1994, when the Danish Ministry of Research published objectives for developing an "information society" by 2000. Denmark's Ministry of Health followed up on this publication by developing an "Action Plan for Electronic Health Records" (EHRs) in 1996 and creating a parallel effort in 2000 by outlining a national strategy for health IT use in hospitals. In 2003, the ministry launched a national effort focused on using IT to directly improve health-care service. In 2007, a new cross-governmental organization was formed to ensure a consistent national strategy on health IT that emphasized a stronger role for the national government.

Like Denmark, Finland was early in establishing a national strategy for health IT adoption. In 1996, Finland's Ministry of Social Affairs and Health established the first strategy focused on using IT to create a more integrated, patient-focused health-care system. The government revised the strategy in 1998 to target specific goals for health IT, including an EHR for every patient, interoperability with legacy systems, and high levels of security and privacy.[75] Since 1998, Finland has launched a number of initiatives to further adoption of health IT, one being to move toward the goal of nationwide EHR adoption by 2007. The initial priority of the Finnish e-health strategy was to implement tools for health-care providers, such as sharing patients' information, and the secondary priority was to develop e-health services for citizens.[76]

Do Countries' Innovation Policies Work?

The countries at the frontiers of innovation shift dynamically—and have, in fact, changed considerably during the past quarter century. Professors Jeffrey Furman and Richard Hayes assessed changes in the national innovation capacity of twenty-three countries from 1978 to 1999.[77] Starting in 1979, they classify countries as either world-leading innovators (like the United States, Germany, and Japan), middle-tier (like Britain, France, and Australia), third-tier (like Spain and Italy), or "emerging" innovators (like Ireland and Taiwan) based on countries' patenting activity per capita (a proxy for commercialized innovations). Their analysis correlates changes in countries' national innovation policies with their innovative productivity during the two-decade period.

Furman and Hayes found that although a gap in innovative activity remains between the world's most innovative economies and other innovator countries, it has decreased substantially. Moreover, the set of countries that generates numerous new-to-the-world innovations has expanded significantly, as a number of formerly industrializing countries dramatically increased their levels of innovative productivity. A number of these "emerging innovators"—Ireland, Finland, Singapore, Korea, Denmark, and Taiwan, in particular—achieved remarkable increases in innovative output per capita, moving to the world's technological frontier and *overtaking* the innovative capacities of many mid- and third-tier countries—notably Britain, France, and Italy—whose economic conditions started off much more favorably in the early 1980s.

These late-innovating countries accelerated their growth rates by both adopting technologies from leader countries and leapfrogging them by developing institutions that dealt with emerging challenges more effectively than nations bogged down in an older economic order. Furman and Hayes conclude that innovation leadership among countries requires not only the development of innovation-enhancing policies and infrastructure (including strong IP protections, openness to trade, highly competitive markets, and strong industry clusters), but also a commitment to maintaining substantial financial and human capital investments in innovation. They observe that these "once follower" countries now lead the world in developing—and funding—integrated national innovation policies that seek to tip the global economic playing field in favor of their domestic industries and corporations. While several of these countries are admittedly smaller and have the advantage of more easily generating the political will to implement aggressive innovation policies, many larger countries—notably Germany, Canada, Japan, and the United Kingdom—have studied these once-follower countries and started to implement similar approaches. As Furman and Hayes found, a country's innovation policies can have a significant impact in its standing in the race for global innovation advantage.

Other research has reached similar findings. As Richard Lipsey, Kenneth Carlaw, and Clifford Bekar write in *Economic Transformations*, "when specific needs and major externalities can be identified, and when capture and other pitfalls can be avoided," a country's innovation policies "can provide effective assistance to specific technologies, industries, and even firms." The authors cite a number of programs, including Canada's Industrial Research Assistance Program and the Defense Industry Productivity Program, as well as U.S. initiatives such as the Defense Advanced Research Projects Agency (DARPA), "that seem to have worked for some period of time."[78]

A 2009 study by the German Association of Chambers of Industry and Commerce illustrates the power of countries implementing effective innovation strategies, finding that about 30 percent of all German companies attributed their innovations "to improved research and innovation policies at the federal level."[79] Likewise, a 2011 review of the Swedish national innovation system found that its adaptation and performance had been quite successful during the previous fifteen years and attributed much of this success to Sweden's effective innovation policies.[80] Indeed, constantly measuring the success of a country's innovation policy in order to identify strengths, weaknesses, gaps, and opportunities for improvement is essential for innovation policy to succeed. As the *European Innovation Progress Report 2009* notes, "By linking investment in innovation clearly to productivity improvement," the *UK Innovation Index* "underscores the central importance of innovation to economic growth." Likewise, the *European Innovation Progress Report* concluded that "a major success element for Finland is a strategic policy review of its science, technology, and innovation policy, drawn up by the Science and Technology Policy Council every third year since 1987."[81]

As this chapter has explored, there are a number of constructive policies that countries can implement to accelerate their innovation-based growth. However, to turbocharge their climb up the innovation leaderboard, an increasing number of countries are turning to a set of mercantilist innovation policies that seek to gain unfair advantage in the global innovation competition at the direct expense of their peers, the topic to which we now turn.

7

Cheating as a Way to Win the Race

INNOVATION MERCANTILISM AS THE STRATEGY OF CHOICE

Since the beginning of the Industrial Revolution, communities, states, and nations have sought to gain economic advantage, in part by ensuring that firms in their jurisdiction become more productive and innovative, but also by trying to gain advantage over neighboring jurisdictions with which they trade. For example, after World War II (WWII), U.S. states began to seriously compete with each other for jobs and investment, while European nations increasingly competed within the European Common Market. Now, as global economic integration has become much more widespread, the scope of economic competition has substantially broadened. Today, what China does affects what happens in California, and vice versa. As places around the globe compete with each other for economic advantage, their innovation capacity has become a vital element of this competition.

However, the race for global innovation advantage creates both global opportunities and threats, because countries can implement their innovation policies in ways that are either "good," "bad," or "ugly."[1] As chapter 6 explains, good innovation policies include countries increasing their investments in scientific research, incentivizing industrial research and de-

		World	
		WINS	**LOSES**
Country	**WINS**	Good	Ugly
	LOSES	Self-Destructive	Bad

Figure 7.1 The Good, Bad, Ugly, and Self-Destructive of Innovation Policy

velopment (R&D), promoting information technology (IT) deployment and adoption, and educating a world-class workforce. As figure 7.1 illustrates, a country's "good" innovation policies are positive for the world, as discoveries, inventions, and innovations made in one nation ultimately spill over to the benefit of citizens worldwide.

But many countries are increasingly adopting a negative-sum, beggar-thy-neighbor, "innovation mercantilist" approach that seeks to realize innovation-based growth by manipulating global trade to boost their exports and reduce imports while forcing foreign technology and innovative activity to come to their shores. Policies such as forced technology transfer and intellectual property theft can help the nation that is implementing them but hurt the world, and hence are "ugly" (see figure 7.1). And sometimes countries adopt policies that they think will help them but which only end up hurting them (such as high tariffs on important capital goods, like computers), and thus are "bad."

But in both such cases, countries have bought into a misguided mercantilism that views exports in general and high-value-added exports in particular as the Holy Grail to economic success.[2] As Adam Smith observes in *The Wealth of Nations*, by favoring exports, "nations have been taught that their interest consisted in beggaring all their neighbors. Each neighbor has been made to look with an invidious eye upon the prosperity of all the nations with which it trades, and to consider their gain as its own loss."[3]

Classic free-trade theory holds that free trade benefits all countries by allowing each to specialize in producing the products or services for which it has comparative advantage. This in theory maximizes international economic welfare, benefiting consumers worldwide by giving them access to the highest-value, lowest-cost products and services. Thus, in a global market-based innovation economy, free trade can be a positive-sum game in which everybody wins—but only if everybody plays by the rules.

Yet, notwithstanding the benefits that accrue to all countries from free international trade, this system is under assault by a number of innovation mercantilist countries. Such nations are not as focused on innovation as they are on innovation mercantilism, specifically the manipulation of currency, markets, intellectual property (IP) rights, standards, foreign technology and direct investment, and so forth, to gain unfair advantage favoring their technology exports and companies in international trade. Their goal is not to increase the global supply of jobs, productivity, and innovative activity, but rather to induce their shift from the rest of the world to themselves through means that are sometimes "good," but that in all too many cases are either "ugly" or "bad."[4] As more and more nations adopt innovation mercantilist practices, it becomes even more compelling for additional nations to join them. As such, the most important challenge from innovation mercantilism is that it will fragment and drag down the entire global trading system. While innovation mercantilism is the dominant logic of several nations' innovation policies, China is by far the most egregious practitioner.

China: How to Win Enemies and Influence Industries through Systemic Mercantilism

Because it is the largest and most pernicious innovation mercantilist, China gets the lion's share of attention when it comes to innovation mercantilism. While China is engaged in many "good" policies (as chapter 6 describes), the Chinese government does not believe that these are enough for them to win the race—and to China, winning the race doesn't just mean winning, but beating its competitors in the process. To dominate the race, China has turned to a wide array of innovation mercantilist practices.

Perhaps China's most pervasive and damaging mercantilist practice is its rampant and widespread currency manipulation. China manipulates its currency by pegging the renminbi near to the dollar at artificially low levels in an attempt to shift the balance of trade in its favor. This currency manipulation is a central feature of China's export-led growth strategy, designed to make its exported products cheaper and thus more competitive on international markets, while making foreign imports more expensive. The overall intent is to induce a shift of production to China, but the effect is all too often to shift production from more productive and innovative locations to a less productive and innovative one in China. And one result of refusing to spend the money it earns from exports is massive current account reserves. As of November 2011, China had accumulated $3.2 trillion worth of foreign currency reserves, a jump of 33 percent since 2009 and larger than any nation's reserves at any time in history.[5]

China has staked its political and economic stability on export-led job creation driven by artificially cheap currency that puts foreign competitors at a distinct disadvantage. As Robert Cassidy, President Clinton's assistant U.S. trade representative for Asia and China and principal negotiator of the agreement that led to China's World Trade Organization (WTO) accession, argues, "China has adopted an export-led development strategy, the centerpiece of which is a currency that is undervalued by 20 to 80 percent, with the consensus leaning toward 40 percent."[6] China's government strictly controls the flow of capital in and out of the country. Every day, China buys about $1 billion in the currency markets, holding down the price of the renminbi and thus maintaining China's artificially strong competitive position. China has actually doubled the scale of its currency intervention since 2005, now spending $30–40 billion a month to prevent the renminbi from rising.[7] This subsidizes all Chinese exports by approximately 25 to 40 percent, while placing the equivalent of a 25 to 40 percent "tariff" on Chinese imports. Such currency manipulation is a blatant form of protectionism. Fred Bergsten of the Peterson Institute for International Economics observes: "Largely as a result of this competitive undervaluation, in 2007, China's global current account surplus soared to almost $400 billion and exceeded 11 percent of GDP, an unprecedented imbalance for a major trading country."[8]

China is not alone in intervening in markets to manipulate the value of its currency. Trade analysts at the Peterson Institute for International Economics have found that at least fifteen other countries—including Argentina, Brazil, Hong Kong, India, Indonesia, Israel, Malaysia, Singapore,

Korea, the Philippines, Taiwan, Thailand, Turkey, South Africa, and even Switzerland—also intervene in currency markets, substantially undervaluing their currencies against the dollar and other currencies.[9] In part, they do so in an effort to remain competitive with China.[10] As William Cline and John Williamson of the Peterson Institute write, "A handful of high-surplus countries are intervening in a fashion that is perverse for the reduction of international imbalances. These are the principal countries with major undervaluations of currencies (and correspondingly large excesses of current account surpluses over targets for international norms) that are nonetheless preventing market correction of currency valuation."[11] China, of course, is in that category, as it has long fixed the value of the renminbi to the dollar, but Japan, Hong Kong, Malaysia, Singapore, and Taiwan are also in this category.

Even nations with large and sustained trade surpluses manipulate their currencies, addicted to the high that below-market priced currency provides. In 2010, Japanese companies urged that their government take action to devalue the yen for fear of being undercut by exporters in China, Korea, Singapore, and Taiwan.[12] Despite the fact that Japan has run trade surpluses with the world for more than twenty-five years, on September 16, 2010, Japan intervened in world currency markets to drive down the exchange rate of the yen by selling an estimated two trillion yen ($23 billion)—at that time, the largest such intervention ever—in an effort to devalue the yen against the dollar in order to make Japanese exporters more competitive. Japan came back to the well again in August 2011, with the largest-ever single-day currency intervention, valued at an estimated 4 trillion yen ($48.29 billion).[13] Nevertheless, China is the linchpin to the system of currency undervaluation that compels other nations to also intervene in markets to manipulate the value of their currencies, and this ends up hurting European and American economies in particular, especially since neither the dollar nor the euro is manipulated for competitive advantage.

Despite the fact that currency manipulation directly violates international trade law (under International Monetary Fund rules, it is prohibited, and it may be actionable under WTO rules), virtually nothing is done to combat it. Yet currency manipulation undermines confidence in globalization by severely distorting trade, increasing the cost of other countries' exports, and costing those countries jobs. By raising the costs of foreign exports, currency manipulation retards the development of innovation-based jobs in foreign countries that may have a more natural comparative advantage, thereby retarding the development of innovation globally. This is because currency adjustment is the principal way that high-wage nations compete with low-wage ones. If a low-wage nation has an absolute advantage over a high-wage one, a falling currency in the high-wage nation is the natural adjustment mechanism to restore comparative equilibrium.[14] By disabling the adjustment mechanisms of international commerce, currency manipulators have succeeded in running up unsustainable trade surpluses and undermining confidence in trade's ability to produce shared global prosperity.

But currency manipulation has another, perhaps even more destructive impact. By artificially reducing the cost of labor compared to capital, it is moving the world production system more toward labor and away from capital. In other words, it reduces global productivity because it distorts the global production system into using relatively fewer machines. The Boston Consulting Group (BCG), in an analysis of low wage competition from China and India, describes the phenomenon this way:

> In the developed world, most industries have invested heavily in automation and have also simplified product design in order to reduce labor content. In low cost countries, where high labor content is less costly than high automation, the tradeoff between capital and labor is radically altered. . . . Product design and manufacturing processes will need to be adjusted accordingly; screws may once again be cheaper than welds, and built-up assemblies may become cheaper than more complex integral designs.[15]

BCG goes on to write in biased and overblown but accurate terms, "This source of advantage is rooted in the reintroduction of skillful human hands into highly sophisticated assembly processes, replacing costly monolithic machines." The BCG report even describes how one Western company eliminated all conveyer belts in its Chinese factories. In other words, we are heading backward as a world, to an era when companies used much more hand labor. It's one thing if this process happens naturally in an unmanipulated marketplace where more labor comes onto the global marketplace.

But to artificially exacerbate this trend through currency manipulation and large subsidies hurts global productivity.

Yet currency manipulation is just one arrow in the Chinese mercantilist quiver. It has many more. One is tariffs, a process like currency manipulation, but that targets higher prices for only select imports. For example, China—despite its massive trade surplus and although it has entered into the WTO's Information Technology Agreement (ITA)-accession protocol to reduce trade barriers on IT products—places 30 percent tariffs on color video monitors with TV tuners and turntable record decks; 24.5 percent on video monitors; 20 percent on printers, copying machines, and facsimile machines; and 20 percent on video recording or reproducing apparatus.[16] Overall, China's most-favored nation (MFN) applied tariff rates (simple average of all products) of 9.6 percent are almost three times higher than America's (3.5 percent).[17] Moreover, only 46 percent of imports enter China duty-free, whereas 76.3 percent of imports enter the United States duty-free.[18]

Production and export subsidies are also among China's favored innovation mercantilist practices. Despite the fact that the Chinese government committed to eliminating or substantially reducing subsidies (particularly those for loss-making state enterprises) as a condition of its WTO accession agreement, China spent more than $15 billion on export-enhancing subsidies for its steel industry in 2007 alone.[19] Looking at production subsidies by examining firm-level data encompassing nearly a half-million Chinese firms from 1999 to 2005, Girma et al. found that a doubling of production subsidies led, on average, to a 2.1 percent increase in China's level of exports, showing that China's unfair production subsidies have boosted the country's export performance.[20]

But China's subsidies go far beyond steel. According to Caing Statistics, over 90 percent of Chinese-owned companies listed on public markets in 2010 were granted government subsidies.[21] This compelled the U.S. Trade Representative's Office in October 2011 to counter-notify nearly two hundred Chinese subsidy programs to the WTO that China had failed to notify, the majority of them pertaining to China's solar and wind power industries.[22] Irrespective of whether or not those subsidies are found to violate the WTO, the very fact that China did not report them violates the country's commitments under the WTO agreement. Subsidies notifications are required annually under WTO rules, so that other countries can study the subsidies and determine whether any of them violated trade rules that prohibit using government money either to help companies buy market share in other countries or to discourage imports. However, since becoming a WTO member in December 2001, China's only notification came in 2006 and was very incomplete, in part because it only addressed subsidies at the national level, but not the numerous subsidies offered by China's provinces and municipalities. As U.S. Trade Representative Ron Kirk notes, "This lack of transparency severely constrains the ability of WTO members to ensure that each government is playing by the rules."[23] And some of these subsidies are contingent upon Chinese companies not buying imported supplies. For example, the central government provided subsidy grants of $6.7 million and $22.5 million to Chinese wind turbine manufacturers that agreed not to buy imported components.[24] Such subsidies are doing extensive damage to U.S. and foreign firms in not just the clean energy but also many other industries. As Ben Santarris of SolarWorld, a German solar panel manufacturer, explains, "Pervasive and all-encompassing Chinese subsidies are decimating our industry."[25]

The Chinese government also provides tax subsidies, particularly to Chinese-owned companies to help them compete with foreign-owned companies in China. A case in point is the German enterprise software provider SAP. Because Germany's SAP does well in China's enterprise resource planning (ERP) software market, the government gives hefty tax rebates to domestic players such as the Kingdee International Software Group, which has become the biggest ERP software supplier to midsized Chinese enterprises.[26] Likewise, in an effort to favor Chinese-owned car companies, China exempted forty-nine Chinese electric and fuel cell cars from sales taxes but made sure that no imported cars were eligible for the exemption.

A principal arrow in China's mercantilist quiver is to force requirements on foreign companies with respect to intellectual property, technology transfer, or domestic sourcing of production as a condition of market access. While the WTO prohibits China from requiring companies to comply with specific provisions as a condition of market access, it is a paper tiger when it comes to requiring China to live up to the rules. More than any nation, China can use this tactic to dramatic effect because it has such a large market of more than one billion customers to which multinational corporations desperately want to have access. Because China is still largely a technologically developing nation, forcing companies from developed nations to transfer their technology (or, in many cases, just downright stealing it) is a faster way to innovation success than engaging in the hard work to move up the technology learning curve, as European and American companies have had to do. And then China uses this newfound technological prowess to turn the tables on the "developed" companies, by combining their newly acquired advanced technology with low wages (and government subsidies) to take global market share away from them.

China is indeed the undisputed master of the joint venture and R&D technology transfer deal. China's government unabashedly forces multinational companies in technology-based industries—including IT, air transportation, power generation, high-speed rail, agricultural sciences, and electric automobiles—to share their technologies with Chinese state-owned or influenced enterprises as a condition of operating in the country. For example, Chinese officials normally force multinational companies to form joint ventures with its national champions and transfer the latest technology in exchange for business opportunities. Companies that resist are simply excluded from projects and refused permission to invest. The Chinese government uses the restrictions to drive wedges between foreign rivals vying to land big projects in the country in order to induce them to transfer their technologies that state-owned enterprises require to catch up. Although the WTO prohibits mandatory technology transfers, the Chinese government maintains that incentivized transfers, whereby companies trade technology for market access, are purely business decisions.[27] Thus, China continues to violate the WTO, only more covertly, getting the technology of developed countries and paying nothing in return. Foreign companies continue to capitulate because they have no choice; they either give up their technology or lose out to other competitors that are willing to make the essentially Hobson's choice.[28] Industrial organization economists refer to this type of market as monopsonistic: having one buyer that can set largely whatever terms it wants against competitive sellers.

One example is the evolution of China's high-speed rail market. In early 2009, the Chinese government began requiring foreign companies that wanted to bid on high-speed railway projects to form joint ventures with the state-owned equipment producers, CSR and CNR. Certainly not willing to just import the trains and equipment, China stipulated that multinational companies could hold only a 49 percent equity stake in the new companies, that they had to offer their latest designs, and that 70 percent of each system had to be made locally. Competing foreign rail manufacturers— like France's TGV, Japan's Kawasaki, and Germany's Siemens—had no choice but to go along with these stipulations, even though they realized that their joint-venture partners would soon become their rivals outside China.[29] But this was not sales; this was sales and tech transfer. The winning bidder, Kawasaki, had to develop the local supply chain for train components and teach the Chinese engineers—by sharing their entire know-how and catalog of technologies, and even bringing Chinese engineers to its Japanese manufacturing facilities for training.

While the foreign multinationals are still importing the most sophisticated components, such as traction motors and traffic-signaling systems, today they account for less than 20 percent of China's high-speed rail market. Meanwhile, CSR and CNR have acquired many of the core technologies, applied them with stunning quickness, and now dominate China's local market. Moreover, they have become major players in the $110 billion international rolling-stock market, having built high-speed railways in several developing countries, including Saudi Arabia, Turkey, and Venezuela (several for which the Chinese government has cofunded the railway modernization projects).[30] They've also made inroads in developed markets, with CNR recently winning rail contracts in Australia and New Zealand, all the while outbidding their forced mentor Kawasaki because they got much of their technology for free and then massively subsidized production and exports.

And now the Chinese companies are in negotiations to supply high-speed rail to the state of California. As the *New York Times* surreally explains, "Nearly 150 years after American railroads brought in thousands of Chinese laborers to build rail lines across the West, China is poised once again to play a role in American rail construction. But this time, it would be an entirely different role: supplying the technology, equipment, and engineers to build high-speed rail lines."[31] Without a trace of irony about how China came to be so competitive in high-speed rail, Zheng Jian, director of high-speed rail at China's Railway Ministry, said: "We are the most advanced in many fields, and we are willing to share with the United States." And not only is China offering to build California's 215 mph bullet train, it even generously offered to finance some of the construction (no doubt out of its trade surplus with the United States). Of course, California would still have to invest billions, including for Chinese rail components and engineering services. Imagine that—America's own stimulus dollars potentially going to help deepen its trade deficit with China. But as any neoclassical economist would advise, if the free market dictates that China's firms are bringing the most attractive offer to the table, then why not?

Rail is far from the only industry where China uses unscrupulous practices against foreign multinationals. We see it in industry after industry. For example, Ford Motor Company has opened several automobile plants in China, but as a condition of access, it had to do so as part of a joint venture with Chinese automobile producer Chang'an Motors so that Chang'an could learn from Ford. Moreover, the Chinese government required Ford to establish two R&D laboratories employing at least three hundred Chinese engineers. In another gambit to squeeze advanced electric vehicle technology out of Western auto manufacturers, the Chinese government announced in September 2011 that it will not let General Motors or Ford qualify for tax incentives that Chinese residents can receive for purchasing electric cars unless GM and Ford transfer proprietary and valuable electric vehicle technology to China.[32]

The CEO of a large multinational telecommunications equipment company shared with us that he opened a large R&D facility in Beijing employing more than five hundred scientists and engineers. When asked if he did this to access Chinese engineering talent, he responded bluntly: "Unless I promised the Chinese government that I would open up an advanced technology lab there, I was told that I would not be able to sell to the Chinese telecommunications providers" (most of which are de facto controlled by the Chinese government).

China knows it can get away with these threats because its market is so large and fast growing. Another case in point involved a Chinese state-owned enterprise engaged in dumping the chemicals for a particular herbicide that a U.S. company sold (that is, selling it below what it costs to make in order to gain market share). The company told the Chinese agricultural minister that it was planning to bring a complaint before the WTO. The minister responded that if the case were brought, the company would lose access to the Chinese market. Needless to say, the U.S. firm did not bring the case, even as it continued to lose global market share and jobs in the United States.

At least these "tech transfer" efforts have the veneer of being voluntary agreements between two parties (even if one of the parties has a proverbial gun to its head). But China doesn't stop there. It engages in outright theft and in fact is the world's leading IP thief. Some might object to this term as too harsh, but it's not clear what other term to use when one party takes property from the owner without compensation.

The U.S. International Trade Commission estimates that in 2009 alone Chinese theft of U.S. intellectual property cost almost one million U.S. jobs and caused $48 billion in U.S. economic losses.[33] Microsoft CEO Steve Ballmer estimates that as much as 95 percent of the copies of Microsoft's Office software and 80 percent of its Windows operating systems in China are pirated.[34] That estimate is backed up by the Business Software Alliance's *Global Software Piracy Study, 2009*, which provides data on unlicensed software units as a percentage of total software units installed in a country and which finds that 79 percent of software units installed on Chinese computers have been pirated.[35] There are 240,000 Internet cafés in China that rely on illegal copies of entertainment software.[36] Chinese firms even export technology to the United States that allows users to illegally circumvent encryption protection so they can pirate video games without paying for them. As bad as it is that private citizens and companies steal foreign software, the fact that government agencies fail to legally procure—or outright pirate—products or services made by foreign companies is downright outrageous. Despite a ten-year-old government order, at least 80 percent of Chinese government computers run versions of Microsoft Windows operating systems that were illegally copied or otherwise not purchased, not to mention scores of other Western software packages that are also unfairly pilfered. It's no wonder the United States runs an outlandishly large trade deficit with China when U.S. consumers, businesses, and government agencies pay for their products and services, but even the Chinese government fails to pay for America's.

And China is not only going after the technology of developed countries. China's insatiable voraciousness for foreign technology includes pilfering it from impoverished developing countries as well. Consider the case of Step Technologies, a small start-up based in Accra, Ghana, that allows customers to monitor and control their home security system through mobile devices. Step Technologies partnered with a Chinese manufacturer to make the control devices for the home security system, and transmitted the technical details of what was required for the device's production to the manufacturer. However, over the next several months, Step Technologies noticed something peculiar—devices identical to Step Technologies' began appearing in the market without the company's permission and without the manufacturer paying a licensing fee. Veterans of Ghana's IT sector were unsurprised, telling us outright: "Of course the Chinese manufacturer stole the idea."[37] Despite the fact that China's gross domestic product (GDP) is 192 times greater than Ghana's (and its GDP per capita seven times greater), China is unrepentant in its systemic national strategy to take IP from whomever, and wherever, it can.

Nor is China's piracy confined to digital products; it's rampant on analog products as well. For example, the U.S. Customs and Border Protection agency found that 79 percent of imports of U.S. trademark-infringing goods came from China (and an additional 10 percent came from Hong Kong).[38] In a telling example of this "analog" piracy, the global agriculture firm Monsanto decided to open production and research facilities for advanced corn technology in China and proceeded to develop experimental fields growing genetically enhanced corn. It wasn't long, however, before the advanced corn was systematically stolen, clearly an effort by the Chinese government to gain access to the IP embedded in Monsanto's corn. Shortly after that, one Chinese producer of corn seeds saw a dramatic acceleration in its technological capabilities. In Guangzhou recently, Rob Atkinson visited an "electronics mall" (in actuality, a large building with hundreds of independent, inefficient vendors) and saw scores of vendors selling fake iPods with the Apple logo clearly affixed (and also clearly fake). When asked if these were real, the vendors insisted that they were. Now, this was not in some back alley far away from official eyes, but within a mile of the provincial government headquarters. More recently, Chinese "entrepreneurs" even opened twenty-two fake Apple stores, unlawfully mimicking Apple's brand and logo, to the extent that its employees wore Apple branded shirts.[39]

Many in China view piracy as simply a different kind of business model. There's the make/buy IP business model, and the steal IP business model. Both are seen as legitimate. In an article in *The Journal of Science and Technology Policy in China*, edited by the Chinese Academy of Sciences, Sheng Zhu and Yongjiang Shi write about how the cell phone "cluster" in Shenzen called Shanzhai is "turning to the Shanzhai ethos, starting with producing counterfeited mobile phones to rebel against the expensive world-leading brands. . . . The Shanzhai idea of rebellion has evolved into a desire to take on global corporations by producing copies of the world leading brands."[40] The view is that this kind of rebellion is almost "Robin Hood-like" as it provides cell phones for the masses at the expense of the greedy, rich Apples, Nokias, and LGs of the world. The authors go on to note how those in central government "tend to tacit consent the phenomenon."[41]

So great is China's desire to incorporate and assimilate Western technology that it supports industrial espionage to steal trade secrets. A case in point was the charges made in 2012 by the U.S. Department of Justice against a business person with alleged links to the Chinese Communist Party. He is charged with paying former DuPont engineers for help in designing a chemical compound that Chinese firms are not yet capable of making.[42]

This kind of rampant technology theft not only hurts foreign companies (and jobs back in their home countries) it also gives Chinese companies a significant leg up on the competition because they can get IP without having to pay for it. A case in point is Autodesk, based in San Rafael, California, and the global leader in making computer-animated design software (used to design bridges, buildings, manufactured parts, and so forth) and computer-generated imagery. Autodesk's software brought you the world of Pandora in James Cameron's *Avatar*. But now Autodesk is experiencing a Pandora's box of Chinese IP theft, finding its software widely pirated by Chinese manufacturing firms. Furthermore, Chinese firms are competing against U.S. manufacturers who have to factor the cost of the Autodesk software into the prices they charge, a cost that most Chinese manufacturers avoid. We can call this the "piracy subsidy" they enjoy, but try bringing a court case to get compensation. In China, even when the law is enforced, the penalties are usually a slap on the wrist. One example is *Wuyang Company v. Microsoft, Adobe, and Autodesk*. This was a case where Guangzhou Wuyang Steel Structure Corporation was found to have systemically used pirated copies of U.S. software from these three U.S. companies. While it is one of the few cases that have been prosecuted, the company received a fine of just 1.3 million yuan ($198,000), presumably much less than the actual value of the software it pirated.[43]

China also has used its judicial system to gain unfair advantage, designing its monopoly policies to block foreign companies from competing against entrenched domestic monopolies. For example, a monopoly controlled by the People's Bank has been allowed to operate electronic payment systems for Chinese currency credit cards, cutting leading foreign companies out of the sector. This forced the United States to bring a case against China before the WTO in September 2010, alleging that unfair restrictions were preventing foreign companies from providing electronic payment services in China.[44] And China's new antimonopoly law has struck fear into the hearts of many U.S. and European Union (EU) antitrust experts, who fear that it will be used as a club against foreign companies operating in China.

Another way China gains unfair advantage is through its government-owned and government-influenced enterprises. Output of state-owned enterprises (SOEs) still accounts for about 40 percent of GDP.[45] And despite Chinese promises to curb SOEs, they have grown in the last decade. For example, the state-owned Assets Supervision and Administration Commission indicates that the assets of its firms have grown from the equivalent of 60 percent of GDP in mid-2003 to 62 percent of GDP in mid-2010.[46] Given their control over vast sectors of the economy, China's central and provincial governments use the power of the purse strings for unfair mer-

cantilist practices as well. These enterprises, many of which compete directly with foreign firms, receive significant benefits from all levels of
Chinese government. A major benefit is not to have to make a profit. An
in-depth study by the Unirule Institute, an independent Chinese think
tank, found that in 2009 the return on equity for SOEs was about half the
rate of non-state-owned enterprises, a substantial "subsidy" in and of itself.
But for their government granted advantages, including preferential financing from state banks and free land, Chinese SOEs would have operated at a 6.29 percent loss during the period 2001 to 2009.[47] The ability
to consistently lose money amounts to a considerable subsidy compared to
private foreign firms that must charge enough to make a reasonable profit.[48]

China also uses government procurement as a mercantilist tool. Though
China promised to accede to the Government Procurement Agreement as
soon as possible as part of its entrance to the WTO in 2001, ten years have
elapsed without it doing so. China's government procurement law even includes a provision requiring that goods and services be purchased domestically. This is a considerable policy tool since at least 20 percent of goods
and services in China are purchased by government.[49]

But China goes beyond just buying domestically, to preferentially buying from Chinese firms rather than foreign ones producing in China. For
example, a U.S. auto manufacturer with a joint venture in China has told
some of its U.S.-based suppliers that the provincial authorities where it is
based have required it to source from Chinese-based and -owned suppliers. China uses the same practices in clean energy. China's government
requires that most new wind energy equipment purchased by Chinese
companies (most of which are state-owned anyway) be: (1) made in China;
(2) based on Chinese-owned IP; and (3) compatible with Chinese technical
standards. These indigenous innovation policies contributed to foreign
wind turbine producers seeing their share of China's wind turbine market
crater from 75 percent in 2004 to 15 percent in 2009.[50] In fact, foreign companies did not win a single central government–funded wind energy project in China between 2005 and December 2010.[51]

China went even further in 2009 with its "indigenous innovation product
accreditation" scheme—a list of products invented and produced in China
that would receive preferences in Chinese government procurement.[52] To

be eligible for preferences, products would have to contain Chinese proprietary IP rights. Moreover, the original registration location of the product trademark needed to be within China. Not surprisingly, almost no products made at foreign-invested Chinese facilities received accreditation. For example, of the 523 accredited products listed in the Shanghai municipal government's catalog, only 2 were made by foreign-invested enterprises (FIE)—both from Chinese-foreign joint ventures with majority Chinese ownership.[53] Of 42 products listed in the Beijing catalogue, only 1 came from an FIE. On Nanjing's list, there were none.[54]

Discriminating in government procurement on the basis of intellectual property rights lies outside accepted international practice and acts as a barrier for most foreign companies—even those that have invested significantly and manufacture in China—seeking to sell to China's significant government procurement market. But China sees it as a powerful tool to unfairly gain advantage. As Thomas Hout and Pankaj Ghemawat describe in the *Harvard Business Review*, China's goal with its indigenous innovation policy is no less than "creating a tipping point in which multinational corporations will have to locate their most-sophisticated R&D projects and facilities in China, enabling it to eventually catch up with the U.S. as the world's most advanced economy."[55]

It was only after considerable pressure from foreign companies and governments that the Chinese State Council rescinded these indigenous innovation product catalogs at all levels of government in December 2011. Whether this will have any real effect is too early to tell. The Chinese governments could very well continue to use the product catalogs as informal guides to procurement decisions.[56]

Finally, China uses discriminatory product standards to keep out foreign products and avoid paying IP royalties. Most standards are developed by a voluntary standards process led by the private sector—think Internet and e-mail standards, for example. But China wants to use standards to unfairly gain advantage and has been perhaps the world's most aggressive country in manipulating technology standards. In fact, in 2007, only 46.5 percent of China's national standards were equivalent to international standards.[57] In addition to mandating specific standards, the Chinese government dominates the process and runs it without international consensus. It drafts most standards without foreign, or even public, input. If foreign representatives are allowed to participate at all, they can only be observers without voting rights.[58] For example, China has attempted to give its wireless telecommunications equipment manufacturers and operators a competitive advantage by developing a proprietary 3G wireless standard and then forcing foreign companies to adopt it for their Chinese products and operations.[59] Thus, Datang Corporation developed China's domestic 3G standard (TD-SCDMA—Time Division-Synchronous Code Division Multiple Access) with explicit Chinese government support, little foreign participation, and without global consensus. China's goal was to force foreign telecommunications equipment manufacturers to adopt the standard in order to sell their products to Chinese service providers in China's potentially huge and lucrative 3G wireless market. Not only would they be forced to design their equipment to conform to the standard (thus raising their costs) but they also would have to pay royalties to Datang to use it.

Because the Chinese government knows that it has considerable "market power" over foreign companies due to its market's sheer size, it knows that unless challenged by other governments or the WTO, it has significant leeway in unilaterally setting standards that favor domestic firms and force foreign ones to pay licensing fees. Such was the Chinese government's motivation when it announced that by June 2004, the Wireless Local Area Network Authentication and Privacy Infrastructure (WAPI) standard would be mandatory as the wireless protocol for all computers sold in China, even though the international standard, WiFi, already included four different security methods. While the government claimed that WAPI was justified because it was more secure than the existing standard, the consensus is that, in fact, it is a technically inferior standard.[60] Its true motivation was to force foreign companies to pay licensing fees to Chinese companies and to surrender U.S. technology. In particular, before American companies could use the standard, they needed to obtain the encryption algorithms, which required them to give up proprietary technical specifications to their Chinese competitors. It took the U.S. government threatening to file a WTO complaint against China for violating the WTO's Technical Barriers to Trade Agreement (for creating a standard that constituted a trade barrier) for China to drop its mandate.[61]

However, this has not deterred the Chinese government from continuing to support the standard by requiring that WAPI be used in all government procurement. Nor has it deterred China from trying to extend the WAPI standard (which originally applied only to computers) to mobile devices. China has now made it a de facto requirement that any mobile handset device with wireless capability sold in the country have the WAPI chip in order to receive approval for sale on the Chinese market. While manufacturers can still place WiFi chips in mobile devices, China's requirement means that companies must also include a WAPI chip (the user has to figure out which to enable). This will only add costs for handset manufacturers (and customers) while degrading the customer experience.

These are not isolated examples. In fact, there are dozens of international IT standards that most countries have adopted through a regular, open, industry-led standards-setting process, for which China is currently trying to establish its own domestic standards, many of which the Chinese government is seeking to make compulsory in products sold in China.[62] What's the value to the global economy of having a competing standard such as WAPI, when the global community has already collaboratively developed an effective standard such as WiFi? The answer is none, of course. In fact, it makes IT more expensive and less effective. But China continues to manipulate technology standards so Chinese firms won't have to pay royalties on embedded foreign IP while at the same time creating indigenous technology standards that it requires to be used for products sold in China, thereby forcing foreign firms to pay royalties to Chinese firms.

Thus, while Western countries predominantly play by the rules of free trade, China is playing by its own set of rules, all the while brazenly refusing to adhere to the commitments it made under its WTO accession protocol or to enter into subsequent WTO agreements, such as the Government Procurement Agreement, despite repeated promises to do so. Charlene Barshefsky, who as U.S. Trade Representative under President Bill Clinton helped to negotiate China's 2001 WTO entry, argues that the rise of powerful state-led economies like China undermines the international trading system. When such countries decide that "entire new industries should be created by the government," they tilt the playing field against the private sector. Barshefsky argues that such mercantilist actions raise "significant and profound—almost theological—questions about the rules [of international trade] as they exist."[63] Indeed, the threat is profound and how it evolves will determine the shape of the global economy for the next century.

Other Players in the Mercantilist Game

To be sure, China is not the only nation that relies on innovation mercantilism to gain position in the race for global innovation advantage. Argentina, Brazil, India, Malaysia, Russia, Taiwan, and Vietnam, among others, also pursue mercantilist-based, export-led growth strategies, although none to the extent of China. Again, we see these types of mercantilist practices with regard to intellectual property theft, steep tariffs on IT products and services, discriminatory procurement and regulatory practices, and export subsidies.

Take IP theft, for example. IP theft reduced global trade by 5 to 7 percent in 2007.[64] IP theft hits the United States particularly hard, as eighteen million Americas are employed in IP-intensive industries and more than half of all U.S. exports rely on IP.[65] In the United States, IP-intensive industries pay their employees nearly 60 percent more than others, and output and sales per employee are more than double those of non-IP-intensive industries.[66] But according to the U.S. Commerce Department, counterfeiting of U.S. merchandise alone is estimated to top $250 billion annually and cost the United States approximately 750,000 jobs.[67]

Yet recognition of IP rights remains a contentious issue. In 1994, the Trade-Related Aspects of Intellectual Property Rights (TRIPS) Agreement obligated all WTO members to offer and to honor product and process patents for twenty-year terms for nearly all types of inventions "in all fields of technology, provided they are new, involve an inventive step, and are capable of industrial application."[68] But a number of countries that have pursued export-led growth practices, including Argentina, Brazil, China, and India, oppose the TRIPS Agreement, believing that TRIPS amounts to a form of "economic imperialism" on the part of developed countries.[69] Argentinean law and economics scholar Carlos Correa argues that "the monopoly rights granted by intellectual property rights [are] regarded as an instrument to avoid further catching-up based on imitative paths of industrialization, that is, as a tool to freeze the comparative advantages that had so far ensured U.S. technology supremacy."[70] This perspective is not limited to developing country proponents. A report by the United Kingdom's Commission on Intellectual Property Rights (IPR) asserted that "the immediate impact of intellectual property protection is to benefit financially those who have knowledge and inventive power, and to increase the costs of access to those without. This is obviously relevant to the distribution of gains between developed and developing societies."[71] And even a Lord of the British parliament claimed that the impact of TRIPS on the world economy is that "the monopolies of the rich countries help to perpetuate a world in which one-half of the people are affluent and the other half are starving."[72]

Despite the fact that negotiators enshrined IP-access rights into TRIPS, requiring developed countries to provide incentives for their companies to transfer technology to least-developed countries, for mercantilist nations this is not enough. Despite the fact that many of the technologies these countries are using to improve their quality of life and to spur their economic growth were produced because companies and governments in developed nations invested hundreds of billions of dollars in risky R&D to create them, mercantilist developing nations want the technology for free or at a steep discount. Moreover, they already enjoy advantages from low wages and minimal regulations; on top of this they want to be able to steal technologies that developed nations have a competitive advantage in. Two reasons these countries reject TRIPS and want to continue pilfering IP from others is because it's easier than making expensive investments themselves and because, at least over the short term, IP theft works. Indeed, research by Grossman and Helpman shows that IP theft actually does help countries in the short run.[73] However, they also find that IP theft stifles the incentives of countries to embark on homegrown technology development, thus hurting countries over the long run.

Some, like New Democrat Network's (NDN) Rob Shapiro, argue that America shouldn't really worry about IP theft because "in the end, developing nations will have no other option [than] to adopt modern IP protections."[74] But to paraphrase John Maynard Keynes, in the long run, we're all dead. In other words, developing countries can do significant damage to developing economies through IP theft in the near and moderate terms.

Others argue that because China's rampant IP theft shows little sign of abating, we should just give up fighting it. Zachary Karabell argues that since China steals so much IP, it's a waste of time to try to fight it (or forced technology transfer) and that the United States would be better off just trying to stay ahead and keep developing new IP faster than the Chinese can steal it.[75] But this is as nonsensical as saying during the cold war that it made no sense to try to stop the Soviets from stealing U.S. weapons technology.

Western countries need a far more nuanced and unified approach to IP theft. While Karabell thinks we should give up altogether and Shapiro suggests that developing countries will eventually just have to give in to adopting modern IP protections, what's needed is for the United States, Europe, and Japan to: (1) make a continued and concerted push for strong IP rights in international trade agreements; (2) staunchly enforce existing IP rights; and (3) develop and adhere to a consensus among policymakers that—in contrast to what U.K. parliamentarians or its IPR Commission believes—IP protections are beneficial for developed and developing countries alike.

Ultimately, developing countries' own economic development opportunities and IP development potential are inhibited by their weak IP protections. For instance, the lack of effective protection for IP rights has limited the introduction of advanced technology and innovation investments by foreign companies in China, reducing potential benefits to local innovation capacity.[76] Likewise, Brazil's insistence on tampering with IP rights has severely damaged the development of its pharmaceuticals industry. For example, in 1999, Brazil passed its Generics Law, which allowed Brazilian companies to legally produce generic drugs that are perfect copies of patented drugs, a clear violation of TRIPS. While Brazil's government claims that generic manufacturers must demonstrate that they behave within the "laws and rights" of the global economy, even Brazil's government has moved to violate the patent rights of foreign firms. During price negotiations with U.S. manufacturer Abbott Laboratories, Brazil's minister of health threatened the company's patent on Kaletra, an anti-AIDS drug, if Abbott did not lower its price on the drug in Brazil.[77] Though Abbott relented, slicing Kaletra's price in half, the damage was done.

Jorge Raimundo, president of Interfarma, the Brazilian association for scientific research, explains: "Because of the continued danger that patents will be violated, employment in Brazil's scientific research sector dropped from twenty-four thousand in 1999 to twenty thousand in 2006. Until 1999, Brazil was attracting annual investments worth about $350 million [in pharmaceutical research]. In 2005, that figure dropped to about $90 million. The investments are moving instead into Mexico, Korea, and other countries."[78] In other words, such policies have made the pharmaceutical industry increasingly cautious about making new investments in Brazil. Moreover, there is evidence that corporate R&D intensity is decreasing in Brazil, even as it increases in Mexico and Korea, no doubt in part due to policies like the Generics Law that have caused foreign direct investment (FDI) to depart Brazil for other destinations.[79]

But IP theft is not the only tactic in use. While a major focus of the international trading system has been to remove tariff barriers, countries have gone to great lengths to evade tariff reduction commitments and high tariffs persist on a number of high-tech products and services. For example, despite being a signatory to the WTO's Information Technology Agreement (ITA), the EU attempted to rewrite descriptions of certain IT goods in an effort to circumvent their coverage under the ITA. In 2005, the EU applied duties of 14 percent on LCD TVs larger than nineteen inches, and in 2007, it moved to allow duties on set-top boxes with a communications function, as well as on digital still-image video cameras. While the United States won this trade dispute with the EU through a favorable WTO ruling in August 2010, the case was emblematic of countries' attempts to circumvent existing trade agreements to favor domestic production.[80]

Indeed, a number of countries—even those that are signatories to the ITA, including Indonesia, India, Malaysia, the Philippines, and Turkey—continue to place high tariffs on information and communications technology (ICT) goods. For example, Indonesia applies 10 percent tariffs on video game consoles and video monitors and projectors. India continues to impose tariffs of 10 percent on solid-state, nonvolatile storage devices; semiconductor media used in recording; and television cameras, digital cameras, and video camera recorders. Malaysia imposes duties of 25 percent on ink cartridges, cathode-ray tube monitors, and all monitors not incorporating television reception apparatus. The Philippines imposes tariffs of up to 15 percent on telephony equipment and on computer monitors.[81] In Turkey, smartphones can cost as much as $1,000, due in large part to tariffs.

Countries that are not signatories to the ITA impose even higher tariffs. Argentina imposes 26 percent duties on optical media for sound recording and 20 percent for electronic calculators and telephone sets. Brazil imposes 20 percent tariffs on cordless handset telephones, electronic calculators, and cathode-ray tube monitors. All these measures are designed to unfairly disadvantage foreign IT producers to the advantage of domestic ones—but they hurt domestic IT consumers in the process. Moreover, because they fragment global production, they result in higher prices for consumers in other nations as well.

Though not nearly as overt as China, many nations also favor domestic producers in government procurement. For example, not only has Europe long provided massive WTO-illegal subsidies to Airbus, its regional champion, it also subsidizes Airbus through pressure on airlines to purchase Airbus instead of Boeing planes. Air France, which is partially owned by the French government, operates a fleet that's 71 percent Airbus, while 62 percent of Germany's Lufthansa fleet is Airbus. Seventy-one percent of active planes for Alitalia are Airbus, while 100 percent of Iberia's (Spain's major airline) planes are Airbus. In contrast, for the top six U.S. airlines (American, Continental, Delta, Southwest, US Airways, and United), just 15 percent of active planes are Airbus; the rest are largely Boeing. One might argue—wrongly, as it would turn out—that American airlines are biased toward Boeing, just as European carriers are biased toward Airbus. But we see similar market share in other parts of the world. Just 15 percent of All Nippon Airways (ANA) and Japan Airlines planes are Airbus. Korean Air, Malaysia Airlines, and Singapore Airlines buy 22 percent, 29 percent, and 13 percent, respectively, of their fleets from Airbus. That the overwhelming share of the European airline fleet is Airbus clearly suggests untoward government influence (designed to prevent imports) in the selection of aircraft by European carriers.

Nor is China the only country that manipulates standards to block or to limit foreign company access to their markets.[82] For example, European electrical manufacturers are trying to shape Brazil's new electrical standards so they favor European technology and shut out American products. The European Union also leverages its presence in international standards bodies—such as the International Standards Organization, where it has twenty-seven votes and other countries only a single vote—to shape competition. (By that standard, the United States should have fifty votes, one for each state.) Because it's a more subtle method to gain innovation advantage than blunt-force methods like currency manipulation, standards manipulation has become an increasingly popular mercantilist tool. Yet the damage that standards manipulation does to global trade, innovation, and consumer welfare is real; the Organization for Economic Cooperation and Development (OECD) estimates that complying with country-specific technical standards can add as much as 10 percent to the cost of an imported product.[83]

A number of countries also seek to manipulate regulatory practices to gain innovation advantage by enacting discriminatory antitrust policies or by allowing anticompetitive activities on the part of their state-owned enterprises. These distortions lead to fewer choices and higher prices for domestic consumers, thus hurting the local economy and impeding its innovation ability. For example, the EU appears to be favoring two European suppliers of enriched nuclear fuel by imposing strict limits on imports of nuclear fuel from the United States.[84] Meanwhile, in Japan, a government monopoly manages and strictly limits the import of U.S. rice into the country.

European antitrust officials (and EU courts) still adhere to a Populist approach to antitrust with a greater focus on defending the interests of producers (firms and workers), particularly those of European producers over non-European producers.[85] Europe's industrial policy approach to antitrust has been apparent since the late 1990s. In 2001, the European Commission blocked the merger of Honeywell and General Electric (GE), two U.S. technology companies, on antitrust grounds, despite the fact that the U.S. Department of Justice had already approved the deal. In the Microsoft antitrust case, while both the United States and the European Commission opted for behavioral (as opposed to structural) remedies, the commission's decision went much further than the United States'—both in 2004, when it required Microsoft to sell a separate version of Windows without the Media Player application, and in 2006, when it imposed a fine of $357 million on Microsoft. Most recently, the Commission took action against Intel regarding its sales practices. It's hard to imagine European competition authorities bringing a case against Microsoft if, for example, Microsoft were a French firm headquartered in Paris, or denying the merger of GE and Honeywell if they were German and Finnish companies.

Why Countries Pursue Innovation Mercantilism

Why have innovation mercantilist practices become so prevalent? Perhaps it's a bit like why Willie Sutton robbed banks, because that's where the money is (or at least that's where they think the money is). Countries engage in innovation mercantilism because they hold one or more of the following four beliefs: (1) that mercantilist policies work; (2) that goods, particularly exportable goods, constitute the only real part of their economy; (3) that moving up the value chain is the primary path to economic growth; or (4) that they should become autarchic, self-producing economies. Moreover, countries actually engage in innovation mercantilism because they know they can practice it with impunity because the global trading system as enforced by the WTO is largely toothless, akin to making bank robbers simply occasionally return only a share of their stolen money rather than pay a fine or go to jail.

First, for more than a generation, U.S. policy toward countries employing mercantilist practices has been predicated on the belief that these countries were only hurting themselves. As a consequence, the United States viewed its trade policy as benevolently trying to help these countries by explaining a bit more clearly how mercantilists only harm themselves, hoping they would see the error of their ways and abandon the practice.

But the reality is that while some mercantilist policies do not work, many do—particularly over the near term. China's mercantilist practices clearly were the principal reason the country racked up a current account (trade) surplus of an astounding $426 billion in 2008.[86] The United States' trade balance with China in 2010 was negative $273 billion; in 2011 it was negative $295 billion.[87] Had China paid for all the IP it stole or procured at a massive discount, its trade surplus would be considerably smaller.

Second, many nations believe that tradable goods constitute the only real part of the economy through which they can drive a growth multiplier and create jobs, largely discounting the crucial role boosting productivity in service sectors plays in fostering growth. Take Brazil, for example. Claudio

Nehme and Adriano Galvao, advisers to Brazil's Center for Strategic Management and Studies of Science, Technology, and Innovation, gave a presentation titled "Defining Long-Term Strategy Plans for Industry Sectors in Brazil" at the 2009 World Future Society annual conference. They identified six sectors that the Brazilian government has picked as targets of the country's national innovation strategy. Each of the sectors—such as airplanes, biotechnology, machine tools, and pharmaceuticals—involved export products, with no focus on any service sectors. When asked why there was no focus on services, they replied that services don't export as much. This is why a top official involved in Brazil's broadband plan told us that in contrast to the emphasis the government gives to these export sectors, the government pays scant attention to broadband and IT use because "they aren't export industries."

Building their economies around high-value-added, export-based sectors (such as IT or high-tech, capital-intensive manufacturing) appears to be the path that almost all developing nations—China, Brazil, India, Indonesia, Malaysia, Russia, and others—are following, right in the footsteps of Japan and the Asian tigers Hong Kong, Korea, Singapore, and Taiwan before them. Countries that systematically run large trade surpluses have bought into the perspective that exports are good (and imports bad).

Flowing from this second proposition is the third: mercantilist countries believe that the primary path to economic growth lies in replacing low-wage, low-value-added export industries with high-wage, high-value-added ones. For example, China's strategy seeks to shift from being a successful low- and middle-tech economy to a sophisticated high-tech one by cajoling, co-opting, and often coercing both Western and Chinese businesses.[88] Such countries are willing to take short-term losses in order to grow long-term, high-value-added production. In other words, these countries believe they can sacrifice short-term profits for long-term gains in international markets.

Consider the 1986 case filed by the U.S. company Zenith Radio Corp. against Japan's Matsushista Electric Industrial Co. American electronics firms alleged, accurately, that Japanese electronics manufacturers were colluding to charge high prices on televisions in Japan so that they could engage in predatory pricing in the United States in order to gain market share and ultimately put U.S. producers out of business. Neoclassical economists viewed this as unlikely, not only since firms in a true market economy would have an incentive to break the cartel and charge lower prices in Japan in order to expand their market share, but also because firms would be unlikely to accept low profits in the United States for a long period of time in order to gain monopoly profits in the distant future. Reflecting the received neoclassical economic wisdom that this type of alleged behavior was irrational and therefore simply could not exist, U.S. courts sided with the Japanese firms, and in so doing, contributed to the decimation of the U.S. television industry.

The reality was that "Japan, Inc." (that is, the close collaboration between Japanese government and industry) was able to get producers to collude to charge high prices in the home market and lower prices abroad in order to gain market share overseas. Because of this, they were able to eliminate all competitors in the United States and gain market share and potentially higher profits there as well. Japan's government encouraged such collusion because the country's leaders had decided that their society should pay a short-term societal tax (higher prices paid by Japanese consumers) to gain long-term benefits (a larger global market share for televisions made by Japanese companies). Moreover, Japanese firms faced many fewer short-term pressures from financial markets for quick profits, so they were able to endure short-term losses overseas. China and other mercantilist countries follow a similar strategy, subsidizing exports and lowering current standards of living of consumers to gain competitive advantage in a host of key industrial sectors.[89] By doing this, they hope to erode the production base of advanced industrial nations, with the goal of ultimately knocking industry after industry out of competition in order to reap long-term job and profit gains. Despite the fickle protestations of neoclassical economists that this is irrational or undesirable, this is a principal way that mercantilist countries compete. Yet, while mercantilist countries are prepared to incur short-term losses to gain long-term, high-value-added production, such an accomplishment, as we describe below, is not nearly as valuable to an economy as raising productivity levels across all industries.

Finally, some countries pursue mercantilist strategies out of a desire to realize national economic self-sufficiency. The intellectual foundation that guides the global trading system goes back to the early nineteenth-century work of classical economist David Ricardo. In his famous theory of comparative advantage, Ricardo argued that when two nations trade, both can benefit, even if one is more productive in all industries, as long as each concentrates on the activities where it has a relative productivity advantage.

But trade theory based on conventional comparative advantage assumes that comparative advantage is a given and does not allow for policy to change it, that countries are stuck with what they have. But the "new trade theory" developed after the 1980s advances the notion of "competitive advantage" where nations can shape what they are good at in trade. In part, this can come from industries in which there are first-mover advantages (either from learning or scale economies). But even the theory of competitive advantage is supportive of trade and globalization, for according to it, countries should be exporting products and services in which they have (or want to have) competitive advantage and importing products and services in which they do not.

But the Chinese government in particular is not practicing a policy of comparative advantage or even competitive advantage; it is practicing a policy of absolute advantage. In other words, the Chinese strategy for globalization is to be dominant in virtually all industries. Autarky (a desire to become fully economically self-sufficient and free of the need to import goods or services), not trade, defines the Chinese goal. As hard as it may be for followers of Western neoclassical economics tradition to grasp, the Chinese don't want to make some things and buy others; they want to make virtually all of them (with perhaps the exception of raw material imports, like waste paper from the United States). As such, China's economic strategy consists of two main goals: (1) to develop and support all industries that can expand exports; and (2) to methodically and systemically identify imports and design strategies to reduce if not eliminate them. Chinese economic policy can be explained in terms of these two goals. Indeed, it appears that Chinese policy is to identify every single flow of money exiting the country (that is not a government-approved investment in Treasury bills or equities) to purchase foreign products or services, and shut off the spigot. This ambition is evident in China's effort to establish a domestic base of commercial, wide-body jet aircraft production and its desire to establish indigenous standards across a range of technologies so it need not make royalty payments on IP embedded in foreign technology standards. It's also clearly evident in China's cornering 97 percent of the world's production of rare earth minerals, and in cutting international exports of those minerals so that companies are pressured to produce more products requiring rare earth minerals in China.[90]

Such policies make it apparent that China fundamentally does not believe in the notion of global specialization and comparative advantage; it wants an absolute advantage in every single product category. As economic columnist Robert Samuelson explains, "The trouble is that China has never genuinely accepted the basic rules governing the world economy."[91] China's autarchic policies represent an extreme form of mercantilism, to be sure, but they are fundamentally at odds with the principles of an open international trading system that China committed to when it elected to join the WTO. But what China and other countries practicing innovation mercantilism must understand is that when they joined the WTO, they joined a trading system, not an exporting system.

Why Mercantilist Strategies Are Fundamentally Flawed

While some innovation mercantilist policies can benefit countries—at least for the short run—in general, they represent a fundamentally flawed strategy, hurting the overall global economy as well as the countries practicing them. Apologists for China and other innovation mercantilists contend that the best way for these countries to grow jobs and boost per capita incomes is through mercantilist policies predicated on running up massive trade surpluses. But, in fact, neither jobs nor income growth is dependent on mercantilist policies.

The need to create jobs is the number one excuse offered by China and its foreign apologists for the country's pernicious mercantilism. But while the logic that China must "keep Chinese-made products cheap, so Chinese factories will stay busy" is appealing, it is in fact flawed.[92] China (or any other mercantilist country) could achieve full employment just as readily by implementing a loose monetary policy and an aggressive fiscal policy and creating a better social safety net so citizens wouldn't feel compelled to save most of their money. As one thorough review of the economic literature on trade and job creation explains, "In the long run, aggregate net employment largely is unaffected by international factors, whereas these factors have important allocative effects in the short and long run, both between and within detailed industries."[93] In other words, trade surpluses or deficits can change the industries and firms that jobs are located in, but they don't affect the overall number of jobs or rate of job growth over the medium term.

This is consistent with basic economics, which holds that a change in GDP equals the sum of changes in consumer spending, government spending, corporate investment, and net exports (exports minus imports): $GDP = C + I + G + (Ex-Im)$. This is the classic formula for those who remember their macroeconomics. In other words, mercantilist countries could grow just as rapidly by pursuing a robust domestic expansionary economy that drives growth through increased domestic consumption and business investment or government spending. If countries have the right macroeconomic policies, they don't need trade surpluses to create jobs; expanded domestic activity can maintain full employment.

Even if Chinese officials were to acknowledge that they don't need mercantilist policies to create jobs, they would argue that mercantilist policies are needed for them to raise per capita incomes. The way they do this is to target "key" higher-value-added industries in which to run export surpluses. But far from generating increased incomes, export surpluses actually lower real incomes. China's $426 billion current account surplus in 2008 did not boost the nation's living standards because it represented $426 billion of value that China shipped outside its borders while getting nothing in return other than promissory notes. Consequently, China's residents are actually $426 billion poorer because if China instead had used those promissory notes to buy foreign goods and services, Chinese households would have seen on average a 17 percent increase in their disposable income.

But Chinese officials will argue that they are willing to impose a short-term diminution of income on their citizens in exchange for longer-term productivity growth. But even here, mercantilism is a flawed strategy because the lion's share of productivity growth in most nations—especially large- or medium-sized ones, like China—comes not from growing higher-productivity industries, but from all organizations and industries, even low-productivity ones, boosting their productivity. In fact, about 80 percent of an economy's productivity growth comes from organizations improving their own productivity and only about 20 percent comes from more productive organizations replacing those that are less productive.[94] This is exactly what the McKinsey Global Institute finds in its report *How to Compete and Grow: A Sector Guide to Policy*, concluding that countries that outperform their peers do not have a more favorable sector mix, but instead have individual sectors that are more competitive and productive.[95] In other words, the productivity of a nation's sectors matters more than its mix of sectors.

We can see this when applied to China. Chinese government officials give as a major reason for their high-tech export strategy the supposed fact that they intend to get rich by shifting their industry mix toward higher-value-added, innovation-based sectors. But the amount of productivity growth generated from an industry-mix strategy is quite limited. Consider that the Chinese set a goal for the value-added of "strategic" emerging industries to reach 15 percent of overall GDP by 2020. Conservatively assuming that they are now around 4 percent of GDP and generously assuming that value-added per worker is twice as high in these industries as in the Chinese economy overall, this shift would yield a one-time productivity boost of just 1.4 percent. Assuming that the overall rate of Chinese economic growth will be 8 percent annually, this strategy of promoting strategic emerging industries, the centerpiece of Chinese economic policy, at best will generate the equivalent of fourteen months of Chinese economic growth.

But the net effect is likely to be even lower because this strategy distorts capital goods markets, which are vital to boosting productivity. We can see why by looking at the import substitution industrialization strategies that nations like India, Argentina, Brazil, and Paraguay have adopted. For example, in an attempt to create a domestic computer assembly industry, Argentina has imposed tariffs on assembled computers, though not on computer parts. But this has resulted in Argentina creating an inefficient computer industry, with up to one-third of computers hand assembled in small shops. Likewise, Brazil's imposition of stiff tariffs on foreign computers and components in an effort to seed a domestic IT industry has only had the effect of raising the price Brazilian organizations and individuals pay for IT products and services and inhibiting the diffusion of IT throughout domestic service sectors such as financial services, retail, and transportation, causing productivity growth in these sectors to languish. India followed similar practices for many decades with similar deleterious effects.

These policies raise the price of capital investment goods, in this case, information technology goods and services, which economists classify as general purpose technologies (GPTs). GPTs are technology systems that produce spillover effects by enabling new products or services or by enhancing the productivity of downstream industries.[96] In this era, the fundamental GPT is information and communications technologies. Countries should want to acquire the best GPTs and more broadly the best capital goods they can, from wherever they are produced at the best possible price. Higher import prices, through tariffs or a manipulated currency, end up costing an economy more than it helps. For example, for every $1 of tariffs India imposed on imported IT products, it suffered an economic loss of $1.30. As Kaushik and Singh find in their study of IT adoption in India, "High tariffs did not create a competitive domestic [hardware] industry, and [they] limited adoption [of IT by Indian users] by keeping prices high."[97]

The crucial point missed by countries using mercantilist policies to build capital goods sectors, including IT industries, is that the vast majority of economic benefits from IT, as much as 80 percent, come from their widespread usage, while only 20 percent come from their production. Consider Israel, which has been held out as a poster child for high-tech development and a model for other nations of how to do it right. But Saul Lach, Gil Shiff, and Manuel Trajtenberg found that while Israel's IT sector boomed during the 1990s, becoming "a hotbed of innovation and technological advance by worldwide standards," the country's overall productivity remained sluggish, with traditional manufacturing and services sectors seemingly unable to benefit from the success of the IT sector, leading to the emergence of a "dual economy." The authors conclude that "a fast-growing GPT-producing sector is not enough to guarantee sustained growth. The notion of one sector serving as the 'locomotive' that pulls the rest of the economy is simply wrong; there are virtually no examples of such cases in economic history. For an economy to experience sustained growth, most of the sectors have to grow in tandem and the productivity gains, which underlie growth, have to be widespread and pervasive."[98]

Thus, raising productivity in domestic, "less exciting" sectors of the economy such as retail trade can have outsized economic impacts. Yet many countries protect small-scale mom-and-pop stores through barriers to FDI and competitive entry, zoning laws, and restrictions on the size of stores.[99] For example, Argentina's grocery retail sector is one of the few in the world to have experienced declines in productivity growth since the early 1990s, primarily because its large, productive firms have lost market share due to extreme regulatory restrictions placed on them.[100] In this case, rather than creative destruction leading to the exit of less productive firms, Argentina sought uninspired preservation. Discriminatory policies against efficient (larger) firms coupled with the lack of enforcement of regulations on smaller and informal firms meant that less efficient firms actually gained market share. For example, small stores can sell products whose void date has expired, while larger firms are forced to "donate" food to grassroots neighborhood associations. Small grocery stores pay much less in taxes. It can take four years to obtain a permit for a large grocery store, and regulations limit the size of stores and the maximum number of stores any one firm can operate in an area. Buenos Aires even has zoning laws that ban larger stores. Furthermore, only in the larger stores does the government impose price controls on food and limit imports of certain items. Sunday work must be paid overtime in many large stores and some regions even require hardship pay increases for working in large stores.

Such policies recall scenes from Kurt Vonnegut's classic short story "Harrison Bergeron," which pictured a dystopian future in which social equality was achieved by handicapping the more intelligent, athletic, beautiful, or capable members of society. Ballerinas had to wear lead weights, and the most intellectually gifted had to wear headphones that played distracting noises every thirty seconds, carry three hundred pounds of weight strapped to their bodies, and wear distorting eyeglasses designed to give them headaches. It was only then that true equality could be achieved. Just like the Handicapper General in Vonnegut's story, whose duty it was to impose handicaps so that no one would feel inferior to anyone else, Argentina has put lead weights on its efficient big-chain grocery store retailers. And by no means is Argentina alone; governments in France, India, Japan, Korea, and even some U.S. localities have likewise handicapped the most effective companies in their retail sectors. Of course, this is an example from just one industry sector. Scores of countries jealously guard many of their incumbent firms in nontraded sectors, whether it's European restrictions on cross-border licensing of legal or medical professionals, or constrained competition in financial services because of regulatory restrictions.

In stark contrast, countries that have liberalized their retail sector have seen dramatic improvements in sector productivity, with consequent strong contributions to economic growth. In Sweden, the liberalization of opening hours and zoning regulations unleashed competition, contributing to its retail sector productivity growing 4.6 percent per year for ten years after 1995.[101] Russian retail productivity more than doubled since 2000, from 15 percent to 31 percent of U.S. levels, because of the increasing market share won by more modern retailers. In Mexico, opening the food retail sector to international competition has lowered prices and increased choice. Mexico saw an explosion in the number of convenience stores (from one thousand to six thousand in five years). Mexican consumers are beneficiaries of this increased competitive intensity, as food prices have grown significantly less rapidly than other prices.

Indeed, raising the productivity of domestic nontraded sectors can have profound economic impacts. Overall productivity in India is but 8 percent of U.S. rates, in part because the productivity rates of its retail goods and retail banking sectors are just 6 percent and 9 percent of U.S. levels, respectively.[102] If India could raise productivity in these two sectors to just 30 percent of U.S. levels, it would raise its standard of living by more than 10 percent. Therefore, attracting more high-value-added export firms is not likely to be the major path to growth in the long run; countries should instead boost productivity across vast swaths of the economy, including in sectors the are not traded internationally.[103] But it's often politically easier to turn a blind eye to IP theft, to subsidize traded industries, and to manipulate currency than it is to take on the hard political fight of supporting productivity and innovation-based transformation of domestic-serving sectors. Yet, as we explain in chapter 11, innovation mercantilism is fundamentally unsustainable if the world is to achieve a robust global innovation economy.

8

Winning the Race for Innovation Advantage *with* the Eight "I's" of Innovation Policy

How can the United States apply the lessons learned from other countries in crafting its own effective innovation policy? We've seen that the United States suffers from many of the same ailments that led to the United Kingdom's industrial decline, including a persistent blindness to the problem. But like someone who goes on a diet and starts exercising after an overweight friend suffers a heart attack, perhaps America can learn from Britain's economic "heart attack" and begin a rigorous diet and exercise program for industrial renewal.

The key is whether America can act before it's too late. The lesson learned from the United Kingdom (as we discuss in chapter 3) is that if a nation passes a critical inflection point, it becomes extremely difficult to restore lost industrial innovation capabilities. To understand why, consider that after World War II (WWII), U.S. industrial innovation leadership was built on a complex, interlocking, and mutually reinforcing ecosystem. This involved original equipment makers producing complex products; spin-offs, many of which became successful companies in their own right; suppliers; providers of specialized business services (e.g., venture capitalists);

educational institutions producing skilled workers, knowledge, and discoveries; testing labs, standards, and other innovation infrastructures; and a growing market of sophisticated customers—all knit together by a complex system of interactions among the players. As each component became stronger, others followed suit, and a positive upward cycle resulted.

However, leadership is never assured, either for companies or nations. Advantages can become disadvantages, particularly if the environment changes. Companies and nations can become committed to conventional ways of doing things and fail to take advantage of new opportunities. To paraphrase former Intel CEO Andy Grove, problems start when companies and nations stop being paranoid about competitive threats. When this happens, a virtuous cycle can transform into a negative one.

America is not yet at the precipice that the U.K. economy fell from, though the economic ship of state is sailing dangerously close. While it's not yet too late to turn things around, there will come a time, perhaps in the very near future, when regardless of how attractive the United States makes science, technology, engineering, and math (STEM) education; how much money it invests in research; how much it lowers its corporate tax rate; or how low the dollar falls, it will not be able to easily regain a robust industrial innovation capability. Many of the key pieces will have been too fully dismantled. We don't mean to imply that America needs to restore all jobs in all industries. That is neither possible nor desirable. We do mean that the United States should seek to be an economy that runs trade surpluses in complex, technology-based industries (in order to pay for the imports of commodities and low-skill products) and that is competitive not just in the research and development (R&D) of new products (including intangible products like software and content) but also in the ability to manufacture many of those complex products domestically.

What would it take to achieve this? Clearly, many specific issues need to be addressed. Numerous reports, books, and articles have proposed solutions, such as improving the patent system, improving education, or reforming the corporate tax code. As in chapter 6, rather than offer a laundry list of programs and policies, we present the seven "I's" of innovation policy: Inspiration, Intention, Insight, Incentives, Investment, Institutions,

and IT (information technology); except this time we add an eighth—
International—and apply them in terms of how the United States needs to
get each right.

Inspiration: Setting Ambitious Goals

If the United States is going to act, it first must overcome its shortsightedness, partisanship, and ambivalence toward innovation. Inspiration can
come from "stretch" goals. Fifty years ago, President John Kennedy proclaimed that the United States "should commit itself to achieving the goal,
before this decade is out, of landing a man on the moon and returning
him safely to the earth." This was an audacious goal that many said could
not be achieved. But by bringing together the genius of American engineering talent, dynamic companies, and government commitment, America
achieved it. Likewise, in the 1990s, America set a goal of sequencing the
human genome in a decade and by combining government support and
private-sector initiative, America again accomplished its goal.

Landing a man on the moon is now trotted out as the inspirational
metaphor for solving an array of problems, but it's not the right one for this
crisis. While the moon landing was difficult, it was after all a relatively
straightforward and discrete engineering challenge. Restoring U.S. innovation leadership is a profoundly more complex and less tangible task than
going to the moon. But that does not mean that the United States should
fail to set similarly audacious goals. Here are five ambitious goals worth
achieving by 2020:

1. Eliminate the trade deficit and turn the $100 billion deficit in high-
technology products and services into a $100 billion surplus. Neo-
classical economists will recoil in horror at any such goal because
for them the trade deficit either poses no problem or simply results
from our low savings. But the trade deficit is a problem because it
represents both a loss of U.S. global competitiveness and a debt that
future generations must repay. There is no reason why the United
States could not balance its trade terms within a decade.

2. Add two million new jobs in technology industries, expanding tech
jobs (e.g., IT, biotech, pharmaceutical, clean energy, and advanced

manufacturing) by one-third. Overall U.S. employment is expected to expand by just 10 percent by 2020, so this would be an ambitious goal. Achieving it would not only create two million high-wage jobs but also millions of related jobs from the multiplier effect.

3. Raise the rate of productivity growth by 50 percent. From 1957 to 2009, the average rate of productivity growth per decade (not compounded) ranged from a high of 34.6 percent from 1957 to 1966 to a low of 11.9 percent from 1973 to 1982. From 2000–2009, it averaged 26.4 percent. Looking at five-year periods, productivity growth ranged from 21.2 percent between 1948 and 1952, to just 4.2 percent between 1977 and 1982, to 8.7 percent between 2005 and 2009. If we can raise the annual productivity rate from 1.65 percent per year (the average from 2005–2009) to 2.45 percent, it will take just twenty years, instead of thirty, to boost per capita incomes by 60 percent.

4. Leverage IT to transform U.S. government, transportation, health care, and education systems. The United States leads the world in the use of IT within business, but it lags in the use of IT in many other areas. Thus, it should make it a goal to have all medical data in digital format (such that all patients have electronic health records), for all travelers to have access to real-time information for roads and transit, for all information-based government functions to be digitized and online, and for higher education to provide a significant share of education online.

5. Develop clean energy sources whose unsubsidized price is lower than fossil fuels. Absent subsidies or carbon taxes, clean energy is not cost competitive with fossil fuels. Until it is, the planet will not transition away from carbon-based fuels. But driving sustained energy innovation has the potential to make using clean energy a money-saving decision.

Intention: Make Innovation-Based Competitiveness a National Priority

In 2010, the *Washington Post* series "Top Secret America" described the rapid growth of the national intelligence establishment after the terrorist attacks of September 11, 2001, reporting that "some 1,271 government organizations and 1,931 private companies work on programs related to counterterrorism, homeland security, and intelligence in about ten thousand locations across the United States."[1]

Whether this apparatus is too large or too small is not the point. The point is that when the United States feels that its national security interests are threatened, there is bipartisan support for a massive response. The message to America's adversaries is unambiguous: threaten U.S. national security and America will spare no expense in responding and defending itself. This is not new. Once the United States committed to winning WWII, it was all-in. Once it committed to winning the cold war after George Kennan's 1946 Long Telegram, it was all-in. John Kennedy's inaugural address summed up the view: "Let every nation know, whether it wishes us well or ill, that we shall pay any price, bear any burden, meet any hardship, support any friend, oppose any foe, in order to assure the survival and the success of liberty. This much we pledge—and more."[2]

But no U.S. president has said: "Let every nation know, whether it wishes us well or ill, that we shall pay any price, bear any burden, meet any hardship, support any friend, oppose any foe, in order to assure the survival and the success of U.S. innovation leadership." In fact, when it comes to economic security through innovation and competitiveness, the American hawk turns into a dove. Even bringing up the idea of defending U.S. economic interests produces such responses from the Washington economic policy elite as: "Getting tough on mercantilists will just promote a trade war"; "It's okay for developing nations to cheat, after all, America did too in the 1800s"; "We don't need an innovation policy, the private sector handles that"; "Competition between nations is a myth"; and, of course, the old chestnut, "We're still number one, so stop worrying."

Imagine if members of the U.S. national security community suggested that "Getting tough on our enemies will just encourage them to attack us" or "It's okay for rogue nations to get nukes, after all we've got our nukes." They would be ridiculed and expelled from the Washington national security establishment. Yet, when it comes to national economic security, this kind of thinking not only goes unpunished but instead is rewarded as prudent and insightful.

So the most important step for the United States is not to pass a particular bill to make the tax code more supportive of innovation, to spur technology transfer from universities, or to make any other discrete move toward
renewal (though all are needed). Rather, foremost, the United States needs
a new "Washington Consensus" that is focused not on the rest of the world
but on America. The term Washington Consensus was first coined by
economist John Williamson in 1989 to describe ten specific economic policy prescriptions that he recommended global institutions like the World
Bank and the International Monetary Fund (IMF) impose on developing
nations seeking their assistance.[3] But there is another implicit Washington
Consensus that has to do with broadly shared views about U.S. domestic
economic policy and innovation. And the United States needs a new domestic Washington Consensus among the Washington economic policy
elite about how to revive the U.S. economy.

Who are these Washington economic policy elites? While membership
changes with new entry and retirements, it consists of leading academic
neoclassical economists focused on economic policy as well as current and
former leading government policymakers (particularly those at the Treasury, the Office of Management and Budget [OMB], the White House Council of Economic Advisors, and the National Economic Council, along with
members of the Congressional Finance and Budget Committees and the
Congressional Budget Office). Also among the elite are prominent scholars
at think tanks like the Council on Foreign Relations, Brookings Institution,
American Enterprise Institute, Peterson Institute for International Economics, and the Center for Strategic and International Studies.

It is immaterial whether these elites are Democrats or Republicans, for
they share many of the same underlying beliefs and policy views. They do
so in large part as a manifestation of what social psychologist Irving Janis
famously termed "groupthink." Groupthink refers to a "deterioration of
mental efficiency, reality testing, and moral judgment that results from in-
group pressures."[4] When the head of the White House National Economic
Council says that the United States doesn't need a manufacturing strategy
because manufacturing is declining in all nations (though it's not, as we
describe in chapter 4) and the response is silent assent, the Washington
Consensus groupthink is at work.

Ten key principles constitute the current Washington Economic Consensus:

1. The United States is the world leader in innovation-based competitiveness and likely always will be because it is the most open, entrepreneurial, and market-driven economy.
2. Government's job is to ensure that markets are competitive and that entry, exit, and prices are not distorted.
3. Fiscal discipline is the key and in efforts to balance the budget, "everything should be on the table."
4. Globalization is an unalloyed good for the United States, even if other nations engage in innovation mercantilism.
5. Mercantilist nations only hurt themselves.
6. America's role in the global economy is to be a shining "city on the hill" that, by force of example, shows misguided nations why mercantilism and "industrial policy" are wrong.
7. Government can do little to spur innovation; it's something that just happens. In the words of Nobel Prize–winning economist Robert Solow, it is "manna from heaven."
8. The best tax code is a simple one, with a broad base and low rates.
9. To the extent that a more active government role is needed, it should be to support basic "factor conditions," such as science and education.
10. Government should refrain from "picking winners."

These views are almost never questioned—that is why they represent a consensus. In fact, questioning the consensus is risky. To enjoy the perks of being in the "club" (for example, being invited to the right dinners, being asked to join an administration in the right position, being on the board of the right organization or company), one not only must subscribe to the consensus but also defend it against all enemies, foreign and domestic. Not doing so opens one up to the risk of being seen as odd at best, irrelevant at worst.

Despite these risks, as it becomes clearer that the U.S. economy is not doing so well in innovation-based global competition, a few respected individuals have begun to speak out against components of the consensus, including Intel CEO Paul Otellini, former Intel CEO Andy Grove,[5] Eli Lily CEO John Lechleiter, Dow Chemical CEO Andrew Liveris, Boeing CEO James McNerney, General Electric (GE) CEO Jeffrey Immelt, Harvard Business School's Willy Shih and Gary Pisano, and MIT's Paul Samuelson.[6] As the structural nature of the U.S. economic challenge becomes clearer, other elites will likely join in. The critical question is whether it will become safe enough for people other than CEOs and retired economists to challenge the Washington Consensus. In either case, the critical first step is to replace the dysfunctional Washington Economic Consensus with a new Washington Innovation Consensus based upon the following ten principles:

1. While the United States retains important strengths, it is no longer the leader in innovation-based competitiveness and likely will continue to decline unless business, labor, academia, and government work together.

2. The major economic role for government is to ensure that institutions (e.g., businesses, governments, nonprofits) support and foster innovation.

3. Fiscal discipline is important, but funding for policies to spur innovation and competitiveness (including lowering corporate tax rates, even if it is not "revenue-neutral") should not "be on the chopping block"; rather, funding for such policies should be expanded.

4. Globalization can be an unalloyed good for the United States, but only if other nations generally play by the rules and America steps up its innovation game.

5. Mercantilist nations sometimes help themselves and almost always hurt the United States.

6. America's role in the global economy is to be a tough competitor that looks after its own economic interests first and joins with other like-minded nations committed to enforcing the global rules of fairly growing an innovation economy.

7. Innovation is a product of intentional human action that can and should be encouraged by policy.

8. The best tax code is one that includes incentives for spurring innovation and competitiveness.

9. While government needs to support "factor conditions" (e.g., basic scientific research and education), that alone is not enough to ensure a nation a pioneering position in innovation activity. More proactive innovation policies are needed.

10. Government can and should "pick winners" in the sense of identifying general industries and broad technology areas of national economic importance and playing a catalytic role in marshaling public and private resources to meet clear opportunities and challenges.

To be clear, we are not advocating merely exchanging one groupthink paradigm for another. Rather, we are recommending trying something new, thinking in new ways, and adjusting our frame of reference. The Washington Economic Consensus has its roots in the post-WWII economic reality, and it worked for a long time. But the world of 2012 is nothing like that of 1945, and U.S. economic elites need to shake up their thinking. Perhaps in 2050 the Washington Innovation Consensus will itself have become stagnant in its orthodoxy. If so, economic thinkers should reassess it. For now though, we are a long way from revitalizing our prevailing thinking.

Insight: Improving Understanding of Innovation Performance

Inspiring the nation and developing the intention to win are key first steps. But without insight on how the United States is doing with regard to its strengths, weaknesses, threats, and opportunities, the best of intentions will fall short.

Notwithstanding the hundreds of millions of dollars spent every year and the thousands of economists working for the federal government, the exact nature of the challenge and U.S. capabilities are only weakly understood. A Treasury Department official recently e-mailed a colleague, asking: "In what sectors is China catching up, so that Chinese companies are increasingly competitive with U.S. companies? I'm hoping we can find some subjective assessment that points to certain particular firms/industries. For example, we've seen some information that suggests Huawei is a real competitor for Cisco and others in the world of wireless and network infrastructure." Can you imagine a Department of Defense (DOD) official e-mailing a Washington think tank, asking: "What areas of the Chinese defense system are strong?" This was not the fault of the Treasury official, and kudos to him for reaching out to try to get better information. But it is emblematic of the fact that the United States has never felt that it needed to develop this kind of strategic economic intelligence to really understand the competitive position of the U.S. traded sector.

As George Washington University scholar Andrew Reamer notes, the opaqueness and limitations of our national statistical system for measuring innovation, productivity, and competitiveness make achieving this insight daunting.[7] Established after WWII, the system was designed to help policymakers avoid another Great Depression, and therefore measured things like the number of houses built and cars manufactured. It did not measure innovation in the construction industry, how competitive the auto industry was, or any other number of important matters regarding the competitiveness and innovativeness of the U.S. economy; the assumption was that these things took care of themselves. Besides, we were so dominant, it didn't matter.

If government is going to effectively support private-sector innovation in America, it needs to get much smarter. The very existence of government policies (tax, trade, regulation, spending, and so forth) means that government inevitably influences innovation and competitiveness, sometimes for good, sometimes for ill, but almost always by happenstance. Government would be much better positioned to effectively support innovation if it were more strategic and knowledgeable.

The place to start is to develop a national innovation and competitiveness strategy and to engage in a comprehensive analysis of the key factors contributing to the competitiveness of traded-sector establishments. Private-sector firms like Intel, General Electric, and Microsoft have strategies. Nations like Britain, Canada, Finland, Japan, and Korea have strategies, as we discuss in chapter 6. U.S. states like Massachusetts and Washington have strategies. But the United States does not, at least not a strategy based on a comprehensive analysis of traded-sector strengths and weaknesses, opportunities and threats, and the viability of a range of public policies affecting them. Whereas many other countries have coherent, strategic

game plans to compete and win in the highest value-added sectors of economic activity, the United States relies on makeshift reports and one-off
policies that all too often are not tied to any serious, analytically based, and
coordinated strategy.

Components of the national innovation and competitiveness strategy
should include an assessment of: (1) current U.S. competitiveness, including for traded sectors at the major industry level (three-digit North American Industry Classification System [NAICS] codes); (2) current business
climate for competitiveness (including tax and regulatory policies, as well
as the overall system for private-sector business investment) and how it
stacks up to major competitors; (3) trade and trade policy issues; (4) education and training; (5) science and technology policy; (6) regional issues in
competitiveness (including the roles of state and local governments and
federal policy impacts on innovation and competitiveness in rural and ur-
ban regions); (7) measurement and data issues; and (8) proper organization
of government to support a comprehensive innovation and competitiveness agenda. The National Competitiveness and Innovation Strategy Act of
2010 (S. 3620), passed at the end of 2010 and signed into law by President
Obama, charged the administration to undertake this, but unfortunately
the report took only a broad-brush look at the challenges.[8]

To take the next steps, the federal government should start by getting
more strategic about promoting the competitiveness of high-value-added
sectors. Currently, federal agencies work to advance their own particular
missions and are largely unwilling to take into account the impact of their
actions on innovation competitiveness or to coordinate with other agencies. Medical devices are a good example. The Food and Drug Administration (FDA) reviews the safety and effectiveness of medical devices. The
Department of Health and Human Services sets reimbursement schedules. The DOD and the Veteran's Administration procure such devices.
But there is little or no coordination across agencies to develop a unified
strategy to orient government policies to support the competitiveness of
the U.S. medical device industry, even though it is a high-value-added sector in which the United States still retains competitive advantage, even
though that position is at risk.[9] Accordingly, the Department of Commerce
should develop strategic road maps and guide interdepartmental collaboration to ensure that the regulatory policies and activities of disparate gov-

ernment agencies are, wherever possible, aligned to promote the global competitiveness of strategic sectors of the U.S. economy.

One can almost hear the howls of outrage, whether from the "Glenn Becks" of the Right that this amounts to "a secret government plan to take over private business" or from the "Al Sharptons" of the Left that this is "some kind of secret plan to maximize corporate profits." But developing a national innovation and competitiveness strategy is not the same as developing a heavy-handed industrial policy. A thorough analysis of U.S. innovation-based competitiveness is just as likely to find problems from too high a corporate tax rate, too many regulations, and too many tort lawsuits as from inadequate federal support for collaborative industry-university research institutes. Nor does helping corporations become more competitive constitute a plot against workers. To the contrary, U.S. workers cannot thrive unless U.S. business establishments are innovative and productive.

Incentives: Encouraging Innovation, Production, and Jobs in the United States

Nondemocratic nations can force companies to innovate, or at least make them try. Democratic countries cannot and should not. Harangue, pressure, and other "sticks" won't produce innovation or competitiveness. But that has not stopped some from trying. In the United States, the Obama administration is trying to induce American companies to produce more domestically by proposing to end their ability to defer U.S. foreign-source income. In February 2012, the administration announced a series of tax reform proposals whereby the overseas earnings of U.S. corporations would be taxed at a "minimum" rate regardless of whether or not the earnings are repatriated. The administration argued that permitting U.S. corporations to defer recognition of their foreign source income until they repatriate the income encouraged them to ship jobs overseas and deprived the U.S. Treasury of revenue. Ending deferral, the administration contends, would stop "subsidizing" the export of jobs.

If it were as simple as that, what's not to like? Government revenue and jobs would both go up. But it's not that simple. If U.S. affiliates in a lower-tax nation sell much of what they produce there to nations other than the United States, then requiring these facilities to pay the higher U.S. tax rate will make them less competitive with firms from other nations that are subject to the lower national rate. Since these competitors would enjoy relatively lower costs, they would export more, including to the United States, taking market share away from U.S. firms. Thus, making foreign affiliates of U.S. firms pay the higher U.S. rate could shift imports to non-U.S. foreign firms and reduce global market share of firms headquartered in America. As Reed College economist Kimberly Clausing notes, ending deferral would "exacerbate concerns regarding the international competitiveness of U.S.-based multinational firms, as U.S. firms would face a tax disadvantage relative to firms based in other countries when operating in low-tax markets."[10] At best, it appears that ending or limiting deferral could have mixed results, perhaps spurring some activity to locate or to remain in the United States, but also reducing jobs offered in America by U.S.-headquartered companies that serve global operations (such as R&D, management, sales, or marketing jobs).

In this specific case, lowering the effective corporate tax rate, rather than ending deferral, is the preferred strategy. More generally, the better way to spur innovation-based competitiveness is to provide more incentives to invest in the United States. Indeed, to maximize innovation, countries need to provide organizations with incentives. Nobel Prize–winning economist Douglass North summed up the secret sauce of innovation success this way: "We must create incentives for people to invest in more efficient technology, increase their skills, and organize efficient markets."[11]

Figuratively speaking, most nations were absent for the lecture in Economics 101 that incentives are bad because they distort allocation efficiency. But unlike other pupils, Uncle Sam went to class that week, wrote a term paper on why incentives are bad, and got an A for it. The U.S. government has no "war chest" from which it can draw incentives to attract or retain multinational establishments. Its workforce training, R&D, and capital expenditure tax incentives are either nonexistent or anemic. And at 39.1 percent, the combined state-federal statutory corporate tax rate on U.S. companies is now the highest in the world, after Japan cut its corporate tax rate on April 1, 2012.[12] Indeed, while statutory corporate tax rates fell, on average, by 16 percent across all the Organization for Economic Cooperation and Development (OECD) economies from 2000 to 2009, they remained constant in the United States. In contrast, the statutory corporate tax rate fell by 48 percent in Ireland (from a tax rate of 24 percent to 12.5 percent); by 43 percent in Germany (from a rate of 52 percent to 29.8 percent); and by 19 percent in Canada (from a rate of 44.6 percent to 36.1 percent). In fact, the United States was the only country in the OECD in which the statutory corporate tax rate did not decline between 2000 and 2010.[13]

Some argue that while the U.S. statutory rate is high, the effective tax rate is actually low. After all, just look at companies like GE that supposedly pay very little in taxes. However, with respect to the effective corporate tax rate, which takes account of credits, deductions, and other incentives that corporations receive, the U.S. rate is also quite high. According to the World Bank, at a combined state-federal rate of 32 percent, the U.S. effective corporate tax rate is one of the highest in the developed world.[14] In a cross-country analysis of effective corporate tax rates, business school professors Kevin Markle and Douglas Shackelford found that among multinational firms, U.S. multinationals "are among the highest taxed" and that U.S. manufacturers (domestic and multinationals) were the third-highest taxed of the group of countries analyzed, paying taxes 37 percent higher than manufacturers in Asia.[15]

This negative incentive clearly hurts America's ability to maintain a globally competitive industrial economy, since lower effective corporate tax rates spur greater foreign direct investment (FDI) coming into a country while reducing outward FDI. This effect has become more pronounced as the race for innovation advantage has intensified. Altshuler finds that a 1 percent reduction in an average country tax rate in the 1980s raised FDI by 3 percentage points; by the 1990s, a 1 percent reduction in average country tax rates raised FDI levels by 3.7 percentage points.[16] Moreover, a 10 percent increase in a country's effective corporate tax rate reduces its investment-to-gross domestic product (GDP) ratio by 2.2 percent and reduces its FDI inflows by 2.3 percent.[17]

While this international tax-based competition is relatively new, it has been going on at the state level for more than half a century. Indeed, when the U.S. economy became fully national in scope after WWII, states were forced to compete for mobile corporate investment. They had no choice but to lower their corporate tax rates, increase their corporate tax incentives, or both. Because of this, from 1970 to 2008, corporate taxes as a share of state tax revenues fell from an average of 8.3 percent to 6.2 percent. Now the United States finds itself in the same position; it has to compete for internationally mobile investment and it needs a more competitive corporate tax code to succeed. The reality is that the U.S. government lost the freedom to unilaterally design its own corporate tax system twenty years ago. It just doesn't know it because it continues to wrap itself in the comforting illusion that it is not in competition or that the unique characteristics of the U.S. economy allow it to have a higher corporate tax rate with no penalties.[18]

What would the U.S. corporate tax code look like if the federal government recognized the competitive reality? Clearly, the effective rate would be lower. Cutting the effective rate will be important not only to making the U.S. economy more competitive but also to reducing the amount of corporate tax deferred inside other nations. But the real question is how to do this. There are two main choices: the first is to reduce the statutory rate of 35 percent; the second is to reduce the effective rate, but mostly through incentives.

Most companies and virtually all neoclassical economists favor a lower statutory rate; the former want certainty in the tax code and the latter object to the idea of the tax code substituting for the wisdom of the market. Indeed, for many tax policy experts, effective corporate tax reform means simplifying the code by removing some or even all exemptions, including critical ones such as the R&D tax credit and accelerated depreciation, and using the savings to reduce statutory rates.[19] However, any revenue neutral tax reform that reduces or eliminates key incentives for investing in research, capital equipment, and manufacturing will make things worse, not better.

In fact, the tax code should substitute for the wisdom of firms and it should not be certain. When there are significant economy-wide benefits from firms investing in a particular way, it is entirely appropriate for a bargain to be made: business can pay less in taxes if it takes steps that maximize economy-wide benefits. And it should be uncertain in the sense that firms will pay lower taxes only if they take certain actions.

What are those actions? We know that three types of corporate investment—research and development, investments in new capital equipment (including software), and training frontline workers—drive growth and innovation.[20] Because incentives make a difference in encouraging companies to make these types of investments, the United States needs to take three key steps: First, the R&D tax credit needs to be significantly expanded—and made permanent. There is a consensus in the scholarly literature that R&D tax incentives spur firms to invest more in R&D than they would otherwise.[21] Twenty years ago, the U.S. R&D credit was the most generous in the world. Today, because many nations have instituted their own, more generous R&D tax incentives, U.S. R&D tax credit generosity has dropped precipitously in rank, to twenty-seventh in the world. Expanding the credit would help make the United States a more attractive location for internationally mobile R&D and lead to greater R&D investment in America.

But while R&D is one critical component of an innovation economy, so too are worker skills. While training and ongoing education are critical components of robust productivity growth, companies in the United States are investing about half as much in training as a share of GDP as they did a decade ago, in part because the payoffs increasingly flow to other firms since workers switch jobs more frequently and in part because companies are under increasing pressures for short-term profits.[22] To spur greater workforce training, Congress should institute a tax credit for expenses associated with that training.[23] Finally, an effective innovation policy needs to lower after-tax prices for equipment and machinery (including software). Providing a tax credit on equipment and machinery will spur more domestic investment and enhance productivity.

Rather than provide three separate credits, however, Congress should create a unified Innovation and Investment Tax Credit (IITC), building off the Alternative Simplified Credit (ASC) for R&D. The ASC provides a credit of 14 percent on R&D expenditures above 50 percent of the average of the last three years. The credit could be even more effective if the rate were increased and applied only to investment above 75 percent of the base. Thus, we propose that the IITC provide a credit of 45 percent on expenditures in R&D and skills training above 75 percent of base-period expenditures. Because capital expenditures are much greater than expenditures for workforce training, we propose that companies receive a lower credit of 25 percent on capital expenditures made in excess of 75 percent of their base-period expenditures.

To understand how this would work, consider the following hypothetical example. From 2009 to 2011, a company invests an annual average of $10 million in R&D, $10 million in workforce training, and $50 million in new machinery, equipment, and software in the United States. In 2012, it invests $12 million in R&D, $12 million in training, and $60 million in machinery, equipment, and software. Under the IITC, it would be eligible for a credit of $9.67 million (45 percent of $9 million for R&D and training, and 25 percent of $22.5 million for machinery and equipment).

A robust IITC would go a long way toward helping establishments in the United States become more competitive globally, both by reducing their tax liability and by encouraging them to invest more in the drivers of innovation and productivity. It also would make the United States a more attractive location for inward foreign direct investment. Moreover, when compared to an across-the-board corporate rate reduction alone, these incentives would be more targeted toward those industries and firms that are most exposed to international competition. Software companies would get more incentives, law firms fewer. Automobile producers would get more, automobile rental companies fewer.

Opponents will raise at least three objections. To start with the most valid one—cost—the IITC would not be cheap. It would cost approximately $75 billion per year to reduce corporate tax payments by 17 percent through incentives. Can the federal government afford this in a time of fiscal constraint? It can, for two reasons: First, because the IITC spurs growth, it provides offsetting revenues. One reason for this is that higher tax rates lead to less investment (and, therefore, lower tax revenues) and also to more income shifting. Indeed, a study by the World Bank finds precisely this, reporting that, "high tax rates do not always lead to high tax revenues. Between 1982 and 1999, the average corporate income tax worldwide fell from 46 to 33 percent, while corporate income tax collections rose from 2.1 percent to 2.4 percent of national income." While the notion that lower marginal tax rates produce more, not less revenue (the "Laffer curve") does not apply to individual taxes (at least at today's rates), it can apply for corporate taxes.[24] Clausing finds that the combined revenue-maximizing corporate income tax rate in the United States is 33 percent, significantly lower than the current combined U.S. federal-state rate of 39 percent. The proposed IITC would lower the combined rate to just below that, to 32.4 percent. So lowering the rate this way would in theory not reduce revenue. Moreover, these incentives can also partially or fully pay for themselves because they will spur greater competitiveness and productivity, which will also lead to greater tax revenues. For example, boosting the R&D tax credit would pay for itself, albeit after fifteen years, because productivity, and therefore tax revenues, would be increased.[25]

For those who would insist on up-front offsetting revenue raisers to pay for the IITC, there are several options. Eliminating the 2001 tax cuts for the wealthiest 2 percent of earners (those earning above $250,000) would almost completely close the gap, producing about $65 billion a year. Does anyone really believe that the better way to grow the economy is to let high-income individuals keep $65 billion more of their earnings to buy another Armani handbag or Jaguar car, instead of letting the business engines of competitiveness and innovation save $65 billion in taxes to invest in research, skills, and equipment?

Another way would be to restore the tax rates on dividend income to their pre-2003 levels. This would have the added advantage of encouraging companies to invest more in their firms, rather than disburse the money out as dividends. Congress also could institute a border-adjustable corporate activity tax (like a value-added tax), such that imports would be taxed, not exports.[26] (More than 150 countries apply such a border-adjustable consumption tax on their imports, which imposes a tax burden on U.S. exports.)[27] Carbon taxes are another source. A $15 per ton carbon tax would raise $90 billion a year, of which only about $17 billion would be borne by manufacturers. When one nets out the fact that U.S. manufacturers would see tax reductions from the innovation-based tax incentives described above, the United States could impose a carbon tax and on net still improve the competitive position of its manufacturing sector.[28]

Moreover, even increasing the budget deficit in the short term to pay for these incentives would be more than worth it. Cutting these types of tax investments to balance the budget is penny-wise and pound-foolish. As conservative columnist George Will wrote in reference to federal support for science, "Making the government lean by cutting the most defensible—because most productive—federal spending is akin to making an overweight aircraft flight-worthy by removing an engine."[29]

The second reason many holders of the Washington Consensus will oppose the IITC proposal is because it violates one of the central tenets of the consensus, that the best tax code is a simple one with a broad base and low rates. But this was not always a part of the Washington Consensus. From the 1950s to the early 1980s—a period of robust growth—the federal government provided incentives for companies to invest more in capital equipment. Under the Kennedy administration, two measures were enacted to spur investment: shortened depreciation schedules and a 7 percent investment tax credit. But by the 1980s, neoclassicists, who embrace the simplicity principle, had taken over. As a result, the 1986 Tax Reform Act was a Holy Grail for neoclassical economists, for it not only eliminated the investment tax credit but also increased corporate taxes while cutting individual taxes. Talk about getting it wrong all the way around.[30]

One influential assault on the view that the tax code should favor investment in plant and equipment came from none other than Larry Summers, former director of the White House National Economic Council (NEC). In a 1979 article, Summers and fellow economist Alan Auerbach modeled the impact of instituting an investment tax credit (ITC). Not surprisingly, they found that a 12 percent ITC would increase the stock of equipment by 18 percent while also boosting GDP.[31] Sounds good, right? Wrong. Their model also showed that the credit would lead to slightly higher interest rates and a crowding out of other "investment sectors." What exactly were these sectors? Housing! As a result, they opposed a pro-growth investment tax credit because it would distort allocation efficiency by leading to more investment in manufacturing and less in housing. Thus, since the late 1970s, the Washington Economic Consensus has been against investment incentives.

The third objection (as if the first two weren't enough) goes something like this: "How can you propose cutting taxes on multinational corporations when American workers are struggling?" For many on the Left, helping corporations is the last thing to do when workers are hurting. But just as neoclassical thinking on corporate taxes reflects a twentieth-century mind-set, so too does this kind of Populist thinking. Rob Atkinson was former executive director of the Rhode Island Economic Policy Council, a public-private partnership established in the mid-1990s to help develop and guide an economic strategy for the state. After the council prepared a strategic economic development plan, it "went on the road" to present its recommendations to key stakeholders. One of the first stops was the Rhode Island Senate Democratic Caucus policy retreat. Accompanied by George Nee, president of the Rhode Island AFL-CIO, we presented the recommendations, including calling for Rhode Island to institute the most generous R&D tax credit in the nation and an investment tax credit. When we finished, one senator asked Nee: "I know we need to do things to help create jobs, but is there any possible way we can do this without having to help business?" To which Nee answered: "No." To their credit, the Senate Democrats supported this legislation, allowing Rhode Island to have a more competitive corporate tax structure, and to attract and grow more R&D and investment. If even some of the most liberal states in the nation have figured out that a competitive corporate tax code is not a choice but a requirement if workers are to prosper, surely Washington can do the same.

Investment: More Public Funding for Innovation and Productivity

If the United States is to ensure that companies expand R&D, commercialization, and production at domestic establishments, it needs to provide significantly more support for research, commercialization, technology adoption, and education and training.

America once led the world in investment in innovation. But the United States has fallen to eighth place among OECD countries in R&D intensity, and U.S. investment in R&D as a share of GDP increased by just 3 percent from 1987 to 2008. One major reason for this slippage has been a slowdown in federal R&D investment, as it grew in constant dollars at just 0.3 percent per year from 1987 to 2008—much lower than its average annual growth of 4.9 percent from 1953 to 1987, and ten times lower than the rate of GDP growth.[32] In fact, to restore federal support for research as a share of GDP to 1987 levels, Congress would have to increase federal support for

R&D by almost $110 billion—per year. When a nation underfunds research by such a whopping amount, industrial decline should not be a surprise.

If we are optimistic and assume that the United States will increase investment in innovation by just a fraction of what it should—at least $30 billion per year—where should this funding go? To be sure, we need funding increases at agencies like the National Science Foundation (NSF), the National Institutes of Health (NIH), and the Office of Science at the Department of Energy. But while necessary, these increases are not enough. If we are to win the race for global innovation advantage, we need to also expand funding for programs targeted explicitly toward supporting industrial innovation. Funding for programs like the NSF and NIH are important, but the days when we could expect the discoveries coming from scientific research to flow predominantly to companies in the United States are long gone. Now knowledge flows across the globe, benefiting U.S. establishments (albeit more) as well as our competitors. Without other programs focused on the transfer of innovations to U.S. establishments, America won't fully reap the benefits of these investments.

Congress should increase funding for the Defense Advanced Research Projects Agency (DARPA) and the National Institute of Standards and Technology (NIST). But as chapter 6 notes, to even come close to matching the investments of peer countries, the United States should be investing at least $5 billion more per year on efforts to spur industrial innovation. A number of programs deserve increased support. Congress should expand support for NSF programs that work more closely with industry, including the Engineering Research Center and the Industry/University Cooperative Research Center programs, Partnerships for Innovation, and the Advanced Technical Education Program. These programs receive less than 2 percent of the NSF's budget.[33] The United States should significantly expand the industrially oriented programs at NIST, including the Technology Innovation Program and the Manufacturing Extension Partnership. The latter program is particularly important to helping restore U.S. manufacturing competitiveness since it works to help small manufacturers become more innovative and productive, but as noted, it is significantly underfunded compared to peer programs in competitors such as Canada, Germany, and Japan.

One key to supporting industrial renewal is to help firms in the same industry conduct collaborative research that helps the entire industry. One of the best examples of this is the Semiconductor Research Corporation (SRC). Thirty years ago, the U.S. semiconductor industry faced challenges from foreign competition. In response, visionary industry leaders, with help from the Defense Department, formed the SRC to invest in and to manage long-term research addressing the industry's technology needs and to create a pool of experienced university researchers and a pipeline of graduates knowledgeable about semiconductor science and technologies. Based on alignment of industry and government needs, including recognition of the need for a robust technology workforce, the SRC established research programs jointly funded with DARPA, NSF, and NIST. The SRC has had a substantial impact on both industry and academia. SRC investment has built a network of more than one thousand university collaborators working in the semiconductor field. Materials, design tools, and processes based on SRC research are widely used across the industry. Just as significant as the technological output has been the impact on human capital. The SRC has supported more than 8,400 graduate and undergraduate students, almost all of whom remain in the semiconductor field as researchers and innovators.[34]

The SRC would not have been formed or continued without government support. We should replicate this model across other industries and technologies. NIST is attempting to do this with the Advanced Manufacturing Technology Consortia (AMTech) program, which is a public-private partnership initiative that provides federal grants to leverage existing consortia or to establish new ones focused on long-term industrial research needs. The grants would fund development of research road maps and projects in advanced manufacturing and enhance the research productivity of consortia members through improved coordination and efficiencies. The program's goal is to accelerate the innovation process—from discovery, to invention, to development of new manufacturing process technologies—in order to support the creation of new high-skilled, high-wage manufacturing jobs. But AMTech's initial funding request was at just $12 million per year, and the Obama administration is seeking only $21 million in FY' 13; funding for the program should ramp up to at least $500 million annually. The National Network for Manufacturing Innovation (NNMI), a $1 billion proposal announced in March 2012 by the Obama administration, would provide such a framework by establishing fifteen institutes acting as hubs of manufacturing excellence across key manufacturing technologies and sectors.[35]

We also need to foster a better state-federal innovation partnership. Since the 1980s, all fifty states have established technology-based economic development (TBED) programs. Republican and Democratic governors and legislators support these programs because they recognize that businesses will not always create enough high-paying jobs in their states without support. But states only invest about $2 billion annually in these activities, an amount dwarfed by the tens of billions they spend recruiting firms from other states. Because states are key partners in the U.S. innovation system, the federal government needs to better support their technology efforts. One way to do that would be to create a performance-based challenge grant program to cofund state TBED programs that would build off the Obama administration's well-intentioned but significantly underfunded regional innovation clusters initiative.

However, if we really want to get smart about promoting technological innovation, we could take a page from the playbooks of other nations and create a National Innovation Foundation (NIF). The NIF's goal would be straightforward—to help establishments become more innovative and competitive. It would do this by:

- catalyzing industry-university research partnerships through national-sector research grants;
- expanding regional innovation promotion through state-level grants to fund activities like technology commercialization and support for entrepreneurship;
- encouraging technology adoption by assisting small and midsized firms in taking on existing processes and organizational forms that they do not currently use;
- supporting regional industry clusters with grants for cluster development;
- championing innovation to promote innovation policy within the federal government and serving as an expert resource on innovation to other agencies.

Finally, one area that deserves its own focus is energy innovation. As chapter 4 notes, many nations are making major bids for clean energy leadership by funding R&D and deployment efforts. As a result, the United States is at risk of getting left behind. One reason is limited funding for clean energy innovation. For example, while the stimulus legislation provided $400 million to fund the Department of Energy's new Advanced Research Projects Agency-Energy (ARPA-E, modeled on the DOD's DARPA), the agency could only fund 1 percent of the 3,700 applications it received.[36] Unfortunately, Congress cut ARPA-E's funding to $180 million in 2011.

Spurring an energy innovation revolution will require an array of policies, but the single most important one is to increase funding for clean energy R&D. This should include expanding funding for ARPA-E to at least $1 to $2 billion annually and providing funding for Energy Frontier Research Centers, which support small groups of researchers focused on breakthroughs in science and on working to solve specific technical problems that are blocking clean energy development. We should support the development of clean energy "clusters" to accelerate collaboration between multidisciplinary researchers in academia or government and corporate and venture capital partners that can contribute market insight and expertise. Total new funding for energy R&D should be on the order of at least $5 billion annually.

Institutional Innovation: Doing New Things in New Ways

For most neoclassical economists, the royal road to prosperity is paved with price-mediated markets. If everyone sells and buys things based on the prices they agree to, economic welfare is maximized. To be sure, price-mediated markets are useful, but when it comes to innovation they are not enough. Adaptive efficiency—the ability of economies and institutions to change over time to respond to successive new situations, in part by developing and adopting technological innovations—is the key to growth and competitiveness. As innovation economist Joseph Schumpeter pointed out more than half a century ago, "A system which is efficient in the static sense at every point in time can be inferior to a system which is never efficient in this sense, because the reason for its static inefficiency can be the driver for its long-term performance." Where does this adaptive efficiency (that is, innovation) come from? One key place is institutional evolution. Douglass North explains: "We are far from knowing all the aspects of what makes for adaptive efficiency, but clearly the overall institutional structure plays a key role to the degree that the society and the economy will encourage the trials, experiments, and innovations that we can characterize as adaptively efficient. The incentives embedded in the institutional framework direct the process of learning by doing and the development of tacit knowledge that will lead individuals in decision-making processes to evolve systems that are different from the ones that they had to begin with."[37] In other words, to win the race for global innovation advantage, nations cannot just be content with high rates of technical innovation; they also need high rates of organizational innovation. In particular, the United States needs to shake off complacency, move beyond partisan gridlock and ideological rigidity, and approach the task of institutional innovation with the same urgency that some of America's leading companies, such as Apple and IBM, did when faced with crises. Institutional innovation is critical. It is also hard. But when it occurs, it can be transformative.

Take the case of engineering education. In the early 1990s, a small cadre of visionaries from the corporate and academic sectors got together to examine the state of U.S. engineering education. What they saw gave them pause. Too much of engineering education was rooted in a model of teaching and research that was more than one hundred years old. This didn't help students become engineering innovators, nor did it effectively link engineering to businesses. Given the increasingly global and collaborative nature of engineering, this cadre began urging the addition of teamwork, project-based learning, entrepreneurial thinking, and communication skills to engineering curricula, as well as a greater emphasis on social needs and human factors in engineering design.

In 1997, an entirely new college was created in the suburbs of Boston to put that vision into practice. The Franklin W. Olin College of Engineering was created as a highly selective undergraduate engineering institution designed to prepare students "to become exemplary engineering innovators who recognize needs, design solutions, and engage in creative enterprises for the good of the world."[38] But the founders of Olin realized that they had to completely change the model of engineering education for this to work. They started with perhaps the most radical change: doing away with academic departments and faculty tenure. They decided that engineering ed-

ucation had to be interdisciplinary and integrated with hands-on learning
and research opportunities for students. And they made a commitment to
diversity, with the result that, in 2010, 44 percent of their all-engineering
student body was female (compared to approximately 20 percent nation-
ally), with minorities comprising 17 percent of the student population.

By all measures, Olin has been a tremendous model of institutional innovation. Approximately 80 percent of Olin graduates go into STEM fields
and 25 percent are involved in start-up entrepreneurial enterprises (either
full- or part-time), with 10 percent starting their own businesses. Moreover,
on the National Survey on Student Engagement (NSSE), which assembles
annual data from first- and senior-year students attending hundreds of colleges and universities, Olin's "Active and Collaborative Learning" Benchmark Score is among the highest in the nation. Employers of Olin graduates
see them as exceptional.

If we want to win the innovation race, it's not enough to create just one
Olin; we need hundreds or thousands, not only for engineering education,
but in area after area of American society: K–12 education, health care,
university technology transfer, surface transportation, electric utilities,
government services, social services, and so forth. Over the years, these
institutions have become stagnant, bogged down by the weight of convention, tradition, and inertia. We need to be engaged in systemic innovation
in our institutions, trying many experiments and recognizing that many
or even most will fail, but then widely adopting the ones that succeed (just
like the private sector does). Most important, this means that our conception of innovation policy needs to be broadened from its current focus on
science and technology to include institutions.

Unfortunately, institutional innovation is barely on Washington's radar
screen. Democrats regularly resist institutional innovation out of fear that
the new systems will not provide the kind of universal service characteristic of the bureaucratic, managerial government programs established after
WWII, or worse, that they will act as a stalking horse for a Tea Party–like
attack on government itself. And all too often, in their zeal to rein in big
government, Republicans would rather shrink it than drive it to innovate.

On top of this, a deeply inherent conservatism in the field of public administration leads congressional and federal agency staff to view too many

policy areas and institutions as simple, mechanistic systems. And it leads them to view their jobs as a matter of pouring more resources into the front end to get more outcomes at the back end, as adding a regulation here or there that will force the system in question to behave differently, or as mandating that organizations do certain things. And when they do legislate or regulate, much too often their proposals are premised on the view that our public, private, and nonprofit institutions are working just fine—all they need is more: more money, more authority, and so forth.

Occasionally, institutional innovation breaks through. The 1996 Welfare Reform Act is an example, as are some components of the Obama administration's "Race to the Top" education reform initiative. And, to be sure, there are leaders on both sides of the aisle who embrace institutional innovation. For example, former Republican House Speaker Newt Gingrich has been a leader in calling for new kinds of institutions, such as the creation of what he terms a "21st Century Intelligent Health System." But these actions and leaders are the exception rather than the rule.

America needs to do better. For the U.S. innovation economy to succeed, American institutions must themselves embrace innovation and constantly adapt and evolve to improve and to do things in new and creative ways. And to drive institutional innovation, policymakers need to view policy areas as complex systems with multiple actors having different motivations, multiple feedback loops, uncertainty, and a host of other complex factors, such that simple and "obvious" solutions are not always right. There are no stock formulas to drive institutional innovation. While the right answer will depend on the particular context, a number of approaches can be used, including the following:

Prizes

Most organizations respond to incentives. If we want organizations to innovate, we should offer prizes. For example, rather than simply give more money to colleges and universities and hope they increase U.S. graduation rates in STEM disciplines, we should award cash prizes to colleges and universities that have dramatically increased STEM degrees and maintained those increases over five years.

Markets

In too many areas, organizations fail to innovate because there is too little competition. We see this in the slow pace of adoption of the smart electric grid by electric utilities, of intelligent transportation systems by state departments of transportation, and of new forms of schooling and pedagogy by public schools. In all cases, enabling more competitive markets can help create incentives for change. For example, Congress should pass legislation to require electric utilities to share data on electricity use with customers so they can use that data with any smart grid application service provider. It should dramatically reduce federal restrictions on tolling federal highways and use the highway trust fund to reward states that shift more to tolling and pricing of roads. It should also support more experimentation with school vouchers and charter schools. The list goes on and on.

Information

One reason organizations do not change is that many times their customers are not aware of just how poor their poor performance is. Open information can change that. In higher education, for example, the federal government should require all colleges and universities receiving federal money to report their results from the National Survey of Student Engagement, the survey in which Olin excels. This information would allow parents, teachers, students, funding agencies, and other stakeholders to compare institutions of higher learning based on real performance, not just on the superficial information they get in rankings like the *U.S. News and World Report* survey.

Congress could also help establish stronger university entrepreneurship metrics. This could be achieved in several ways. First, the United States could collect better data on the number of new businesses started by a university's faculty and on the total number of spin-off companies created by each university. Congress could direct the National Science Foundation (NSF) to develop a metric by which universities report that information annually. NSF could use this data to reward universities that do a better job, for example, by also giving bonus points on research grant proposals they receive. Applicants from universities that do a great job of promoting entrepreneurial spin-offs/start-ups would be more likely to have their private investigator grants funded. In addition, the Department of Commerce should use data available through the ES-202 form (Unemployment Insurance Tax Records), which tracks how many employees an establishment has every quarter. The form could also be made to note the university that the founder of the organization attended, and then that information could be combined, anonymously, to find out which colleges and universities have graduates that are founding and running the most high-growth businesses.

New Kinds of Organizations

Even with these incentives, many institutions will still resist change. As a result, sometimes the best approach is to start from scratch and create entirely new institutions. A case in point is science, technology, engineering and math education. One promising strategy for helping more American high school students graduate with expertise and interest in science is to create new high schools explicitly focused on STEM education. To date, there are only about one hundred of these innovative math and science high schools in the United States, but their graduates pursue undergraduate and graduate degrees in STEM fields in relatively greater numbers than graduates from traditional high schools.[39]

Funding Targeted to Innovation

While lack of resources is not always the problem, sometimes money matters. Cases in point are the numerous federal agencies that play a key role in innovation but that are woefully underfunded. The U.S. Patent and Trademark Office (PTO) used to be the envy of other nations for its effectiveness and efficiency. But today a backlog of more than seven hundred thousand patent applications at the PTO means that most applicants will wait at least three years for a decision. Likewise, there have been increased delays at the FDA for drug and device approval and difficulties in upgrading the scientific expertise needed to expeditiously and effectively evaluate new drugs and biological submissions.[40] The U.S. Trade Representative's Office brings relatively few cases before the World Trade Organization (WTO) to challenge the mercantilist practices of other nations. And the U.S. statistical system needs to do a better job of providing the kinds of data that would help policymakers understand the true condition of the U.S. innovation system. In all of these cases, lack of funding has been the principal cause of suboptimal performance and more resources would boost performance.

Innovation Impact Analysis

Innovation is the poor stepchild of cost-benefit analysis. For more than thirty years, the OMB's Office of Information and Regulatory Affairs (OIRA) has reviewed proposed federal agency actions on the basis of cost-benefit analysis. In other words, will the agency regulation or action lead to benefits that exceed their costs? This is certainly important, but there is almost no analysis of how federal actions will affect innovation. To remedy this, Congress should establish a small Office of Innovation Review (OIR) within the OMB whose mission would be to champion innovation within these processes.[41] Such an entity would add an important new voice to the regulatory conversation. There would now be an entity speaking clearly and forthrightly on the centrality of innovation. More important, the OIR would not merely have a voice: it would be able to remand agency actions that harm innovation. It would also propose regulations that foster innovation. This is no small matter. Indeed, it would change the regulatory playing field overnight.

Funding Tied to Performance

The federal government routinely provides monies to other organizations (state and local governments, educational institutions, health-care providers, and the like) to achieve some public purpose. But all too often, the accountability is process-based—did the funds get spent the way they were supposed to?—not outcome-based. Moreover, to achieve process-based accountability, federal rules often stifle creativity and innovation in organizations receiving support. The federal government could be a catalyst for innovation if it tied its funding more closely to performance. Indeed, the federal government should explicitly use its power of the purse strings to drive innovation among the recipients of those funds. It should allocate money to agencies, departments, or other benefactors that implement innovative policies or approaches. The idea is to take the same amount of money, but allocate it as an incentive to drive performance improvements and innovation.

The Department of Education's "Race to the Top" initiative is a model for spurring organizational innovation. The department offered $4 billion in grants to states committed to reforming their education systems. States that are unwilling to leverage data and accountability systems to improve measurable performance outcomes, that have legislation preventing the development or expansion of innovative school approaches, or that cannot demonstrate effective alliances with local teachers' unions on performance accountability are not eligible. After Tennessee and Delaware were awarded the first $600 million, nonqualifying states worked to pass conforming legislation, including addressing long-standing union issues.[42] "Race to the Top" should serve as a model for using performance incentives to drive innovation across a range of government agencies. For example, as noted, the federal government could make funding to universities partially contingent on how well universities commercialize their research. Likewise, the Department of Transportation could allocate funding from the Highway Trust Fund on the basis of how effectively states reduce traffic congestion.

Information Technology Transformation

One of the defining features of many of today's innovations is their basis in information technologies—computers, software, and telecommunications.[43] As such, economic success depends upon accelerating digital transformation and the widespread use of IT in all sectors of the economy. The United States performs well when it comes to enterprise-level adoption of

IT. However, the United States lags behind in the adoption of IT in other areas, particularly those confronted with chicken-or-egg conundrums.

One prominent example is the smart electric power grid. The smart grid is intended to be a new kind of network that will deliver power more efficiently and reliably than our existing power grid. The smart grid will facilitate the seamless integration of new technologies, including "smart" appliances that respond to dynamic price signals, plug-in hybrid electric vehicles, distributed generation (for example, residential solar panels), and energy storage solutions. However, U.S. electric utilities have been slow to embrace it, in part because as regulated monopolies they have little incentive to do so and in part because the public utility commissions that regulate them have been risk-averse. (It's made worse by neo-Luddite citizen groups that oppose smart grids on completely fallacious grounds.) And, at least until the 2009 stimulus legislation, there was little help from government.

This suggests a key role for government: supporting "digital platforms." Neoclassical economics ignores technology platforms. But throughout U.S. economic history, technology platforms have served as powerful launching pads for new industries and jobs. In the 1920s, there was no point in GE or RCA inventing a new electric appliance if people did not have electricity. In the 1950s, there was no point in Sears or Macy's opening stores in sub-urban shopping malls if customers could not drive on highways to get to them. In the 1990s, there was no point in Amazon.com trying to sell books online if the World Wide Web didn't exist. And in the early 2000s, there was no point for YouTube to host videos if people didn't have broad-band in their homes.

Today is no different. There is no point in creating an online application to let people manage their health information if that information consists of paper records. There is no point in creating a smart washing machine that turns itself on when electricity costs are low at night if the supportive electric grid isn't smart as well. There is no point in creating mobile appli-cations that require high transmission speeds if the 4G network is not de-ployed with adequate spectrum allocated to it. In fact, there are thousands of job-producing new products, services, and business models ready to be launched once the needed digital platforms are in place.

There are at least six key digital platform technologies today. The first is broadband, which is a critical enabler of a host of new applications like telehealth and cloud computing. Yet, only about two-thirds of Americans subscribe to broadband, it is not universally deployed (about 6 percent of homes have no access other than satellite), and broadband speeds, while improving, can get much faster still. One reason so few Americans subscribe to broadband is that they don't have a personal computer or don't know how to use one. Taking steps to get more than 90 percent of households online would be a significant step forward in building a universal broadband economy.

Second, next-generation 4G wireless communications promise to provide services with speeds that are twenty to fifty times faster than today's 3G networks, enabling a mobility revolution to emerge. Yet, many places today cannot even get cell phone coverage, much less advanced data services, and it is not clear that the government will free up enough spectrum, especially spectrum now used by TV networks, for these data-hungry wireless applications. Third, health IT gives patients and their caregivers an easily accessed, comprehensive view of the patient's health information. But compared to some other nations, America lags far behind.[44] Fourth, intelligent transportation systems can bring real-time intelligence to travelers. Imagine that you could get real-time, in-vehicle traffic information that dynamically reroutes your navigation route based on information such as current road conditions (e.g., avoid icy spots or that traffic accident that just occurred moments ago and is backing up the interstate). Fifth, a smart electric grid could sense the location of power outages; charge customers based on time-of-day use; and enable the use of new technologies like plug-in hybrid electric vehicles, distributed generation, and energy storage solutions. Sixth, contactless mobile payments can let consumers use their cell phone to pay a taxi fare, check in and out of a parking garage, present a boarding pass at the airport, or serve as a hotel room "key."

Without government help to catalyze deployment of these platforms, we will not see the progress that is possible. In fact, as noted previously, a key reason why some nations are ahead of us in deploying these platforms is that foreign governments have engaged in smart partnerships to help the private sector build the platforms, in part by using a combination of tax incentives; smart, but limited, regulations that drive change; and having the government act as a lead purchaser. The U.S. federal government should do the same.

International Framework for Innovation

Competing effectively in economics, sports, or any other area depends not only on competing at the highest level but also ensuring that the opponents play by the rules. While the United States needs to improve its innovation game, it also needs to fight more vigorously against foreign innovation mercantilism.

Indeed, it will be difficult for the United States to regain global innovation leadership if it continues to largely turn a blind eye to rampant foreign policies and practices that distort the spirit, if not the letter, of the WTO agreement, with the goal of limiting U.S. imports of high-tech products and services while promoting their exports. These countries want it both ways; they want access to the U.S. market but do not want to buy U.S.-produced goods and services. They want U.S. FDI, particularly high-tech investment, through outsourcing, joint ventures, and other types of investment, but they want to weaken the competitive advantage of U.S. companies in favor of their own. They want U.S. technology and intellectual property, but they don't want to pay for it.

For decades after WWII, the United States benignly aided the development of other countries' manufacturing and export capacity, believing that the expansion of commerce would create a bigger pie for all and that it would be years before emerging countries became formidable competitors. Well, those years have arrived. The fledglings have grown into formidable birds of prey in some cases, and the United States can either take cover or engage them as serious opponents on an equal footing.

To stop the continued erosion of America's technology leadership, the federal government will have to make fighting foreign innovation mercantilism, particularly but not solely from China, a top priority, as important as national security. Both the administration and Congress need to let countries know that they cannot expect to get the WTO's benefits if they fail to meet its obligations.

The first place to start is currency. The U.S. government needs to affirm that it will no longer defend the dollar and that it expects other nations to stop their own currency manipulation. Presidents should appoint Treasury secretaries who see their job not as "borrowers in chief" who want a strong dollar to keep their borrowing costs low, but as "defenders of a level playing field" who will publicly work to drive the value of the dollar lower. They should bar the words "defend the dollar" from all Treasury speeches, memos, and thinking. This means allowing the dollar to weaken while pressuring other nations that manipulate their currencies to strengthen theirs, at least until the United States once again achieves a balance of trade.

Fighting currency manipulation is only one component of the struggle the United States (and hopefully its like-minded allies) must engage in. The United States also needs to dramatically increase its pressure on other nations and global organizations (like the WTO) to stop the wide array of unfair trade practices targeted at boosting exports, particularly in high-value-added, innovation-based sectors.[45] These include discriminatory tariffs and taxes, export subsidies, intellectual property (IP) theft, blocking market access by foreign firms, forced technology transfer, unfair subsidies to state-owned enterprises, standards manipulation, and the use of regulations and laws (including antitrust) to discriminate against firms.

Unfortunately, all too often, U.S. agencies see the race for innovation advantage as a game in which U.S. industrial advantage can be traded away for foreign policy goals, as chapter 4 explains. Moreover, agencies like the State Department sometimes take the side of other nations, especially developing nations. The fact that there are even debates inside the State Department over whether to pressure developing nations that are stealing U.S. intellectual property (with one side arguing that doing so would hurt poor nations) suggests that the U.S. government is still not of one mind when it comes to defending America's economic interests.

Moreover, the agency supposedly charged with defending U.S. economic interests internationally, the United States Trade Representative's Office (USTR), suffers from two key limitations. First, its budget and manpower are too modest given today's global trade challenges. Second, political leadership in the USTR more often than not focuses on promoting trade opening rather than on enforcing existing trade agreements. Because success for the USTR is often defined as signing new trade agreements, it has less incentive to be a tough negotiator. You cannot win at negotiation if you need the deal more than the other guy. Different reforms to trade enforcement have been proposed, including expanding the USTR budget for enforcement, moving the enforcement function out of the USTR to the U.S. Department of Justice, or setting up the USTR as a separate agency outside the Executive Office of the President (combined with some related functions from the Commerce Department).

Wherever the USTR is situated, it needs access to more talent and resources that can help it think strategically about how trade and globalization are impacting U.S. competitiveness. The USTR is still fighting the last war—the tariff war and the war to sign trade agreements. It's not set up, either institutionally or philosophically, to fight the current war—the war against rampant innovation mercantilism fueled by a wide array of nontariff barriers. To help address this, Congress should allocate $5 million to create an Office of Globalization Strategy within the USTR, run by a deputy for globalization strategy. The office would be staffed by an interdisciplinary team of about twenty individuals with a diverse set of skills, including economists (as of 2011, there were only three at the USTR), policy analysts, attorneys, and so forth, experienced across competition policy, regulatory policy, standards, technology policy, and other realms. This group would be charged with systems thinking about the design of U.S. trade policy in the context of globalization to ensure renewed U.S. competitiveness.

Affected businesses must also become more willing partners in enforcement efforts. The USTR cannot bring legal actions if companies will not supply the evidence. Companies often rightly assert that they will face retribution in foreign markets, particularly China, if they are associated with WTO actions. But unless other countries begin to honor their global trade commitments soon, the U.S. hand will become ever weaker and companies will completely cede their ability to level the playing field. One way for the government to address this challenge is to make it clear that USTR will bring cases whenever U.S. interests are being hurt, even if U.S. companies don't want them to proceed. This policy would make it clear to countries like China that their threats to punish American firms for bringing cases won't work.

Beyond facing retaliatory threats, there are two other reasons why U.S. companies don't bring more trade enforcement cases. First, they are expensive. Second, the "free rider" problem means that companies can benefit if they can convince other firms in their industry to bear the burden of helping the USTR to bring a trade case. In order to remedy this, Congress should encourage companies to build WTO cases by allowing them to take a generous tax credit for expenditures related to bringing the cases.[46]

One other area the United States must better compete in with regard to international trade is by providing increased export financing assistance to U.S. exporters. As a share of GDP, competitors such as Brazil, China, India, France, and Germany provide seven to ten times more export credit assistance than does the United States.[47] (In fact, as a share of GDP, in 2008, China provided seventeen times more export credit assistance to its exporters than the United States did.) To address this, Congress should expeditiously reauthorize funding for the U.S. Export-Import Bank, which provides export credit financing to U.S. businesses, while increasing the statutory lending authorization of the bank from $100 billion to at least $160 billion. Furthermore, Congress should allow the bank to use $20 billion in unobligated authority to lend directly to domestic manufacturing companies that are in competition with subsidized competitors and can demonstrate that the funds would support expanded manufacturer activities in the United States.

A final component of the international issue is high-skill immigration. Talent is a key resource in the global knowledge economy.[48] High-skill immigration plays a critical role in contributing to a country's knowledge and skills pool. The United States has benefited immensely from attracting foreign-born talent. For example, at least seven studies have examined the role of immigrants in launching new companies in the United States, and all conclude that immigrants are key actors in this process, creating from 15 percent to 26 percent of new companies in the U.S. high-tech sector over the past two decades.[49] While many nations, such as Canada, have implemented explicit strategies to attract internationally mobile skilled workers, the United States has a de facto low-skill immigration policy.[50] To change that, Congress should provide automatic permanent residency status (green cards) for foreign students who graduate with a master's or Ph.D. degree in STEM fields. We should also create a system whereby fees for

H-1B visas (a nonimmigrant visa that allows a U.S. company to employ a foreign individual for up to six years) float directly with the unemployment rate, with H-1B visa fees being low when unemployment rates are low and vice versa.

Recognizing that the United States is falling behind in the race for global innovation advantage is hard; developing the political will to take action is even harder. However, there is no reason the United States has to succumb to the same malady its British cousins did. While America often avoids action on problems for much too long, as Churchill once said, "The Americans will always do the right thing . . . after they've exhausted all the alternatives."[51] Certainly there will be deniers, resisters, and opponents, as there are now, but it's also likely that there will be increasingly vocal calls for action. If a growing consensus develops about the nature of the problem and the need to act, this ultimately could get translated into political action. But developing this consensus for action will require a better understanding of the political economy of innovation.

9

Why Don't We Have More Innovation and Innovation Policy?

Ef innovation is the elixir that amplifies incomes and advances economic competitiveness, and if innovation policy is required for an even more potent elixir, why don't we have more of both? With the proliferation of innovations in our daily lives—iPads, smartphones, and new drugs, to name a few—these may seem like odd questions. But in contrast to some who marvel at the innovations appearing almost daily, we wonder why there aren't more. George Bernard Shaw wrote: "You see things; and you say 'Why?' But I dream things that never were; and I say 'Why not?'" Why is India still so poor? Why can't Japan accelerate its growth? Why does the United States lag behind leading nations in the adoption of digital platform technologies? Why do educational systems in most nations look the same way they did fifty years ago? Why haven't we cured cancer? Why aren't robots intelligent? Why does renewable energy still cost more than coal and oil? The real question is about the innovations that could be here but aren't.

It took almost a quarter century, 1984 to 2008, for world economic output to double. Why couldn't we double it again by 2026 instead of 2034? For this to happen, global productivity growth would have to increase from

3.1 percent per year to only 4.1 percent. If we could maintain that rate, the billions stuck in poverty would see their incomes increase by a factor of five in forty-one years instead of the fifty-four years it will take at current rates. Companies and governments across the globe invest approximately $1.1 trillion a year on research and development (R&D). Why couldn't they invest $2.2 trillion and more quickly develop cures for major diseases, affordable clean energy, smart robots to do routine work, real-time language translation, brain-computer interfaces, autonomously controlled cars, much faster jet aircraft, and other innovations?

This list of potential innovations could go on and on. All of them will eventually emerge, for the simple reason that science and technology will enable them to and people will want them. But why do we have to wait so long? Only antitechnology Luddites would not leap at the opportunity to wave a magic wand and reach into the future to transport every innovation that will exist in 2042 to the present day. As such, a principal mission of the international community should be to do that—to deliver the promise of the future to the world's 7 billion inhabitants as quickly as possible.

For the United States, the innovation imperative is especially critical because innovation is a key way to effectively compete with the Chinas and Indias of the world. The principal way to spur global innovation and to renew the U.S. industrial economy is to vigorously support innovation and the policies that support it. But all too often the political process in the United States, as in many other nations, fails in doing so. In far too many nations, the forces and ideologies committed to stasis are powerful. As this chapter explores, three key factors particularly limit innovation: interests that fight it, ideologies that oppose it, and governments that ignore it. Given the forces allied against it, it's a wonder that innovation occurs to the extent it does. Maximizing innovation requires understanding these forces and identifying and implementing strategies to overcome them.

Interests Opposing Innovation

Too many interests (businesses, professions, unions, governments, educational institutions, and civic groups, among others) see innovation as a threat to their livelihood and translate that opposition into action that retards both innovation itself and the introduction of policies to enable and spur innovation.

Incumbent Opposition

John Stuart Mill once stated: "One person with a belief is a social power equal to ninety-nine who have only interests." Yet, when it comes to technological innovation, ninety-nine persons with a belief in the power and potential of the innovation can be thwarted by just one with a special interest. Given the benefits of innovation, why would anyone be against it? Niccoló Machiavelli provided the answer as early as 1532, when he wrote in *The Prince* that "there is nothing more difficult to execute, nor more dubious of success, nor more dangerous to administer than to introduce a new system of things, for he who introduces it has all those who profit from the old system as his enemies, and he has only lukewarm allies in those who might profit from the new system."[1] Or, as innovation economist Joseph Schumpeter explained in his seminal treatise *Capitalism, Socialism and Democracy,* "The resistance which comes from interests threatened by an innovation in the productive process is not likely to die out as long as the capitalist order persists."[2] Schumpeter might have been more prescient if he had said that such resistance would only intensify over time, for that appears to have happened, particularly in developed nations.

It wouldn't be so bad if the health of economies did not depend on innovation. But as Schumpeter also famously wrote, "It is the process of industrial mutation—if I may use that biological term—that incessantly revolutionizes the economic structure from within, incessantly destroying the old one, incessantly creating a new one. This process of creative destruction is the essential fact about capitalism."[3] This creative destruction—that is, innovation—forces individuals, organizations, and even whole regions and nations to adapt or suffer the consequences of not doing so. It turns industries (and occupations) into vestigial "buggy whip industries" with little purpose. For those invested in the old—old products, services, industries, occupations, institutions, forms of work organization, and production processes—innovation is risky and often met with trepidation at best. While the rest of us gain handsomely from innovation—after all, the definition of innovation is bringing new value to consumers and citizens—those invested in the old sometimes lose. And all too frequently they fight, often vigorously and effectively, to protect their interests against particular innovations.

As Mancur Olson noted thirty years ago in *The Logic of Collective Action*, while the benefits from innovation are widely dispersed, the losses associated with it are usually borne by a small minority.[4] This risk of imminent economic hanging focuses the mind and the pocketbook, leading these groups to spend time and money to defeat, or at least slow down or limit, innovation. Moreover, it is incumbents who are often hurt by innovation, and they usually have more money, more people to mobilize, and more and better connections with policymakers and legislators. Innovators, because they are in many cases new to the scene, usually have less money and fewer connections. They often have little more than the merit of a new and better idea. In *The Rise and Decline of Nations*, Olson extends this theory to try to explain why some societies innovate more than others. He hypothesizes: "Stable societies with unchanged boundaries tend to accumulate more collusions and organizations for collective action over time."[5] And they use this collective action to thwart change. While it's not necessary to agree with Olson's mechanistic theory of societal change—that the longer a society is stable the more it will grow the barnacles of resistance—he is right that societies differ in the extent to which vested interests can organize to limit innovation and that this is an important factor in explaining rates of growth and innovation.

Sometimes opposition to innovation is manifest. In 2008, peasant farmers, left-wing activists, environmentalists, and their political supporters in the Indian state of West Bengal demonstrated against the Tata Corporation's acquisition of farmers' land to build a car factory to produce the ultra–low cost Nano car. Tata was forced to abandon the almost-completed factory, wasting $300 million and losing the potential to create twelve thousand relatively good-paying jobs. The interests of a few farmers trumped the interests of tens of thousands of workers and citizens in West Bengal.

But it's not just underdeveloped nations with socialist political traditions that oppose innovation. It happens in developed nations, too. A case in point is France, a developed nation with socialist political traditions. As many as three million people, 5 percent of the French population, marched in more than two hundred protests in March 2009, most against plant closings and workforce reductions needed to allow French companies to survive the downturn and remain globally competitive.[6] Some of the marches were even supplemented by "boss-nappings," where workers temporarily held company executives hostage to force negotiations to reduce job cuts or stop plant closings.

Opposition to innovation is not always about militant confrontation. More often it is inconspicuous and cloaked in the mantle of the public interest. An example is union resistance to self-checkout scanners. In recent years, many retail stores have installed systems that let consumers scan products and pay without the assistance of a retail clerk. These systems lower costs, but also reduce the number of checkout workers, and not surprisingly cause unions to oppose them. The United Food and Commercial Workers (UFCW) union stated: "We don't like self-checkout scanners because they put cashiers out of work."[7] Knowing it would get little support from legislators if it sought legislation banning self-checkout outright, the UFCW instead pushed for the introduction of a bill in the California legislature that would require alcohol sales be made with the assistance of a cashier.[8] Instead of it being obvious that legislators were doing the bidding of one union to make the lives of millions of consumers more difficult, the legislators cloaked their actions in the mantle of protecting California's youth, even though there was no evidence of any problems associated with minors purchasing alcoholic beverages through self-service checkouts in California.[9] When the bill passed California's legislature in 2010, then California governor Arnold Schwarzenegger promptly vetoed it. But in 2011, Democratic governor Jerry Brown signed the legislation into law, meaning that California consumers will now pay higher prices and wait longer in lines.

Unions representing grocery store workers are hardly alone in opposing innovation. Unions often oppose innovation that boosts productivity. One International Association of Machinists and Aerospace Workers leader stated: "At this point, the objective is not to block the new technology, but to control its rate and manner of introduction, in order that it is adapted to labor's needs and serves people, rather than being servile to it or its victims."[10] Translation: We want to slow down the introduction of new technology so that none of our members lose their jobs.

It's not just unions that wrap protectionist claims in the mantle of the public interest; businesses do so as well. U.S. car dealers helped pass legislation in all fifty states prohibiting auto manufacturers from selling directly to the customer, including over the Internet, claiming that such restrictions were needed to protect consumers against rapacious car manufacturers.[11] Realtors seeking to protect their 6 percent sales commissions have colluded to keep online discount brokers from getting access to real estate listings, claiming that discounts are not in the consumer's interest.[12] Optometrists helped pass state legislation making it hard for consumers to fulfill their prescriptions online, purportedly to protect consumers from suffering eye damage.[13] Travel agents sought to enlist the U.S. Justice Department against the airlines' formation of the online travel site Orbitz, claiming to "act as the public's representatives and help keep prices low."[14] Gas station owners in Oregon and New Jersey have successfully fought legislation allowing self-service gas stations because consumers might cause damage if they pump their own gas. Wine wholesalers have successfully pushed for state laws limiting online sales from wineries and out-of-state retailers to protect against underage drinking.[15] The list goes on and on. Insurance agents, mortgage brokers, investment bankers, securities traders, college professors, music and video stores, radiologists, pharmacists, veterinarians, and even undertakers selling caskets are among the professions and industries that have sought government protection, often successfully, from more efficient and lower cost (frequently e-commerce) competitors, all claiming that they simply wanted to protect the public.

Such restrictions are not limited to the United States. The European Commission is considering rules for member states that would permit manufacturers to require retailers selling their products to maintain brick-and-mortar stores for a certain proportion of sales.[16] To protect small booksellers from larger or online booksellers who can sell at a discount, France prohibits bookstores from giving discounts of more than 5 percent. Germany and Norway go even further, allowing no discounts. Australia imposes "parallel import restrictions" on imported books to limit competition. In Japan, laws limiting the entry of large supermarkets and providing incentives for small retailers to stay in business explain the country's high share of family retailers, and their low productivity. India also has long precluded competition in its retail sector by keeping foreign competitors such as Walmart out of its markets. In fact, Walmart has only been able to enter India through a $100 million joint venture with an Indian company, Bharti, which runs Walmart's stores in India on a cobranded basis. Moreover, in an effort to protect smaller merchants, the Indian government astonishingly required that Walmart sell only to wholesalers, business owners, and their family and friends. These buyers then resell the products directly to consumers, often at a substantial additional markup. In December 2011, the Indian government proposed rescinding this protectionist law, but then backed down in the face of ferocious opposition from left-wing politicians and retailers.

We recognize the rational self-interest of people wanting to maintain their livelihoods. Even if they understand that change is inevitable, people often hope that it will occur a little later, as they get closer to a secure retirement. But the examples cited here serve to point out that the proconsumer, prosafety rationales are actually thin reeds used by those whose chief interest is thwarting change. A better approach would be to move forward with an innovation strategy that includes ample opportunities for education and retraining for the jobs that increased productivity and innovation will create. Ultimately, however, it is the responsibility of citizens and their elected officials to keep the long term in mind and support innovation.

"Main Street" Welfare

A national economy can be innovative even if interest groups occasionally fight against innovation, especially if the rule of law applies and the political process is relatively transparent and open. However, it becomes much harder when entire political coalitions are forged for the purpose of redistributing, rather than growing, the innovation pie. American politics in particular has devolved into this kind of zero-sum battleground. While the common view is that Democrats are focused on redistribution and Republicans focused on growth, in fact, both parties have quite formidable redistributionist factions. As each marshals its forces, they collide in political battle, each seeking to seize a bit more and each blithely unconcerned with, or even hostile to, efforts to fuel the competitiveness, innovation, and productivity engine—what we refer to as the "CIP Engine."

U.S. economic politics is often framed as a clash between "Main Street" and "Wall Street." Wall Street is portrayed as filled with greedy financiers, counting their huge end-of-year bonuses and concerned only with getting rich by manipulating financial deals, even if it means destroying communities, companies, and jobs in the process. In contrast, Main Street, the story goes, is populated by mom-and-pop businesses owned by red-blooded Americans who work hard, create jobs, and drive this great country. This meme has become deeply embedded in the American political culture. Just enter "Main Street vs. Wall Street" in a search engine and one gets statements like those below, the first two from conservative commentators and the second two from liberal pundits:

- "Rising costs and taxes and declining income have mugged Main Street while Wall Street revels in the Fed-engineered 'recovery' in the stock market."[17]
- "This bailout [to Wall Street] isn't as bad as Main Street thinks. It's worse."[18]
- "My biggest disappointment in President Obama, a man I voted for, is that he has consistently sided with Wall Street over Main Street."[19]
- "Wall Street vs. Main Street: Final Showdown Threatens Reform."[20]

The perceived dichotomy is so embedded that the TV news magazine show 60 Minutes has even bought into it. In a segment about the suffering of local, small businesses in Newton, Iowa, caused by the closing of the Maytag appliance factory (the washers and dryers will now be made in Mexico), host Scott Pelly bemoaned the fact that these companies weren't getting help: "Three years after the beginning of the Great Recession, with interest rates the lowest they have ever been in history, banks are lending less money to the engines that create jobs."[21]

But this Wall Street vs. Main Street framing misses the point that neither is a CIP engine. What will determine whether America thrives in the global economy is not whether Fred's clothing shop on Main Street sells more pants or whether Goldman Sachs' profits soar even higher. It is whether companies that export goods and services and compete in tough international markets do well; whether companies that drive productivity in their operations through the introduction of new technology do well; and whether high-growth entrepreneurial companies, especially ones that develop and commercialize innovations, do well. These are not Main Street or Wall Street companies. These are "Industrial Street" and "Office Complex Street" companies; the former being manufacturing firms, particularly those competing in international markets, and the latter being technology-based nonmanufacturing companies (e.g., information industries such as software, Internet, telecommunications, movies and music, and global engineering services firms).

Defenders of Main Street and champions of Wall Street will, of course, argue otherwise. A healthy Wall Street is critical, the latter assert, because it provides the capital that enables companies to grow. To be sure, well-functioning capital markets are important, especially to the extent they channel capital to activities that boost innovation and productivity. But this is a two-way street. Without companies that take in capital and yield high returns from innovation, productivity, and growing sales, Wall Street couldn't make a profit on the capital it manages. As a result, financial markets would shrink. But the last thing Wall Street wants to do is downsize. Like any good redistributionist, it will fight change any way it can, as the industry did in the early 2000s by investing in the Ponzi scheme known as subprime mortgages and collateralized debt obligations and resisting real financial services industry reform legislation. As University of Massachusetts economist Gerald Epstein states: "The usual economists' argument for financial innovation is that it adds to the size of the pie. But these types of things [like collateralized debt obligations (CDOs)] don't add to the pie. They redistribute it—often from taxpayers to banks and other financial institutions."[22] Given that Wall Street came close to driving the global economy off the cliff, and would have had taxpayers not bailed it out, its defenders are a bit muted these days. But claims of Wall Street primacy still lurk in the background, ready to be reasserted once the present outrage over the financial collapse and bailout subsides.

Main Street's backers are even more vocal in their claims. "How can you say that corporations, and not small Main Street businesses, are the CIP engines?" they will protest. "We all know that Main Street creates the jobs, produces the innovations, and drives the growth." We may think we know this; but what we know is wrong.

Let's start with the claim that Main Street is the source of jobs. To understand why the jobs claim is wrong, it's important to understand the difference between what regional economists refer to as local-serving and export-serving businesses. Consider the closed Maytag factory; it was an export-serving business, meaning that it shipped products outside of the local labor market. While a small share of the washers and dryers coming off the assembly line were sold to local Newton residents, most were sold to customers throughout the nation or even the world, who sent money back to Maytag, who gave some of it to their local workers. In contrast, the local restaurants, dry cleaners, clothing stores, and barber shops are local-serving, as the lion's share of their output is sold to Newton residents, including Maytag workers. If one of these local-serving "Main Street" businesses had gone out of business, it would have had virtually no effect on the output of the Maytag factory; moreover, another business would more or less automatically expand or emerge to meet local demand. But the Maytag factory closure had an immediate negative impact on the local-serving businesses, whose customers (Maytag workers, its suppliers, and their workers) had much less money to spend locally on meals, haircuts, dry cleaning, and other needs and desires.

The reality is that the majority of U.S. businesses are local-serving. These include, for example, the 219,986 doctors' offices, 166,366 auto repair facilities, 151,031 food and beverage stores, 115,533 gas stations, 111,028 offices of real estate agents and brokers, 93,121 landscaping companies, 75,606 nursing homes, 36,246 furniture stores, 28,336 veterinary offices, 15,666 travel agencies, 4,571 bowling alleys, 2,463 amusement arcades, 858 radio networks, and 26 commuter rail systems. These and millions of other local-serving businesses will neither prosper nor suffer principally on the basis of economic policies targeted at them. Providing them easier credit, cutting their taxes, giving them subsidies, exempting them from regulations, or any of the myriad "remedies" offered by Main Street backers are largely irrelevant to their collective survival (although perhaps not to their owners' income) and to U.S. economic vitality. What is relevant is the strength of the demand for their goods and services. To come back to the *60 Minutes* story, the small business owners Pelly interviewed weren't in trouble because they couldn't get loans. They couldn't get loans because they were in trouble. And they were in trouble because they had fewer paying customers than before the Maytag factory closed. Let's say that the government decided to help these Newton companies by saying that they could pay taxes at a rate of 10 percent instead of 35 percent. No new jobs would be created because the same number of people would need haircuts and pants. It would even be the same if the government provided them with low-cost loans. If we want to help Main Street create jobs, the best way to do so is to help Industrial Street and Office Complex Street create good-paying jobs while boosting productivity, thereby driving up demand for Main Street goods and services.

Moreover, most small businesses don't create jobs. One study of a sample of companies created from 2004 to 2008 found that only 3 percent added more than 10 employees during that time.[23] Another study found that among small companies in their second, third, fourth, and fifth years of business, more jobs were lost to bankruptcy than were added by those still operating.[24] In fact, only a relatively small number of high-growth "gazelle" firms create most of the jobs. So the focus should be on entrepreneurial, high-growth firms, not on small business per se.

In addition to not being the jobs engine, Main Street is not the innovation, the productivity, or the export engine. Firms with fewer than five hundred employees employ 49 percent of U.S. workers but account for just 25 percent of U.S. exports.[25] The companies that export and successfully compete against foreign companies in global markets are much more likely to be large Industrial Street and Office Complex Street firms. Main Street firms account for only 19 percent of the funds invested in R&D.[26] This is not to say that some small technology-based firms are not highly innovative. But to assume that small always equates with innovative or entrepreneurial is not accurate.

Indeed, small firms are significantly less productive than large ones. Workers in large firms earn 57 percent more than workers in companies with fewer than one hundred workers.[27] And besides getting paid more, workers in large companies get 3.5 times more retirement benefits than workers at Main Street companies, 2.7 times more paid leave, and 2.4 times more health-care benefits.[28] The only area where workers at Industrial Street and Office Complex Street companies get less than Main Street workers is workers' compensation and unemployment insurance (9 percent less), presumably because they get injured and laid off less often. This is not in any way to denigrate small Main Street businesses. Their owners take risks, work hard, and contribute to their communities. But we should not let our emotions get in the way of reality. The engines of a nation's competitiveness, innovation, and productivity are not mom-and-pop small businesses, but rather the firms in traded sectors, high-growth entrepreneurial companies, and U.S.-headquartered multinational corporations. Although the latter comprise far less than 1 percent of U.S. companies, they account for about 19 percent of private-sector jobs, 25 percent of private-sector wages, 48 percent of goods exports, and 74 percent of nonpublic R&D investment. And, since 1990, they have been responsible for 41 percent of the nation's increase in private labor productivity.[29]

In short, it's Industrial Street and Office Complex Street, not Wall Street and Main Street, that predominantly drive the nation's jobs, competitiveness, innovation, and productivity growth. To be clear, Industrial Street and Office Complex Street include companies of all sizes, but they are characterized particularly by companies that compete internationally, that are high-growth and innovative (regardless of their size), and that are manufacturing-, research-, or information-based.

Notwithstanding this economic reality, members of both parties continue to swoon over Main Street, while core factions of the Democratic Party go as far as to attack Industrial Street and Office Complex Street. And both parties seek to exempt Main Street from rules and regulations. While it is true that many small businesses have very small profit margins and the costs of taxes and regulations eat into those profit margins, it is also important to remember that this is not a reason to subsidize them or exempt them from regulations, as they usually are today. If some go out of business because of this, other companies with stronger balance sheets and higher productivity will automatically take their place. The one area where government should not pick winners is with regard to firm size.

Let's start with the Republican Main Street business coalition, which fights for policies to redistribute wealth from wage earners to coalition members (business owners). It is one thing to redistribute wealth in the short run from workers to CIP companies (for example, by increasing the R&D credit so that companies invest more in R&D, which in turn helps the overall economy). If done right, workers and consumers benefit later through more and better jobs, lower prices, and more innovative products and services. It's quite another to redistribute wealth to the owners of Main Street small businesses, with the principal result being a bigger number on line 37 of their 1040 IRS tax form (Adjusted Gross Income) and a smaller number on line 76 (Amount You Owe). And that is largely the goal of the small business coalition supporting the Republican Party. At its center is the National Federation of Independent Businesses (NFIB), the leading organization of small and independent businesses. The NFIB portrays itself as the defender of the companies that create jobs and wealth, and woe to any politician who dares to threaten these American-as-apple-pie economic engines. But while the NFIB's membership may include a smattering of high-growth, innovation-based firms, the lion's share are small Main Street firms that are almost completely dependent on Industrial Street or Office Complex Street companies for their well-being. But to listen to the NFIB and many in the media who have bought into their folklore, it's the family-owned pizza parlors, dry cleaners, print shops, car dealers, and clothing stores that drive the U.S. economy.

This is a mythology that the NFIB plays for all it's worth. Anytime Congress, the administration, or state governments consider action that might require businesses to do anything—such as provide health insurance or unpaid leave for workers having a child—the NFIB fights to ensure that its small-business members are exempt. After all, they object, if you force our members to actually give their workers health insurance coverage, the economic engine would sputter and stall. The NFIB doesn't just lobby to ensure that Main Street is exempt from regulations that apply to Industrial Street and Office Complex Street, it also lobbies to exempt Main Street from taxes. Rather than fight for expensing for all companies (letting companies take a tax deduction for all their capital expenditures in the first year), the NFIB supports this only for its members. Rather than lobby to expand the R&D tax credit that spurs companies to invest more in research, the NFIB lobbies for repeal of the estate tax. Rather than lobby to reduce the corporate tax rate, which would help Industrial Street and Office Complex Street compete in global markets, it works to lower the top individual tax rate, which, while helping NFIB members, would have virtually no effect on U.S. competitiveness or innovation.[30] Rather than support expanding unemployment insurance and workforce training expenditures so that workers are more likely to support rather than oppose automation and globalization, it pushes to cut unemployment taxes.[31] And NFIB makes sure that anyone who questions their agenda is painted as antibusiness.

Unfortunately the NFIB has been successful. In the two decades before 2010, when President Obama proposed having first-year expensing apply to companies of all sizes, any equipment expensing provisions enacted applied only to small companies. While the NFIB succeeded in getting the estate tax reduced by 50 percent in 2001, the U.S. R&D tax credit remains anemic. While the NFIB worked with Republicans to lower the top marginal individual tax rate, the corporate tax rate is now the highest in the world. And while the NFIB successfully lobbied for reduced unemployment insurance taxes in many states, federal workforce training expenditures have been cut.

Redistributionists also populate the other side of the aisle. Liberal redistributionists, however, see their mission as redistributing money from rich people and corporations to low-income Americans and workers. A case in point is Citizens for Tax Justice (CTJ). CTJ is a liberal advocacy group whose "mission is to give ordinary people a greater voice in the development of tax laws. Against the armies of special interest lobbyists for corporations and the wealthy, CTJ fights for fair taxes for middle- and low-income families . . . and closing corporate tax loopholes."[32] Like the NFIB, CTJ, and its allies in the Democratic Party, fight for redistribution, but unlike the NIFB, it is explicit in its opposition to most policies that would help Industrial Street or Office Complex Street boost innovation, productivity, or competitiveness. In fact, it wants to tax these engines even more in order to pay for increased social welfare.

The result is that Washington economic politics has become a redistributionist battleground between the NFIBs on the Right, seeking to funnel resources to their Main Street members (small business), and the CTJs on the Left, seeking to funnel resources to their Main Street members (low- and moderate-income Americans). The NFIB and CTJ spend much of their time battling over which of these respective redistributionist schemes will prevail. The NFIB fights for "low tax rates so that small business owners keep more of their money." CTJ calls for its members to "Tell Congress: Don't Choose Tax Cuts for the Rich over Help for the Unemployed."[33] The NFIB fights against unionization. CTJ fights for unionization. The NFIB fights against cap and trade legislation. CTJ not only fights for cap and trade but also for making sure that even more of its costs are borne by large corporations. The NFIB fights to weaken tort liability for small business, CTJ to strengthen it. And so on. No wonder the United States has failed to put in place the kinds of innovation policies needed for the CIP engine to thrive in tough global economic competition.

To be sure, in a democracy, the NFIB and CTJ have every right to lobby for societal resources to be redistributed to their members, just as AARP has a right to lobby to funnel more societal resources to retirees. The problem is that not only do they portray these redistributionist policies as growth and innovation policies, but also that too many elected officials believe that helping Main Street helps the CIP engine. Even Democrats have bought into the Main Street small business myth. The Kerry-Edwards 2004 platform promised to help "encourage investments by small business."[34] House Democrats promise to "fight for America's Small Business" because they are "the engine of America's economy."[35] The 2008 Obama-Biden platform promised to support "Small Business and Entrepreneurship." But where's the platform to ensure high productivity and globally competitive U.S. establishments?

If we want to restore American competitiveness, it's time to rethink programs designed to help Main Street small business broadly, as opposed to the subset of small manufacturers or high-growth entrepreneurial companies. Why enact bonus depreciation only for small firms? Why exempt small firms from the regulatory requirements that large firms face, such as the Family and Medical Leave Act? Why have procurement set-asides for small business? Why have a corporate tax rate that is progressive, with lower rates on lower levels of income? Why have lower application fees for small business, such as the lower fees small companies pay to file for a patent? Why even have Small Business Administration loans for mom-and-pop businesses, as opposed to small manufacturers and high-growth start-ups? The sum of these policies results in smaller, less productive, lower-wage nontraded firms being a larger share of the economy than they would be otherwise. But the policies survive, and even thrive, since it's a way for both parties to be seen as business friendly.

Ideological Resistance to Innovation and Innovation Policy

It's not just action based on naked self-interest that limits innovation and innovation policy; action based on ideology does as well. By ideology, we mean an organized system of thought that influences views and positions on issues. In many nations, including the United States, many advocacy groups, journalists, and intellectuals have adopted a distinctly anti-innovation worldview, making it harder for businesses to innovate and for government to support innovation. Moreover, even when some ideologies favor innovation, they reject innovation policy. And in some nations, particularly the United States, the ideology of many business leaders compels them to maintain that government has little or no role to play in fostering innovation. Finally, in some nations, particularly the United States, the United Kingdom, and other Commonwealth nations, neoclassical economists' ideology leads them to question or to reject innovation policy.

Neo-Luddites and Traditionalists

Incumbents fighting to protect their interests are not alone in opposing innovation. A wide array of groups and individuals ideologically oppose innovation. For example, neo-Luddites (named for Englishman Ned Ludd, whose followers destroyed textile machines at the beginning of the Industrial Revolution) view innovation not as a force for progress to be encouraged, but as something to be stopped. They want a world in which a worker never loses a job; consumer rights trump all else, even lower prices; no personal information is shared, even if sharing benefits society and enables a vibrant Internet ecosystem; the environment is protected whatever the costs; and cities are designed for residents who live in apartments and travel by transit to patronize small, local merchants. In short, they want a world in which risk is close to zero, losers from innovation are few, and change is glacial and managed.

And just like the Luddites of almost two centuries ago, today's Luddites also believe that innovation kills jobs. This has become a pervasive view, even among media outlets, academics, and policymakers who should know better. In a *Forbes* series on the world of 2020, Martin Ford wrote: "The economy of 2020 may well be characterized by substantial, broad-based and ever increasing structural unemployment, as well as by stagnant or plunging consumer spending and confidence."[36] In their book *Race against the Machine,* MIT professors Erik Brynjolfsson and Andrew McAfee agree, stating that workers are "losing the race against the machine, a fact reflected in today's employment statistics."[37]

Even President Obama has bought into this fallacy that technology's ability to boost productivity costs jobs. During a June 14, 2011, interview with Ann Curry of NBC's *Today* program, he suggested that technology and automation were in part responsible for the U.S. economy's sluggish job growth. The president explained that "there are some structural issues with our economy where a lot of businesses have learned to become much more efficient with a lot fewer workers. You see it when you go to a bank and you use an ATM, you don't go to a bank teller, or you go to the airport and you're using a kiosk instead of checking in at the gate."[38]

These arguments play to people's fears and at first glance appear correct. But they are wrong. The president's suggestion that technology leads to job loss is simply not the case.[39] In fact, U.S. productivity gains were higher before the Great Recession than they are now (and productivity gains were higher still in the 1990s, when job growth was booming), meaning that technological-based productivity gains are not the culprit behind recent sluggish U.S. job growth. In contrast, the vast majority of economic studies show that productivity gains—including through self-service technologies such as ATMs, kiosks, and self-checkout machines—actually lead to more jobs.[40]

When innovations (for example, tractors, disease-resistant crops, and chemical fertilizers) boosted agricultural productivity, the nation needed fewer farmworkers; however, as food became cheaper, consumers spent the money they saved on other things like cars, appliances, travel, and entertainment, thus creating employment in other sectors. This is why the Federal Reserve Bank found that "productivity grew noticeably faster than usual in the late 1990s, while the unemployment rate fell to levels not seen for more than three decades. This inverse relationship between the two variables also can be seen on several other occasions in the postwar period and leads one to wonder whether there is a causal link between them."[41] This is not to say that productivity-enhancing technologies do not sometimes result in job displacement or short-term job loss. But on net, most studies find large gains in jobs from productivity-enhancing technologies in the moderate and long run.[42] A definitive Organization for Economic Cooperation and Development (OECD) review of the impact of technology on jobs found that "technology both eliminates jobs and creates jobs. Generally it destroys lower wage, lower productivity jobs, while it creates jobs that are more productive, high-skill and better paid. Historically, the income-generating effects of new technologies have proved more powerful than the labor-displacing effects: technological progress has been accompanied not only by higher output and productivity, but also by higher overall employment."[43] If economies want to create jobs, innovation—including innovation that drives efficiency and productivity—is a key way to do so.[44]

This kind of opposition to new technology is not unfamiliar. What's new is that, in contrast to a generation ago when neo-Luddites were largely consigned to the fringes of the U.S. political debate, today they are accorded widespread legitimacy. Twenty years ago, if someone wrote that the U.S. government is hatching a secret plan to forcibly implant radio frequency identification (RFID) chips under the skin of all Americans, akin to the mark of the beast as prophesied in the Book of Revelation, he or she would have been dismissed as a crackpot. Today, one person making this claim—Katherine Albrecht, in her book *Spychips*—is widely quoted by the mainstream media, testifies at government hearings, and contributes to *Scientific American*, a journal that is increasingly a voice for neo-Luddites. One reason for the rise of neo-Luddism is that it sells. Technology pessimist Nick Carr couldn't sell many books or articles titled "IT Does Matter" or "Why Google Is Making Us Smart." Most people think that information technology (IT) does matter, and that Google is making us smarter. Who wants to buy a book or an article that restates the obvious? But saying that "IT Doesn't

Matter" or that Google is making us "stupid" is bound to get your Amazon ranking up. In reality, the evidence is clear that IT does matter, both to firms and to the economy,[45] and that IT is making us smarter.[46]

Just like self-interested incumbents, today's neo-Luddites couch their opposition to innovation in terms that make it appear they are fighting for general, as opposed to narrow, interests. By equating productivity and innovation with corporate profit, opponents portray the battle as one between big powerful, multinational corporations on the one hand and honorable civic interests (family farms, mom-and-pop Main Street businesses, privacy, a neutral Internet, competition, or "smart growth") on the other. When the choice is presented this way, rather than between increased standards of living and the narrow interests of neo-Luddites, it is much harder for the advocates of innovation to prevail. Moreover, opponents do not just cast progress as damaging to the little guy, but as risky, uncertain, and dangerous, which helps them mobilize constituencies and raise money. Of course, most opponents are quick to deny that they are actually against innovation; they just want to slow it down, control it, manage it, make sure it is introduced fairly, etc.

The epicenter of the neo-Luddite movement is Europe, where organized campaigns oppose a wide array of innovations, including biotechnology, nanotechnology, information technology, and industrialization generally. Perhaps the poster child of opposition to innovation is Switzerland, given its recent decision to regulate research on bioengineered plants on the basis that plants have "feelings" that deserve respect. Now, researchers in Switzerland must get the government's permission to conduct research on plants to make sure that they don't violate the inherent dignity of their subjects. But Switzerland may be just the most extreme case of this anti-innovation sentiment when it comes to biotechnology and food. In another example, police watched as protestors uprooted genetically modified grapevines at France's National Institute for Agronomic Research. In Spain, dozens of people recently destroyed two fields containing genetically modified crops.

The result is that Europe has fallen behind in both human- and plant-based biotech innovation. In Germany, as reported in *Newsweek*, "a powerful coalition of environmental activists, church leaders, politicians, and journalists mobilized fears against medical biotechnology as a dangerous meddling with nature, an attack on human dignity reminiscent of Nazi eugenics. With much of the public behind them, lawmakers tightened regulations, bureaucrats refused to grant permits, and even academic research facilities became targets of righteous protest."[47]

Unfortunately, since the early 1990s, these movements have gained considerable strength in the United States and in the Commonwealth nations as well, in part because of generous funding by foundations and some wealthy individuals of so-called public-interest organizations (we say "so-called" because their positions often favor a small group of ideologically like-minded individuals, not the broad public interest). In America, conservative neo-Luddites pressed the Bush administration to place severe restrictions on stem-cell research.[48] While the Obama administration reversed those restrictions, it has been pressured to act in other areas by Luddites on the Left. For example, left-wing organic food activists pressured the U.S. Department of Agriculture to rule that two additives in baby food (omega-3 fatty acid DHA and omega-6 fatty acid ARA) did not meet guidelines for the agency's organic certification. While not contesting the safety of the ingredients, the activists claim that because they are derived synthetically, they should not be considered organic. Now, parents can feed their infants food that is entirely organic. Yet in doing so, they may put their children at risk. The two ingredients, which had been used in more than 90 percent of organic baby food, were originally adopted by baby formula producers because they more closely mimic breast milk and have been shown to promote cognition and eyesight development in babies.

To be sure, consumers have the right to know what "organic" means. But the effort to set a standard should not be a backdoor way to stop innovation. In addition, while it is prudent and rational to ask serious questions about the moral and societal consequences of scientific change, answers should be based on science and not merely reflect discomfort.

Underlying much of the eco-left's opposition to innovation is an ideology of simple living and local self-sufficiency. Ecotopian Bill McKibben is perhaps the intellectual leader of this movement. Regularly quoted by the mainstream media as a leading voice on climate change and solutions to it, McKibben is, in fact, a radical anti-innovationist. Anyone who calls Kerala, a state in India with a per capita income less than 5 percent of America's, "profoundly more successful" than America and who pins the hopes of solving climate change on rich nations becoming poor and poor nations staying poor doesn't understand the power of innovation, and probably never has been poor.[49] Only sustained clean energy innovation, not sustained impoverishment (or for that matter top-down regulation), is the answer to climate change. And it won't arise from a bunch of self-sufficient communities composting their kitchen waste and burning cords of hardwood.

Food and the environment are just two areas among many that innovation neo-Luddites fight. Today, they actively oppose information technology even though IT is the source of more innovation than any other technology. These Internet traditionalists believe the Internet is having unintended and dire consequences. They invoke the purported loss of privacy and net neutrality, and complain that corporations are controlling the use of digital content. As such, these groups press for regulations that would severely limit Internet innovation, while making almost no effort to support policies that would fuel the Internet innovation engine—such as policies to support widespread use of IT in health care, transportation, education, government, and industry.

The poster child of the "stop Internet innovation" movement is the net neutrality movement. Net neutrality refers to the notion that broadband networks should not discriminate (either in quality or price) among packets delivered on their networks. The proponents of strong net neutrality regulations (strong in the sense that they would limit good network discrimination as well as bad) fear that the Internet's unique nature is under threat by the forces of incumbent broadband companies. If "Big Broadband" gets its way, neutralists fear that the Internet will go the way of cable TV, the "vast wasteland" where elitist programming such as *The Wire* competes with advertising-supported, Populist programming such as *American Idol*. But the reality is that the Internet still needs substantial amounts of innovation—both in the core and on the edge—including better tools to manage networks to optimize performance, especially for latency-sensitive applications like two-way video communications such as Skype.

But even innovation on the edge of the Internet scares neutralists. A case in point is how Web companies are using new ways to serve up more targeted ads to Web users in order to better monetize free Internet content and applications. Like over-the-air television, much World Wide Web content is free because, like television, it is supported by advertising revenue. But as the free Web ecosystem has gotten larger (and seen increased costs) and as technologies have enabled consumers to more easily avoid ads (for example, pop-up blockers), Web sites have increasingly tried to deliver ads that are more relevant to users' actual interests, with the idea that users will be more likely to click on them. They do this by matching what you might have clicked on in the past to build a profile, usually an anonymous one (for example, the person visiting this Web site is likely to be interested in sports).

Yet, for many "privacy fundamentalists," this is part of the development of a surveillance society, where people are tracked in order to limit free speech and to boost corporate profits. For many neo-Luddites, privacy is a fundamental human right that should not be traded in exchange for innovation or productivity, or even quality of life or life itself (in the case of health IT).[50] Even if most ad targeting is anonymous, neo-Luddites see the use of information about themselves for marketing purposes as dehumanizing. For this reason, they seek rules whereby organizations would not be able to use data for more than the most basic purposes without the affirmative consent of the individual involved.

But limiting Internet innovation has clear costs. Avi Goldfarb and Catherine Tucker found that after the introduction of the European Union's Privacy and Electronic Communications Directive, the effectiveness of online ads fell by approximately 65 percent. The authors note that if European advertisers were to reduce their spending on online advertising in proportion to the loss in effectiveness, "revenue for online display advertising could fall by more than half, from $8 billion to $2.8 billion."[51]

Nevertheless, opposition such as that to directed Web advertising explains in part why so many governments have not implemented advanced IT innovations. When it comes to the collection and use of data by government, Luddites from both the Left and the Right emerge and make common cause in their crusade against "Big Brother." It largely does not matter whether the goal is to crack down on deadbeat dads, catch red light runners, or prevent terrorist attacks: if it involves the government collecting more information or using existing information for new purposes, these groups will generally oppose it. In protesting against the growing practice of cities installing red light cameras, former Republican House majority leader Dick Armey railed: "This is a full-scale surveillance system. Do we really want a society where one cannot walk down the street without Big Brother tracking our every move?"[52] In fact, the use of technology to isolate crucial data or to allow a free Internet to thrive is far removed from the terrifying prospect of an Orwellian world. Just the same, the imagery works and the foes of innovation often dominate the debate.

As Mancur Olson's theory would suggest, neo-Luddites thrive in the fertile ground of nations with less support for innovation. And in many nations, the culture of innovation has become less supportive over time. A case in point is the United States, which came to lead the world in innovation in part because it was willing to accept and embrace risk and change, and then not overreact if there was a problem. There was a general belief in the inevitability of social and economic progress. The stirring musical pageant "Our Country 'Tis of Thee," written by Walter Ehret in the 1950s, is filled with optimistic statements such as: "There was no stopping a nation of tinkerers and whittlers, long accustomed to making, repairing, improving and changing," and "So when you're spellin' the word America, do not forget the 'I' for the inventors," and "Progress! That was the word that made the century turn." This optimistic sense was reflected not just in story and song but also in the writings of intellectuals who saw technology as a powerful force for liberation and enlightenment. Economist Benjamin Anderson wrote in the 1930s: "On no account must we retard or interfere with the most rapid utilization of new inventions."[53]

Today, many pundits are more likely to carry on about the risks of technology. In 2009, when Toyota was accused of having made cars with problems with sudden acceleration that initially couldn't be explained, *Washington Post* columnist Eugene Robinson didn't attack Toyota for faulty engineering, he attacked technology itself, writing that cars are "fly-by-wire too, thus equally at the mercy of information age technology, the fire we purloined from Olympus."[54] Six months later, a definitive U.S. government assessment showed that the electronics were not faulty. New York University's Neil Postman sums up the Luddite view: "I think the single most important lesson we should have learned in the past twenty years is that technological progress is not the same as human progress. Technology always comes at a price."[55]

Resistance to the future has become so pervasive that it has almost become second nature. One only has to visit the Smithsonian to see it on display. The Smithsonian was once known as the National Museum of History and Technology, but when Roger Kennedy became director in 1979, in a period when technology was equated with nuclear war and Three Mile Island, he dropped "technology" from its name. While the deletion was symbolic, it reflected the new attitude toward technology. Rather than celebrate it, the Smithsonian began to focus on "the social impact of machines and technology," a code for technology's purported negative and disruptive effects. After reviewing a 1994 "Science in American Life" exhibit, one commentator stated: "There is not much on pure science or the thrill of scientific discovery, and there is a great deal on science's unintended consequences."[56] Again, this is not to say that it's not appropriate to ask questions about the full impacts of innovation, but all too often this becomes a smoke screen for neo-Luddite opposition.

Just as America once led in innovation and no longer does, it used to lead in public attitudes supporting innovation, but now lags. Consider the World Values Survey (WVS), which asks people in more than sixty nations a range of questions about their values, many having to do with attitudes toward economic growth, technology, and innovation.[57] One question asked what respondents believe the major aim of their nation should be: (1) a high level of economic growth, (2) strong defense forces, (3) greater say in how things are done, and (4) more beautiful cities and countryside. The differences among nations are striking. Not surprisingly, growth is the top goal in many developing nations. After a half century of Communist-controlled economic failure, Eastern Europeans clearly want growth: 80 percent of Bulgarians and Romanians and 75 percent of Russians and Ukrainians put growth first. Likewise, now that they have discovered the benefits of globalization and innovation, most Southeast Asian nations want growth: 82 percent of Indonesians, 70 percent of Taiwanese and Vietnamese, and 65 percent of Malaysians favor growth. Surprisingly, less than half of Chinese and Indians put growth as their top goal, in part because relatively large shares favor strong defense and a clean environment. But while many of the emerging nations that compete with the United States put growth first, fewer than half of Americans, and even smaller proportions of Western Europeans and Japanese, believe that economic growth should be their nation's top goal. With the exception of civil war–torn Rwanda, no nation has a larger share of citizens choosing a strong defense (30 percent) than the United States.[58] Europeans and the Japanese rank even lower on growth than the United States because a large share put "having a greater say in how things are done" as a higher priority than growth. When fewer than half of a nation's population favors growth as the most important aim for their nation, it's hard to mobilize support for innovation and innovation policy.

We see similar attitudes when people are asked about whether more emphasis on technology is good or bad. Again, many other parts of the world strongly favor technology. People in Asian nations in particular see technology as an unalloyed good. The net "good" score (the percent of people favoring technology minus those who see it as bad) was 84 percent in Vietnam, 70 percent in Taiwan, and 53 percent in Malaysia and Indonesia. Even the Asian nations that didn't put growth at the top of the list favored technology. Japan's net "good" score was 62 percent, while China's was a whopping 87 percent. In contrast, the United States' "good" score was just 44 percent and Western Europe's about the same. In other words, citizens in most Southeast Asian nations have a much more positive attitude toward technology than those in the United States and Europe. These attitudes appear to matter, as there is a strong positive correlation (0.44) between the extent to which a nation's citizens think that more emphasis on technology is good and those nations' overall per capita gross domestic product (GDP) growth rate during 2000–2010.

To be sure, in an economy and society buffeted by the winds of change and risk, stability has a certain appeal. But in a world in which innovation is consciously limited, incomes will increase more slowly, and technological progress to improve health and provide new products and services will decelerate. Winning countries will be those that embrace risk and change, see neo-Luddite arguments as special-interest pleading, and resist giving in to neo-Luddite pressures. Asian countries seem to have an advantage here; they appear more aggressively focused on driving economic growth, face fewer social factors inhibiting innovation, and possess a citizenry eagerly clamoring to experiment with and adopt new technologies.

Businessmen Who Distrust Their State

We've seen how both interest-based and ideologically based neo-Luddites fight innovation. Perhaps this kind of opposition is to be expected. But at least industry should be a natural supporter of innovation policy since the goal of such policy is to spur more competitiveness, innovation, and productivity, particularly in enterprises.

However, as David Vogel argues in "Why Businessmen Distrust Their State: The Political Consciousness of American Corporate Executives," because of historical differences in development patterns and the role of the state, nations differ in the extent to which business leaders favor state support of innovation and competitiveness. Vogel writes: "There is, in fact, relatively little principled opposition toward strong government by French, German, or Japanese businessmen."[59] However, the prevailing view of U.S. (and U.K., as we note in chapter 3) business executives is that government has little role to play, other than to get out of the way and "do no harm." Vogel continues: "What is so striking about American business ideology is the remarkable consistency of business attitudes toward government over the last one hundred and twenty-five years. A sense of suspicion toward the state has managed to survive the most impressive and decisive political triumphs."[60] Vogel is not suggesting that business should support central government planning. Rather, his point is that if a nation is to win the race for global innovation advantage, its business community should not reflexively reject any action by government (other than cutting tax rates and supporting education and basic science) as inappropriate.

At a recent roundtable on innovation policy, several experts, including Dr. Atkinson, expressed support for a more active U.S. government role to promote innovation, including the development of a national innovation and competitiveness plan that identifies key technology areas, such as electric batteries. One business executive immediately took exception, arguing that the United States didn't need an "industrial policy"; rather, the government should just "let a thousand flowers bloom." Ironically, the executive worked for the American division of a Japanese car company that had benefited from the Japanese government's well-funded strategy to develop batteries for electric cars. Upon questioning, the executive confirmed that, yes indeed, the Japanese government's "industrial policy" to support battery innovation played an important role in his company's success in the marketplace, but even so, the United States should not copy these kinds of policies. It was his mind-set as an American executive that shaped his opinion, for such views are in the DNA of U.S. business executives.

It's not just individual executives who hold such beliefs. Much of organized business views government this way. When the U.S. Chamber of Commerce touts such bromides as "We know that only American free enterprise is capable of meeting this challenge and creating the innovation and opportunities of America's future," it sends a clear signal that government policy to spur innovation is not wanted. Despite the fact that U.S. manufacturing has been losing in the race for global innovation advantage, the National Association of Manufacturers (NAM) is hardly any better in its lack of robust support for government policies to spur industrial renewal. NAM proclaims that "the private sector generates economic growth that benefits all citizens. Therefore, a central objective of federal fiscal policy should be to provide a favorable climate in which the private sector can flourish."[61] For NAM, goverment just needs to leave its members alone and all will be well. And of course, the National Federation of Independent Businesses is on the same page, as exemplified by Chief Executive Dan Danner's statement that "politicians do not create jobs. Jobs will be created by the hard working small business men and women when these entrepreneurs have taken enough calculated risks needed to expand their businesses."[62]

One could argue that the Chamber of Commerce and the NFIB have these views because they represent Main Street companies that do not need a government supportive of innovation. Indeed, other innovation-based industries are in fact more favorable toward government innovation policy. For example, the Information Technology Industry Council, a trade association representing major IT hardware, software, and device companies, actively supports government innovation policies in the areas of science and science education, trade policy, and technology platforms like health IT and the smart grid.

Surely, the individuals who work in entrepreneurial technology companies must hold a similarly supportive view. After all, the federal government has played a key role in the development of the IT, biotech, and energy industries. But often they don't. In testimony to the House Science Committee, Paul Holland, general partner at the Silicon Valley venture capital firm Foundation Capital, worried that prior testimony had implied that government should have too much of a role, and argued (incorrectly) that government had nothing to do with the success of companies like Intel, Apple, or Google.[63] Paul Mason, managing director for Starnet, LLC, a San Francisco firm that operates R&D partnerships, echoes this dismissive view, stating: "In our system, our government is not organized to innovate. Government . . . only collects taxes and divides up power."[64] Michael Arrington, founder of the Silicon Valley blog "TechCrunch," complained that it was time for Washington to "just leave Silicon Valley alone."[65] No need for a more generous R&D tax credit, intellectual property (IP) protections, federal funding of research, or a trade policy to protect open markets? To say that such ideologically inspired statements blithely ignore history is an understatement.

While distrust of a proactive role for government in innovation is deep in the psyche of American business, perhaps this is beginning to change, in part because more business leaders see their own companies challenged by foreign companies that are backed by their states. In 2010, General Electric CEO Jeff Immelt acknowledged that China is becoming increasingly hostile to foreign multinational firms, stating: "I really worry about China. I am not sure they want any of us to win, or any of us to be successful. We are a pathetic exporter . . . we have to become an industrial powerhouse again but you don't do this when government and entrepreneurs are not in synch."[66] Immelt went on to volunteer his time and leadership to chair President Obama's Jobs Council. Former Intel CEO Andy Grove writes: "Our fundamental economic beliefs, which we have elevated from a conviction based on observation to an unquestioned truism, is that the free market is the best of all economic systems—the freer the better. Our generation has seen the decisive victory of free-market principles over planned economies. So we stick with this belief, largely oblivious to emerging evidence that while free markets beat planned economies, there may be room for a modification that is even better."[67] Former Microsoft CEO Bill Gates has called on the United States to develop a major clean energy innovation strategy: "To achieve the kinds of innovations that will be required, I think a distributed system of R&D with economic rewards for innovators and strong government encouragement is the key."[68] Dow Chemical CEO Andrew Liveris has written a book, *Make It in America*, about renewing American manufacturing.[69] Only time will tell whether Immelt, Grove, Gates, and Liveris are anomalies or representative of a maturing U.S. business community as it wakes up to the nature and scope of the international competition it faces.

The Neoclassical Economics Naysayers

In most nations, policymakers look to economists for both guidance and blessings on their economic policies in general and innovation policies in particular. Unfortunately, depending on the economic doctrines subscribed to by these economists, policymakers can get very different advice about how or even whether to spur innovation.

It would be one thing if economics were like physics. When the Chinese government wants advice on how photons are transferred on fiber-optic cables, their physicists will tell them the same thing that American, Brazilian, or French physicists would tell their governments. But if they want advice on how to grow their economy, their economists will tell them very different things than would U.S. economists. For the dirty little secret in economics—as much as economists wish it weren't so—is that economics is more an art than a science, and different economists have quite different views. This means that nations whose economists understand the importance of innovation and the need for smart innovation policies will more likely do well in the race for global innovation advantage.

Unfortunately for some nations, especially the United States, the experts charged with dispensing economic advice and passing judgment on economic policy proposals are neoclassical economists, who neither understand nor appreciate innovation. What's worse, they look suspiciously at even the most "light-touch" attempts to spur innovation through proactive policies as being destructive "industrial policy."

Who are neoclassical economists? The short answer is most economists, at least most of those advising policymakers in the United States and Commonwealth nations. The membership card for this club is a Ph.D. in economics, not from just any Economics Department but from one at an esteemed university teaching the right (that is, neoclassical) brand of economics. At the top of the economics hierarchy are either leading scholars at the top economics departments or scholars who have also done a stint in government, usually as secretaries or undersecretaries in Treasury Departments or Finance Ministries, advisers to national leaders (in the United States, this means being on the Council of Economic Advisors or National Economic Council), or heads of budget agencies. Lower-ranking but still top-quality economists hail from less renowned universities and occupy less important government posts (such as assistant secretaries). Members span the political spectrum. In the United States, for example, Greg Mankiw and Glenn Hubbard spent time in the Bush administration before going back to academia (Harvard and Columbia, respectively). Likewise, Robert Lawrence and Alan Blinder served as top advisers for President Clinton before returning to ivy-clad halls (Harvard and Princeton, respectively), while Larry Summers (Harvard), Peter Orszag (Brookings), and Christina Romer (Berkeley) all advised President Obama.

Neoclassical economics is a straitjacket when it comes to innovation policy. To understand why, consider its basic tenets. A guide to help high school students study for the Advanced Placement Macroeconomics test defines economics as "the study of how to allocate scarce resources among competing ends." In other words, neoclassical economists don't study "how societies create new forms of production, products, and business models to expand wealth and quality of life" (that is, innovation). Rather, they study how commodities are exchanged in price-mediated markets— why, for example, one manufacturer sells more widgets than others. Federal Reserve Bank economist Stephen LeRoy notes: "The single most important proposition in economic theory, first stated by Adam Smith, is that competitive markets do a good job in allocating resources."[70] But the unasked question is how companies produce widgets in the first place. Innovation doesn't come from allocating widgets more efficiently; it comes from making widgets more efficiently and, more to the point, by inventing better widgets and then developing better models by which to sell them (maybe selling widgets over this new thing called the Internet). In short, the real issue is how to expand the economy's supply potential (in economics-speak, how to move the long-run supply curve to the right). Conventional economists know little about this issue, and much of what they think they do know is wrong. As noted innovation economist Joseph Schumpeter once stated: "The problem that is usually visualized is how capitalism administers existing structures, whereas the relevant problem is how it creates and destroys them."[71]

U.S. policymakers interested in crafting policies to achieve an additional 15 percent increase in per capita GDP in ten years will get little in the way of guidance from the neoclassical economics guild residing at think tanks or government agencies, especially the Treasury and the Office of Management and Budget (OMB). Seeking such guidance would be a fool's errand because neoclassical economists would just report that there is little government can do to boost long-term growth. At best, they hope government will avoid missteps that would reduce the fixed rate of growth the "market" will produce on its own. No wonder economics is known as "the dismal science."

Alan Blinder summed up the conventional view when he stated: "Although economics can tell the government much about how to influence aggregate demand, they can tell it precious little about how to influence aggregate supply. . . . Nothing—repeat, nothing—that economists know about growth gives us a recipe for adding a percentage point or more to the nation's growth rate on a sustained basis. Much as we might wish otherwise, it just isn't so."[72] And it doesn't really matter much whether the economists are Democratic or Republican; the advice is largely the same. Greg Mankiw, former CEA director in the Bush administration, states that "the sources of strong productivity growth [in the 1990s] are hard to identify."[73] With advice like this, no wonder the U.S. political dialogue gives scant attention to innovation-led growth and policies needed to promote it.

To the extent that conventional economics focuses on growth at all, it is based on what is called the Solow growth model, named after MIT economist Robert Solow, who in the 1950s tried to explain how the U.S economy expanded. In this pioneering work, he found that the likely factors (for example, capital investment and education levels) accounted for very little. The residual—the part not explained by the variables—was actually much larger. Solow called it "technical change." But this wasn't really saying much, for as Stanford economist Moses Abramovitz famously stated, the residual represented "the measure of our ignorance." And after more than fifty years, this is still the case. Conventional economists continue to look at innovation as Solow did: it falls like "manna from heaven." Or, to put it more formally, conventional economics sees innovation as exogenous—or outside their models—and therefore beyond legitimate economic inquiry. As Harvard's Elhanan Helpman notes in *The Mystery of Economic Growth*, "The subject of growth has proved elusive and many mysteries remain . . . the mystery of economic growth itself has not been solved."[74]

If innovation is so important, why does conventional neoclassical economics ignore it? Akin to the drunk who looks for his keys under the streetlamp, conventional economics ignores innovation because so much of it is in the dark and hard to measure. As Mankiw states, "Knowledge is an unmeasurable variable." For neoclassical economists, if you can't measure it and put it in a complex mathematical equation, it simply doesn't matter. What is under the streetlamp of these economists? Sitting under the bright lights of macroeconomic statistics are measurable processes of exchange (such as investment levels, interest rates, inflation rates, sales of goods and services, and money supply). Consequently, they rely on complex, calculus-filled mathematical models incorporating these variables rather than on actual studies of how businesses, industries, and national economies work.

When neoclassical economists acknowledge any role for government, they envision it as simply to ensure a good business climate, including protecting property rights and providing public goods like science and education. Anything beyond that is derided as "industrial policy," or even worse, socialism. And while liberal economists want the government to intervene, it's not to spur growth but to ensure a fairer allocation than the market will produce. But they see this as coming at a price. As Alan Blinder writes, "Policy changes that promoted equity (such as making the tax code more progressive or raising welfare benefits) would often harm efficiency."[75] But as a liberal neoclassical economist, he would sacrifice growth for fairness, arguing that "we need not summarily reject a substantial redistributive program just because it inflicts some minor harm to economic efficiency."

In other words, conventional economists believe that the pretax marketplace is efficient and that government policy (like taxes, regulation, and spending) distorts Adam Smith's "invisible hand." When asked if the government should be focusing on key industries (like robotics), former Obama economic czar Larry Summers reflected this conventional view and dismissed the idea out of hand, claiming: "I think anyone who has studied some of the countries that we compete with, who's studied our own country's experience with synfuels, for example, has to recognize that it's a mistake to think that people sitting here in Washington, no matter how well motivated, are going to be as attentive to what customers want, what can and what cannot be commercialized."[76] It's okay for California (if a country, the world's eighth largest) to pick winners, but not the United States. In dismissing the need for actions by the government to help boost U.S. competitiveness, Mankiw framed the choice in this overly simplistic way: "Policymakers should not try to determine precisely which jobs are created, or which industries grow. If government bureaucrats were capable of such foresight, the Soviet Union would have succeeded as a centrally planned economy. It did not, providing the best evidence that free markets are the bedrock of economic prosperity." Thus, he makes a bold leap from having a modest government role in guiding innovation to Stalinism.

If nations want to craft effective innovation policies, they must be guided by economic thinking grounded in the twenty-first century, not the twentieth. As we discuss in chapter 5, the innovation economy is rife with "market failures" and leaving it only to "what customers want" is leaving it to less innovation and competitiveness. This is why an increasing number of nations, including many in Western Europe and Southeast Asia, look for guidance not to neoclassical economics but to "innovation economics," a new theory of economic growth based on an explicit effort to understand and incorporate innovation into economic models.[77]

Innovation economics reformulates the traditional economic growth model so that knowledge, technology, entrepreneurship, and innovation are central goals, resulting from intentional activities by economic actors, including government. It is guided by three key principles: First, that the central focus of economics should be on growth as opposed to business cycles or the neoclassical goal of allocative efficiency. Innovation economists focus on the actual processes of production and innovation, such as trying to determine why firms develop and adopt new technologies and what policies can spur them to do more. Thus, while neoclassical economists tend to rely on complex mathematical models, innovation economists care and study more about how businesses, industries, and national economies actually work.

The second principle is that innovation drives growth. In some studies, innovation economists have found that as much as 90 percent of per capita income growth comes from innovation.[78] In fact, the major changes to the U.S. economy since the mid-1990s have occurred not because the economy accumulated more capital to invest, but from innovation. The economy developed and used a wide array of new technologies, particularly information technologies. Although capital was needed for these technologies, it was not the driver; nor was capital a commodity in short supply, as evidenced by the glut of capital flowing into subprime loans in the 2000s. As such, innovation economics is focused on spurring economic actors— including individuals, enterprises and organizations, industries, and even cities, states, and entire nations—to be more productive and innovative.

Finally, innovation economics holds that while markets are important, left to themselves they will not produce the amount of innovation and growth possible without supplementation by strong public innovation policies. As Harvard's F. M. Scherer explains, the conventional model "assumes perfect competition, constant returns to scale, and the absence of externalities. . . . All three assumptions have been questioned, often convincingly, by new growth theorists."[79] Or, as innovation economists Philipe Aghion, Paul David, and Dominique Foray counter with reference to neoclassical assertions that markets alone almost always get it right, "The empirical foundations for such sweeping statements remain remarkably fragile."[80]

Governments That Ignore Innovation

Interests and ideologies that support, not oppose, or are indifferent to innovation are key to enabling nations to enjoy robust innovation rates. But to maximize innovation, nations also need a political system that supports it. Governments that put innovation at the center of their economic policies will do better, all else being equal, than governments that let other issues dominate the political process. And as we discuss in chapter 6, many nations have developed and implemented national innovation policies in order to better position themselves to win the race for global innovation advantage. Yet as we have also seen, in some economies, innovation never makes it on the stage because the stage is crowded with redistributionists. Since the early 1990s, U.S. redistributionists from both the Right and the Left have created a politics that ignores important economic issues in favor of either unimportant or destructive ones. Some interests fight for policies that do nothing to help Industrial Street and Office Complex Street; some fight against policies to help these sectors; and neither side fights for policies that would help them. Even worse, U.S. politics is increasingly dominated by hot-button, red state-blue state issues such as abortion, health care, gun control, immigration, and other sociocultural issues. Innovation policies seem always to remain the bridesmaid, never the bride. Congress talks about making the R&D credit permanent, but never does. Legislators recognize the importance of high-skill immigration, but get caught up in politics over broad-scale immigration reform. Lawmakers pass legislation authorizing more investment in science, but then don't appropriate the funding. They talk about reducing the effective corporate tax rate, but don't. They complain about ineffective trade enforcement, but can't find a way to give the U.S. Trade Representative's Office more resources for enforcement. But why would they do these things when the core economic constituencies of each party are onstage, putting on a passion play featuring Main Street redistributionists? Elected officials have only so much time and attention, and if they are spending most of it on these sidetrack issues, they can't focus on the real issues of how to keep the innovation engine healthy.

But even if we could wave a magic wand and confine the redistributionist NFIBs and CTJs to a small stage over on K Street (the street where many lobbying firms reside), Washington would still find it hard to actively support innovation, because Washington is hamstrung not only by political but also ideological gridlock. Republicans are all too often focused on limiting government's role in the economy, while Democrats want to increase it, but often in ways that would limit innovation. At the end of the day, both parties see it as the job of businesses to spur innovation. Government's job, if you are a Republican, is to give people "freedom" from taxes and regulations; and if you are a Democrat, it's to give people "fairness," entitlements, and protection from big business. As a result, both conservatives and liberals frequently leave questions of innovation and productivity off the political stage.

For many Republicans, particularly the more conservative "Tea Party" wing, a proactive innovation policy is synonymous with heavy-handed "industrial policy" or even state socialism. They believe that "government failure" is always worse than market failure. As a result, for many conservatives, the best innovation policy is a minimalist agenda focused on creating a favorable environment for the private sector through a simple and less burdensome tax code, limited government regulation, a trade agenda that simply signs more trade deals, and the devolution of many functions back to the states.

While many Democrats support public investment in science and education, social issues such as expanding health-care coverage, regulating carbon emissions, protecting consumers and workers, and helping disadvantaged individuals and communities all too often take precedence. And when tough choices have to be made between promoting innovation and supporting redistribution, their choice is usually for the latter. For example, rather than fund the America COMPETES Act in 2007—which authorized increased funding for science and science education—Congress increased funding for items like farm subsidies, income security, and health care. (Congress did later provide a one-time allocation of funds for COMPETES in the stimulus bill.) Moreover, much too often, their inclination is not to support innovation but to protect Americans from it by erecting regulatory and trade barriers. To be sure, it's important to get social policies right, particularly in an era of increasing income inequality and heightened economic risk. But absent innovation policies to produce desirable economic opportunities for American workers, social policies will be at best a limited backstop.

Both conservatives and liberals need to recognize that their long-standing views are a deterrent to success in the twenty-first-century race for global innovation advantage. Both liberal and conservative anticorporate and antigovernment stances amount to an abandonment of U.S. corporations and high-growth entrepreneurs in their fight for global market share and U.S. jobs. We should want American establishments and entrepreneurs to win this fight. We should want American establishments to have the best workforce, science, and technology transfer systems in the world. We should want American establishments to benefit from competitive tax and regulatory systems. We should want other nations to pay for U.S. exports and not steal them or force American companies to sell at lower than market prices. We should want U.S. companies to be able to innovate around technology platforms that government helps support. We should want them to have access to the best and the brightest from around the world. And we should want them to be able to access foreign markets, but in nations that are playing by the rules.

Conclusion

Innovation is in some ways quite simple: organizing societal resources (research, finances, knowledge, skills, and entrepreneurial effort) to generate new products, processes, and business models. And the way societies can support innovation is to erect as few roadblocks as possible and devote the resources needed to make it easy to improve the status quo. Recognizing the need for innovation is central. As we have seen, all of this is easier said than done. The next chapter assesses nations' and regions' prospects for overcoming these barriers to innovation.

Can Nations Overcome the Barriers to Innovation?

T here is no doubt that winning at innovation involves hard work, although a measure of luck doesn't hurt. Just ask Mark Zucker- berg, who happened to get Facebook to market and gain a critical mass of users faster than the social network's competitors. But at the end of the day, if the result of any individual effort to innovate involves a set of odds, the chances of success escalate if the individual takes the right steps. Societies are no different. If nations are organized so that individuals and organizations have the right incentives to innovate, the resources needed to innovate, and access to the customers who want innovation, then the odds increase significantly that they will be an innovation leader.

Balancing the Yin and Yang of Innovation

As we have seen, national innovation success requires not only putting in place the right policies to support innovation, but also reducing the bar- riers to innovation. Both depend on finding the right balance between three key sets of potentially competing factors: (1) individual versus collective

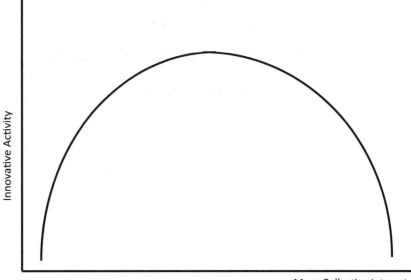

Figure 10.1 The Inverted "U" Curve for Innovation

interests, (2) current versus future generation interests, and (3) stability versus dynamism. Nations poised to do well in the race for global innovation advantage likely will be those that find the right balance between these competing interests. Such nations will have found a balance at the top of the inverted "U" curve between the two poles of these three factors (figure 10.1). Being too far in one direction will likely mean suboptimal innovation performance.

Enabling Individual Freedom versus Providing Collective Support

All societies balance an inherent tension between the public and the private good, and between individual freedom and collective responsibility. Throughout history, different societies have placed their emphasis at different points on the continuum, as have different political philosophers, from Hobbes (individual) to Marx (collective). Where to establish this balance is a key question that nations must address. Investment analyst Vinny Catalano writes: "What is the right balance? What serves the greater good:

acting in one's own self-interest even to the seeming detriment of the greater good or deferring one's self-interested benefits at potentially great individual expense (for the moment or longer) and thereby allowing others to gain?"[1] We postulate here that the nations effectively balancing the tension between individualism (emphasis on individual rights and freedom) and communitarianism (emphasis on the collective good) better position themselves to win the innovation race.

If there is too much communitarian focus and public intervention, individuals (and firms) lack the freedom and incentives to innovate. Likewise, if nations are too top-down in their efforts to innovate, they risk not only picking the wrong technologies, but limiting innovations that would emerge from entrepreneurs acting in response to market signals. By definition, innovation is about challenging the status quo, identifying unmet market opportunities, and swiftly and effectively bringing new solutions to the marketplace. No matter how "reinvented" government is, it can never do this job solely or even principally on its own. As we learned from the seventy-five-year experiment with Communism, societies that focus principally on the collective interest at the expense of the individual cannot build an innovation economy or society. As conservatives are rightly fond of pointing out, centrally directed economies that limit individual incentive cannot be innovative.

But to go from that statement to the other extreme and claim that only unfettered free markets are best for a country to succeed at innovation is equally misguided. Societies that minimize the importance of the collective, societal interest will also underperform with regard to innovation, not to the same degree as centrally directed economies, but certainly in relation to economies that find a more appropriate balance. While innovation is undoubtedly about entrepreneurs bringing new value to the marketplace, in many cases, it's not just some lone, creative entrepreneur seeing beyond where others can. Innovation more often than not involves collective action. When Sir Isaac Newton famously stated "I stand on the shoulders of giants," he meant that the advancement of knowledge requires building on what others have done before, as Steven Johnson explains in *Where Good Ideas Come From: The Natural History of Innovation*.[2] But innovation not only requires building on the work that others have done before, it usually requires coordinating with others' current work. In this sense, entrepreneurs acting on their own will not produce all the innovation that is possible. Indeed, a wide array of new economic research suggests that markets acting alone will underperform in producing innovation. As chapter 5 discusses, because of these market failures around innovation, unless society actively supports innovation, entrepreneurs will underproduce it.

Thus, the critical issue in the dynamic relationship between the individual and the community should not be framed—as it is by many economists, pundits, and policymakers—as the state *versus* the market. Instead, as *The Origin of Wealth* author Eric Beinhocker writes, the issue should be framed as "how to combine states *and* markets to create an effective evolutionary system."[3] How to craft this effective evolutionary system (Beinhocker's term for an innovation system) in the most effective way is a practical problem that should not be guided by broad sweeping ideological statements such as "government always gets it wrong" or "government should direct innovation."

One way to assess where nations stand on the continuum between the market and the state is the World Values Survey (WVS). The most recent WVS asks individuals in fifty-four countries their views on a wide range of issues, one of which is whether government ownership or private ownership of business should be increased.[4] While government ownership of business is not usually the way to maximize innovation, the question is a useful indicator of where nations stand on the continuum of individual versus collective. It is important to keep in mind that individuals' answers to the question may reflect existing levels of ownership: people in nations with higher levels of government ownership might actually want less. Notwithstanding this, the survey finds significant differences between nations.

It is perhaps not surprising that the United States ranks highest in thinking that government ownership of business should decrease, with a weighted net score of 54 for less ownership (58 for less ownership minus 4 for more ownership).[5] Commonwealth nations also favored less government ownership, with New Zealand, Canada, and Australia scoring 41, 35, and 18, respectively. Continental European nations varied. Spain and Germany, which scored 2 and 11, respectively, were only slightly more in favor of more private ownership. In contrast, individuals in Sweden (20), Finland (23), and Switzerland (24) were more strongly in favor of private ownership, but nowhere near as strongly as Americans.

Again, perhaps not surprisingly, Asian nations favor more, not less, government ownership. China had one of the highest negative scores (−38), reflecting a strong desire for even more government control of the economy than it already has. Citizens in Indonesia (−20), Malaysia (−5), Thailand (−21), and India (−7) also wanted more government control. Surprisingly, Vietnam was positive (14), but this may reflect dissatisfaction with the already high levels of government ownership there. Given the general trust in government in Asian nations, it is surprising that Japanese citizens also wanted less government, scoring in the same range (22) as Commonwealth and Nordic nations. Reflecting its long tradition of socialist thought and dictatorial governments, Latin America had very high negative scores, with Argentina scoring the highest of any nation in the survey (−56), and Chile (−30), Columbia (−29), and Mexico (−5) all favoring more government ownership.

While it is overly simplistic to say that the middle ground is the optimal place from which to drive innovation, these scores do reinforce the view that, compared to other nations, the United States is too far to the free-market side of the continuum to win in the innovation economy. In the United States, government and market are usually seen as antithetical forces, with a society only able to choose one; kind of like the old beer commercial: "Tastes Great! No, Less Filling!" And our public discourse is usually about the dangers of tilting too far toward the collective side of the continuum. Indeed, Adam Smith's widely quoted statement that the individual who "intends only his own gain" will, in the course of maximizing his needs, be "led by an invisible hand to promote . . . the public interest" is touted as Talmudic-like proof that there is no trade-off and that the right place is on the individual side of the continuum.[6] It's worth noting that devotees of Smith are asking policymakers in today's global, knowledge- and technology-based economy to base their actions on the works of someone who wrote well over two centuries ago about a preindustrial economy. Physicists don't refer back to the sacred texts of Sir Isaac Newton. Doctors don't base their treatment decisions on the writings of Dr. Charles Mayo.

Yet many U.S. economists and economic policymakers repeatedly quote an eighteenth-century tract, making the case for innovation policy a tougher one than in nations that are more balanced.

But if the United States is too extreme on the side of individual freedom and markets, other nations, most notably China, are just as extreme on the side of collective interest and state control. The Chinese government still exerts a strong role over the economy, with many enterprises still state owned and others significantly guided by the very visible hand of government. The idea that markets and entrepreneurs should be in the lead in determining the course of innovation is as foreign to China as the idea that government should be in the lead is to the United States. Absent a shift toward the individual side of the continuum, it will be difficult for nations like China to develop truly entrepreneurial economies.

Balancing the Interests of the Current and Next Generations

To maximize innovation, nations must also find the right balance between the interests of present and future generations. A nation focused only on the present generation would not invest in the future. Why pay higher taxes to support government investments in research, education, and infrastructure when the benefits accrue to future generations? But in even the most present-oriented society, people agree as part of the social contract to sacrifice at least some benefit now for greater gains in the future.

Conversely, a nation focused only on future generations would invest too much of its wealth for the future good and spend too little on current consumption. But while it's clearly a problem if nations invest too little in innovation, can nations invest too much? They can if they reduce current consumption so much that it dampens opportunities for innovation to meet consumer needs or if the future investments become big, expensive boondoggles. Innovators need a market for their goods and services, and if current consumption is limited too much, the market for innovators is artificially limited.

We only have to look at the United States and China to see this yin and yang of future versus current consumption. America's challenge is that because it has become overly focused on individual consumption today, it significantly underinvests for the future. China's problem is the opposite; it's impoverishing its current generation to prepare for the future, in sometimes wasteful ways that also retard present-day innovation.

One only has to look at policies toward currency and trade balances. America's strong dollar policy is designed to maximize present consumption. With the U.S. dollar stronger than the economy's underlying capabilities allow—as signified by accrued trade deficits running into the trillions of dollars—America's 310 million consumers can buy their imported DVD players, T-shirts, and cars cheaply, but the production base that would produce wealth in the future is hollowed out. While some of the effects of a weaker manufacturing and technology base are felt already by the 5.5 million manufacturing workers who have lost their jobs from 2000 to 2011, they will be most keenly felt in the future in the form of relatively lower U.S. productivity and a trade debt that future generations are on the hook to pay off by producing more than they consume and exporting the difference.

The U.S. trade debt is like any other debt—it will have to be paid back.[7] China, Germany, Saudi Arabia, and other nations running big trade surpluses with the United States are not just giving us DVD players, luxury automobiles, and oil. They want something in return. And while they are willing to accept pieces of paper (U.S. Treasury bills, or T-bills) now, those bills are only worth something when they are traded for real goods and services. And at some point, these nations will demand this, forcing future generations of Americans to pay off the current generation's trade debt. It's as simple as this: every DVD player, luxury automobile, and barrel of oil that Americans consume now by expanding our trade debt is a DVD player, luxury automobile, and barrel of oil that a future generation will be responsible for paying for in the form of reduced consumption of real goods and services.

If the U.S. political economy leads to a focus on maximizing current consumption, China's focus is on minimizing consumption. In part because of its culture of caring about future generations, and in part because China is ruled by an authoritarian government that can impose austerity with little fear of public backlash, Chinese policy limits citizens' after-tax income and uses the surplus to maximize future investment. The primary way China does this is by undervaluing its currency. As noted, the $426 billion current account surplus China accumulated in 2008 did not boost the living standards of present-day Chinese citizens; all that value was transferred outside China's borders. If China balanced its trade and purchased more foreign products instead of foreign T-bills, the average Chinese household would see a 17 percent increase in disposable income, as represented by the increased imports they could enjoy. So why is Chinese economic policy designed to impoverish its current generation by running huge trade surpluses (instead of importing more)? Because it hopes to gain global industrial market share that could benefit future workers—and because China's Communist leaders believe that it is only by expanding exports that it will create enough jobs to perpetuate the regime's political stability.

We see this tension between present and future consumption not just in currency policy, but in many other areas, including infrastructure policy. Infrastructure—the basic facilities, services, and installations needed for the functioning of a society—entails tangible physical infrastructure such as bridges, roads, rails, airports, pipelines, water systems, electrical networks, and energy storage facilities. It also entails digital infrastructure such as smart electric grids, fixed and mobile broadband communications networks, digital databases, and standards. For at least three decades after World War II (WWII), the United States led the world with the most advanced physical infrastructure and made large and sustained investments year after year. Yet today, near gridlock on many roads in large metropolitan areas, crowded airports, collapsing bridges, and electric grid failures are all a consequence of America's unwillingness to invest for the future. In fact, the United States ranks just twenty-third out of 139 countries in the overall quality of its infrastructure.[8] In 2009, the American Society of Civil Engineers gave America's infrastructure an average grade of D. The society estimated the five-year investment need to restore crumbling infrastructure at $2.2 trillion.[9]

The United States reaped the benefits of previous generations' foresight and investment, generations that developed and built a transportation system that became the envy of the world. But since the early 1980s, Americans have violated the pact by which current generations invest to make the future better than the present. An ever-expanding backlog of investment needs is the price of our failure to maintain funding levels. Revenues raised by all levels of government for capital investment total only about one-third of the roughly $200 billion necessary each year to maintain and improve the nation's highways and transit systems.[10] While Americans have expected to be served by high-quality infrastructure, they have been increasingly less willing to contribute the money needed not only to maintain the infrastructure but also to expand it to meet the needs of a growing population. As figure 10.2 shows, the average age of the government capital stock (which includes assets such as roads, bridges, and water systems) has increased by almost 50 percent since 1970 as the nation has failed to invest adequately to replace aging infrastructure.[11] It's interesting to note that the average age of nonresidential infrastructure (the buildings and machines used by the private sector) also grew during 2000–2010 by about one year, as U.S. companies cut back investment in favor of paying higher dividends to shareholders who demand their fair share now.

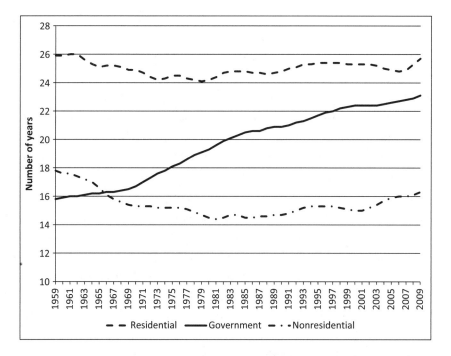

Figure 10.2 America's Aging Infrastructure: Average Age of Capital Stock
Source: Based on statistics from the U.S. Bureau of Economic Analysis.

Compare this to China, which is enjoying an infrastructure boom, spending more than 15 percent of its gross domestic product (GDP) on domestic infrastructure projects.[12] In 2010 alone, China invested 682 billion yuan (about $100 billion) in twenty-three major new projects. Between 2000 and 2009, China invested more than 2.2 trillion yuan ($330 billion) in 120 major infrastructure projects.[13] For example, in transportation infrastructure, China plans to double the size of its high-speed rail network—already the largest in the world—by laying down more than twenty-six thousand miles of additional track by 2020.[14] For automobiles, it's building tens of thousands of miles of expressways and will surpass the United States in highway mileage in less than a decade.[15] From 1997 to 2009, China invested 4.3 trillion yuan ($650 billion) in Internet infrastructure, constructing an optical communications network five million miles long and providing broadband access to 96 percent of Chinese towns.[16] China's investment also includes the most expensive infrastructure project in the world, the enormous South-North Water Transfer Project, which will divert fresh water from the Yangtze River to dry northern cities like Beijing at a projected cost of up to 420 billion yuan ($60 billion)—more than twice the cost of China's recently completed Three Gorges Dam, the largest hydroelectric power station in the world.[17]

But where the United States is underinvesting in infrastructure, China may be investing too much too rapidly, and without enough attention to quality, as several recent derailments of its high-speed trains attest. Moreover, while China is building massive research parks, at least some are underutilized with quite low levels of occupancy. One such industrial park had room for a thousand companies, but had only forty-two tenants. For many of these investments, there is no serious consideration of return on investment, even though infrastructure investment only makes sense if the expected net present value returns exceed the cost of capital.

With regard to scientific research, we see the same dynamics. Investments in science can take as many as forty years to pay off, but on net provide very high societal rates of return. But as with infrastructure, while the costs are borne by the present generation, many of the benefits accrue to future generations who didn't pay for the research. From WWII until the 1970s, the United States led the world in investment in research. But now, with 2.8 percent of GDP devoted to research and development (R&D), the United States ranks just eighth among countries tracked by the Organization for Economic Cooperation and Development (OECD) in R&D intensity, behind Israel, Finland, Sweden, Korea, Japan, Denmark, and Switzerland. Each of those countries has a R&D intensity greater than 3 percent, with Israel leading the way with an astounding R&D intensity of 4.3, followed by Finland and Sweden with exceptionally strong rates of 4.0 and 3.6 percent, respectively. Compared with these countries' commitment to investing in R&D, the United States is lagging considerably. As noted, the primary reason for this decline has been a decrease in federal funding. In the first decade of the 2000s, federal investment in R&D as a share of GDP was just 44 percent of levels in the 1960s (1.75 percent versus 0.77 percent). In fact, from 1987 to 2008, federal R&D investment grew at just 0.3 percent per year in constant dollars—much lower than its average annual growth of 4.9 percent from 1953 to 1987—and ten times lower than the rate of GDP growth over that period. Among thirty-six nations, the United States ranked only twenty-eighth in the growth of government investment in R&D from 1999 to 2009, with a growth rate seventeen percentage points below the average of the other nations.

What is especially troubling about these trends is that while Americans as a whole have gotten richer, they have also become more shortsighted and self-interested. In the 1960s, when R&D was 1.75 percent of GDP, this meant that Americans were willing to invest 2.8 percent of their income in government R&D. Today, with per capita incomes almost three times higher in real dollars, Americans are only willing to invest 0.48 percent of their income in government R&D (just 17 percent of the 1960s level). To see the extent of this shift to the present-day side of the continuum, consider that in the 1960s, the total of government investment in R&D, infrastructure, and education, plus the trade surplus (or deficit) minus the national debt, equaled 3.1 percent of GDP. In the 1970s, this figure fell to 0.8 percent, but was still positive. In the 1980s, it went negative, to −3.3 percent of GDP. In other words, we were cutting investments in the future while running up bills for the future. In the 1990s, with the decline in the trade and budget deficits, this composite figure improved slightly, to −1.3 percent. However, from 2000–2010, it plummeted to −4.5 percent of

GDP. In other words, from the 1960s to 2010, there has been a shift of 7.6 percentage points in the amount of investment for the future and future debt. And this doesn't include the estimated shortfall in state and local government public pensions of at least $2.5 trillion.[18]

While the WWII generation ran up huge budget deficits to pay for the war effort, its members also largely paid off that debt, leaving their children a legacy of low debt, modern infrastructure, great research facilities, and trade and capital account surpluses, which the Baby Boom generation then promptly squandered. Yet today, the Baby Boomer generation has done the opposite. Today, the Left rejects cutting entitlements—including to people ages sixty-five to seventy, most of whom could work—as a way to pay for needed investments and reduce future debt, while the Right rejects increasing taxes on individuals as a way to pay for needed investments. What do they have in common? A short-term individualistic orientation: "Me, now!" As James Lincoln Collier wrote in *The Rise of Selfishness in America*, "A nation in which most people cannot even occasionally put the good of the whole society above their own immediate gratification is bound to grow steadily worse."[19]

If the United States is all about "Me, now," China is about "Us, then." Not only is China impoverishing its own current generation, it's impoverishing future generations of Americans through its huge trade surplus. China is investing hundreds of billions of dollars in the future—in research, infrastructure, and overall economic subsidies, including currency manipulation. And while some of this investment is surely efficient in the sense of providing a reasonably high social rate of return, some of it—and perhaps much of it—is inefficient and wasteful. Japan recycled its trade surpluses of the 1990s back into building physical infrastructure and proceeded to waste a significant share of it on "white elephant" projects. The Chinese are doing the same today, and, through forced societal savings, they are limiting domestic markets that could spur entrepreneurial growth.

Balancing Employment Stability and Dynamism

To maximize innovation, societies have to be able to accept what Schumpeter called "creative destruction"—the development of new kinds of organizations and technologies that often displace old ones. While all change involves risk, if a nation's residents view change as too risky, they are likely to resist change and press for stasis and stability. But conversely, dynamism can be too high in nations if employment security is too low. Take Japan and the United States as examples of this yin and yang.

In the 1980s, many who studied the Japanese economic miracle praised Japan for its system of lifetime employment, arguing that it gave workers the security they needed to accept the innovations their firms might make. In contrast, U.S. workers, who had less employment security and a very weak social safety net, were more likely to resist organizational innovations. Today, the problem for Japan and similar nations (including many in Europe) is that a system of security through employment gives companies little incentive to adopt innovations that boost productivity since there is almost no way to reduce head count. In Japan, at a 2011 Chief Technology Officer (CTO) forum on innovation at which Rob Atkinson spoke, the discussion turned to why Japanese enterprises invest so little in information technology (IT) (less than half the rate of U.S. enterprises). The CTO of a major Japanese electronics corporation explained: "Why invest in IT when if it successfully raises productivity you are limited in your ability to reduce head count?" Indeed, when Japanese companies do lay off workers to become more productive, they are often publicly castigated. In June 2010, Naoto Kan, Japan's prime minister, criticized Nissan CEO Carlos Ghosn for firing workers, even though Ghosn had rescued Nissan from bankruptcy. Much of the resistance to laying off Japanese employees stems from the fact that it can be quite difficult for them to get new jobs. And if they do get one, they usually suffer a loss in salary, seniority, and pension.

If entrepreneurial ventures were plentiful in Japan, that would be one thing. But disruptive entrepreneurial ventures that might displace existing organizations are viewed with suspicion in Japan. At the same forum, the moderator raised concerns about clean energy innovation because it might lead to job losses for Japanese oil refining and gas station workers. The conversation then turned to attitudes toward entrepreneurship. Atkinson mentioned that his nineteen-year-old son was studying computer science and hoped to be part of a successful IT start-up by the time he turned twenty-five, something his parents heartily endorsed. At best, their son

would be part of a successful company, and at worst he would learn valuable skills that he could take to his next company. In response, a Japanese
executive fretted: "In Japan, most parents would be extremely worried if
their son wanted to go down this path, for if the start-up failed, what would
he do next? He would likely be unemployed or face a series of low-wage,
dead-end jobs. Better that he go to work for a large, stable corporation."
This, in a nutshell, explains why there is so little entrepreneurship in
Japan. But it also explains why the Japanese government has worked to
limit mergers and bankruptcies, since both usually result in firm restructuring and employment loss. This overriding focus on stability leads to a
society where elevators in many stores are still operated by pretty young
women, even though most countries phased out elevator operators decades
ago. Yukio Hatoyama, leader of the ruling Democratic Party in Japan, bases
his political philosophy on what he calls "fraternity," which means empathy
toward workers, rather than a concern with corporate profits. But what about
empathy toward Japanese consumers who are stuck with higher prices?
Japan's quest for a "humane" and stable economy is a recipe for a low-
growth economy.

Japan is by no means the only nation where employment security acts as
a barrier to innovation. While it's easier for French employers to lay off
workers, they pay a high price, usually having to pay tax-free redundancy
benefits to employees and, even then, they are not off the hook. In France,
when Molex, an electronics parts maker, closed a plant that had been un-
profitable for years, it paid out $42 million in redundancy payments, but
affected employers sued the company demanding even more. When the
company stopped payments in response, the French government's minister of industry publicly called the firm's behavior "scandalous" and ordered
French car makers to stop doing business with the supplier.[20] In Argentina, states such as Santa Fe have even outright banned large grocery
stores from laying off employees.[21]

If the Argentines, Japanese, and French resist change because their employment security is so strong, Americans resist it because their employment security is so weak. U.S. workers have few protections, and companies
can and do engage in corporate restructuring that leads to layoffs. The
upside is that companies can more easily reengineer work to boost produc-

tivity and to lower prices for consumers. The downside is that this makes it simple for companies to take the easy way out and move jobs offshore to cut costs rather than doing the hard work of automating labor domestically and investing in the skills of their workforce (leading to some layoffs, rather than an entire plant being shuttered). Another upside of the U.S. environment is that American workers are much more likely to start new companies, in part because if they fail, they can more easily get back in the workforce as compared to Japanese workers. But if American workers are "free agents" as compared to Japan's "organization men," they also are free agents working without a net. If U.S. workers lost their jobs, at least before the recent health-care reform legislation, they risked losing health insurance coverage (if they even had it through an employer), their home, and more. In most cases, the newly unemployed are eligible for only minimal short-term unemployment insurance benefits. For these reasons, many Americans have turned against globalization and innovation, seeing it as a threat to the fragile security they might have at work.

The key to success for nations is to combine flexibility for organizations to restructure and to innovate (including the ability to go out of business when entrepreneurial competitors come up with a better widget) with security for workers. But the security should not be tied to employment, as it is in Japan, but rather to employability. This describes a model that several Scandinavian nations have adopted called "flexicurity" (a combined term for "flexible security"). Flexicurity systems include:

- comprehensive lifelong learning strategies to ensure the continual adaptability and employability of workers;
- effective active labor market policies that help people cope with rapid change, reduce unemployment spells, and ease transitions to new jobs; and
- modern social security systems that provide adequate income support, encourage employment, and facilitate labor market mobility.[22]

Flexicurity is based on the reality that employment security is decreasing. To help workers manage, they will need new kinds of security—not to help them stay at a particular job, but to help them effectively transition into new employment through viable skills.

One model is Finland. It has created a flexicurity program that includes features such as requiring employers to give workers who are to be released paid time off during the notice period for the purpose of job seeking, giving employees a right to a reemployment program, and providing increased and more effective employment office services.[23] It also helps in Scandinavian nations that health insurance is not a function of employment; thus, if workers lose their jobs, they don't lose their health coverage. All of these factors are why a Swedish labor union leader stated: "Swedish unions don't fear new technology; we fear old technology." In other words, if the companies they work for don't continually modernize, they will risk losing all their jobs. So they are willing to risk having their companies restructure work through new technology because they know that loss of a particular job is not catastrophic.

The Innovation Success Triangle

If national balance with respect to the three "yin and yang" factors is the key to success in the race for global innovation, there are a number of specific individual components that nations must also master. Indeed, national innovation success depends on a range of factors, and nations need to get most of these right to win the race. One way to understand these factors is to conceptualize an "Innovation Success Triangle," with business environment factors along one side, the regulatory environment along another, and the innovation policy environment along the third (figure 10.3). Success requires correctly structuring all three sides of the innovation triangle.

Factors comprising an effective business environment include the activities, institutions, and capabilities of a nation's business community. Innovation-friendly factors include: vibrant capital markets, but also ones that discourage short-term investing; a population that accepts and even embraces churn and change; high levels of entrepreneurship; a culture in which interorganizational cooperation and collaboration is accepted; high levels of university licensing and patenting; strong IT adoption, especially among business; strong executive management skills; and a business investment environment that strikes the right balance between short- and long-term goals.

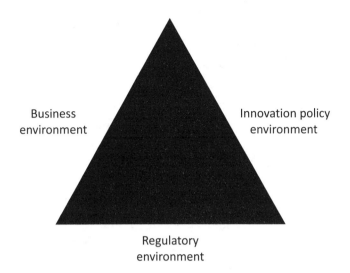

Figure 10.3 The Innovation Success Triangle

An effective regulatory environment features a competitive and open trade regime, including an aggressive stance by government to protect its businesses against foreign mercantilist attacks; processes by which it's easy to launch new businesses and to bring innovations to market; transparency and the rule of law; a reasonable business tax burden; robust and competitive product and labor markets; a strong patent system and protection of intellectual property; and limited regulations on the digital economy. To be sure, a good regulatory climate does not mean simply the absence of regulations. As we saw with the recent financial crisis, the right kinds of regulations are critical to ensuring that markets work and innovation flourishes. But nations need a regulatory climate that supports rather than blocks innovators and that creates the conditions to spur ever more innovation and market entry.

The final leg of the triangle is a strong innovation policy system. This includes generous support for public investments in innovation infrastructure (such as science, technology, tech transfer systems, and rural broadband and other digital infrastructures); channeling R&D into spe͏ci͏f technology or industry research areas; funding sec university-government research partnerships; reshapin code to spur innovation and IT investment, including expenditure incentives; a skills strategy, including high-skill immigration and support for science, technology, engineering, and math (STEM) education; encouraging private-sector technology adoption, especially by small and midsized manufacturers; supporting regional industry technology clusters and regional technology-based economic development efforts; active policies to spur digital transformation in the private and nonprofit sectors; and championing innovation in the public sector.

Innovation Prospects for the World

As nations compete to win the global innovation race and try to master the innovation policy triangle, some will sprint out ahead, others will remain stuck in the middle of the pack, and still others will struggle to get out of the starting gate. Nations and regions face different challenges in the race. No nation has it entirely right just yet, although a few come close. While some nations—such as Japan and much of Europe—have strong innovation policy systems, many of them suffer from limited regulatory and business environments. Others, like the United States, have reasonably good business and regulatory environments, but weak innovation policy environments. The nation that can put together all three sides of the triangle most effectively while managing the yin and yang of innovation is likely to be the nation that wins the race.

The United States: Boston or Buffalo?

A century ago, two of the fastest growing, most dynamic metropolitan areas in America were Boston, Massachusetts, and Buffalo, New York. As historian Mark Goldman writes, "In 1901, the year Buffalo hosted the Pan American Exposition, the city was buoyant and rapidly expanding. With more than 350,000 people its population was growing rapidly while its economy was strong and diversified. Commerce, Buffalo's traditional source of wealth, gave every sign of remaining prosperous. . . . Meanwhile, the development of heavy industry, particularly of steel, pointed to still more growth and greatness. Buffalo's growth had already been remarkable and its future seemed filled with promise."[24] But the greatness lapsed as

Buffalo's economy declined. Goldman continues, "By the 1970s and early 1980s, all the high hopes that the people of Buffalo had once had for the city had been dashed." By the mid-2000s Buffalo's population was around 270,000, half of what it was at midcentury, and 80,000 less than a century before. Its once monumental steel mills are largely shuttered, and the economy now depends on a mix of service sectors, including higher education, regional banking, and government services.

In 1900, Boston looked like it faced similar prospects. It hosted thriving textile and shoe industries and had long been a commercial trading center. But by the Great Depression and especially after WWII, many of the textile and shoe firms fled the Boston region for cheaper labor in the South, just as many manufacturing firms have now decamped for cheaper wages in China. Boston looked like it was on the same path to decline as Buffalo. But as chapter 1 explains, Boston subsequently reinvented its economy on several occasions, notably after WWII and again in the 1980s, and today boasts a diverse innovation-based economy with thriving biotechnology, IT, and financial services sectors.

The history of the American economy shows that some places, partly through a combination of luck and location, but also grit, have been able to rebound from adversity and transform themselves as the overall economy transforms. But other places were not as adaptive and suffered as a result. The key question, therefore, is whether over the course of the next two decades the United States will be like Buffalo and sink further into relative decline or, like Boston, rise again from its decline through innovation and economic transformation.

There are certainly reasons to believe that the United States is on the Buffalo path. America has become a society obsessed with short-term gain, both in business and society at large, and does not seem to be able to summon the will to invest for the long term. Moreover, American society and politics have become much more concerned with protecting, preserving, and redistributing our previously accumulated wealth than with growing wealth anew. It has had significant difficulty summoning any kind of moderate, pro-market but also pro-government policies.[25] Our foreign policy is focused on military, not economic, issues. We have schizophrenic positions on immigration and attracting foreign talent. We have developed a perverse egalitarianism and anti-elitism that bode ill, for it means that efforts to enable excellence—whether it's separate toll lanes or high schools for those gifted in math and science—are branded as antidemocratic and elitist. Finally, the federal balance sheet is deeply in the red with no more money available for investment in the future. America has spent it all and has refused to cut wasteful spending, especially the massive entitlements for retirees who are retiring earlier and living longer, or to raise taxes on individuals, with the result that there is nothing left to make the kinds of public investments in innovation the nation needs. In addition, the nation has a political economy culture that seeks to minimize the role of government in supporting companies' innovation efforts.

Yet notwithstanding this array of challenges, America is not necessarily destined to become Buffalo because, like Boston, it comes to the race with enduring strengths. It retains a creativity and risk-taking orientation that other nations and regions lack, particularly Asia. Its IT companies continue to be global leaders. It has a strong network of universities and national laboratories. And it's wealthy enough to make big bets on future investment should it choose to do so.

Returning to the innovation success triangle, the U.S. business environment—with the exception of a shortsighted investment focus on the part of U.S. businesses, no small deficit—is mostly strong. And while the regulatory environment weakened some in the 2000s, it generally supports private-sector innovation. The big challenge for the United States is its innovation policy environment, where the federal government underperforms in terms of what we call the four Ts (tax, trade, technology, and talent).

However, it's possible that there is an emerging awareness that the path America has been on is not sustainable. And should this awareness broaden, it could very well lead to action, just as the Japanese/German challenge to the United States of the late 1970s and early 1980s led to action. If Churchill was right when he said that you could count on the Americans to do the right thing once they've exhausted all the other options, Americans have to recognize that they have come close to exhausting all the other possibilities and need to begin to take bold action. And they will have to recognize that success in this new twenty-first-century race has to be won with help from all three sides of the triangle, including a much more coherent and robust innovation policy side. To date, such recognition has not been apparent, although, in some pockets, it is growing.

Europe: Italy or Finland?

For most of the postwar period, productivity grew faster in Europe than in the United States, partly as Europe caught up to the American lead established in the last quarter of the nineteenth century and the first half of the twentieth century. But after 1995, the trend reversed, with U.S. productivity growing faster, even after the European Commission stated its intention with the 2000 *Lisbon Strategy* to become the world's innovation leader by 2010. If the challenge for the United States is whether it will be Buffalo or Boston, the challenge for Europe is whether it will be Italy or the Nordics.

Italy was not always a study in economic decline. While the United Kingdom was losing its industrial advantage in the 1950s and 1960s, Italy was enjoying what many at the time called the Italian economic miracle—called in Italy, "il boom." But since 2000, the boom became a bust, with one result being that "a fairly large amount of Italy's economic literature has recently focused on the country's stagnation."[26] Italy's numerous small enterprises, which were once an advantage because of their flexibility, are now a disadvantage because they can't boost productivity enough to compete with firms in nations like China and they can't diversify fast enough into industries and technologies that low-wage nations have difficulty moving into. Marco Annunziata, the London-based chief economic analyst at Unicredit, stated: "The country has stagnated for at least the last ten years. We have an enormous public debt with no room for maneuvering in the budget. We have low productivity, and growth probably the lowest in Europe. And because of global competition, the system is only going to get worse."[27] Italy is, in fact, one of the few old European nations that has a net outmigration of college graduates.[28]

Compare that with Nordic nations like Denmark, Finland, and Sweden, which have been able to stay competitive in global markets by boosting productivity and continuing to invest in R&D and education. Two decades ago, most pundits wrote off the Nordics, claiming that their social democratic model of high taxes, high social benefits, and worker security was antithetical to innovation and growth. But unlike many European nations, the Nordics took action. They lowered their corporate tax rates and introduced investment incentives. For example, Sweden slashed its corporate tax rate from 52 percent in 1989 to 26.3 percent today.[29] The Nordic countries invested in innovation to a significant degree, through their universities and through specialized national innovation agencies. They developed national innovation strategies. Even the unions got in the game, with many of the private-sector unions understanding that employer innovation and adoption of new technologies were instrumental to their own future. And their citizens appear to have a much greater appreciation of the importance of innovation than Italian citizens.

It's important to note that there is considerable variability within Europe in how countries are doing on innovation, particularly by region and over time. Northern and Western European countries considerably outperform those in Southern and Eastern Europe, with Spain, Italy, Portugal, Slovenia, Slovakia, and Greece all in the bottom half of the Information Technology and Innovation Foundation's (ITIF's) *Atlantic Century II* assessment of the innovation capacity of forty-four countries and regions. At the same time, several of the larger European economies have demonstrated slow progress in improving their innovation capacity since 1999. Out of forty-four countries and regions, France ranks thirty-seventh, Germany thirty-eighth, and Italy forty-fourth in improving their innovation capacity during 1999–2011.[30] The Baltic nations have performed much better in this regard, with Estonia, Latvia, and Lithuania placing fifth, seventh, and twelfth, respectively.[31]

Assessing Europe through the Innovation Success Triangle yields mixed results. European businesses actually perform fairly strongly on innovation. In fact, the European Union's (EU's) *Sixth Community Innovation Survey* (CIS) found that 52 percent of EU-27 enterprises reported innovation activity between 2006 and 2008.[32] By comparison, the U.S. National Science Foundation's 2008 *Business R&D and Innovation Survey* (BRDIS), which covered the same period and asked the exact same questions as the CIS, found that just 9 percent of surveyed U.S. firms were active innovators from 2006 to 2008 (although about 22 percent of U.S. manufacturing companies reported innovation activity).[33] A 2004 OECD report prepared by Eric Bartelsman found that the "rates of innovation" between U.S. and EU enterprises were actually the same, and that in contrast to popular belief Europe was not behind.[34] However, Bartelsman found that the United States did a much better job than Europe of more quickly allocating capital and labor to the most promising innovative concepts and start-up businesses, so the United States was spawning more "winners," even though the underlying rates of innovation were analogous. This points to the weaknesses many European countries face with regard to bureaucratic regulatory environments that impede capital and labor movement and place unnecessary burdens on firm creation and dissolution. With a regulatory system that embraces the precautionary principle—which holds that if an action or a policy has a suspected risk of causing harm to the public or to the environment, in the absence of scientific consensus that the action or policy is harmful, the burden of proof that it is *not* harmful falls on those taking the action—Europe's regulatory approach is actually biased against innovation and is clearly the weakest link in its innovation success triangle.

Yet it's not as if the countries in the European Union—not to mention the European Union itself—aren't trying to win the innovation race. In fact, at least they know they are in a race and need innovation policy to help them win. And, as we have seen, many European countries do have strong innovation policy environments, supported in many cases by national innovation foundations and cogently articulated national innovation strategies. Several Northern or Western European countries, including Denmark, Germany, Finland, France, the Netherlands, Sweden, and the United Kingdom, are clearly toward the front of the pack in terms of their innovation policy efforts.

However, if all it took was intention to win, Europe would be a lot farther ahead, for European policymakers have at least conceptually said many of the right things, as evidenced by proclamations such as Europe's *Lisbon Strategy*. While the *Lisbon Strategy* produced some benefits, it's generally regarded as having failed to meet its goals, and thus the European Union launched an updated *Europe 2020 Strategy* in June 2010 that set concrete goals for the EU and each of its member states around five core objectives—employment, innovation, education, social inclusion, and climate/energy—to be reached by 2020.[35] To be sure, such strategies are laudable and, in pockets, European countries have made strides. But such strategies have yet to transform the continent into the world's clear innovation leader, in large part because Europe still has not realized that it cannot achieve an innovation economy without embracing at least a modest amount of Schumpeterian creative destruction while rejecting a smothering and unaffordable welfare state.

Regarding the first problem—the lack of full implementation—a challenge for Europe is that it is still a collection of different nations with different languages, laws, and regulations, which makes the emergence of continental-wide markets difficult to achieve, particularly in services sectors such as law, accounting, and medicine. The halting efforts to create a European patent system provide another example of the difficulty in developing an integrated European innovation ecosystem. And the fiscal crisis within Europe in 2011 and 2012 has shown how tenuous the entire European project is. Moreover, as an entity, the European Commission has not had the budgetary power to enact European-wide innovation policies, particularly science and technology (S&T) policies, at the right scale. To date, the continent has relied instead on underfunded national policies. However, recognizing these challenges, on November 30, 2011, the European Commission announced Horizon 2020, a new financial instrument for research and innovation funding for Europe that seeks to invest €80 billion ($106 billion) from 2014–2020 in both scientific and technological-based innovation and also nontechnological and social innovation. Though the proposal awaits approval by the European Parliament, Horizon 2020 represents a significant financial commitment toward bolstering Europe's innovation competitiveness.

But as for the second challenge, as much as European leaders embrace innovation, they have a decidedly schizophrenic view of it. When they refer to innovation, they really mean science- and technology-based jobs, not innovation. This is because innovation is the constant transformation of an economy and its institutions, and one thing Europe does not want is constant transformation, especially if it has the potential to upset the delicate balance of their social democratic societies. Even though Schumpeter was a European, Europeans are not Schumpeterians. They want the benefits of a knowledge-based technology economy without the creative destruction that not only accompanies it but also is required to achieve it. Some in Europe get this. For example, one of the goals of SITRA, the Finnish Innovation Fund, is to "promote systemic innovation in Finnish society."[36] But the visionaries are working uphill to convince fellow Europeans. Paul Giacobbi, a member of the French Assembly, states: "The idea that nothing will change, no factory will ever close, and restructuring will not be a permanent feature is contrary to everything that the direction of the world tells us every day."[37] Unless Europe can accept that innovation entails plant closures and job losses, new technologies with uncertain social or environmental impacts, and new kinds of business models and organizations, it's not likely that it will be able to keep up in the race for global innovation advantage.

Southeast Asia: Export Mercantilists or Model of Balanced, Productivity-Led Growth?

When looking at the more developed economies of Southeast Asia, including Japan, Singapore, Korea, and Taiwan, one must certainly be impressed with their ability to become technology leaders, particularly in high-tech manufacturing. China has developed into a manufacturing powerhouse and India seeks to be a leader in IT. Many of these nations have been able to maintain or even to grow manufacturing as a share of their economies. Japan, in fact, remains a leader in sectors like electronics and manufacturing, and is well positioned in emerging industries such as robotics and nanotech-based materials. Remember, it was General Motors (GM) and Chrysler that went bankrupt and had to be rescued by the government, not Toyota and Honda. In fact, as the *Economist* notes, Japanese firms hold more than 70 percent of world market share in thirty industries worth more than $1 billion, including digital cameras and car navigation devices.[38] And Japan and Korea are extremely well positioned to lead in clean energy, as their global leadership position in batteries and hybrid cars demonstrates.

ITIF's *Atlantic Century II* study found several Asian nations toward the lead in the race for global innovation advantage. Moreover, it found that Asian countries scored well, both on overall scores and on change scores. While China ranked thirty-fourth overall, it is quickly catching up to—and in some cases surpassing—the United States and Europe in terms of aggregate scientific publications, patent applications, and science and engineering graduates. China's rapid ascent is reflected in the fact that it ranked first in rate of change in enhancing its innovation capacity during 1999–2011 in ITIF's 2011 *Atlantic Century II* study. China's technological prowess can no longer be dismissed with a simple wave of the hand. But China is not alone among major Asian economies in significantly bolstering its innovation capacity since 1999. In fact, in ITIF's *Atlantic Century II* report, Korea ranks second, Singapore eighth, and Japan seventeenth on improving their innovation capacity since 1999.[39] Put simply, these four Asian nations, plus Taiwan, are strong innovation competitors—and getting stronger.

For its part, Korea has the distinction of being one of the fastest-growing economies in history, having the same per capita income as Afghanistan in the 1950s, and now having a per capita income equivalent to that of the United States in 1979. Like Japan, Korea focused societal investment on manufacturing industries, and its companies moved up the value chain to produce better-quality and more complex products. (Remember the poor quality of the original Hyundai cars?) Taiwan also has grown rapidly, first being an assembler of commodity technology products, but quickly moving up the value chain to become a force in its own right in manufacturing high-tech products. And Japan, ignored by many U.S. economic pundits as an economic basket case, is in fact much healthier than overall GDP figures indicate, in large part because this number reflects the declining age of its working population as the Japanese society ages. In fact, Japan has slightly outperformed the United States in per capita income growth since the early 2000s.[40]

But historically, much of the innovation in Southeast Asian nations has been a matter of copying innovations produced elsewhere, particularly in the United States, perfecting and building on them, and then exporting them, usually to the United States. The strength of these nations has largely been around engineering prowess. Two questions in particular face these nations: First, will they be able to develop truly entrepreneurial economies and at the same time grow the productivity of their anemic nontraded sectors? As these nations advance, development through adoption of existing innovations will prove harder. They will need to develop stronger abilities to truly innovate on their own. This will require real risk taking and break-the-mold entrepreneurship, which to say the least is hard in Southeast Asia. Japan in particular has very low levels of venture capital investment and its new business starts are quite low. And in China, the educational system and the culture continue to produce individuals who do not question the status quo, a key factor in enabling entrepreneurship.

The second question facing Southeast Asian nations is whether they can find a way to grow without relying almost solely on exports. While Japan boasts world-leading exporters of manufactured products—think Hitachi, Panasonic, and Toyota—its nontraded sectors are decidedly subpar. Japan's service sectors have achieved but a fraction of U.S. service-sector productivity levels. Japan's retail sector has achieved barely half of U.S. retail productivity levels, while its construction and food-processing industries have reached only 40 and 33 percent of U.S. productivity levels in these sectors, respectively.[41] Low levels of service-sector productivity explain why the whole of Japan's economy, even with some of the world's most productive manufacturing industries, is only 80 percent as productive as America's. When only about one-quarter of your economy is growth oriented, you can't grow very fast. Low service-sector productivity also afflicts Korea. As Kim Jung-Woo of the Samsung Economic Research Institute notes, "Compared to the biggest OECD economies, the productivity of South Korea's service industries appears to be low. If South Korean service industries' productivity continues to remain low while their weight in the GDP grows, it could undermine the productivity of the nation's whole economy."[42] But this should come as no surprise. Fifty years of economic policy in almost all Asian countries have focused on only one goal: becoming export power-houses. The domestic serving sectors were left to atrophy.

This same dynamic is even worse in other Southeast Asian nations, especially China and India. Thus, the challenge for the poorest Southeast Asian nations like China and India is simple: Can they embrace productivity and markets? What probably strikes many visitors to India and China is the building boom, which is evident almost everywhere. But what visitors may not notice as readily are the rampant levels of inefficiency and over-manning. What's done in the United States by one or two workers is often done in China and India by a multitude. At a recent visit to China, we found our hotel's front desk staffed with seven or eight clerks, even though we never saw more than two or three other guests there. At the pool, three workers staffed the cabana, although this being December, we saw only one hearty guest braving the unheated pool. At a nearby park, seven government workers were huddled together to weld one chain. At a local deli, three people handled paying for the sandwiches: one put your sandwich in a bag, another took your money, and a third put the money in the register and handed change back to the second person. A shopping "mall" might have hundreds of tiny vendors all selling pretty much the same small selection of items (toys, jewelry, electronics, and the like). India is even worse. At airports, five workers accept passengers' boarding passes, a job that would be done by one worker in the United States. To fill potholes on a street, fifteen workers went back and forth carrying the gravel in buckets atop their heads. The examples could go on and on.

This is why, despite industrialization and technological advancement, output per Chinese and Indian worker is just 14 percent and 8 percent, respectively, of U.S. levels. Perhaps they were taking Milton Friedman's tongue-in-cheek advice literally: While visiting a developing Asian country where a new canal was being built in the 1960s, he was shocked to see that instead of modern tractors and earthmovers, the workers had shovels. When he asked why there were so few machines, the government official explained: "You don't understand. This is a jobs program." To which Friedman replied: "Oh, I thought you were trying to build a canal. If it's jobs you want, then you should give these workers spoons, not shovels." China and India are by no means the only nations who prescribe "spoons."

Why is this featherbedding so high and productivity so low? We spoke to a CEO of a major Indian manufacturing company and expressed puzzlement as to why so many Indian operations were so overmanned. Instead of agreeing and complaining about how Indian workers and governments force companies to be inefficient as we expected him to, he replied "India cannot afford productivity, we need the jobs." Like so many business and government officials in developing nations, he had bought into the myth that productivity kills jobs. When the CEO of one of India's largest companies says this, you know there is real resistance to change. But India has a long tradition of supporting inefficiency. After independence from Great Britain, the new government passed laws limiting the size of certain enterprises in order to create jobs. For example, pencil makers could grow no larger than fifty employees, which resulted in India having one of the world's most inefficient pencil industries, meaning that few Indians could even afford a pencil. India, after all, was the inspiration of much of the nonsense spouted by E. F. Schumacher in his best-selling antiproductivity book *Small Is Beautiful.*

With productivity so low, you'd think that raising it would be job number one for countries like China and India.[43] But it isn't. To the extent that China and India are focused on growth, it's on high-tech growth for export markets. Both nations want to get rich not by across-the-board productivity gains, but by restructuring their industrial mix toward more productive sectors. For India, this means sectors like computers, biotechnology, and IT services. For China, it means pretty much every technology-based export industry. This approach is much easier politically than actually encouraging the domestic competition and "creative destruction" that are needed to drive across-the-board growth.

Even if they could succeed in increasing their global share of high-tech production, it's not the path to growth. For example, if India could raise productivity in its retail trade and banking sectors to just 30 percent of U.S. levels (currently, they are at 6 percent and 9 percent, respectively), it would raise its standard of living by more than 10 percent. This would create more wealth than the entire Indian IT services industry. Likewise, Chinese economic officials are on a campaign of "industrial restructuring" to move away from low-value-added industries to higher-value-added ones such as autos, electronics and information, and petrochemicals. But even if they can expand these industries by 50 percent and even assuming that they account for around 10 percent of Chinese jobs and are 50 percent more productive than the industries they replace, China only will have generated the equivalent of fourteen months of economic growth.

These dual economies (a few world-class exporters and a lot of subpar domestic serving firms) in Southeast Asia are no accident. Southeast Asian economies are not set up to be high-productivity economies for the simple reason that the raison d'être of their economic strategies since WWII has been export-led growth. In other words, economic planners bought into the notion that the way to grow your economy is to shift your industrial base to high-value-added, export-based sectors. And they did so quite successfully.

Yet countries like Japan, with their myopic focus on export-led growth, largely missed the greater opportunity to improve national economic growth by increasing the productivity of their domestic sectors, particularly through the application and diffusion of general-purpose technologies such as IT. Indeed, Japanese firms have invested much less than U.S. firms in productivity-enhancing IT. Economists Jorgenson and Nomura find that investments in IT can explain the productivity differences between the United States and Japan since 1990. The authors found that Japanese productivity levels increased from 52.4 percent of U.S. productivity levels in 1960 to 86.1 percent in 1990 (during the Japanese economic miracle). Yet, since the mid-1990s, the productivity gap between the two countries has widened to 79.5 percent. Fukao and Miyagawa suggest that sluggish Japanese productivity growth after 1995 has been due to insufficient investment in IT capital.[44] Japanese firms may know how to make computers, but they do not use them as well as U.S. firms do. This is not because they don't know how to use them, but because using them the right way is too disruptive. Japanese corporations continue to rely on custom-designed software instead of standard, off-the-shelf software that American firms use, in part because this is a way to keep their workers from moving to competitors' firms where they'd have to learn a whole new system. It may keep their workers tethered, but it keeps their productivity low.

If Southeastern Asian nations wish to raise their living standards, they would be much better off abandoning their mercantilist, export-led strategies in favor of a broad-based innovation and productivity strategy. The path to higher incomes lies in raising domestic productivity by all firms in all sectors, including in unglamorous sectors like hotels, restaurants, retail distribution, utilities, and government services. To take just one example, the use of IT in all sectors of the Chinese economy was responsible for 38 percent of the increase in the country's productivity growth from the late

1990s to the mid-2000s.[45] Boosting efficiency in the economy, in part by using more IT but also by creating the competitive and market conditions for firms to become more efficient, is the royal road to growth.

Countries relying predominantly on export-led strategies risk being a one-trick pony: They may reach the technological frontier and boost growth for a while, but they are liable to languish there, or perhaps even decline if global export markets become saturated and as countries with more robust service sectors pass them by. Clearly, this explains Japan. Once it caught up to the world technological frontier by the 1980s in industries like automobiles, consumer electronics, and semiconductors (by using an imitative catch-up strategy based on export-led growth) its growth slowed, not having as much success in several key technologies that have subsequently emerged, notably biotechnology and IT usage.

But it also explains China, Korea, India, and many other Asian nations that all looked to Japan as the model: crank up the export machine, including through a wide array of unfair or dubious trade practices, and sit back and reap the benefits. For example, Jong-Won Yoon, a leading Korean economist, reflected this when he wrote: "The Korean economic miracle has been based on efficiency in mass production and an export-orientation strategy. . . . [But] for a recovery in the potential growth rate it will be necessary to shift to a high-value-added industry structure."[46] In other words, just find an even higher-value export sector to ride to prosperity.

For Japan, the benefits are over; for the Koreans and Singaporeans, they are coming to an end soon; and for China, they will continue but plateau at some point in the future unless China changes course. There's pretty much no way Japan can continue to grow through the tech-mercantilist model. It remains to be seen whether it can summon the understanding and political will to shift strategies—for doing so risks alienating powerful political constituencies that enjoy the safety of lack of competition domestically. It's even worse for the Japanese "wannabes." Nations like China are on a path to becoming Japan, with competitive export sectors but woefully lagging domestic services sectors. However, unlike Japan, China will never get there: it will not be able to generate the needed trade surplus because the United States and Europe are no longer in a position to import at high enough levels. You can only take out "bank loans" for so long before the bank won't lend to you. And, eventually, China will have to stop giving other nations products for nothing in return.

Japan in particular has its own unique challenges. In many ways, Japan is a contradiction. It's home to companies that dominate global markets in many areas. Government works closely with industry to help it remain technologically cutting-edge, including having leading-edge broadband Internet networks. This is the Japan Inc. that was so much in the news in the 1980s and 1990s and is still a force to be reckoned with. But at the same time, Japan is a nation where true innovation is rare, where entrepreneurship is looked down upon, and where most young people want the security of large corporations. It's a place where many industries, especially ones serving national markets, are protected from real competition. It's a place with relatively slow productivity growth, and very low levels of corporate adoption of IT.

For Japan, we posit that the choice is between the vision of Japan Inc. or the one exemplified by Takfumi Horie. A relatively young entrepreneur who founded Livedoor, a Web site design operation that grew into a popular Internet portal, Horie became a billionaire, the likes of similar high-tech millionaires in America. Similar to his typical American counterparts, he tried to buy a sports team. He also tried to take over a broadcasting company without its approval. And he was criticized by conservative business circles in Japan for his unconventional manner—including his informal attire (such as wearing T-shirts to business meetings). Horie was everything Japan Inc. was not. Perhaps this is why in 2007 he was convicted of securities fraud. Whether he was guilty or simply a target of the establishment because he had the audacity to shake things up, we have no idea. However, it is clear that Japan would benefit from more people like Horie (leaving aside the purported securities fraud).

In other words, the challenge for Japan is whether it embraces a more dynamic and entrepreneurial economy and the risks that brings, or tries to optimize Japan Inc. the best way it can. Sticking with the latter brings significant risks, the two primary ones being failure to increase productivity in Japanese firms and difficultly in developing new, entrepreneurial companies.

China has different challenges. At the risk of being flip, perhaps the best analogy with regard to the choice confronting China is whether it will be the Borg or the Klingons. In the futuristic TV series *Star Trek: The Next Generation*, the United Federation of Planets, a collection of largely democratic, freedom-loving planets in the galaxy, faces its greatest threat: the Borg. The Borg is a pseudo race of cybernetic beings that exists as a collective. It operates solely toward the fulfillment of one purpose: to add the biological and technological distinctiveness of other species to their own in the pursuit of perfection. This is achieved through forced assimilation, a process that transforms individuals and their technology into the Borg.

The Borg is a useful analogy for what appears to be Chinese innovation policy: to forcibly assimilate all foreign technology into the Chinese collective so that China can become completely self-sufficient. This appears to be the Chinese strategy: don't trade for things in industries China is weak in, try to dominate every industry. Indeed, China's 2006 Medium and Long Term Technology Plan reads like a plan to dominate virtually every advanced technology sector. The problem with the Borg strategy is twofold, as chapter 7 discusses. It's ultimately a costly strategy for China since its citizens must give up massive amounts of current consumption for the hope of future consumption, partly because so much is wasted. And it ignores the vast benefits from boosting the productivity of sectors that aren't traded in global markets. But unlike the Borg, China can't entirely consume other worlds. China's dependence on the U.S. economy—especially given its own underdeveloped services economy—means that if China continues to do too much damage to the U.S. economy, it's only dampening its long-term growth prospects, especially if it seeks to continue to grow primarily through exports.

The alternative to the Borg scenario is for the Chinese to follow the Klingons. The Klingons, a race in the galaxy and once enemies of the Federation, realized that they would prosper if they aligned with and joined the Federation as partners—which they did, to their clear advantage. In some ways this describes China's choice. They can continue to follow the Borg strategy, which ultimately will result in conflict with the rest of the world, or they can join the "United Federation of Nations" as a full partner, and behave responsibly. Behaving responsibly means renouncing IP theft (including cyber-theft and industrial espionage), letting their currency shift in response to international market signals, abiding by the rule of law, and generally moving away from state capitalism. The choice is theirs, although as we note in chapter 8, America and Europe can and should help them move in this direction.

Finally, India has its own question and challenge: Can it reduce corruption and ineptitude by government officials? As the *Economist* recently asked, "Is Indian capitalism becoming oligarchic?" For all of its success as a global IT offshoring hub, India suffers from uncompetitive domestic markets and inept and sometimes corrupt governments.[47] One Indian corporate lobbyist described the central government as an ATM machine and "our shop." It can take years if not decades to get infrastructure and other projects through the government approval maze. And much of the economy is still operated by state-owned enterprises and long-standing private enterprises with connections to the government. According to the World Bank, only four out of every ten thousand Indian firms go bankrupt each year, compared to three hundred in the United States. Without effective churn to weed out inefficient and inept firms, it's hard for an economy to be innovative. India could take an important and symbolic step in this direction by allowing big-box retailers such as Walmart and Tesco to sell directly to consumers and not be required to enter into joint ventures.[48]

Finally, it's important to point out that Asia and America face almost opposite challenges. By and large, America has a highly productive and innovative domestic services sector. Its hotel, insurance, logistics, and retail sectors are the best in the world. New business models in services industries appear all the time. Companies use high levels of IT and in effective ways. But it's America's export sector that is in crisis. For much of Asia, it's the opposite; their export sectors are vibrant and productive and their domestic service sectors languish. But for both, innovation is the answer: for America, an innovation and innovation policy built around traded sectors; for Asia, one built around domestic sectors.

Latin America: Can Government Get Out of the Way?

A century ago, Argentina was one of the richest nations in the world. Anyone visiting Buenos Aires sees the evidence of this in magnificent, century-old cathedrals and promenades. Today, it barely qualifies as a developed nation. But this is the tragedy of Latin America. Like the Eastern Bloc nations after WWII, Latin America wasted decades, in large part due to misguided economic policies and fragile, often corrupt, political regimes. With Latin American nations switching between socialist regimes that want to regulate and even confiscate private-sector growth and corrupt dictatorial right-wing regimes, it has been difficult to achieve market-based entrepreneurialism supported with smart innovation policies. On top of this, a culture that gave short shrift to science and engineering, preferring the elegance of political theorizing, made it hard to develop a real innovation economy. Finally, a deep distrust of competitive markets in many Latin American nations, including Argentina, Brazil, and Uruguay (each with the rate of citizens' favoring competition lower than the United States by 40, 66, and 41 percent, respectively), has meant a willingness to tolerate uncompetitive markets and the inefficiency and stagnation that come with them.

Perhaps the most significant barrier was that in the 1960s and 1970s, many Latin American nations latched on to the failed import-substitution industrialization (ISI) model of economic development, thereby rejecting the liberal, GATT-based, free-trade and open investment regime institutionalized after WWII.[49] Whether the measure has been growth rates, current account balances, or income distribution, the ISI strategy has performed poorly, for several reasons. ISI failed because it depended on markets that were too small or too poor to provide economies of scale and on demand conditions that were too isolated to produce globally competitive industries. This typically resulted in inefficient production of bad products by insulated state-owned and private enterprises.[50] The stiff tariffs and restrictions that Argentina and Brazil place on imports of foreign computers and components in an attempt to spur development of local high-technology industries, such as computers, are an excellent example of failed ISI policy. These policies have only had the effect of raising IT prices for domestic players, causing productivity growth in the service sectors of these economies to languish. But the political system keeps them in place, despite their costs to consumers and the economy. For example, in 2009, Argentina's new president, Cristina Kirchner, revived the country's 1970s-era protectionist industrial policies by imposing restrictive import-licensing requirements and applying what's known as *el impuestazo*, or the Big Tax—a doubling of the value-added tax on imported electronics.[51] Moreover, the Argentinean government is requiring some manufacturers to match every dollar worth of products they import to the country (such as component parts) with a dollar's worth of exports, an approach it's calling export equalization.

Unfortunately, the damage done by such poor Latin American economic policies continues to impact the innovation capacity of countries like Argentina, Brazil, and Mexico today. ITIF's *Atlantic Century II* study found Brazil to rank just thirty-eighth, Mexico fortieth, and Brazil forty-second out of forty-four nations and regions in innovation capacity. Worse, these countries are in the bottom half at rates of improvement in innovation capacity since 1999, with Brazil coming in twenty-sixth, Mexico twenty-seventh, and Argentina thirty-second.

Thus, the challenge for most of Latin America is to embrace democratic, rule-of-law regimes combined with free markets and robust innovation policies. Fortunately, there is evidence that the forces of innovation and innovation policy are emerging in several Latin American countries. Colombia has launched an ambitious and thoughtful innovation strategy called Colombia 2025.[52] Uruguay has developed a national innovation strategy and launched a national innovation agency, which has as a key mission assisting Uruguay's entrepreneurs. After the fall of the Pinochet government, Chile embraced a democratic path that both respects markets and supports a role for government in innovation policy. Brazil has developed a national industrial strategy that includes a focus on innovation and industrial leadership in sectors like pharmaceuticals, aviation, and renewable fuels, although it will do better to focus on its services sectors too. But for now, these are the exception rather than the rule. For Latin American nations to begin to move up the rankings in the race for innovation advantage, such measures will have to become the norm.

Conclusion

No country or region has it right just yet. Each has at least some strengths, although some have more than others. Finding that sweet spot (balancing individuals and society, present and future, dynamism and security) that most favors market-based innovation and government innovation policy will be an enduring challenge for every nation. To go back to our sports analogy, winning the global race for innovation requires hard work and commitment on the part of individual nations. And if they can do that, they will see their standings go up relative to their competitors. But that won't be enough to maximize global innovation. We need to move innovation from the minor leagues to the major leagues, and the way to do that is to rethink the overall global innovation governance system.

11

Creating a Robust Global
Innovation System

We want to end this book the way we started it, with a vision. We envision the global race for innovation advantage as one in which virtually all nations win, with higher productivity and per capita incomes, new and better products and services, and a better quality of life for all. We picture a world in which potentially catastrophic problems of hunger, disease, and environmental degradation are effectively tackled, reducing the risks of wars over scarce resources. In our vision, transformative technological and scientific advances help unite nations and people in common pursuits. And finally, we see old global institutions upgraded and redesigned for a global marketplace characterized by cooperation and fair play. The old-age Washington Consensus, designed sixty years ago for a postwar world, would be replaced with a newly minted Innovation Consensus designed for today's geopolitical and economic arrangements. It sounds too good to be true. But it doesn't have to be.

Why can't the world enjoy much higher rates of innovation and productivity? Why can't major, pressing global challenges be solved, such as curtailing climate change and curing major chronic diseases? And why can't we do so in ways that benefit both individual nations and the world as a whole? The pessimists will proffer their usual rebuttals, such as: the environment can't handle humankind getting richer; too many nations are corrupt or inept; corporations and the wealthy will capture the benefits of innovation;[1] the markets will get us there in their own sweet time, while any effort to push the envelope is doomed to failure; and innovation only ends up creating winners and losers.

While it's not clear that we can achieve this vision, there is really no compelling reason why not. Even if there is an inherent "speed limit" for innovation that we can't exceed, we are not anywhere close to approaching it. At the end of the day, maximizing innovation requires the will and the resources to do the right thing. Unfortunately, too few nations are organized in ways to maximize innovation. Nations underinvest in innovation because many of its benefits spill over to the rest of the world. Too many nations are focused on innovation mercantilism, which sometimes boosts innovation within their borders, but reduces innovation elsewhere. And the de facto system of global governance is not designed to spur nations to do the right thing or to deter nations from doing the wrong thing. As a result, the world produces significantly less innovation than is possible and is needed. The major challenge for the community of nations, therefore, is to create a robust global innovation system with considerably higher rates of win-win innovation and considerably lower rates of win-lose innovation.

The Failure of Global Economic Institutions

The international economic system is governed by institutions and norms rooted in a past era. The years after World War II (WWII) were characterized by the paramount leadership and power of the United States, the advent of the cold war, and chronic poverty and underdevelopment in what came to be known as the third world. In essence, the global trading and financial system was a closed club. The Communist and developing world, a majority of countries, were not integrated into that system. Now that they are largely integrated, the international order has failed to produce a sustainable globalization system, in part because it is still organized to deal with finances and the flow of commodity goods across borders, not with innovation, and because many of the nations that have joined have not embraced market-based globalization. As such, the global system does little to promote innovation policies and even less to pressure countries engaged in innovation mercantilism to play fairly. In essence, there is no one in charge of supporting and refereeing the global innovation competition. Not only are the three major international economic organizations—the International Monetary Fund (IMF), the World Bank, and the World Trade Organization (WTO)—not designed to play this role, but to the extent that they try, they act largely as if they were in charge of a soccer game and getting paid by the teams they referee.

Let's start with the IMF. Established after WWII, the IMF was charged with overseeing the international monetary system—the system of exchange rates and international payments that enables countries and their citizens to buy goods and services from one another. The new global entity was designed to ensure exchange rate stability and encourage member countries to eliminate exchange restrictions that hindered trade. This was critical, for according to the IMF, "During the Great Depression of the 1930s, countries attempted to shore up their failing economies by sharply raising barriers to foreign trade, devaluing their currencies to compete against each other for export markets, and curtailing their citizens' freedom to hold foreign exchange. These attempts proved to be self-defeating."[2]

As a result, under rules established by the IMF, each member country has agreed not to engage in "protracted, large-scale intervention in one direction in the exchange market." These are nice words, but it's too bad they are largely meaningless. The IMF has proven unwilling to take action to curtail currency manipulation or to create a sustainable global innovation system. Case in point, the IMF's Executive Board concluded its 2010 Article IV consultations with China mostly by praising the Chinese authorities. The board stated that their "quick, determined, and effective policy response [to the global financial crisis] has helped mitigate the impact on the economy and ensured that China has led the global recovery."[3] Yes, China led the global recovery, but by massively subsidizing its export industries, thereby cranking up its mercantilist export machine, which in turn slowed the recovery in other nations. Amazingly, the IMF's directors "welcomed China's recent decision to return to the managed floating exchange rate regime," even while they "agreed that the exchange rate is undervalued."

Moreover, they noted, "In the twelve months to May, the nominal effective exchange rate has depreciated by 1.25 percent while the real effective exchange rate has depreciated by 0.1 percent." Thus, the IMF praised China for moving toward a more freely floating exchange rate regime, even as Chinese currency rates actually depreciated because China was committed to manipulating its currency to beggar thy neighbor—exactly what the IMF said helped extend the Great Depression.

To the extent that the IMF even views mercantilism as a problem, it sees it as being caused by the nations that are hurt by it, not by those engaged in it. As stated on the IMF Web site: "IMF policy advice called for countries that ran excessively high external deficits before the crisis to put in place plans to consolidate their public finances to maintain investor confidence, again in ways that were as growth-friendly as possible. The onus would then fall on those countries that ran excessive current account surpluses to power global demand by shifting from export-propelled growth toward domestic demand. As the currencies of economies with excessive deficits depreciated, then it would follow that those of surplus countries must appreciate."[4] In other words, the IMF is advising nations whose economies are damaged by innovation mercantilists to cut government spending (the standard IMF answer to virtually any problem), in order to devalue their currency and reduce demand for imports. This would then reduce innovation mercantilists' exports and maybe help them see the error of their ways. Ah, a devious and subtle plan. Talk about blaming the victim.

One key reason why the IMF is unwilling to enforce its own guidelines is that it's dominated by neoclassical economists. They look at China and argue that Chinese growth has spurred growth in the rest of the world because it imports more than it used to and provides low-cost exports.[5] But they fail to examine the negative impact of currency manipulation on global growth (for example, as we discuss in chapter 7, it results in a substitution of labor for capital and lowers global productivity growth). But perhaps more to the point, above all else the IMF does not want to make waves. It recently hired Min Zhu as special advisor to the IMF's managing director. Zhu was most recently deputy governor of the People's Bank of China, China's central bank. Now he is advising the IMF on what to do. Does he urge the IMF to force nations, including China, to start playing by the rules? Of course not. Rather, his advice is for the IMF to press the United States to give up on manufacturing. As he states, "You see most advanced economies are service-oriented, and emerging economies are manufacturing-oriented, partly reflecting the division of labor . . . [this] complementarity will make the world more productive and more sustainable, and the IMF should play a central role in this process."[6] This is akin to having the head of the Soviet Union's central bank being appointed to the IMF in the 1960s and advising America to stop spending money on defense. But what's worse is that in the 1960s, the IMF would have rejected Zhu's recommendation that advanced economies give up on manufacturing, but now the IMF considers it sage advice.

The World Bank is even worse, if this were possible. It not only does almost nothing to pressure innovation mercantilists to shape up, but actively supports their policies. We see this with regard to the Bank's support for China. While it might have made sense for the Bank to support China in the 1970s and the 1980s, it certainly doesn't now. China has been growing at more than 10 percent annually, in large part by engaging in innovation mercantilism that takes jobs from other nations. But this, however, has not deterred the Bank.

In 2008, the World Bank provided more than $2.4 billion in loans to China, which by 2009 was supporting seventy-five active projects. This pretty much says it all: a nation that has the largest current account surplus in world history, accrued through innovation mercantilism, can go to the World Bank to borrow money (much of it from the United States) to finance development projects to increase their exports to the United States even more. For example, the Bank funds highway and freight rail projects enabling Chinese manufacturers to more easily move their products to ports for export and to help open the interior of the country (and the hundreds of millions of untapped low-wage laborers there) to global supply chains. It provided a loan to the Chinese government to help it become more effective in economic policy (it appears to have worked, given China's massive trade surplus). A part of that loan went to support "enhanced governance in power sector." Apparently, the governance didn't include the commitment to unbiased government procurement, for the Chinese government mandated in 2005 that Chinese electric utilities buy only Chinese-made wind turbines, and not foreign ones.[7]

But it gets worse. The World Bank funded the development of a project to assess the viability of China developing high-tech research parks (that would directly compete with U.S. innovation leadership) and one to support the development of the Yangling Agricultural Hi-tech Industries Demonstration Zone, which includes twenty-two foreign companies.[8] At the same time, China actually lent more money than the World Bank to developing countries during 2009–2010. China signed at least $110 billion of loans to other developing country governments and companies in 2009 and 2010, while the World Bank made loan commitments of $100.3 billion to such countries from mid-2008 to mid-2010.[9] And Chinese loans came with strings attached to buy Chinese-made products. So, China desperately needs development assistance from the World Bank, but can loan out more money than the Bank does to others? In essence, China is using the West's own capital to curry favor and influence with developing countries.

In response to criticisms such as this, the Bank might point to projects that helped improve how the Chinese government operates as evidence that they were pushing reform. For example, the Bank made a loan to the Chinese government so it could establish a "regulatory mechanism for improving the balance of payments." The Bank initiated this project because China had a "large surplus pattern . . . shown in the balance of payments." In other words, it ran chronic trade surpluses. The project's goal was to make "recommendations on improving the balance of payments." So far, so good. At its conclusion in late 2007, the Bank noted that the project had achieved its goals, having trained more than two hundred Chinese officials on why they shouldn't run big trade surpluses and having its recommendations "adopted by the Communist Party of China Committee, the National People's Congress and the concerned government agencies. . . . For example, the Seventeenth Congress of the Communist Party of China called explicitly for 'adopting comprehensive measures to improve the balance of payments.'"[10] Maybe the Bank actually thought that when China said "improve the balance of payments" it meant reduce its massive trade surplus, rather than expand it. The Bank declared mission accomplished just six months after China's trade surplus with the world had set a record. And for the next three years, Chinese trade surpluses continued at record levels, while the Chinese government continued its staunch refusal to stop manipulating its currency. And the Bank said and did virtually nothing. Mission accomplished.

In fact, this was such a "success" that the World Bank decided to have another go at it, giving the Chinese government $20 million for a second "China Economic Reform Implementation Project." This time the Bank supported a number of studies, including ones on "the external debt status in China against the backdrop of global capital flows," and "the statistics of external debt denominated in local currencies."[11] But this wasn't the end of it. Not content to fund a study to help the Chinese manage their huge foreign currency surpluses and get higher returns from them, it helped the Chinese increase them.[12] It provided the Chinese Export-Import Bank (Eximbank) funding in 2006 to "formulate a medium-and-long-term development strategy . . . including the strategic guiding ideology, the choosing of the medium-and-long-term development strategy together with feasibility analysis, the guidelines, policies and measures for the implementation of the strategic goals." The project funded experts to consult with the Bank as well as the travel of Chinese Eximbank officials overseas to study best practices, "such as export credit, trade financing, ship financing, ODA [overseas development assistance] loan and financing for small and medium sized enterprises."[13]

Keep in mind that the main purpose of the Chinese Export-Import Bank is to fund Chinese companies so they can export, including to the United States. And they have been doing so with gusto. The Bank reports: "With China Eximbank credit support, China First Heavy Industries has seen enhanced market competitiveness and facilitated its exports of complete sets of large equipment . . . to regions worldwide," including America, to take market share away from Peoria-based Caterpillar.[14] It also provided the Aviation Industry Corporation of China with $15 billion to help China's aviation industry "achieve leaps and bounds development and seek further integration into the international aviation industry." The World Bank's actions are nothing short of extraordinary. The United States provides the World Bank with U.S. taxpayer dollars so they can fund a Chinese government agency that, in turn, can fund Chinese government corporations whose mission is to take away some of the best and highest-paid U.S. jobs.

Nor has the World Bank stopped there. In February 2012, the World Bank issued a report called *China 2030* aimed at helping the country find new growth drivers. For example, the report noted that "new technological opportunities make green development not just a realistic possibility but a potential driver of economic growth. If successful, green development will create new business opportunities, stimulate innovations in technology, and potentially make China globally competitive in sunrise industries."[15] Again, U.S. taxpayer dollars are funding an international agency seeking to directly bolster the competitiveness of an international competitor in emerging technologies and industries. It's not as if the World Bank could not have made recommendations to ensure robust Chinese growth without encouraging them to ramp up high-tech exports.

At no time according to Bank documents did the Bank in any way pressure China to stop stealing foreign intellectual property (IP), stop manipulating its currency, end subsidies to its state-owned enterprises (SOEs), or cease procurement and tax policies that discriminate against foreign-owned firms. It's not because the Bank personnel are incompetent. It's that their overriding mission is to help lower-income countries grow (even ones that need no help, like China), and they don't differentiate between legitimate policies and innovation mercantilist policies. This is because the World Bank isn't really the "world" bank; it's a collection of country desks (for example, the China desk or the Zimbabwe desk). Its development professionals appear to be evaluated primarily on one question: Did they support projects that spurred economic growth in the respective countries for which they are responsible? And if the China desk can get China to export more earthmovers, routers, biotech products, and airplanes to the United States, they get rewarded. It doesn't matter if the result is fewer U.S. workers employed making earthmovers, routers, biotech products, or airplanes. It doesn't matter if they did it through mercantilist means. It doesn't matter that by doing this they completely ignored boosting innovation and productivity in the domestic-serving parts of countries' economies.

The World Bank has become an agent and enabler of innovation mercantilists, as a function of the incentives that the Bank's organizational structure and mission dictate. We asked a World Bank official why the Bank doesn't press innovation mercantilists to change their ways. She responded with incredulity: "But countries don't want to be told what to do" (with the implication that if the Bank told countries what to do, they wouldn't want to use Bank services). And if they didn't want their services, the Bank would have to lay off Bank workers. Of course countries don't want to be told what to do. But they also don't like paying back World Bank loans, and the World Bank requires them to do that. Besides, if a country doesn't want to be told what to do, the Bank should focus even more resources on nations that will allow themselves to be told what to do. In other words, don't engage in innovation mercantilism if you want our help.

Even if the IMF and the World Bank have chosen not to make the most important global economic task—globally sustainable innovation—their mission, one might think that the WTO would. After all, the primary purpose of the WTO is "to open trade for the benefit of all." But, like the other two bodies, the WTO also has largely abdicated its role in fighting innovation mercantilism. Unfortunately, the WTO views what is actually systemic innovation mercantilism on the part of many countries as being merely occasional and random infractions of certain trade provisions that should be handled on a case-by-case basis. For them, we're all occasional mercantilist sinners and those without sin should be the ones to cast the first stone. In reality, the dominant logic toward trade in many nations, including many WTO members, is thoroughly predicated on export-led growth through mercantilist practices.

The explanation for the WTO's lassitude is that it's populated by free-trade absolutists who favor trade and even more trade, even if it's based on innovation mercantilism. Let's be clear here. This is not an argument for a return to national economies or a call for protectionism. In fact, the exact opposite is needed: the breaking down of systemic innovation mercantilism that distorts trade and innovation today. But for the WTO, this means risking a reduction in trade, since likely the only way to fight innovation mercantilism, at least in the short run, is to limit exports from mercantilist nations. The organization is loath to do that since facilitating trade is its cardinal goal.

In fact, like the IMF, rather than attack innovation mercantilist policies, the WTO would rather blame the nations hurt by those policies. Pascal

Lamy, head of the WTO, reflects the neoclassical consensus when he opines: "Current account imbalances between countries are primarily a macroeconomic phenomenon, a sign of international differences in aggregate savings and investment behaviour and have little to do with trade policy. A current account deficit of a country reflects dissaving by domestic residents—an excess of total expenditures, both private and public, over national income. A current account surplus, on the other hand, represents savings by domestic residents with national income exceeding total expenditures."[16] He even goes on to praise "imbalances," stating that they are a sign that savings in one country are being deployed or used in another country: "If investment prospects are plentiful in a country, but its residents are unable to generate a sufficient amount of saving to exploit them, foreign savings can fill the gap."[17] He doesn't seem to stop to consider that investment prospects are not in fact plentiful (the Chinese invest in low-yield U.S. Treasury bills) or that foreign savings come at the expense of domestic savings because of mercantilist-generated trade surpluses.

The reality is that the global trading system is so distorted by mercantilists that many people in many nations have lost faith in it. But rather than understand why, Lamy laments that people don't understand the benefits of free trade. It's a bit like asking why people aren't going out shopping, when every third time they go out they get mugged. Maybe they like shopping but don't like getting mugged. Lamy's answer would be to run ads saying "go shopping, it's good for you." Maybe the answer is to arrest the muggers (e.g., crack down on the systemic mercantilist violators) instead of asking, "What's the matter with you people? Why are you opposed to shopping (e.g., trade)?"

But why do these organizations, charged with making the global economy function, either sit on the sidelines or actively support nations engaged in destructive innovation mercantilism? As with most policy questions, the simplest explanation is most likely the correct one (the Occam's razor principle). Thus, the IMF, the World Bank, and the WTO don't work to support sustainable global innovation because it is either not their mission or not thought to be important. For the World Bank, two goals are most important: responding to individual national economic fiscal crises and ensuring robust international capital and trade flows. It doesn't ask if the robust international capital and trade flows are the result of deeply dysfunctional, high-tech mercantilist policies. For the World Bank, helping poor countries get richer is paramount, regardless of how this is done and who else it hurts. For the WTO, trade flow is all that matters. Going after systematic mercantilism might disrupt those flows. And overriding all of this, getting tough on mercantilism and mercantilists would rock the boat, exposing all three bureaucratic agencies to unwelcome conflict. It's easier to just go along to get along.

A Bretton Woods for the Innovation Economy?

In 1945, representatives from forty-four nations met in the small resort town of Bretton Woods, New Hampshire, during the height of WWII to make financial arrangements for the postwar world after the expected defeat of Germany and Japan. It was then that the plans for the World Bank and the IMF were created, with the General Agreements on Trade and Tariffs (GATT), precursor to the WTO, created two years later. And the global trading system more or less worked for about forty years. But as the commodity-based manufacturing system evolved into the specialized global innovation economy, the strains on the Bretton Woods framework have become ever more pronounced.

If we are to create a robust global innovation economy, the most important place to start is with the recognition that we need an international innovation policy framework. Just as the Washington Consensus rejects the need for a national innovation policy in the United States, the Geneva Consensus (the consensus of global governance institutions like the IMF, the World Bank, the WTO, and others) rejects the need for an international innovation framework. Instead, finance and trade ("capital and goods flows") are considered the key to global allocation efficiency. The notion is premised in two-hundred-year-old economic theory, which holds that each nation has a "comparative," not absolute, advantage in some things. Originally developed in the late 1800s by economist David Ricardo, the theory of comparative advantage postulates that even if one country is superior to another in the production of two different goods, if that country focuses production on the good for which it has the highest *relative advantage*, and the other country focuses on the second good, both countries will benefit from trade. For example, England may produce cloth 40 percent more efficiently and wine 20 percent more efficiently than Portugal, but if England specializes in cloth production and Portugal in wine, aggregate output will be higher and both countries will benefit.

This has become economic religion for the holders of the Geneva Consensus. The problem with the Geneva Consensus is not so much that free-trade theory is necessarily wrong (although as new trade theory has shown, it can be),[18] but that ensuring the removal of all remaining trade barriers (principally seen as tariffs) should no longer be seen as the world's foremost economic objective—promoting global innovation should be. To be sure, enabling further global integration of product and capital markets would help boost global gross domestic product (GDP), but actually not by that much, especially when compared to policies that would boost innovation. One way to see this is to examine how much reducing existing trade barriers would benefit the U.S. economy. At the high end, the Peterson Institute—a subscriber to both the Washington and Geneva consensuses—claims that elimination of remaining global barriers to trade flows would add another $500 billion to annual U.S. GDP.[19] Other studies, however, suggest that this figure is significantly overstated. The U.S. International Trade Commission estimated that removing all remaining barriers to imports into the United States would add just $3.7 billion to U.S. GDP. The World Bank's LINKAGE model estimates that the United States would gain about $16.2 billion from the removal of these barriers. But let's assume for argument's sake that the number is in fact $500 billion. This is roughly 3.5 percent of U.S. GDP. If we can instead boost productivity through innovation just one percentage point faster, the U.S. economy would grow by 3.5 percent of GDP by year four and by double that amount by year seven, far exceeding the benefits of removing barriers to trade flows.

Again, this is not to say that more integrated global markets are not useful or that unilateral "protectionism" cannot be harmful. It is to say that innovation is vastly more important. Put another way, designing a global economic system to maximize trade and capital flows (to in turn maximize allocation efficiency) is like trying to get the global economic car to go faster by replacing the spark plugs rather than by installing a souped-up engine. Just as neoclassical economists promote allocation efficiency at home, they see it as the goal globally. But dynamic efficiency (innovation) and productive efficiency (productivity) are much more important, domestically and globally.

As such, the first and central task of global economic policy should be to encourage all nations to put boosting innovation and productivity as their top economic priority. Doing this means working to develop a new Geneva Consensus that puts the promotion of sustainable innovation at the top of the list. And by sustainable innovation, we mean innovation in the "good" category (as we define in chapter 6), especially innovation focused on boosting productivity and adding to the global stock of knowledge. This means focusing more on issues of IP protection, enactment of voluntary, industry-led global standards, reduction of discriminatory indigenous innovation policies, and other similar actions.

The second step is to revamp the mission of existing international bodies, not only to better support sustainable global innovation but also to fight against innovation mercantilism. This means stronger enforcement by global bodies like the WTO against beggar-thy-neighbor mercantilist strategies. It means organizations like the World Bank and the IMF, along with regional and national development organizations, including the U.S. Agency for International Development, the Inter-American Development Bank, and the European Development Bank, no longer promoting export-led growth as a key solution to development. Such institutions need to begin tying their assistance to steps taken by developing nations to move away from such negative-sum mercantilist policies. They should instead reward countries whose policies are focused on spurring domestic productivity instead of protecting the status quo or growing solely by exporting (or limiting imports).

The IMF should start by calling out nations that are chronic currency manipulators. The fact that the IMF has not yet formally declared China a currency manipulator suggests that the IMF is a paper tiger. After getting tough with currency manipulators like China, the IMF should tie any future financial assistance not to whether nations adhere to the Geneva Consensus (cutting government spending to get budgets under control), but to whether they follow what should become a global innovation consensus (putting in place policies to drive domestic innovation and productivity).

Enacting these true innovation policies risks the opposition of powerful interests: unions and workers who may be displaced; domestic producers, including small businesses, who enjoy cozy relationships and low levels of competition; able-bodied individuals who are paid for not working; and government bureaucrats whose top-down control is challenged. But it is only by spurring competition, allowing new business models to take hold (e.g., allowing big-box retailers to displace inefficient mom-and-pop retailers), and deploying the best production tools—often by increasing the use of information technology (IT)—that these nations will see fast increases in standard of living. But without carrots and sticks to move in this direction, these nations will continue to take the easy way out: innovation mercantilism. Nations that work in the direction of sustainable innovation should be rewarded with support; nations that do not should be left to fend for themselves.

For its part, the World Bank should make a firm commitment that it will stop encouraging policies designed to support countries' export-led growth strategies. Indeed, the World Bank should place a moratorium on all such policies. If countries insist on pursuing innovation mercantilist practices, the World Bank should cut off its support. At the same time, the World Bank sorely needs institutional innovation to begin seeing its mandate as achieving a more globally balanced international economic system. The G-20 countries, as the primary sponsors of the World Bank, must tackle this issue head-on. Specifically, the G-20 should demand from the World Bank, within a year, a new strategic plan for completely revamping its approach with a focus on win-win innovation policy.

To be sure, the innovation strategy that the World Bank crafts for truly lagging developing countries, notably in Africa, should be distinct from those for more developed nations. And exports are certainly part of any nation's economic growth strategy. But an export-focused strategy must be revised to reflect today's world. Innovation-based growth in Africa will be much more about adopting and leveraging information technologies, such as by improving access to broadband Internet and improving education, health care, and public infrastructure.

Indeed, IT has played a vital role in raising productivity and contributing to more efficient markets in many developing countries. For example, a 10 percent increase in broadband penetration increases per capita GDP growth in low- to middle-income countries by 1.38 percent.[20] Likewise, a 10 percent increase in mobile phone penetration in low- and middle-income economies adds 0.81 percent to annual per capita GDP growth.[21] And a survey of twenty thousand businesses in low- and middle-income countries found that firms using IT have faster sales and employment growth and also higher productivity.[22] Accordingly, a recent World Bank study urged nations to adopt more balanced policies regarding IT adoption and use, arguing that doing so could lead to stronger economic growth.[23] These are the ways the global community should be supporting economic growth in developing countries, not by encouraging businesses to decamp from the developed world to relocate to the developing world.

For its part, the WTO needs to worry less about preserving the myth that the current global trading system is based on free trade, and more about aggressively attacking innovation mercantilism. In addition, the WTO, a hidden, Geneva-based institution, whose workings are opaque at best, is long overdue to become more transparent and open. For example, the WTO routinely classifies documents as internal "JOB" documents, not "official WTO documents," allowing them to remain hidden to the public.[24]

The third step toward an innovation-oriented global economic policy is that developed countries will need to work alongside international development organizations to reformulate foreign-aid policies as carrot and stick tools to draw and prod countries toward the right kinds of innovation policies. Two economic principles should guide developed countries' foreign-aid policies. First, foreign aid should be geared to enhancing the productivity of developing countries' domestic, nontraded sectors, not to helping their export sectors become more competitive in global markets. Second, countries that impose significant barriers to trade and blatantly engage in IP theft, currency manipulation, and other mercantilist policies should have their foreign-aid privileges withdrawn. And countries running up huge trade surpluses should simply not be receiving any foreign aid, regardless of how poor they are. The message to these countries should be that if they want to engage the global community for development assistance, mercantilist practices cannot constitute the "dominant logic" of their innovation and economic growth strategies.

Developed countries should start by withdrawing foreign aid to countries fielding egregious mercantilist practices. For example, Japan gave China $1.66 billion in official bilateral development assistance in 2005.[25] It was not until the end of 2009 that Germany stopped giving foreign-aid assistance to China. Germany had given China €67.5 million ($91 million) in 2007 and India €64 million ($86 million) in 2008. Amazingly, German left-wing opposition parties denounced the decision to suspend foreign aid to the world's second-largest economy as a "bad joke" and an "arrogant first move in office" by Dirk Niebel, Germany's development minister, predicting the move would have "disastrous consequences."[26] And the United States gave China $120 million in foreign-aid assistance from 2005 to 2008, even as China continued to accrue huge trade surpluses with America.[27]

Another astounding example is the Global Fund to Fight AIDS, Tuberculosis, and Malaria, which pools countries' donations to fight these pernicious diseases into one coordinated fund. Resource-strapped countries receive grants to purchase medicines, build health programs, and prevent these diseases from spreading. The fund's founders envisioned the resources going to places like Lesotho, Haiti, and Uganda, where these diseases have reached crisis levels.[28] But during the eight years since the fund was launched, China, a country with more than $3 trillion in foreign currency reserves, has become the fourth-largest recipient of funds, having been awarded nearly $1 billion, or almost three times more than South Africa, one of the countries most affected by these diseases. While the United States has committed $5.5 billion and France $2.5 billion to the fund during the past eight years, China has donated a paltry $16 million, and recouped this spending by a factor of sixty. While China has legitimate health concerns, its needs stack up poorly against the expensive opportunity costs exacted on poorer countries; indeed, China was able to afford a $586 billion stimulus package that included new health and education spending of $27 billion. As Jack Chow, chief U.S. negotiator at the talks that established the fund, contends, "It is audacious for China to assert that it needs international health assistance on par with the world's poorest countries."[29] Yet no one in Washington has raised concerns that an amount equivalent to President Barack Obama's entire fiscal 2011 Global Fund budget request of $1 billion has gone to a country that not only can afford to pay its own way, but that also unrepentantly uses mercantilist practices to rack up enormous current account surpluses. Unfortunately, in November 2011, the Global Fund announced that it would not be able to fund new programs until 2014, in part because of global financial woes, but also because countries like China continue to insist on being net recipients rather than net contributors to the program.[30]

Developed nations also need to stop directly enabling innovation mercantilism on the part of the nations they assist. There are many examples of this. For instance, the Overseas Private Investment Corporation (OPIC), a U.S. governmental corporation whose mission is to help American companies invest overseas, funded a venture investment bank that made high-tech investments in India in technology companies that were competing directly against U.S. companies. OPIC's Web site, which is targeted to American businesses, has included links to organizations such as the Indian Investment Center—a government agency that seeks to induce American companies to move jobs to India—and the Federation of Indian Chambers of Commerce and Industry. OPIC also has guaranteed investments in overseas venture capital funds, many of which invest in high-tech ventures that potentially compete with U.S. companies. For example, the OPIC India Private Equity Fund, administered by CIBC World Markets (a Canadian company), has made investments in Indian companies in banking, computer, and other industries.[31]

In an even more stunning example, during George W. Bush's presidency, the U.S. Department of Commerce's International Trade Administration actually hosted conferences for U.S. companies that were designed to help them invest in foreign nations such as China, even if these companies were closing their U.S. plants and opening up plants in China to sell into the U.S. market.[32] U.S. businesses signing up to attend one such conference could list among their interests "opening up an office, warehouse/distribution center, [or] manufacturing facility."[33] They could find information on "How to Select Locations for Your Businesses and Who to Partner with in China" and learn about "China's Taxation for Foreign Companies and Joint Ventures post-WTO." The logic behind the Bush administration's actions was that if U.S. companies were manufacturing in China, they would be more likely to be competitive in a global marketplace. But the result was to contribute to the loss of 5.5 million manufacturing jobs in the 2000s.

It has been only modestly different with the Obama administration, which, as noted, has promised to help China develop commercial jetliners— despite commercial jet aircraft being one of the preciously few manufacturing industries in which the United States is a strong exporter.[34] During the same visit to China at which President Obama made that announcement, General Electric (GE) announced it was joint venturing its entire avionics business with China's state-owned avionics company, which could not have happened without U.S. government participation because of national security considerations and export license requirements. It's one thing for the United States to help companies make investments overseas that help struggling domestic economies with things like water and electricity supply, energy extraction, or enhancing medical care, but it's quite another to subsidize investment in foreign countries' high-tech industries that compete directly with ours.

The notion of a rising tide lifting all boats has merit, and we do not suggest that international efforts to boost economic development are inherently bad or are part of a zero-sum game. To the contrary, developed nations should be doing more, not less, to help poor countries get richer. But, economic development policies should not reward and encourage mercantilist and distorting policies. The aid examples cited above are tantamount to the governor of Michigan setting up meetings to host delegations from Alabama to come and meet with manufacturers in Michigan to see if they could compete and produce more effectively in Alabama. Now, if U.S. manufacturers decide that they can compete more productively offshore than in the United States, they should be free to make that decision, but they don't need assistance from the U.S. government to offshore U.S. jobs.

Just as the United States exerted leadership to reshape the postwar global manufacturing economy, it will need to exert leadership, along with key allies, to reshape the twenty-first-century innovation economy. To do this, America must work with the Australians, Canadians, Europeans, and whomever else will come aboard to lay out a renewed vision for globalization grounded in the perspective that markets should drive global trade; that countries should adhere to their trade agreements; that genuine, value-added innovation drives economic growth; and that fair competition forces countries to ratchet up their game by putting in place constructive innovation policies that leave all countries better off. This task won't be easy, but it should be the top foreign economic policy goal of these nations. But even if these nations will not join with the United States, America can't afford not to act on its own.

For the United States, the tendency will be to let global political and national security concerns trump concerns about economic competitiveness, as chapter 4 discusses. All that has to happen is for North Korea to threaten making a nuclear weapon, and the United States will likely cease to place any economic pressure on China. But the attitude that the United States has had since WWII—that it can afford to put economic competitiveness second—is no longer tenable, especially because a weak U.S. economy increasingly imperils both our defense industrial base and our national security and foreign policy priorities.

For Europe, the problem is twofold. First, both the European Union (EU) and its individual states have been loath to stand up to innovation mercantilists for the simple reason that they hope to benefit from their practices. Perversely, by playing "the good cop" against America's "bad cop," European leaders hope that the mercantilists will punish American companies, not theirs, and that for once Europe will be on top of the innovation economy. While we have shown that the United States is lagging behind many European countries in several measurements of innovation progress, Europe still sees the United States as a formidable competitor that needs to be checked. As one British scholar explained to us after a private roundtable on innovation policy held at 10 Downing Street: "We Europeans would like to see you Yanks taken down a notch. Then we could be the innovation leaders." But there is no reason to think that mercantilists won't turn their sights on European leadership, just as they have done on American supremacy. Countries like China play the "divide and conquer" game all too well.

Finally, innovation mercantilist nations like China, Brazil, and others will likely oppose any efforts to create a new global innovation framework. China will likely claim that what they do in their own economy is no one's business but theirs. That claim is completely without justification when their activity affects the global economy unfairly and violates the spirit if not the letter of the WTO. If they want to be left alone, they should pull out of the WTO and all other international economic agreements—and stop receiving any and all foreign aid, including from the World Bank. Brazil and its fellow travelers in the developing world will likely rely on guilt to make their case: "We're just a poor Southern Hemisphere nation oppressed by you northern developed nation imperialists." In fact, the North-South divide that was a central theme for many years has begun to give way to a more complex system marked by the arrival of advanced developing countries and global supply chains that transcend the geographic location of a country. The reality is that without innovations like computers, the Internet, and biotechnology— which were introduced by developed nations that invested hundreds of billions of dollars to create them—developing nations would be significantly worse off. Even leaving this aside, the fact that nations are developing simply does not give them the moral standing to steal intellectual property or engage in a host of other mercantilist practices.

If developed countries can muster the will and the ability to cooperate, a first priority should be to reformulate their trade and aid agendas. One of the biggest challenges for the United States and European nations is that their trade policies are structured to play "whack a mole." They expend enormous resources to identify, respond to, and combat particular instances of foreign countries' contravening international trade agreements to the detriment of their businesses (the actual harms from which must also be legally established). U.S. or European trade policy rarely rises to the level of broader principles, such as insisting that other countries "desist with this generalized practice." Because U.S. and European trade policies are organized in a legalistic framework to combat unfair trade practices on a case-by-case basis, it becomes difficult for them to put in place a comprehensive trade strategy designed to stimulate competitiveness and innovation.

At the end of the day, developed countries are going to have to abandon the notion that unrepentant mercantilist nations are somehow going to play by the rules if we just play nice with them. Accordingly, the United States, Europe, the Commonwealth nations, and perhaps Japan should create a new global trade zone, involving those countries genuinely committed to adhering to the principles of open, free, and fair trade. Countries that insist on pursuing mercantilist strategies would not be welcomed into this new arrangement. The Trans-Pacific Partnership (TPP) could provide a model for how to organize such a new trade zone. The TPP represents a vehicle for economic integration and collaboration across like-minded Asia-Pacific region countries—including Australia, Brunei, Chile, Malaysia, New Zealand, Peru, Singapore, Vietnam, and the United States—that have come together voluntarily to craft a platform for a comprehensive, high-standard trade agreement.[35] But it's unlikely that the TPP will work out this way, since a number of the nations involved have extensive mercantilist policies.[36]

Countries that would like to participate in such expanded trade partnerships, whether the Trans-Pacific Partnership or a potential Trans-Atlantic Partnership, must abandon wholesale their mercantilist practices. This proposal is not meant to be Pollyannaish; to be sure, every country, including the United States, has at least some mercantilist policies, often as a result of internal political forces. It's not to say that only perfect countries with unblemished trade records can participate. The point is that countries whose dominant logic toward trade is predicated on export-led growth and the use of beggar-thy-neighbor mercantilist practices would simply not be invited to participate. If countries want the benefits of participating in a global trade system, then they must play by the rules of that system.

Finally, we need more capable international institutions to support global science and innovation. Now more than ever, the benefits of research flow throughout the world. As a result, nations that set aside some of their current consumption to invest in science and research are helping not just themselves but the entire world. But there is less investment in science and research than is globally optimal because some countries free ride off of others' investments in research. We see this in Europe, for example, where most science investment is the responsibility of individual nations, not the European Commission. As a result, the EU as a whole invests less in research as a share of GDP than does the United States. Moreover, there is less investment than warranted on challenges that are global in nature. We see this in particular on research that could produce noncarbon energy sources or address future potentially pandemic diseases. Leading nations should therefore establish a Global Science and Innovation Foundation (GSIF). The mission of the GSIF would be to fund scientific research around the globe on key global challenges and in particular support internationally collaborative research. For any nation to be eligible to receive funds, it would have to commit one-tenth of 1 percent of its GDP in funding and be certified by the GSIF (with guidance from the IMF) as a nation not committed to innovation mercantilism.

Moving from Resistance and Indifference to U.S. Innovation Policy Leadership

In the sixty-five years following WWII, most nations looked to the United States to lead the process of global economic governance. And given that the United States renounces innovation mercantilism, it should also play a leadership role in ensuring that the global economy is structured in a way that maximizes innovation. But as discussed above, this means developing a new understanding that global action should be designed not to maximize flows of goods across borders, as important as that is, but to maximize global innovation.

Ensuring that the community of nations moves to a more sustainable, nonmercantilist global innovation system will certainly be important in enabling the United States to more effectively compete in the race. It's difficult to win a race when one's opponents are engaged in systemic mercantilism. But this isn't just about U.S. interests. The United States was right that moving to a more integrated global trading system after WWII was good, not just for the United States but also for the entire world. And the United States would be right today to insist that moving to a system that maximizes global innovation is in everyone's interest.

But for the United States to reassert its leadership, it's critical that it regain its innovation lead. America needs to want to win the race. And to exert new global leadership, it will need to see fighting global innovation mercantilism and supporting global innovation policy as the most important international economic challenge of this era. Achieving such aspirations will not be easy. There are three substantial prerequisites.

The first, as we describe in chapter 8, is for the Washington Consensus to acknowledge that the United States has fallen behind in the race for global innovation advantage—both because some countries are using innovation mercantilist practices and others are using good innovation-promoting practices. But, good or bad, they're all doing something to try to win the innovation race. Second, it will have to then acknowledge that losing the race has had and will continue to have serious economic consequences for the nation, including higher unemployment, reduced income growth, and a hollowed out defense industrial base. Third, the Washington Consensus will have to recognize that government has a key role in helping America win the race. Yet the Left will not acknowledge that to win the race we need to help U.S. companies, including U.S. multinationals, while the Right argues against government intervention.

We suggest that the principal reason why Washington elites deny American innovation decline and ignore foreign innovation mercantilism is that they fear admitting such problems would open up the floodgates of reactionary xenophobic and protectionist forces. On the verge of the French Revolution, Madame de Pompadour famously said: "After us, the deluge." Washington elites somewhat similarly fear that "after us" there could be a surge of Populist fever. And, unfortunately, they may be right. In particular, the American Left reacts to any business failure, real or perceived, by calling not for government support of private-sector success, but for regulation of private-sector action. We can see this by looking at two recent high-profile cases: the U.S. fall in broadband rankings and U.S. offshoring of service-sector jobs.

When reports began to emerge after about 2005 documenting the falling U.S. rank in international broadband adoption, most liberal groups, led by the advocacy group Free Press, argued that the U.S. rank was falling because of too little competition and Big Broadband's sole focus on profits. Now they had real ammunition for their anti-private-sector policy agenda. Rather than call for policies to address the real causes of slippage in the rankings (the fact that too few Americans own computers and possess digital literacy and that there are too many places where connecting broadband has not been economically viable without subsidies), the broadband Left pressed for extreme policies. Like the Populists of the late 1800s, who wanted to nationalize the telegraph and the railroads, these new Populists abhorred the notion that broadband should be provided by for-profit companies and wanted a government takeover. And if it was not to be, then at least government should heavily regulate broadband providers, including requiring them to treat all bits alike (the notion of "net neutrality"), even if some bits (like those traveling on Skype) needed to travel to users' computers much faster (with less latency) than other bits (like those in an e-mail). Free Press and their fellow travelers even went so far as to argue, against any shred of logic, that "net neutrality" legislation was needed if the United States was to avoid continuing to fall in the broadband rankings.

Free Press and the broadband Left were vociferously opposed to doing what virtually every other leading broadband nation did, which was to provide subsidies to for-profit telecommunications providers to deploy broadband to low-income individuals and high-cost areas. When, in crafting the 2009 American Recovery and Reinvestment Act, some senators proposed that in addition to providing $7.2 billion in grants for broadband deployment, government should give tax credits for high-speed broadband investments made in 2009, Free Press came out with guns blazing. The incentives would have spurred billions of dollars of new capital investment, employed tens of thousands of workers and gotten broadband to areas without it, and all in 2009, when the economy most needed a shot in the arm. But Free Press, despite their claim to be for more broadband, would have no truck with any policy that helped Big Broadband capitalists, and played a key role in killing the provision, including by running ads attacking the incentives as "corporate welfare."

The Left's broadband innovation message struck other parties as an extreme call for more regulation/government ownership. Thus, instead of acknowledging that the United States was falling behind in the broadband rankings and supporting government policies to help companies deploy broadband and individuals become digitally literate and adopt broadband, most conservatives spent much of their time denying the reality that the United States was behind. Not surprisingly, the result has been that virtually none of the proactive broadband policies that enabled many other nations to become broadband leaders have been implemented in the United States, while our broadband rank continues to languish (largely because America has a much higher percentage of its households who don't own a personal computer).[37]

This brings us to the second prerequisite for change, recognizing the need for government to help the United States win the innovation race. When many U.S. companies began to offshore jobs more extensively in the early 2000s in part because IT networks and systems now enabled doing so, we saw a similar dynamic between political factions. Former Clinton economic adviser Alan Blinder wrote a widely read article in *Foreign Affairs* entitled "Offshoring: The Next Industrial Revolution," which argued (incorrectly) that the offshoring of service-sector jobs was not just a routine extension of international trade, but a "third industrial revolution," likely to lead to one out of every three American jobs being shipped overseas. He warned: "We have so far barely seen the tip of the offshoring iceberg, the eventual dimensions of which may be staggering."[38] In response, many on the Left called for measures to limit trade, including "Buy American" provisions and a moratorium on new trade agreements, among other measures.[39] It wasn't just that they called for measures to limit globalization; they attacked the companies themselves. During his 2004 presidential campaign, Senator John Kerry called U.S. CEOs who moved jobs offshore "Benedict Arnolds." Lou Dobbs accused U.S. corporations of fighting a "War on the Middle Class." Russell Shaw, a technology writer and *Huffington Post* blogger, even went so far as to call CEOs who move jobs offshore "evil."[40] Not callous. Not greedy. Evil.

And just as with broadband, industry and conservative groups spent most of their energy denying that offshoring was even a problem. Perhaps the crescendo came when Tom Donohue, the president of the U.S. Chamber of Commerce, declared at a conference in 2008 that for every dollar of work U.S. companies offshored, the U.S. economy received $42 of benefit![41] The highest estimate from any credible study up to that time was $1.46 of benefit for every dollar of offshored work, and even this estimate was viewed by many as too high.[42] But if we really believe Donohue, we should offshore every job in America, stop working, and overnight become forty-two times richer! What a deal.

As debate over the race for global innovation advantage intensifies, this type of bifurcated narrative will play out again and again. Just as the Left used America's falling broadband rank to push for public ownership and regulation of broadband companies, the Left will also use America's falling innovation and competitiveness rank as an opportunity to push their true goal: "economic democracy." Economic democracy first began to gain currency among the Left when the U.S. economy began to struggle in international competition in the late 1970s and early 1980s. Then, Martin Carnoy, a liberal economist, and Derek Shearer, a community activist, wrote a book titled *Economic Democracy: The Challenge of the 1980s* that called for "greater democratization of economic decision making [and] an economy with diverse, diffused, pluralist and heterogeneous patterns of ownership."[43] Diverse means some enterprises were owned by the government, some by workers, some by the community, and some by women and minorities. Fast-forward to 2011. Harold Meyerson, a liberal columnist for the *Washington Post,* wrote: "Our economic woes, then, are not simply cyclical or structural. They are also—chiefly—institutional, the consequence of U.S. corporate behavior that has plunged us into a downward cycle of underinvestment, underemployment, and under-consumption."[44] While his analysis is right, his solution is not to do what other nations have done—enter the race on the side of your establishments to help them win the race and structure market incentives to align corporate interests with national interests—but to call for economic democracy. As Meyerson states, "Our solutions must be similarly institutional, requiring, for starters, the seating of public and worker representatives on corporate boards. Short of that, there will be no real prospects for reversing America's downward mobility." The thinking goes: "If *we* could just control corporations, rather than leaving it up to the managers and by extension, shareholders, *we'd* be fine."

By taking such anticorporate and often antiglobalization positions, champions of the Left have done two things: First, they have made it harder for the Washington Consensus to publicly acknowledge that the United States is no longer winning the race and that globalization, as currently structured, is not an unalloyed good for U.S. companies or workers. In other words, they prompt a knee-jerk defensive reaction from the Washington establishment, making it difficult for them to rationally and publicly acknowledge America's challenges. Without this acknowledgment, mobilization of the necessary political forces in Washington to achieve decisive action is virtually impossible. Second, by putting such polarizing issues as economic democracy, Buy American provisions, efforts to halt new foreign market openings,[45] protective tariffs, and increased unionization in domestic and foreign economies at the center of their "competitiveness" strategy, they limit attention to other policies that may gain more support from the center and from businesses that would also improve U.S. innovation and competitiveness.

In short, if the United States is going to move forward in the race for global advantage, the Left will need to abandon its reflexive, anticorporate stance and acknowledge that policies that help, not hurt, corporations are needed. They will need to start by seeing innovation, productivity, and offshoring not as something corporations do because they are greedy, or even evil, profit mongers, but as something they have to do to survive in global competition. They will need to realize that blame is not a strategy. As we note in chapter 8 in the example of the Rhode Island Senate Democratic Caucus getting the message about the importance of allowing Rhode Island to have a more competitive corporate tax structure, at least some on the Left have come to understand that a competitive corporate tax code will be a requirement, not a choice, if U.S. workers are to prosper.

But for their part, members of the libertarian Right deserve their share of the blame for refusing to acknowledge both U.S. decline and the need for innovation policy. The Right is almost hypersensitive to any perceived relative decline in America's global lead in military might, but is strangely oblivious to the deleterious impact that America's declining economic position will have on its security in general and defense capability in particular. If the United States is losing the race for global innovation advantage, members of the Left need to acknowledge that their mission of advancing social justice cannot be effectively met, and the Right needs to acknowledge that America will not be able to maintain superpower status as the arsenal of democracy. Moreover, with their commitment to American exceptionalism and market fundamentalism, the Right is unwilling or unable to acknowledge that the United States has declined in relation to nations with less of a commitment to free markets than America. How can we, that bastion of freedom, possibly lose a race to socialists, Communists, corporatists and other statists?

If the United States is to move forward, the Right will need to accept that America has fallen behind and to acknowledge that it will be virtually impossible to win the race for global innovation advantage when American companies are competing individually against foreign companies that have their government as a partner. The Right needs to abandon its strident antigovernment ideology, and acknowledge the necessary role of government in helping spur innovation and assisting U.S. establishments to win in the global innovation race. It needs to recognize that its idealized world of yeoman entrepreneurs in the Wild West competing in untrammeled market-places is a world long gone. And Republicans need much more sophisticated thinking about how the government can partner with the private sector to drive economic growth rather than blindly flailing about and advocating slashing entire cabinet-level departments without even understanding what those agencies do.[46] For better or worse, U.S. businesses are competing against foreign companies supported by their states. If the Right wants to shrink the state, it should focus on the entitlement state, not the innovation state.

And it's not enough to cry as the economic ship is going down that we were pure to our free-market principles and didn't intervene. Winning should come before principle. The point, after all, is to win (albeit while playing fairly) and this means that government has to be a partner. Athletes without coaches usually lose to athletes with coaches and trainers. Winning in the new race for global innovation advantage requires both competitive athletes (that is, entrepreneurs and companies) and coaches and trainers (government policies to support innovation). To argue that nations can win in global competition without supportive governments is as much of an ideological pipe dream as the notion that the economy would be more productive with better jobs if workers ran the companies. In addition, the Right needs to recognize that not everything government does vis-à-vis innovation policy is "The Technology Pork Barrel," as two neoclassical economists called innovation policy efforts.[47] If they are worried about politicization of innovation policies, they need to push for innovation policies that are determined by objective means, including peer review of grants and requiring industry matching funds.

It is this split between liberals and conservatives, business and labor, that limits Washington from developing a national economic development coalition. Rather than fight over tired old differences, the business and labor camps need to build a coalition for innovation, with business focused more on policies to spur enterprises to invest in America and labor on giving up its protectionist calls.

In the end, the race for innovation advantage will only get more intense and heated. It's therefore critical that the United States and its free-trade allies take the needed steps now to contain and roll back the rampant innovation mercantilism being practiced by countries like China, while ensuring that the global economy evolves in a way that favors free trade and competition based on good and not ugly innovation practices, especially as an increasing number of nations develop and expand their own innovation and competitiveness policies. But as Kennan stated in his long telegram about the rise of the Soviet Union being a test of America's greatness, we can also hope that the new race for global innovation advantage will spur America out of its slumber and divisiveness to again become the global innovation leader, not just as a front-runner in the race, but as a referee to ensure that the race is fair and that everyone benefits from the competition.

NOTES

Chapter 1: The Race for Global Innovation Advantage

1. "Gallup Daily: U.S. Employment," *Gallup*, http://www.gallup.com/poll/125639/Gallup-Daily-Workforce.aspx (accessed October 12, 2011).

2. Alex Parker, "CBO: Longest Period of High Unemployment since Great Depression," *U.S. News and World Report*, February 16, 2012, http://www.usnews.com/news/articles/2012/02/16/cbo-longest-period-of-high-unemployment-since-great-depression.

3. Tyler Durden, "Labor Force Participation Rate Drops to 25 Year Low, at 64.5%," *Zero Hedge* (blog), November 5, 2010, http://www.zerohedge.com/article/labor-force-participation-rate-drops-25-year-low-645.

4. Neil Irwin, "Aughts Were a Lost Decade for U.S. Economy, Workers," *Washington Post*, January 2, 2010, http://www.washingtonpost.com/wp-dyn/content/article/2010/01/01/AR2010010101196.html.

5. Robert D. Atkinson and Scott Andes, *The Atlantic Century II: Benchmarking EU and U.S. Innovation and Competitiveness* (Washington, DC: Information Technology and Innovation Foundation [ITIF], July 2011), http://www.itif.org/files/2011-atlantic-century.pdf.

6. For example, total personal income in the Great Lakes states grew 280 percent, almost the same rate of growth as the nation during this period.

7. From 1969 to the mid-1980s, personal income in the Great Lakes region grew 20 percent slower than it did across the nation as a whole.

8. In the postwar period, those regions grew 2 percent faster and 4 percent slower, respectively, than the nation. The divergence was even starker between particular states and cities. Between 1958 and 1969, Ohio grew 93 percent as fast as Texas, but between 1969 and 1986, it grew just 59 percent as fast. Pennsylvania grew at 80 percent of California's rate before 1969, but afterward it grew at just 31 percent of California's rate.

9. Paul Glader, "To Europeans, U.S. Is a Puzzling Economic Giant," *Washington Post*, February 23, 2012, http://www.washingtonpost.com/conversations/to-europeans-america-is-a-puzzling-economic-giant/2012/02/19/gIQAlhRXWR_story.html.

10. Lawrence J. Peter, *Peter's Quotations: Ideas for Our Time* (New York: Bantam Books, 1979), 112.

11. "It just happens" is a frequent characterization of technological change as postulated by Nobel Prize–winning economist Robert M. Solow in "A Contribution to the Theory of Economic Growth," *Quarterly Journal of Economics* 70, no. 1 (1956): 65–94. See, for example, "The Growth of Growth Theory," *Economist*, May 18, 2006, http://www.economist.com/node/6943519; and David Warsh, *Knowledge and the Wealth of Nations: A Story of Economic Discovery* (New York: W. W. Norton, 2006), 25.

Chapter 2: Explaining U.S. Economic Decline

1. See Carmen M. Reinhart and Kenneth S. Rogoff, *This Time Is Different: Eight Centuries of Financial Folly* (Princeton, NJ: Princeton University Press, 2009).

2. Bureau of Economic Analysis, National Income and Product Accounts Tables (real gross domestic product, quantity indexes, seasonally adjusted), http://www.bea.gov/iTable/index_nipa.cfm (accessed October 12, 2011); Bureau of Labor Statistics, Current Employment Statistics (total nonfarm employment, seasonally adjusted), http://www.bls.gov/ces/ (accessed October 12, 2011).

3. See Michael Hirsh, *Capital Offense: How Washington's Wise Men Turned America's Future Over to Wall Street* (Hoboken, NJ: John Wiley and Sons, 2010).

4. John Cassidy, "What Good Is Wall Street?" *New Yorker*, November 29, 2010, http://www.newyorker.com/reporting/2010/11/29/101129fa_fact_cassidy.

5. Board of Governors of the Federal Reserve System, "Assets and Liabilities of Commercial Banks in the United States (Weekly)," http://www.federalreserve.gov/releases/H8/current/ (accessed October 12, 2011).

6. Bureau of Economic Analysis, Fixed Assets Accounts Tables (Table 3.8ES; chain-type quantity indexes for investment in private fixed assets by industry), http://www.bea.gov/iTable/index_FA.cfm (accessed October 12, 2011).

7. Bureau of Economic Analysis, Direct Investment and Multinational Companies (financial and operating data, nonbank U.S. parent companies, capital expenditures), http://www.bea.gov/iTable/index_MNC.cfm (accessed February 23, 2012).

8. UNESCO Institute for Statistics, Data Centre (R&D expenditure), http://www.uis.unesco.org (accessed February 23, 2012).

9. Battelle, "2011 Global R&D Funding Forecast," *R&D Magazine*, December 2010, 3, http://www.battelle.org/aboutus/rd/2011.pdf.

10. National Science Board, *Science and Engineering Indicators: 2010* (Arlington, VA: National Science Foundation, 2010), http://www.nsf.gov/statistics/seind10/pdf/seind10.pdf; Bureau of Economic Analysis Innovation Account (1959–2007 research and development data), http://www.bea.gov/national/newinnovation.htm (accessed December 7, 2010).

11. "This Time It's Serious," *Economist*, February 18, 2012, http://www.economist.com/node/21547770.

12. Cassidy, "What Good Is Wall Street?"

13. Ron Suskind, *Confidence Men* (New York: Harper-Collins, 2011), 200.

14. Richard McCormack, "The Plight of American Manufacturing," *American Prospect*, December 21, 2009, http://www.prospect.org/cs/articles?article=the_plight_of_american_manufacturing.

15. Suskind, *Confidence Men*, 306.

16. Mara Der Hovanesian and Dean Foust, "Why This Real Estate Bust Is Different," *BusinessWeek*, November 5, 2009, http://www.businessweek.com/magazine/content/09_46/b4155042792563.htm.

17. Charles Himmelberg, Christopher Mayer, and Todd Sinai, "Assessing High House Prices: Bubbles, Fundamentals, and Misperceptions," *Journal of Economic Perspectives* 19, no. 4 (2005): 67–92.

18. U.S. Census Bureau, Historical Income Tables (Table H-8; median household income by state), http://www.census.gov/hhes/www/income/data/historical/household/index.html (accessed January 6, 2011).

19. See Standard & Poor's, "Annual Rates of Change Continue to Improve According to the S&P/Case-Shiller Home Price Indices," October 25, 2011, at http://www.standardandpoors.com/indices/sp-case-shiller-home-price-indices/en/us/?indexId=spusa-cashpidff--p-us-----.

20. Nell Henderson, "Bernanke: There's No Housing Bubble to Go Bust," *Washington Post*, October 27, 2005, http://www.washingtonpost.com/wp-dyn/content/article/2005/10/26/AR2005102602255.html.

21. "Bush Adviser: Housing-Bubble Fears Overblown," *Associated Press*, July 12, 2005, http://www.msnbc.msn.com/id/8552401/ns/business-real_estate/.

22. Himmelberg, Mayer, and Sinai, "Assessing High House Prices."

23. Ibid.

24. Der Hovanesian and Foust, "Why This Real Estate Bust Is Different."

25. Ron Suskind, *Confidence Men*, 21–22.

26. Yves Smith, *ECONned: How Unenlightened Self Interest Undermined Democracy and Corrupted Capitalism* (New York: Palgrave Macmillan, 2010).

27. Deanne Julius, "U.S. Economic Power: Waxing or Waning?" *Harvard International Review* 26, no. 4 (2005): 14–19.

28. Members of the 2005 Rising Above the Gathering Storm Committee, *Rising Above the Gathering Storm, Revisited: Rapidly Approaching Category 5* (Washington, DC: National Academies Press, 2010), 36, http://www.uic.edu/home/Chancellor/risingabove.pdf.

29. Ibid., 65.

30. U.S. Bureau of Labor Statistics, "Evaluating the 1996–2006 Employment Projections," September 2010, http://www.bls.gov/opub/mlr/2010/09/art3full.pdf.

31. Bureau of Labor Statistics, Current Employment Statistics (all employees, manufacturing), http://www.bls.gov/ces/ (accessed February 23, 2012).

32. Stone and Associates and the Center for Regional Economic Competitiveness, *Re-examining the Manufacturing Extension Partnership Business Model* (Gaithersburg, MD: National Institute of Standards and Technology, 2010), 13, http://www.nist.gov/mep/upload/MEP_Bus_Model_Full_Report_October2010_a.pdf.

33. U.S. Bureau of Labor Statistics, Division of International Labor Comparisons, "International Comparisons of Annual Labor Force Statistics," March 30, 2011, 19, http://www.bls.gov/fls/flscomparelf/lfcompendium.pdf.

34. U.S. Census Bureau, *Statistical Abstract of the United States: 1950*, Washington, DC, 1950, http://www2.census.gov/prod2/statcomp/documents/1950.zip.

35. McCormack, "Plight of American Manufacturing."

36. Michael Scherer, "Larry Summers' Warning about the Growth of Government (Transcript)," *Swampland* (blog), *Time*, December 13, 2010, http://swampland.blogs.time.com/2010/12/13/larry-summers-warning-about-the-growth-of-government-transcript/.

37. Peter Marsh, "China Noses Ahead as Top Goods Producer," *Financial Times*, March 13, 2011, http://www.ft.com/intl/cms/s/0/002fd8f0-4d96-11e0-85e4-00144feab49a.html#axzz1lkSaqpZL.

38. "Industrial Metamorphosis," *Economist*, September 29, 2005, http://www.economist.com/node/4462685/.

39. Kevin Williamson, "Red Scapegoat," *National Review*, November 9, 2010, http://www.nationalreview.com/articles/252823/red-scapegoat-kevin-d-williamson/.

40. The sum of annual changes in U.S. gross domestic product (GDP) from 2001 to 2010.

41. Robert D. Atkinson et al., *Worse than the Great Depression: What Experts Are Missing about American Manufacturing Decline* (Washington, DC: Information Technology and Innovation Foundation [ITIF], March 2012), http://www2.itif.org/2012-american-manufacturing-decline.pdf.

42. Susan Houseman et al., "Offshoring and the State of American Manufacturing" (working paper, Upjohn Institute, 2010), http://www.upjohninst.org/publications/wp/10-166.pdf.

43. Bureau of Economic Analysis, National Income and Product Accounts Tables (corporate profits before tax by industry), http://www.bea.gov/iTable/index_nipa.cfm (accessed October 9, 2011).

44. McCormack, "Plight of American Manufacturing."

45. Richard McCormack, "U.S. Precision Machine Tool Industry Is No Longer a Global Competitive Force," *Manufacturing & Technology News*, March 5, 2010, http://www.manufacturingnews.com/news/10/0305/fiveaxis.html.

46. McCormack, "Plight of American Manufacturing."

47. Robert D. Atkinson et al., *Rising Tigers, Sleeping Giant: Asian Nations Set to Dominate the Clean Energy Race by Out-investing the United States* (Oakland, CA: Breakthrough Institute; Washington, DC: ITIF, 2009), 7, http://www.itif.org/files/2009-rising-tigers.pdf.

48. Tom Young, "GE Ploughs $2bn into China Clean Tech Push," *BusinessGreen*, November 9, 2010, http://www.businessgreen.com/bg/news/1895009/ge-ploughs-usd2bn-china-clean-tech-push/.

49. Members of the 2005 Rising Above the Gathering Storm Committee, *Rising Above the Gathering Storm, Revisited*, 9.

50. Stephen J. Ezell and Robert D. Atkinson, *The Case for a National Manufacturing Strategy* (Washington, DC: ITIF, 2011), 29, http://www.itif.org/files/2011-national-manufacturing-strategy.pdf.

51. U.S. Census Bureau, Foreign Trade (U.S. trade in goods and services, balance of payments basis), http://www.census.gov/foreign-trade/statistics/historical/gands.txt (accessed December 1, 2011).

52. Ibid.

53. Stefan Theil, "Why Europe Will Win," *Newsweek*, April 16, 2010, http://www.newsweek.com/2010/04/15/why-europe-will-win.html.

54. "This Time It's Serious," *Economist*.

55. U.S. Census Bureau, "Trade in Goods with Advanced Technology Products," http://www.census.gov/foreign-trade/balance/c0007.html#2011.

56. Ibid.

57. Jessie Jenkins, "Friday Factoids: U.S. Renewable Energy Trade Deficit Soars," *Breakthrough Blog*, January 22, 2010, http://thebreakthrough.org/blog/2010/01/friday_factoids_us_renewable_e.shtml.

58. National Science Board, *Science and Engineering Indicators: 2010*.

59. McCormack, "Plight of American Manufacturing."

60. Winwood Reade, *Martyrdom of Man* (1872; Whitefish, MT: Kessinger, 2003).

61. Semiconductor Industry Association, "Doubling Semiconductor Exports over the Next Five Years," June 17, 2010, http://www.sia-online.org/clientuploads/directory/DocumentSIA/Export/Doubling_Exports_Paper_0610.pdf.

62. Robert D. Atkinson and Scott Andes, *The Atlantic Century II: Benchmarking EU and U.S. Innovation and Competitiveness* (Washington, DC: Information Technology and Innovation Foundation [ITIF], July 2011), http://www.itif.org/files/2011-atlantic-century.pdf.

63. Ibid.

64. This represents infinitesimal improvement over ITIF's initial 2009 *Atlantic Century* report, which found the United States to rank dead last at improving its innovation capacity over the prior decade.

65. Organization for Economic Cooperation and Development (OECD), *OECD Science, Technology and Industry Scoreboard 2011: Innovation and Growth in Knowledge Economies*, September 2011, 76, http://www.oecd-ilibrary.org/science-and-technology/oecd-science-technology-and-industry-scoreboard-2011_sti_scoreboard-2011-en.

66. Jonathan Adams and David Pendlebury, *Global Research Report: United States* (London: Thomson Reuters, 2010), http://researchanalytics.thomsonreuters.com/m/pdfs/globalresearchreport-usa.pdf.

67. European Commission, Joint Research Centre, *2010 EU Industrial R&D Investment Scoreboard* (Luxembourg: European Union, 2010), http://iri.jrc.ec.europa.eu/research/docs/2010/SB2010_final_report.pdf.

68. Stephen Ezell and Scott Andes, "ICT R&D Policies: An International Perspective," *IEEE Internet Computing* 14, no. 4 (2010), http://www.itif.org/files/ICTRandD.pdf.

69. OECD, *OECD Information Technology Outlook, 2008* (Paris: OECD, 2008), 151, http://www.oecd.org/document/47/0,3746,en_2649_33703_46439983_1_1_1_1,00.html. For statistics, see http://dx.doi.org/10.1787/474078101812.

70. Adams and Pendlebury, *Global Research Report.*

71. Authors' analysis of data on scientific articles from the National Science Board, *Science and Engineering Indicators: 2008* (Arlington, VA: National Science Foundation, 2008); population data from World Bank, World Development Indicators (population, total), http://data.worldbank.org/data-catalog/world-development-indicators/ (accessed December 14, 2010).

72. Norman Augustine, *Is America Falling Off the Flat Earth?* (Washington, DC: National Academies Press, 2007).

73. University of Houston Law Center, Institute for Intellectual Property and Information Law, U.S. Patent Litigation Statistics, "Patent, All P-T-C, and All Civil Actions—1970–2005," http://www.patstats.org/Historical_Filings_PatentSuits_OtherSuits.doc (accessed November 10, 2010).

74. National Science Board, *Science and Engineering Indicators: 2010*, Appendix Tables 4-8 and 4-9; Towers Perrin, *2009 Update on U.S. Tort Cost Trends* (Stamford, CT: Towers Perrin, 2009), Appendixes 1–5, http://www.towersperrin.com/tp/getwebcachedoc?webc=USA/2009/200912/2009_tort_trend_report_12-8_09.pdf.

75. Members of the 2005 Rising Above the Gathering Storm Committee, *Rising Above the Gathering Storm, Revisited*, 8.

76. Robert D. Atkinson and Merrilea Mayo, *Refueling the U.S. Innovation Economy: Fresh Approaches to Science, Technology, Engineering and Mathematics (STEM) Education* (Washington, DC: ITIF, 2010), 123, http://www.itif.org/files/2010-refueling-innovation-economy.pdf.

77. Members of the 2005 Rising Above the Gathering Storm Committee, *Rising Above the Gathering Storm, Revisited*, 76.

78. Atkinson and Mayo, *Refueling the U.S. Innovation Economy*, 27.

79. OECD, *OECD Education at a Glance, 2009* (Paris: OECD, 2009), http://www.oecd.org/document/24/0,3343,en_2649_39263238_43586328_1_1_1_1,00.html. Rankings include OECD members and partners. College graduation ranking is based on Tertiary-A institutions; see tables A2.1 and A3.1.

80. Secretary of Education's Commission on the Future of Higher Education, "A Test of Leadership: Charting the Future of U.S. Higher Education," Department of Education, 2006, http://www.eric.ed.gov/PDFS/ED493504.pdf.

81. Justin Baer, Andrea Cook, and Stéphane Baldi, *The Literacy of America's College Students* (Washington, DC: American Institutes for Research, 2006), http://

www.air.org/files/The20Literacy20of20Americas20College20Students_final 20report.pdf. Proficiency in quantitative literacy involves being able to solve problems like computing and comparing the cost per ounce of food items.

82. Members of the 2005 Rising Above the Gathering Storm Committee, *Rising Above the Gathering Storm, Revisited*, 4.

83. Tom Abate, "Why Silicon Valley Faces Fresh Threats," *San Francisco Chronicle*, February 11, 2010, http://www.sfgate.com/cgi-bin/article.cgi?f=/c/a/2010/02/11 /BUMD1BV6A1.DTL.

84. Rebecca Keller, "How Shifting Occupational Composition Has Affected the Real Average Wage," *Monthly Labor Review* 132, no. 6 (2009): 27, http://www.bls .gov/opub/mlr/2009/06/art2full.pdf.

85. "This Time It's Serious," *Economist*.

86. International Monetary Fund, World Economic Outlook Database, April 2010. The twenty-one countries in the IMF's study are: Australia, Austria, Belgium, Brazil, Canada, China, Denmark, Finland, France, Germany, Iceland, India, Israel, Japan, Korea, Mexico, the Netherlands, Norway, Portugal, United Kingdom, and the United States.

87. Paul Samuelson, "Where Ricardo and Mill Rebut and Confirm Arguments of Mainstream Economists Supporting Globalization," *Journal of Economic Perspectives* 18, no. 3 (2004): 135–146, http://www.jstor.org/pss/3216810.

88. See Gregory Tassey, "Rationales and Mechanisms for Revitalizing U.S. Manufacturing R&D Strategies," *Journal of Technology Transfer* 35, no. 3 (2010): 283–333, http://www.nist.gov/director/planning/upload/manufacturing_strategy_paper .pdf.

89. An economy can be said to have "traded" and "nontraded" sectors (and jobs). Traded sectors include industries such as food processing and steel production, where output is sold outside of the relevant market area; nontraded industries are those where economic output is purchased principally by local area residents— for example, haircuts, elementary schools, or local transportation.

Chapter 3: Learning from the Wrong Master

1. Royal Economic Society, "U.K. Industrial Performance since 1960: Does the Failure of Manufacturing Matter?" news release, January 1996.

2. Sydney Pollard, *The Wasting of the British Economy* (London: Croom Helm, 1982).

3. Ajit Singh, "U.K. Industry and the World Economy: A Case of De-industrialisation?" *Cambridge Journal of Economics* 1, no. 2 (1977): 113–136.

4. Rex Pope, *The British Economy since 1914: A Study in Decline?* (New York: Longman, 1998).

5. U.S. Census Bureau, "U.S. Trade in Goods and Services—Balance of Payments Basis," June 9, 2011, http://www.census.gov/foreign-trade/statistics/historical /gands.pdf.

6. Nick Crafts, "Reversing Relative Economic Decline? The 1980s in Historical Perspective," *Oxford Review of Economic Policy* 7, no. 3 (1991): 81.

7. Ibid.

8. Singh, "U.K. Industry."

9. Crafts, "Reversing Relative Economic Decline?"

10. Nicholas Bloom and John Van Reenen, "Measuring and Explaining Management Practices across Firms and Countries," *Quarterly Journal of Economics* 122, no. 4 (2007): 1351–1408.

11. Crafts, "Reversing Relative Economic Decline?"

12. Ibid.

13. Robert D. Atkinson, *Effective Corporate Tax Reform in the Global Innovation Economy* (Washington, DC: ITIF, July 2009), http://www.itif.org/files/090723 _CorpTax.pdf.

14. Singh, "U.K. Industry."

15. Bureau of Economic Analysis, Fixed Assets Accounts Tables (Table 2.1E; chain-type quantity indexes for net stock of private equipment and software by industry), http://www.bea.gov/national/FA2004/Index.asp (accessed August 17, 2010).

16. Michael Kitson and Jonathan Michie, "Britain's Industrial Performance since 1960: Underinvestment and Relative Decline," *Economic Journal* 106, no. 434 (1996), http://www.cbr.cam.ac.uk/pdf/wp014.pdf.

17. Crafts, "Reversing Relative Economic Decline?"

18. Bureau of Economic Analysis, Direct Investment and Multinational Companies (financial and operating data, nonbank U.S. parent companies, capital expenditures), http://www.bea.gov/iTable/index_MNC.cfm (accessed February 23, 2012).

19. Kitson and Michie, "Britain's Industrial Performance."

20. Dean Krehmeyer, Matthew Orsagh, and Kurt Schacht, *Breaking the Short-Term Cycle: Discussion and Recommendations on How Corporate Leaders, Asset Managers, Investors, and Analysts Can Refocus on Long-Term Value* (Charlottesville, VA: CFA Institute, 2006), http://www.darden.virginia.edu/corporate-ethics/pdf /Short-termism_Report.pdf.

21. Kitson and Michie, "Britain's Industrial Performance."

22. Bureau of Economic Analysis, National Income and Product Accounts Tables (Table 6.20; net corporate dividend payments by industry), http://www.bea .gov/national/nipaweb/Index.asp (accessed October 20, 2010); Bureau of Economic Analysis, Fixed Assets Accounts Tables (Table 3.7ES; investment in private fixed assets by industry), http://www.bea.gov/national/FA2004/Index.asp (accessed October 20, 2010).

23. Aswath Damodaran, "Dividends and Taxes: An Analysis of the Bush Dividend Tax Plan" (working paper, Stern School of Business, New York University, 2003), http://pages.stern.nyu.edu/~adamodar/pdfiles/papers/divtaxes.pdf.

24. Crafts, "Reversing Relative Economic Decline?"

25. Krehmeyer, Orsagh, and Schacht, *Breaking the Short-Term Cycle*, 1.

26. National Science Board, *Science and Engineering Indicators: 2010* (Arlington, VA: National Science Foundation, 2010), http://www.nsf.gov/statistics/seind10 /pdf/seind10.pdf.

27. Steve Denning, "Clayton Christensen: How Pursuit of Profits Kills Innovation and the U.S. Economy," *Forbes*, November 18, 2011, http://www.forbes.com/sites/stevedenning/2011/11/18/clayton-christensen-how-pursuit-of-profits-kills-innovation-and-the-us-economy/.

28. Ibid.

29. Maurice Kirby, "Institutional Rigidities and Britain's Industrial Decline," *Business History Review* 63, no. 4 (1989): 930–936.

30. U.S. Chamber of Commerce, "Jobs Challenge," Campaign for Free Enterprise, http://www.freeenterprise.com/2009/10/only-american-free-enterprise-can-meet-our-nations-job-challenge.

31. Ylan Mui and David Cho, "Small Businesses Leery of Obama's Jobs Plan," *Washington Post*, January 29, 2010, http://www.washingtonpost.com/wp-dyn/content/article/2010/01/28/AR2010012803818.html.

32. Pollard, *Wasting of the British Economy*.

33. Jeremy Lott, "Mickey Kaus's Boxer Rebellion," *Real Clear Politics*, June 8, 2010, http://www.realclearpolitics.com/articles/2010/06/08/mickey_kauss_boxer_rebellion_105876.html.

34. Crafts, "Reversing Relative Economic Decline?"

35. Pollard, *Wasting of the British Economy*.

36. Peter Jenkins, "Staggering towards a Socialist Future," *Guardian*, October 1, 1979.

37. Pollard, *Wasting of the British Economy*.

38. Ibid.

39. Ibid.

40. Entering this term into the Google search engine yields 340,000 hits.

41. Pollard, *Wasting of the British Economy*.

42. Robert D. Atkinson, "Don't Believe Amity Shlaes (or Most Neoclassical Economists): Obama's Accelerated Depreciation Proposal Will Boost Economic Growth and Is a Good Idea," *The Innovation Files* (blog), November 24, 2010, http://www.innovationfiles.org/don%E2%80%99t-believe-amity-shlaes-or-most-neo-classical-economists-obama%E2%80%99s-accelerated-depreciation-proposal-will-boost-economic-growth-and-is-a-good-idea/.

43. Pollard, *Wasting of the British Economy*.

44. Ibid.

45. Ibid.

46. Ibid.

47. Pope, *British Economy since 1914*.

48. Pollard, *Wasting of the British Economy*.

49. Organization for Economic Cooperation and Development (OECD), *OECD Science, Technology and Industry Scoreboard 2011* (Paris: OECD, 2011), 119, http://www.oecd-ilibrary.org/science-and-technology/oecd-science-technology-and-industry-scoreboard-2011_sti_scoreboard-2011-en.

50. Kitson and Michie, "Britain's Industrial Performance."

51. Pollard, *Wasting of the British Economy*.

52. "Geithner: U.S. Won't Seek to Weaken Dollar to Spur Growth," *CNBC.com*, November 11, 2010, http://www.cnbc.com/id/40122177/Geithner_US_Won_t_Seek_to_Weaken_Dollar_to_Spur_Growth/.

53. Takashi Nakamichi, "Geithner Affirms Strong Dollar Policy," *Wall Street Journal*, November 11, 2009, http://online.wsj.com/article/SB125792362908743307.html.

54. Emily Kaiser and Tabassum Zakaria, "Bush Says 'We're Strong Dollar People,'" *Reuters*, July 2, 2008, http://www.reuters.com/article/2008/07/02/us-g8-bush-dollar-idUSWAT00972220080702/.

55. Donna Smith, "Bush Says He Believes in Strong Dollar," *Reuters*, February 28, 2008, http://www.reuters.com/article/idUSWAT00899420080228/.

56. Allan Naes Gjerding, "Innovation Economics: Part I: An Introduction to Its Birth and International Context" (working paper, Center for International Studies, Aalborg University, 1997).

57. Pollard, *Wasting of the British Economy.*

58. A notable exception is Jared Bernstein, chief economist for Vice President Joe Biden.

59. Pollard, *Wasting of the British Economy.*

60. Ibid.

61. Ibid.

62. Ibid.

63. Kitson and Michie, "Britain's Industrial Performance."

64. Kevin Hassett, "Obama's Obsession Drives Progress in Reverse," *Bloomberg*, August 15, 2010, http://www.bloomberg.com/news/2010-08-16/obama-s-obsession-drives-progress-in-reverse-commentary-by-kevin-hassett.html.

65. John Eatwell, *Whatever Happened to Britain? The Economics of Decline* (New York: Oxford University Press, 1984).

66. Tania Branigan, "China's Tianhe-1A Takes Supercomputer Crown from U.S.," *Guardian*, October 28, 2010, http://www.guardian.co.uk/technology/2010/oct/28/china-tianhe-1a-fastest-supercomputer/.

67. Pollard, *Wasting of the British Economy.*

68. Pope, *British Economy since 1914.*

Chapter 4: Why Do So Many Refuse to See
U.S. Structural Economic Decline?

1. Members of the 2005 Rising Above the Gathering Storm Committee, *Rising Above the Gathering Storm, Revisited: Rapidly Approaching Category 5* (Washington, DC: National Academies Press, 2010), http://www.uic.edu/home/Chancellor/risingabove.pdf.

2. Titus Galama and James R. Hosek, *U.S. Competitiveness in Science and Technology* (Santa Monica, CA: RAND, 2008), http://www.rand.org/pubs/monographs/2008/RAND_MG674.pdf.

3. Gregory Tassey, "Globalization of Technology-Based Growth: The Policy Imperative," *Journal of Technology Transfer* 33, no. 6 (2008): 560–578, http://www.nist.gov/director/planning/upload/tassey_jtt_2008.pdf.

4. Clyde Prestowitz, *The Betrayal of American Prosperity: Free Market Delusions, America's Decline, and How We Must Compete in the Post-Dollar Era* (New York: Free Press, 2010).

5. Ibid., 91.

6. Judith Stein, *Pivotal Decade: How the United States Traded Factories for Finance in the Seventies* (New Haven, CT: Yale University Press, 2010).

7. Irwin Stelzer, "Chinese Chess," *Weekly Standard*, December 18, 2010, http://www.weeklystandard.com/blogs/chinese-chess_523513.html.

8. RAND Corporation, "U.S. Still Leads the World in Science and Technology: Nation Benefits from Foreign Scientists, Engineers," news release, June 12, 2008, http://www.rand.org/news/press/2008/06/12.html.

9. Robert D. Atkinson, *Innovation in America: Opportunities and Obstacles, before the Subcommittee on Competitiveness, Innovation and Export Promotion, United States Senate*, 111th Cong., June 22, 2010, http://www.itif.org/files/2010-06-RAtkinson-Senate-Innovation-Leadership-Testimony.pdf.

10. David Brooks, "The Crossroads Nation," *New York Times*, November 8, 2010, http://www.nytimes.com/2010/11/09/opinion/09brooks.html.

11. Robert D. Atkinson and Luke Stewart, *University Research Funding: The United States Is Behind and Falling* (Washington, DC: Information Technology and Innovation Foundation [ITIF], May 2011), http://www.itif.org/files/2011-university-research-funding.pdf.

12. Richard McCormack, "Council on Competitiveness Says U.S. Has Little to Fear but Fear Itself; By Most Measures, U.S. Is Way Ahead of Global Competitors," *Manufacturing & Technology News* 13, no. 21, November 30, 2006, http://www.mrcpa.org/pdf/1206g.pdf.

13. Gregory Tassey, *The Technology Imperative* (Northampton, MA: Edward Elgar, 2007).

14. Robert D. Atkinson and Scott M. Andes, *The Atlantic Century II: Benchmarking EU and U.S. Innovation and Competitiveness* (Washington, DC: ITIF, 2011), http://www.itif.org/files/2011-atlantic-century.pdf.

15. Klaus Schwab, Xavier Sala-i-Martin, and Robert Greenhill, *The Global Competitiveness Report 2009–2010* (Geneva: World Economic Forum, 2009), 14, https://members.weforum.org/pdf/GCR09/GCR20092010fullreport.pdf; Confederation of Indian Industry, "GII 2008/2009 Overall Rankings," 2009, http://www.globalinnovationindex.org/gii/main/previous/2008-09/Rankings_08-09.pdf.

16. Klaus Schwab, Xavier Sala-i-Martin, and Robert Greenhill, *The Global Competitiveness Report 2010–2011* (Geneva: World Economic Forum, 2010), http://www3.weforum.org/docs/WEF_GlobalCompetitivenessReport_2010-11.pdf; Soumitra Dutta, *The Global Innovation Index 2011*, (Fontainebleau: INSEAD, 2011), http://www.globalinnovationindex.org/gii/main/fullreport/index.html.

17. Robert D. Atkinson and Scott Andes, *The Atlantic Century: Benchmarking EU and U.S. Innovation and Competitiveness* (Washington, DC: ITIF, February, 2009), http://www.itif.org/files/2009-atlantic-century.pdf.

18. Fareed Zakaria, "Is America Losing Its Mojo?" *Newsweek*, November 14, 2009, http://www.newsweek.com/2009/11/13/is-america-losing-its-mojo.html.

19. Fareed Zakaria, *The Post-American World* (New York: W. W. Norton, 2008).

20. Scott Andes and Daniel Castro, *American Competitiveness in a Post-American World* (Washington, DC: ITIF, November 11, 2009), http://www.itif.org/files/WM-2009-American-Competitiveness.pdf.

21. Robert Shapiro, *Futurecast: How Superpowers, Populations, and Globalization Will Change Your World by the Year 2020* (New York: St. Martin's Griffin, 2009).

22. Ibid.

23. Paul Krugman, "Competitiveness: A Dangerous Obsession," *Foreign Affairs* 73, no. 2 (1994): 28–44.

24. Jane Gravelle, "What Can Private Investment Incentives Accomplish? The Case of the Investment Tax Credit," *National Tax Journal*, September 1, 1993.

25. Kevin Hassett, R. Glenn Hubbard, and Matthew Jensen, *Rethinking Competitiveness* (Washington, DC: American Enterprise Institute, September 29, 2011), http://www.aei.org/files/2011/09/29/HHJ%20Competitiveness%20-2.pdf.

26. Clyde Prestowitz, "Beyond Laissez Faire," *Foreign Policy*, no. 87 (1992): 67–87.

27. James M. Borbely, "Characteristics of Displaced Workers, 2007–2009: A Visual Essay," *Bureau of Labor Statistics Monthly Labor Review*, September 2011, http://www.bls.gov/opub/mlr/2011/09/art1full.pdf.

28. Gregory Tassey, "Rationales and Mechanisms for Revitalizing U.S. Manufacturing R&D Strategies," *Journal of Technology Transfer* 35, no. 3 (2010), http://www.nist.gov/director/planning/upload/manufacturing_strategy_paper.pdf.

29. Nick Carey, "Special Report: Is America the Sick Man of the Globe?" *Reuters*, December 16, 2010, http://www.reuters.com/article/2010/12/16/us-usa-economy-special-idUSTRE6BF28720101216/.

30. Ibid.

31. Bureau of Economic Analysis, Gross-Domestic-Product-by-Industry Data (value added by industry; employment by industry), http://www.bea.gov/industry/gdpbyind_data.htm (accessed October 14, 2011).

32. Mark Perry, "Market Share of Big Three at Record Low of 47%," *Carpe Diem* (blog), April 1, 2008, http://mjperry.blogspot.com/2008/04/market-share-of-big-three-at-record-low.html; "Answer to GM's Market Share Plunge," *Official Harley Earl Website*, http://www.carofthecentury.com/answer_to_gm%27s_market_share_plunge.htm (accessed February 25, 2012).

33. Bureau of Economic Analysis, Gross Domestic Product by State (per capita real GDP by state), http://www.bea.gov/regional/index.htm (accessed October 14, 2011).

34. Tassey, "Rationales and Mechanisms."

35. Richard McCormack, "The Plight of American Manufacturing," *American Prospect*, December 21, 2009, http://www.prospect.org/cs/articles?article=the _plight_of_american_manufacturing.

36. Michael E. Porter and Jan W. Rifkin, "Prosperity at Risk," Harvard Business School, January 2012, http://www.hbs.edu/competitiveness/pdf/hbscompsur vey.pdf.

37. Michael Scherer, "Larry Summers' Warning about the Growth of Government (Transcript)," *Swampland* (blog), *Time*, December 13, 2010, http://swampland .blogs.time.com/2010/12/13/larry-summers-warning-about-the-growth-of -government-transcript/.

38. Neal McCluskey, "A Real Competitiveness Initiative," CATO Institute, March 18, 2006, http://www.cato.org/pub_display.php?pub_id=6010.

39. Erika Kinetz, "Who Wins and Who Loses as Jobs Move Overseas," *New York Times*, December 7, 2003, http://www.nytimes.com/2003/12/07/business/busi ness-who-wins-and-who-loses-as-jobs-move-overseas.html.

40. Robert Samuelson, "A Phony Science Gap?" *Washington Post*, February 22, 2006, http://www.washingtonpost.com/wp-dyn/content/article/2006/02/21 /AR2006022101166.html.

41. James Turner, "The Next Innovation Revolution: Laying the Groundwork for the United States," *Innovations: Technology, Governance, Globalization* 1, no. 2 (2006): 123–144.

42. Richard McCormack, "U.S. Military Fails to Learn Ancient Military Lesson," *Manufacturing & Technology News* 15, no. 18 (2008), http://www.manufacturing news.com/news/08/1017/commentary.html.

43. Denis Fred Simon, "Taiwan, Technology Transfer and Transnationalism: The Political Management of Dependency" (dissertation, University of California, Berkeley, 1980).

44. Amicus Most, *Expanding Exports: A Case Study of the Korean Experience*, (Washington, DC: U.S. Agency for International Development, June 1969), http://pdf .usaid.gov/pdf_docs/PNAAE454.pdf.

45. Ibid., 86.

46. Prestowitz, *Betrayal of American Prosperity*, 94.

47. Richard Nyberg, "Growing Highly Skilled Engineers for a High-Tech Workforce," U.S. Agency for International Development, November 2010, http:// www.usaid.gov/press/frontlines/fl_nov10/p09_workforce101116.html.

48. Prestowitz, *Betrayal of American Prosperity*, 101.

49. Stein, *Pivotal Decade*, 255.

50. Prestowitz, *Betrayal of American Prosperity*, 101.

51. Andrew Bacevich, *American Empire: The Realities and Consequences of U.S. Diplomacy* (Cambridge, MA: Harvard University Press, 2002).

52. Ibid.

53. "Reassessing George Bush," *Economist*, November 11, 2010, http://www.eco nomist.com/node/17463207/.

54. Juliana Gruenwald, "China Agrees to Boost Efforts to Promote Legal Software," *National Journal,* January 19, 2011, http://techdailydose.nationaljournal.com/2011/01/china-agrees-to-boost-efforts.php.

55. Clyde Prestowitz, "The $64 Trillion Question (Part 1)," *New Republic,* June 22, 2010, http://www.tnr.com/article/economy/75733/the-64-trillion-question-part-1/.

56. Prestowitz, *Betrayal of American Prosperity,* 259.

57. N. Gregory Mankiw, "Reflections on the Trade Deficit and Fiscal Policy," *Journal of Policy Modeling* 28, no. 6 (2006): 679–682.

58. Council on Competitiveness, *Competitiveness Index: Where America Stands* (Washington, DC: Council on Competitiveness, 2007), 30, http://www.compete.org/images/uploads/File/PDF%20Files/Competitiveness_Index_Where_America_Stands_March_2007.pdf.

59. Robert A. Blecker, *The Causes of the Trade Deficit, before the U.S. Trade Deficit Review Commission,* 106th Cong., August 19, 1999, http://govinfo.library.unt.edu/tdrc/hearings/19aug99/blecker.pdf.

60. J. Bradford Jensen, "Business Service Exporters" (working paper, Peterson Institute, Washington, DC, 2007).

61. Adam Segal, *Advantage: How American Innovation Can Overcome the Asian Challenge* (New York: W. W. Norton, 2011).

62. Atkinson and Andes, *Atlantic Century,* 19.

63. Dale Jorgenson and Koji Nomura, "The Industry Origins of the U.S.-Japan Productivity Gap," *Economic Systems Research* 19, no. 3 (2007): 315–341; Robert D. Atkinson, *Boosting European Prosperity through the Widespread Use of ICT* (Washington, DC: ITIF, November 2007), http://www.itif.org/files/EuropeanProductivity.pdf.

64. National Science Board, *Science and Engineering Indicators: 2010* (Arlington, VA: National Science Foundation, 2010), http://www.nsf.gov/statistics/seind10/pdf/seind10.pdf.

65. "Where Has All the Greatness Gone?" *Economist,* July 15, 2010, http://www.economist.com/node/16591267/.

66. Justin Lin and Celestin Monga, "Growth Identification and Facilitation: The Role of the State in the Dynamics of Structural Change" (working paper No. 5313, World Bank, 2011), http://papers.ssrn.com/sol3/papers.cfm?abstract_id=1611526.

67. Richard McCormack, "China Takes Big Lead over U.S. In Nanotechnology Research," *Manufacturing & Technology News* 18, no. 18, November 18, 2011.

68. Gary Pisano and Willy Shih, "Restoring American Competitiveness," *Harvard Business Review,* July 2009, http://hbr.org/2009/07/restoring-american-competitiveness/ar/1/.

69. Jeffrey Immelt, Vijay Govindarajan, and Chris Trimble, "How GE Is Disrupting Itself," *Harvard Business Review,* October 2009, http://hbr.org/2009/10/how-ge-is-disrupting-itself/ar/1/.

70. Dick Elkus, *Winner Take All* (New York: Basic Books, 2009).

71. Kenneth Green, "Why the U.S. Shouldn't Panic," *New York Times*, November 9, 2010, http://www.nytimes.com/roomfordebate/2010/11/08/can-the-us-compete-on-rare-earths/america-should-not-panic-about-rare-earths/.

72. "Cash Machines," *Economist*, March 31, 2011, http://www.economist.com/node/18484080?story_id=18484080.

73. Christina D. Romer, "Do Manufacturers Need Special Treatment?" *New York Times*, February 4, 2012, http://www.nytimes.com/2012/02/05/business/do-manufacturers-need-special-treatment-economic-view.html.

74. Galama and Hosek, *U.S. Competitiveness*.

75. Kevin Hassett, "Obama's Obsession Drives Progress in Reverse," *Bloomberg News*, August 15, 2010, http://www.bloomberg.com/news/2010-08-16/obama-s-obsession-drives-progress-in-reverse-commentary-by-kevin-hassett.html.

76. David Yoffe, "Why the U.S. Tech Sector Doesn't Need Domestic Manufacturing," *Harvard Business Review Blog Network*, October 5, 2009, http://blogs.hbr.org/hbr/restoring-american-competitiveness/2009/10/services-can-produce-a-bright.html.

77. Pisano and Shih, "Restoring American Competitiveness."

78. Ibid.

79. Ibid.

80. Tassey, *Technology Imperative*.

81. Pisano and Shih, "Restoring American Competitiveness."

82. Tassey, *Technology Imperative*.

83. Andy Grove, "How America Can Create Jobs," *BusinessWeek*, July 1, 2010, http://www.businessweek.com/magazine/content/10_28/b4186048358596.htm.

84. President's Council of Advisors on Science and Technology, "Sustaining the Nation's Innovation Ecosystems: Report on Information Technology Manufacturing and Competitiveness," January 2004, http://www.whitehouse.gov/sites/default/files/microsites/ostp/pcast-04-itreport.pdf.

85. Louis Uchitelle, "When Factories Vanish, So Can Innovators," *New York Times*, February 12, 2011, http://www.nytimes.com/2011/02/13/business/13every.html.

86. Richard McCormack, "It Is Now Obama's Economy: America's Oldest Printed Circuit Board Company Closes Its Doors," *Manufacturing & Technology News* 16, no. 13 (July 28, 2009), http://www.manufacturingnews.com/news/09/0728/bartlett.html.

87. National Science Board, *Science and Engineering Indicators: 2010*; Bureau of Economic Analysis, Research and Development Satellite Account (1998–2007 research and development data), http://www.bea.gov/national/newinnovation.htm (accessed December 6, 2010).

88. Richard McCormack, "The Plight of American Manufacturing."

89. Battelle and R&D Magazine, *2011 Global R&D Funding Forecast*, December 2010, 30, http://www.battelle.org/aboutus/rd/2011.pdf.

90. Michael Levi, "Misunderstanding High-Tech Trade," *Energy, Security, and Climate* (blog), December 2, 2010, http://blogs.cfr.org/levi/2010/12/02/misunderstanding-high-tech-trade/.

91. Pisano and Shih, "Restoring American Competitiveness."

92. Yoffe, "Why the U.S. Tech Sector Doesn't Need Domestic Manufacturing," citing Milton Marquis and Bharat Trehan, "Accounting for the Secular 'Decline' of U.S. Manufacturing" (working paper, Federal Reserve Bank of San Francisco, 2005).

93. Daniel Bell, *The Coming of Post-Industrial Society* (New York: Basic Books, 1973).

94. Richard McCormack, "Obama's Top Economist Discloses Why the Administration Refused to Support U.S. Manufacturing," *Manufacturing & Technology News* 17, no. 20 (December 30, 2010), http://www.manufacturingnews.com /news/newss/summers123.html.

95. Erin Lett and Judith Banister, "China's Manufacturing Employment and Compensation Costs: 2002–06," *Bureau of Labor Statistics Monthly Labor Review*, April 2009, 31, http://www.bls.gov/opub/mlr/2009/04/art3full.pdf.

96. Organization for Economic Cooperation and Development (OECD) Structural Analysis (STAN) Databases (STAN database for structural analysis), http:// www.oecd.org/sti/stan/ (accessed January 13, 2010).

97. United Nations Conference on Trade and Development, *UNCTAD Handbook of Statistics 2009* (New York: United Nations, 2009), http://www.unctad.org/en /docs/tdstat34_enfr.pdf.

98. Tassey, *Technology Imperative.*

99. David Fenton, "Green Energy Opponents Are the Real Job Killers," *Nation*, January 13, 2011, http://www.thenation.com/article/157727/green-energy-opponents -are-real-job-killers/.

100. Center for American Progress, "Green Jobs 101," December 11, 2008, http:// www.americanprogress.org/issues/2008/12/green_jobs101.html.

101. David Foster, "A National Commitment to Win the Clean Energy Race," *Huffington Post* (blog), January 20, 2011, http://www.huffingtonpost.com/david-foster /a-national-commitment-to-_b_810966.html.

102. Thomas Friedman, *Hot, Flat, and Crowded: Why We Need a Green Revolution— and How It Can Renew America* (New York: Farrar, Straus and Giroux, 2008).

103. Mark Muro, Jonathan Rothwell, and Devashree Saha, *Sizing the Clean Economy: A National and Regional Green Jobs Assessment* (Washington, DC: Brookings Institution, 2011), http://www.brookings.edu/~/media/Files/Programs/Metro /clean_economy/0713_clean_economy.pdf.

104. Ruud Kempener, Laura Anadon, and Jose Condor, *Energy Innovation Policy in Major Emerging Countries* (Cambridge, MA: Belfer Center for Science and International Affairs, Harvard Kennedy School, December 2010), http://belfercenter .ksg.harvard.edu/files/BRIMCS_policy_brief_final_2.pdf.

105. Robert D. Atkinson et al., *Rising Tigers, Sleeping Giant: Asian Nations Set to Dominate the Clean Energy Race by Out-Investing the United States* (Oakland, CA: Breakthrough Institute; Washington, DC: ITIF, 2009), http://www.itif.org /files/2009-rising-tigers.pdf.

Chapter 5: What Are Innovation and Innovation Policy and Why Are They Important?

1. Organization for Economic Cooperation and Development (OECD), *The OECD Innovation Strategy* (Paris: OECD, 2010), 20, http://www.oecd.org/document /15/0,3343,en_2649_34273_45154895_1_1_1_1,00.html.

2. Joseph Schumpeter, *Capitalism, Socialism and Democracy* (New York: Harper, 1975), 82–85.

3. John Kao, *Innovation Nation* (New York: Free Press, 2007).

4. Tekes, "Seizing the White Space: Innovative Service Concepts in the United States," *Technology Review*, no. 205 (2007): 72–74, http://www.tekes.fi/en/doc ument/43000/innovative_service_pdf.

5. OECD, "Economics: Innovation Central to Boosting Growth and Jobs," news release, May 27, 2010, http://www.oecd.org/document/36/0,3343,en_2649_34273 _45324068_1_1_1_1,00.html.

6. Elhanan Helpman, *The Mystery of Economic Growth* (Cambridge, MA: Belknap Press, 2004).

7. National Endowment for Science, Technology and the Arts, *The Innovation Index: Measuring the U.K.'s Investment in Innovation and Its Effects* (London: NESTA, 2009), http://www.nesta.org.uk/library/documents/innovation-index.pdf.

8. Helpman, *Mystery of Economic Growth*, 32.

9. David Leech et al., *92–2 Planning Report: The Economics of a Technology-Based Service Sector* (Arlington, VA: Analytic Sciences Corporation [TASC], 1998), http://www.nist.gov/director/planning/upload/report98-2.pdf.

10. Edwin Mansfield, "Academic Research and Industrial Innovation: An Update of Empirical Findings," *Research Policy* 26, no. 7–8 (1998): 773–776.

11. Patrick Brogan, "The Economic Benefits of Broadband and Information Technology," *Media Law and Policy* 18 (Spring 2009); Robert D. Atkinson et al., *The Internet Economy 25 Years After.com: Transforming Life and Commerce* (Washington, DC: Information Technology and Innovation Foundation [ITIF], 2010), http://www.itif.org/files/2010-25-years.pdf.

12. Arti Rai, Stuart Graham, and Mark Doms, "Patent Reform: Unleashing Innovation, Promoting Economic Growth, and Producing High-Paying Jobs" (white paper, Department of Commerce, April 13, 2010), 1, http://www.commerce.gov /sites/default/files/documents/migrated/Patent_Reform-paper.pdf.

13. Larry Keeley, "The Taming of the New: Larry Keeley Workshop on Innovation," workshop, Puget Sound SIGCHI, Seattle, September 18, 2007; Carl Franklin, *Why Innovation Fails* (London: Spiro, 2003).

14. Erik Brynjolfsson and Adam Saunders, *Wired for Innovation: How Information Technology Is Reshaping the Economy* (Cambridge, MA: MIT Press, 2010), x.

15. Amil Petrin, T. Kirk White, and Jerome Reiter, "The Impact of Plant-Level Resource Allocations and Technical Progress on U.S. Macroeconomic Growth" (discussion paper, Center for Economic Studies, U.S. Census Bureau, December 2009).

16. Curtis Carlson and William Wilmot, *Innovation: The Five Disciplines for Creating What Customers Want* (New York: Crown Business, 2006), 34–35.

17. U.S. Census Bureau, Business Dynamics Statistics, Database List (economy wide), http://www.ces.census.gov/index.php/bds/bds_database_list/ (accessed January 6, 2011).

18. David B. Audretsch et al., "Impeded Industrial Restructuring: The Growth Penalty," *Kyklos* 55, no. 1 (2002): 81–97.

19. Robert Litan, "Inventive Billion Dollar Firms: A Faster Way to Grow," (Ewing Marion Kauffman Foundation, Kansas City, MO, December 2010), 5, http://www.kauffman.org/uploadedFiles/billion_dollar_firms.pdf.

20. Schumpeter, *Capitalism, Socialism and Democracy*, 84.

21. Lori Kletzer, *Imports, Exports, and Jobs: What Does Trade Mean for Employment and Job Loss?* (Kalamazoo, MI: W. E. Upjohn Institute, 2002).

22. Robert D. Atkinson, *Corporate Tax Reform: Groupthink or Rational Analysis?* (Washington, DC: ITIF, July 2011), http://www.itif.org/files/2011-corporate-tax-reform.pdf.

23. "Government's Communication on Finland's National Innovation Strategy to the Parliament," Finnish Ministry of Employment and the Economy, March 2009, 20, http://www.tem.fi/files/21010/National_Innovation_Strategy_March_2009.pdf.

24. Annabelle Malins, speech, National Foreign Trade Council, Washington, DC, April 15, 2010.

25. Adam Smith, *An Inquiry into the Natures and Causes of the Wealth of Nations* (New York: Modern Library, 1937).

26. Stephen Ezell and Robert D. Atkinson, *The Good, the Bad, and the Ugly (and the Self-Destructive) of Innovation Policy: A Policymaker's Guide to Crafting Effective Innovation Policy* (Washington, DC: ITIF, 2010), http://www.itif.org/files/2010-good-bad-ugly.pdf.

27. "Picking Winners, Saving Losers," *Economist*, August 5, 2010, http://www.economist.com/node/16741043/.

28. Ibid.

29. Barry James, "Beyond Minitel: France on the Internet," *New York Times*, January 8, 1996, http://www.nytimes.com/1996/01/08/news/08iht-minitel.t.html.

30. Michael Schrage, "European High-Tech Policy a Poor Model," *Los Angeles Times*, April 4, 1991, http://articles.latimes.com/1991-04-04/business/fi-2825_1_european-computer.

31. Victoria Shannon, "Quaero Gets Off the Ground to Challenge Google," *New York Times*, March 21, 2008, http://www.nytimes.com/2008/03/21/technology/21iht-quaero24.html.

32. Robert D. Atkinson, "For Once and for All, Let's Agree the Government Can and Should Pick Winners," *Huffington Post* (blog), April 22, 2010, http://www.huffingtonpost.com/robert-d-atkinson-phd/for-once-and-for-all-lets_b_548145.html.

33. Gregory Tassey, *The Technology Imperative* (Northampton, MA: Edward Elgar, 2007).

34. Glenn Fong, "Breaking New Ground or Breaking the Rules: Strategic Reorientation in U.S. Industrial Policy," *International Security* 25, no. 2 (2000): 152–186; Henry Etzkowitz, "Innovation in Innovation: The Triple Helix of University-Industry-Government Relations," *Social Science Information* 42, no. 3 (2003): 293–337.

35. Dani Rodrik, "Industrial Policy for the Twenty-First Century" (working paper, Kennedy School of Government, Harvard University, 2004), 38, http://www.hks .harvard.edu/fs/drodrik/Research%20papers/UNIDOSep.pdf.

36. National Economic Council, "A Strategy for American Innovation: Driving towards Sustainable Growth and Quality Jobs," Executive Office of the President, Washington, DC, September 2009, http://www.whitehouse.gov/administration /eop/nec/StrategyforAmericanInnovation/.

37. Douglass North, "Economic Performance through Time," Nobel Prize lecture, Royal Swedish Academy of the Sciences, Stockholm, December 9, 1993, http:// nobelprize.org/nobel_prizes/economics/laureates/1993/north-lecture.html.

38. John Barber, "Setting the Scene," presentation, Six Countries Program Workshop, Bilbao, Spain, September 14, 2009, http://www.6cp.net/downloads/Posi tion%20papers%206CP%20Bilbao%2014%20September.pdf.

39. Iyaz Akhtar, "Eight Companies That Shouldn't Make a Tablet," *PC Magazine*, January 20, 2011, http://www.pcmag.com/article2/0,2817,2375995,00.asp.

40. See Charles Jones and John Williams, "Measuring the Social Return to R&D," *Quarterly Journal of Economics* 113, no. 4 (1998): 1119–1135; Edwin Mansfield, "Social Returns from R&D: Findings, Methods, and Limitations," *Research Technology Management* 34, no. 6 (1991): 24–27; Eric Brynjolfsson, Lauren Hitt, and Shinkyu Yang, "Intangible Assets: How the Interaction of Information Technology and Organizational Structure Affects Stock Market Valuations," *Brookings Papers on Economic Activity* 33 (January 2000): 137–199.

41. J. Tewksbury, M. Crandall, and W. Crane, "Measuring the Societal Benefits of Innovation," *Science* 209, no. 4457 (1980): 658–662, http://www.sciencemag .org/content/209/4457/658.

42. William Nordhaus, "Schumpeterian Profits and the Alchemist Fallacy" (working paper, Department of Economics, Yale University, 2005), http://www.econ .yale.edu/ddp/ddp00/ddp0006.pdf.

43. Lorin Hitt and Prasanna Tambe, "Measuring Spillovers from Information Technology Investments" (conference paper, Twenty-Seventh International Conference on Information Systems, Milwaukee, WI, 2006), http://opim.wharton .upenn.edu/~lhitt/files/itspillovers.pdf.

44. Carmine Ornaghi, "Spillovers in Product and Process Innovation: Evidence from Manufacturing Firms" (working paper, Department of Economics, Carlos III University of Madrid, 2002), http://www.eea-esem.com/papers/eea-esem /2003/2168/spillovers.pdf.

45. Ibid., 37.
46. Ping Lin and Kamal Saggi, "Product Differentiation, Process R&D and the Nature of Market Competition," *European Economic Review* 46, no. 1 (2002): 201–211, http://www.ln.edu.hk/econ/staff/eer.pdf.
47. Elena Cefis, Stephanie Rosenkranz, and Utz Weitzel, "Effects of Coordinated Strategies on Product and Process R&D," *Journal of Economics* 96, no. 3 (2009): 193–222, http://www2.econ.uu.nl/users/rosenkranz/CRW_final_2008july08.pdf.
48. John A. Alic, Lewis M. Branscomb, Harvey Brooks, Aston B. Carter, and Gerald L. Epstein, eds., *Beyond Spinoff: Military and Commercial Technologies in a Changing World* (Cambridge, MA: Harvard University Press, 1992).
49. Atkinson et al., *Internet Economy*.
50. Gregory Tassey, "Globalization of Technology-Based Growth: The Policy Imperative," *Journal of Technology Transfer* 33, no. 6 (2008).
51. Ibid.
52. Michael Gallaher et al., "Economic Analysis of the Technology Infrastructure Needs of the U.S. Biopharmaceutical Industry" (Research Triangle Park, NC: RTI International, November 2007), http://www.nist.gov/director/planning/upload/report07-1.pdf.
53. Tassey, "Globalization of Technology."
54. Daniel Okimoto, *Between MITI and the Market: Japanese Industrial Policy for High Technology* (Stanford, CA: Stanford University Press, 1987).
55. Martin Fransman, *The Market and Beyond: Information Technology in Japan* (Cambridge, UK: Cambridge University Press, 1993).
56. Alfred Rappaport, *Saving Capitalism from Short-Termism: How to Build Long-Term Value and Take Back Our Financial Future* (New York: McGraw Hill, 2011).
57. Francesco Guerrera, "Welch Condemns Share Price Focus," *Financial Times*, March 12, 2009, http://www.ft.com/intl/cms/s/0/294ff1f2-0f27-11de-ba10-0000779fd2ac.html#axzz1nUgIyDFy.
58. National Science Board, *Science and Engineering Indicators: 2010* (Arlington, VA: National Science Foundation, 2010), http://www.nsf.gov/statistics/seind10/pdf/seind10.pdf.
59. William Lazonick, "The U.S. Stock Market and the Governance of Innovative Enterprise," *Industrial and Corporate Change* 16, no. 6 (2007): 983–1035, http://papers.ssrn.com/sol3/papers.cfm?abstract_id=1151065.
60. Ibid., 1031.
61. Adam Brandenburger and Barry Nalebuff, *Co-opetition: A Revolutionary Mindset That Combines Competition and Cooperation: The Game Theory Strategy That's Changing the Game of Business* (New York: Doubleday, 1998).
62. Barber, "Setting the Scene."
63. Erica Fuchs, "Rethinking the Role of the State in Technology Development: DARPA and the Case for Embedded Network Governance" (working paper, Department of Engineering and Public Policy, Carnegie Mellon University, 2010), http://repository.cmu.edu/cgi/viewcontent.cgi?article=1000&context=epp.
64. Ibid., 26.

65. On the conflict between the desires of firms to appropriate university research capacity and the broader social and economic role of universities in promoting the free flow of knowledge, see Richard Lester and Michael Piore, *Innovation: The Missing Dimension* (Cambridge, MA: Harvard University Press, 2004).

66. Stephen Ezell, *Explaining International Leadership in Contactless Mobile Payments* (Washington, DC: ITIF, November 2009), http://www.itif.org/files/2009 -Mobile-Payments.pdf.

67. See *Explaining International IT Leadership* (Washington, DC: ITIF, September 15, 2011), http://www.itif.org/publications/explaining-international-it-application -leadership.

68. Barry LePatner, *Broken Buildings, Busted Budgets: How to Fix America's Trillion-Dollar Construction Industry* (Chicago: University of Chicago Press, 2007).

69. Shane Ham and Robert D. Atkinson, *Modernizing Home Buying: How IT Can Empower Individuals, Slash Costs, and Transform the Real Estate Industry* (Washington, DC: Progressive Policy Institute, 2003), http://www.dlc.org/ndol_ci.cfm ?kaid=140&subid=900055&contentid=251396.

70. Daniel Castro, *Improving Health Care: Why a Dose of IT May Be Just What the Doctor Ordered* (Washington, DC: ITIF, October 2007), http://www.itif.org/files /HealthIT.pdf.

71. James Johnston, *Power of Attorneys: Will the Organized Bar Thwart the Emergence of Online Law?* (Washington, DC: ITIF, 2006), http://www.itif.org/files /powerofattorneys.pdf.

72. Robert D. Atkinson, *The Revenge of the Disintermediated* (Washington, DC: Progressive Policy Institute, 2001), http://www.dlc.org/documents/disintermediated .pdf.

73. LePatner, *Broken Buildings, Busted Budgets*.

74. Joseph Cortright, *Making Sense of Clusters: Regional Competitiveness and Economic Development* (Washington, DC: Brookings Institution, 2006); Andrew Reamer, Larry Icerman, and Jan Youtie, *Technology Transfer and Commercialization: Their Role in Economic Development* (Washington, DC: Department of Commerce, Economic Development Administration, 2003), 57–110.

75. Robert D. Atkinson, *Innovation in America: Opportunities and Obstacles, before the Subcommittee on Competitiveness, Innovation and Export Promotion, United States Senate*, 111th Cong., June 22, 2010, http://www.itif.org/files/2010-06 -RAtkinson-Senate-Innovation-Leadership-Testimony.pdf.

76. Elvio Accinelli, Silvia London, and Edgar Sanchez Carrera, "Complementarity and Imitative Behavior in the Populations of Firms and Workers" (working paper, Department of Economics, University of Siena, 2009), http://www.econ -pol.unisi.it/quaderni/554.pdf.

77. For a detailed treatment of this issue in the context of international trade, see Ralph Gomory and William Baumol, *Global Trade and Conflicting National Interests* (Cambridge, MA: MIT Press, 2000).

78. Benjamin Friedman, *The Moral Consequences of Economic Growth* (New York: A. A. Knopf, 2005).

Chapter 6: Crafting Innovation Policy to Win the Race

1. This is inspired in part by the work of Andrew Reamer, who has proposed a similar framework of "I's." An eighth "I" is added in chapter 8.

2. Azeem Ibrahim, "Every Country Must Have a National Innovation Strategy," *Huffington Post* (blog), January 31, 2011, http://www.huffingtonpost.com/azeem -ibrahim/every-country-must-have-a_b_753255.html.

3. Cong Cao, Richard P. Suttmeier, and Denis F. Simon, "China's 15-Year Science and Technology Plan," *Physics Today* 59, no. 12 (December 2006): 38–43, http:// scitation.aip.org/journals/doc/PHTOAD-ft/vol_59/iss_12/38_1.shtml.

4. Chris Buckley, "China Confirms $1.7 Trillion Spending Plan: U.S.," *Reuters*, November 21, 2011, http://mobile.reuters.com/article/idUSTRE7AK0MT20111121 ?irpc=932.

5. *Overview Hearing: Gas Prices and Vehicle Technology, before the House Appropriations Subcommittee on Energy and Water Development,* 110 Cong. (2008), Testimony of Don Hillebrand, Director, Center for Transportation Research, Argonne National Laboratory, http://www.anl.gov/Media_Center/News/2008/080214 -Hillebrand_oral_testimony.pdf.

6. Robert D. Atkinson et al., *Rising Tigers, Sleeping Giant: Asian Nations Set to Dominate the Clean Energy Race by Out-Investing the United States* (Oakland, CA: Breakthrough Institute; Washington, DC: Information Technology and Innovation Foundation [ITIF], 2009), http://www.itif.org/files/2009-rising-tigers.pdf.

7. Peter Westersträhle, "National Innovation Strategy of Finland" (presentation, Washington, DC, September 28, 2009), http://www.itif.org/files/ITIF_PWester strahle.pdf.

8. Thomas Hout and Pankaj Ghemawat, "China vs. the World: Whose Technology Is It?" *Harvard Business Review*, December 2010, http://hbr.org/2010/12/china -vs-the-world-whose-technology-is-it/ar/1.

9. Organization for Economic Cooperation and Development (OECD), *OECD Main Science and Technology Indicators: 2010* (Paris: OECD, 2010); OECD, *OECD Main Science and Technology Indicators: 2000* (Paris: OECD, 2000).

10. OECD Tax Database (Table II.1; basic corporate income tax rates), http://www .oecd.org/document/60/0,3746,en_2649_34533_1942460_1_1_1_1,00.html (accessed January 21, 2011).

11. Robert Murphy, "An Ironic Twist in Fiscal Policy," *Great Debate* (blog), *Reuters*, September 27, 2010, http://blogs.reuters.com/great-debate/2010/09/27/an -ironic-twist-in-fiscal-policy/.

12. World Bank, World Development Indicators 2010 (GDP per capita, PPP), http:// data.worldbank.org/data-catalog/world-development-indicators/ (accessed February 3, 2011).

13. "The 12 Most Innovative Countries," *Daily Beast*, June 2, 2010, http://www.thedai lybeast.com/galleries/2010/06/01/the-world-s-most-innovative-countries.html.

14. Erica Fuchs, "Rethinking the Role of the State in Technology Development: DARPA and the Case for Embedded Network Governance" (working paper, De-

partment of Engineering and Public Policy, Carnegie Mellon University, 2010), http://repository.cmu.edu/cgi/viewcontent.cgi?article=1000&context=epp.

15. German Federal Ministry of Education and Research (BMBF), *The High-Tech Strategy of Germany* (Berlin, Germany: BMBF, 2006), http://bmbf.de/pub/bmbf _hts_lang_eng.pdf.

16. German Federal Ministry of Education and Research, *High-Tech Strategy 2020 for Germany* (Berlin, Germany: BMBF, 2010), http://www.bmbf.de/pub/hts_2020 _en.pdf.

17. Tekes, "Seizing the White Space: Innovative Service Concepts in the United States," *Technology Review*, no. 205 (2007), http://www.tekes.fi/en/document /43000/innovative_service_pdf.

18. FORA, *New Nature of Innovation* (Copenhagen: OECD, 2009), 69, http://www .newnatureofinnovation.org/full_report.pdf.

19. National Endowment for Science, Technology, and the Arts (NESTA), "Measuring Innovation" (policy briefing, July 2008), http://www.nesta.org.uk/library /documents/Measuring-Innovation-v3.pdf.

20. FORA, *New Nature of Innovation*, 90.

21. Robert D. Atkinson, *Effective Corporate Tax Reform in the Global Innovation Economy* (Washington, DC: ITIF, July 2009), http://www.itif.org/files/090723 _CorpTax.pdf.

22. OECD, *OECD Science, Technology, and Industry Scoreboard: 2009* (Paris: OECD, 2009), 79.

23. Matthew Stepp and Robert D. Atkinson, *Creating a Collaborative R&D Tax Credit* (Washington, DC: ITIF, June 2011), http://www.itif.org/files/2011-creating-r&d -credit.pdf.

24. Robert D. Atkinson and Scott Andes, *Patent Boxes: Innovation in Tax Policy and Tax Policy for Innovation* (Washington, DC: ITIF, October 2011), http://www.itif .org/files/2011-patent-box-final.pdf.

25. Netherlands Ministry of Finance, "Doing Business in the Netherlands: Innovation Box," http://english.minfin.nl/Subjects/Taxation/Doing_business_in_the _Netherlands/Innovation_box/ (accessed August 24, 2011).

26. Neal Stender, Joel Stark, and Forrest L. Ye, "China Income Tax Preferences for High/New-Tech Enterprises (HNTE)" (technical report, Orrick, Herrington and Sutcliffe, Wheeling, WV, 2010), http://www.orrick.com/fileupload/2420.pdf.

27. OECD, *The OECD Innovation Strategy* (Paris: OECD, 2010), 97, http://www .oecd.org/document/15/0,3343,en_2649_34273_45154895_1_1_1,00.html.

28. Wen-Jung Lien et al., "The Economic Impact of Taiwan's Investment Tax Credits and Its Direction of Adjustment," *International Journal of Technology Management* 49, no. 1–3 (2010): 140–154, http://www.inderscience.com/search /index.php?action=record&rec_id=29415&prevQuery=&ps=10&m=or.

29. Ibid.

30. Internal Revenue Service, SOI Tax Stats (Table 21; returns of active corporations), http://www.irs.gov/taxstats/article/0,,id=170734,00.html (accessed January 15, 2011).

31. Deloitte, "International Tax and Business Guide: Malaysia," 2010, http://www
.deloitte.com/assets/Dcom-Global/Local%20Assets/Documents/Tax/Taxation
%20and%20Investment%20Guides/2010/dttl_tax_guide_2010_Malaysia.pdf
(accessed January 15, 2011).

32. Deloitte, "Taxation and Investment Guides and Country Highlights," http://
www.deloitte.com/taxguides (accessed January 15, 2011).

33. Department of Finance Canada, "Tax Expenditures and Evaluations 2010,"
http://fin.gc.ca/taxexp-depfisc/2010/taxexp1004-eng.asp#tocnotes-05 (accessed
January 15, 2011).

34. Tal Barak Harif, "Israel Offers Salary Incentives to Draw Foreign Banks' R&D
Centers," *BusinessWeek,* July 27, 2010, http://www.bloomberg.com/news/2010
-07-27/israel-offers-salary-incentives-to-draw-international-banks-r-d-centers
.html.

35. Ruth David, "India Snoozed, Lost Intel Chip Plant," *Forbes,* September 6, 2007,
http://www.forbes.com/2007/09/06/intel-india-china-markets-equity-cx_rd
_0906markets1.html.

36. Margie Manson, "Intel to Invest $1 Billion in Vietnam as Country Strives to
Raise High-Tech Profile," *USA Today,* November 18, 2006, http://www.usatoday
.com/tech/news/2006-11-18-vietnam_x.htm.

37. Richard McCormack, "Intel CEO Says U.S. Would Lose No Tax Revenue by
Providing Companies with Tax Holidays to Open Plants and Hire Workers,"
Manufacturing and Technology News 17, no. 17 (October 29, 2010), http://www
.manufacturingnews.com/news/newss/intel102.html.

38. Ibid.

39. Government Offices of Sweden, "Government Bill: A Boost to Research and Innovation," November 17, 2008, http://www.sweden.gov.se/sb/d/6949/a/115809/.

40. Jukka Haapamäki and Ulla Mäkeläinen, "Universities 2006," Finnish Ministry of Education, 2007, 23–24, http://www.minedu.fi/export/sites/default
/OPM/Julkaisut/2007/liitteet/opm19.pdf.

41. World Bank, "Doing Business: Measuring Business Regulations," http://www
.doingbusiness.org/ (accessed August 28, 2011).

42. Antonio Ciccone and Elias Papaioannou, "Red Tape and Delayed Entry," *Journal of the European Economic Association* 5, no. 2–3 (2007): 444–458, http://
www.ecb.int/pub/pdf/scpwps/ecbwp758.pdf.

43. "Better Regulation," Business Link, http://www.businesslink.gov.uk/bdotg
/action/layer?topicId=1084828139 (accessed September 21, 2011.).

44. Robert D. Atkinson and Howard Wial, *Boosting Productivity, Innovation, and
Growth through a National Innovation Foundation* (Washington, DC: ITIF,
2008), http://www.itif.org/files/NIF.pdf.

45. Steve Lohr, "Can Governments Till the Fields of Innovation?" *New York Times,*
June 21, 2009, http://www.nytimes.com/2009/06/21/technology/21unboxed
.html.

46. "What Is Oivallus?" *Oivallus,* http://ek.multiedition.fi/oivallus/en/index_copy
.php (accessed November 28, 2011).

47. FORA, *New Nature of Innovation*, 80.

48. Roy Rothwell, "Technology Based Small Firms and Regional Innovation Potential: The Role of Public Procurement," *Journal of Public Policy* 4, no. 4 (1984): 307–332, http://www.jstor.org/pss/3998373.

49. U.K. Department of Business, Innovation and Skills, "OGC Procurement Guide Launched," news release, April 17, 2009, http://webarchive.national archives.gov.uk/+/http://www.dius.gov.uk/news_and_speeches/press_releases /ogc_procurement_guide/.

50. Scott Andes, *Buying Innovation: How Public Procurement Can Spur Innovation* (Washington, DC: ITIF, October 2010), http://www.itif.org/files/2010-buying -innovation-analysis.pdf.

51. Finnish National Fund for Research and Development (SITRA), *Making Finland a Leading Country in Innovation: Final Report of the Competitive Innovation Environment Development Programme* (Helsinki: SITRA, 2005), http://www.edis .sk/ekes/Inno1engl.pdf.

52. Jakob Edler et al., *Innovation and Public Procurement: Review of Issues at Stake* (Munich: Fraunhofer, 2005), http://cordis.europa.eu/innovation-policy/studies /full_study.pdf.

53. Gregory Tassey, "Beyond the Business Cycle: The Need for a Technology-Based Growth Strategy," (Gaithersburg, MD: National Institute of Standards and Technology, February 2012), http://www.nist.gov/director/planning/upload/beyond -business-cycle.pdf.; Data: OECD, *Main Science and Technology Indicators: 2010*, http://www.oecd-ilibrary.org/content/data/data-00182-en/.

54. "About VINNOVA," VINNOVA, November 3, 2010, http://www.vinnova.se/en /About-VINNOVA/.

55. Atkinson and Wial, *Boosting Productivity, Innovation, and Growth*.

56. "Fraunhofer Business Model," Fraunhofer, http://www.fraunhofer.de/en/about -fraunhofer/business-model/ (accessed September 28, 2011).

57. "Facts and Figures at a Glance," Fraunhofer, http://www.fraunhofer.de/en /about-fraunhofer (accessed September 28, 2011).

58. GoAuto.com.au, "VW, Germany Invests in Lithium-ion Batteries," news release, November 27, 2008, http://www.goauto.com.au/mellor/mellor.nsf/story2/5712 F84DC50D73E1CA2573A00082E3CB.

59. Technology Strategy Board, "Innovation Platforms," 2011, http://www.innova teuk.org/ourstrategy/innovationplatforms.ashx (accessed August 24, 2011).

60. Stephen Ezell and Robert D. Atkinson, *International Benchmarking of Countries' Policies and Programs Supporting SME Manufacturers* (Washington, DC: ITIF, September 2011), http://www.itif.org/files/2011-sme-manufacturing-tech-pro gramss-new.pdf.

61. Ibid., 39.

62. M. Cornet et al., "De effectiviteit van de innovatievoucher, 2004," CPB Document No. 95, The Hague, 2005.

63. Barbara Good and Brigitte Tiefenthaler, "Zwischenevaluierung des Programms Innovationsscheck," Technopolis Group, August 11, 2010, http://www.bmvit.gv

.at/innovation/strukturprogramme/downloadsstruktur/zwischenevaluierung
_innovationsscheck.pdf.

64. The Sectoral e-Business Watch, "Chart Report: The e-Business Survey 2006" (slide show, Enterprise and Industry Directorate General, European Commission, 2006), http://www.ebusiness-watch.org/statistics/documents/ChartRep _2006_000.ppt.

65. Hideyuki Oku, "Japan National Strategy for ICT R&D" (slide show, ICT Global Strategy Bureau, Ministry of Internal Affairs and Communications, Tokyo, 2009), http://ec.europa.eu/information_society/activities/foi/research/eu-japan /prog/docs/day1stam/hoku.pdf.

66. Korea e-Government, "Key Achievements," http://www.korea.go.kr/new_eng /service/viewContent.do?enContId=00001264605158939000_151 (accessed August 28, 2011).

67. National Information Society Agency, *Informatization White Paper: Republic of Korea* (Seoul: NIA, 2010).

68. Priscilla Wong and Virginia Cha, "The Evolution of Government Infocomm Plans: Singapore's e-Government Journey (1980–2007)," National University of Singapore, April 2009, http://www.egl.sg/downloads/e-Gov_Journey_Paper.pdf.

69. Infocomm Development Authority of Singapore, "Overview," November 11, 2010, http://www.ida.gov.sg/Infrastructure/20060411230420.aspx.

70. Robert D. Atkinson et al., *Innovation, Trade, and Technology Policies in Asia-Pacific Economies: A Scorecard* (Washington, DC: U.S. Agency for International Development and ITIF, December 2011), http://www.itif.org/publications /innovation-trade-and-technology-policies-asia-pacific-economies-scorecard.

71. U.K. Department for Business Innovation and Skills, and Department for Culture, Media and Sport, *Digital Britain* (London: Crown, 2009), http://webar chive.nationalarchives.gov.uk/+/http://www.culture.gov.uk/images/publica tions/digitalbritain-finalreport-jun09.pdf.

72. Blair Levin, "National Broadband Plan: National Purposes" (presentation, Washington, DC, March 11, 2010), http://www.itif.org/files/2010-national-broadband -plan.pdf.

73. Robert D. Atkinson, Daniel Correa, and Julie Hedlund, *Explaining International Broadband Leadership* (Washington, DC: ITIF, 2008), http://www.itif.org/files /ExplainingBBLeadership.pdf.

74. Daniel Castro, *Explaining International Health IT Leadership* (Washington, DC: ITIF, December 2009), http://www.itif.org/files/2009-leadership-healthit.pdf.

75. Päivi Hämäläinen, Jarmo Reponen, and Ilkka Winblad, *eHealth of Finland* (Helsinki: Stakes, 2007), http://www.stakes.fi/verkkojulkaisut/raportit/R1-2007 -VERKKO.pdf.

76. Persephone Doupi and Pekka Ruotsalainen, "eHealth in Finland: Present Status and Future Trends," *International Journal of Circumpolar Health* 63, no. 4 (2004): 323, http://ijch.fi/issues/634/634_Doupi.pdf.

77. Jeffrey Furman and Richard Hayes, "Catching Up or Standing Still? National Innovative Productivity among 'Follower' Countries, 1978–1999," *Research Pol-*

icy 33, no. 9 (2004): 1329–1354, http://people.bu.edu/furman/html/research/files/Furman%20Hayes%20-%20RP04.pdf.

78. Richard Lipsey, Kenneth Carlaw, and Clifford Bekar, *Economic Transformations* (New York: Oxford University Press, 2005), 532–533.

79. German Federal Ministry of Education and Research, *High-Tech Strategy 2020 for Germany*, 4.

80. Lars Bager-Sjögren and Enrico Deiaco, *The Performance and Challenges of the Swedish National Innovation System* (Östersund, Sweden: Swedish Agency for Growth Policy Analysis, April 2011), 9, 43.

81. European Commission Enterprise and Industry Directorate-General, *European Innovation Progress Report 2009*, 2010, http://www.insme.org/files/4221.

Chapter 7: Cheating as a Way to Win the Race

1. Stephen Ezell and Robert D. Atkinson, *The Good, the Bad, and the Ugly (and the Self-Destructive) of Innovation Policy: A Policymaker's Guide to Crafting Effective Innovation Policy* (Washington, DC: Information Technology and Innovation Foundation [ITIF], 2010), http://www.itif.org/files/2010-good-bad-ugly.pdf.

2. Robert D. Atkinson, "Time to End Rampant Mercantilism," *G8/G20 Summit 2010*, 124–126, http://www.itif.org/files/G8G20_RAtkinson.pdf.

3. Adam Smith, *An Inquiry into the Natures and Causes of the Wealth of Nations* (New York: Modern Library, 1937).

4. Our framework also includes policies that are good for the world but bad for the nation enacting them ("self-destructive"). While in theory this should be a null set, there are cases where countries engage in it, such as keeping corporate taxes high (which hurts innovation and domestic competitiveness). See Ezell and Atkinson, *Good, Bad, Ugly*.

5. Scott Lanman, "China's Cheng Siwei Says Foreign-Currency Reserves Are Too Large," *Bloomberg*, November 1, 2011, http://mobile.bloomberg.com/news/2011-11-01/china-s-cheng-siwei-says-foreign-currency-reserves-are-too-large.

6. Howard Richman, Raymond Richman, and Jesse Richman, "Straight Talk from Clinton's Trade Negotiator," *American Thinker*, June 14, 2008, http://www.americanthinker.com/2008/06/straight_talk_from_clintons_tr_1.html.

7. Fred Bergsten, "Beijing Is Key to Creating More U.S. Jobs," *Foreign Policy*, April 14, 2010, http://www.foreignpolicy.com/articles/2010/04/14/china_the_job_killer/.

8. Ibid.

9. William R. Cline and John Williamson, "Currency Wars," Peterson Institute for International Economics, Policy Brief 10–26, November 2010, 4, http://www.piie.com/publications/pb/pb10-26.pdf.

10. Bruce Katz and Jonathan Rothwell, "Five Myths about U.S. Exports," *Washington Post*, September 5, 2010, http://www.washingtonpost.com/wp-dyn/content/article/2010/09/03/AR2010090302208.html.

11. Cline and Williamson, "Currency Wars," 4.

12. Anatole Kaletsky, "Blaming China Won't Help the Economy," *New York Times,* September 26, 2010, http://www.nytimes.com/2010/09/27/opinion/27kaletsky .html.

13. Gary Dorsch, "Foreign Currency Wars Fuel Gold's Rally to $1,300," *SeekingAlpha* (blog), September 23, 2010, http://seekingalpha.com/article/226610-foreign-cur rency-wars-fuel-golds-rally-to-1-300/; "Japan Forex Move 'Largest for Single Day,'" *Sydney Morning Herald,* August 5, 2011, http://www.smh.com.au/business/world -business/japan-forex-move-largest-for-single-day-20110805-1iesm.html.

14. Robert D. Atkinson, "Globalisation, New Technology and Economic Transfor- mation," in *Social Justice in the Global Age,* ed. Olaf Cramme and Patrick Dia- mond (Cambridge, UK: Polity Press, 2009).

15. Arindam Bhattacharya et al., "Capturing Global Advantage" (Boston, MA: Boston Consulting Group, April 2004), 9, http://www.bcg.com/documents/file14328.pdf.

16. World Trade Organization, "Tariff Download Facility," http://tariffdata.wto .org/ReportersAndProducts.aspx (accessed February 13, 2012.).

17. Robert D. Atkinson et al., *Innovation, Trade, and Technology Policies in Asia- Pacific Economies: A Scorecard* (Washington, DC: U.S. Agency for International Development and ITIF, December 2011), http://www.itif.org/publications /innovation-trade-and-technology-policies-asia-pacific-economies-scorecard.

18. Ibid., 20.

19. Robert Scott, "That 'Buy America' Provision," *New York Times,* February 11, 2009, http://roomfordebate.blogs.nytimes.com/2009/02/11/that-buy-american -provision/.

20. Sourafel Girma et al., "Can Production Subsidies Explain China's Export Per- formance?" *Vox,* July 8, 2008, http://www.voxeu.org/index.php?q=node/1373.

21. Robert D. Atkinson, *Enough Is Enough: Confronting Chinese Innovation Mercan- tilism* (Washington, DC, ITIF: February, 2012), http://www.itif.org/files/2012 -enough-is-enough.pdf.

22. Keith Bradsher, "200 Chinese Subsidies Violate Rules, U.S. Says," *New York Times,* October 6, 2011, http://www.nytimes.com/2011/10/07/business/us-says -some-chinese-subsidies-violate-trade-rules.html.

23. Office of the United States Trade Representative, "United States Details China and India Subsidy Programs in Submission to WTO," October 2011, http:// www.ustr.gov/about-us/press-office/press-releases/2011/october/united-states -details-china-and-india-subsidy-prog.

24. Keith Bradsher, "China Benefits as U.S. Solar Industry Withers," *New York Times,* September 1, 2011, http://www.nytimes.com/2011/09/02/business/global /us-solar-company-bankruptcies-a-boon-for-china.html.

25. Bradsher, "200 Chinese Subsidies Violate Rules, U.S. Says."

26. Thomas Hout and Pankaj Ghemawat, "China vs. the World: Whose Technology Is It?" *Harvard Business Review,* December 2010, http://hbr.org/2010/12/china -vs-the-world-whose-technology-is-it/ar/1.

27. Ibid., 5.

28. Atkinson, *Enough Is Enough.*

29. Hout and Ghemawat, "China vs. the World," 6.

30. Ibid.

31. Keith Bradsher, "China Is Eager to Bring High-Speed Rail Expertise to the U.S.," *New York Times,* April 7, 2010, http://www.nytimes.com/2010/04/08/business/global/08rail.html.

32. Keith Bradsher, "Hybrid in a Trade Squeeze," *New York Times,* September 5, 2011, http://www.nytimes.com/2011/09/06/business/global/gm-aims-the-volt-at-china-but-chinese-want-its-secrets.html?pagewanted=all.

33. Katherine Linton, Alexander Hammer, and Jeremy Wise, *China: Effects of Intellectual Property Infringement and Indigenous Innovation Policies on the U.S. Economy* (Washington, DC: U.S. International Trade Commission, May 2011), http://www.usitc.gov/publications/332/pub4226.pdf.

34. Mark Lee and Bruce Einhorn, "Microsoft's Ballmer Says China Piracy Is a Problem," *BusinessWeek,* May 24, 2010.

35. Business Software Alliance (BSA) and International Data Corporation (IDC), *Seventh Annual BSA/IDC Global Software and Piracy Study* (Washington, DC: BSA, 2010), 6–7, http://portal.bsa.org/globalpiracy2009/studies/09_Piracy_Study_Report_A4_final_111010.pdf.

36. Katherine Linton, Alexander Hammer, and Jeremy Wise, *China: Intellectual Property Infringement, Indigenous Innovation Policies, and Frameworks for Measuring the Effects on the U.S. Economy* (Washington, DC: U.S. International Trade Commission, 2010), http://www.usitc.gov/publications/332/pub4199.pdf.

37. Scott Andes, "China's Reverse Robin Hood: Stealing Intellectual Property from the Poor," *The Innovation Files* (blog), January 19, 2011, http://www.innovationfiles.org/china%E2%80%99s-reverse-robin-hood-stealing-intellectual-property-from-the-poor/.

38. Linton, Hammer, and Wise, *China: Intellectual Property Infringement,* 46.

39. BBC, "Chinese Authorities Find 22 Fake Apple Stores," August 12, 2011, http://www.bbc.co.uk/news/technology-14503724.

40. Sheng Zhu and Yongjiang Shi, "Shanzhai Manufacturing—an Alternative Innovation Phenomena in China: Its Value Chain and Implications for Chinese Science and Technology Policies," *Journal of Science and Technology Policy in China* 1, no. 1 (2010): 31, 46.

41. Ibid., 35.

42. "U.S. Accuses China of Instigating Plot against DuPont," *MSNBC.com,* February 1, 2012, http://www.msnbc.msn.com/id/46216853#.Tyqbh4FcZ50.

43. Owen Fletcher, "Chinese Firm Settles Piracy Suits," *Wall Street Journal,* March 7, 2011, http://online.wsj.com/article/SB10001424052748703386704576186230365798792.html.

44. Kathy Chen and Kris Maher, "U.S. Bill on China Gains Momentum," *Wall Street Journal,* September 16, 2010, http://online.wsj.com/article/SB10001424052748704652104575493791456903512.html.

45. U.S. Department of State, "Background Note: China—Industry," http://www
.state.gov/r/pa/ei/bgn/18902.htm (accessed February 24, 2012).

46. Zhou Xin and Simon Rabinovitch, "China Inc. Gets New Chairman as State-
Owned Firms' Clout Grows," *Reuters*, September 6, 2010, http://uk.reuters.com
/article/2010/09/06/business-us-china-economy-state-idUKTRE685147
20100906; "China State Giants Outstrip Private Firms," *Channel News Asia*, August 30, 2010, http://www.channelnewsasia.com/stories/afp_asiapacific_busi
ness/view/1077996/1/.html.

47. Hong Sheng, *The Nature, Performance and Reform of State-Owned Enterprises*
(Beijing: Unirule Institute of Economics, 2012).

48. David Dollar and Shang-Jin Wei, "Das (Wasted) Kapital: Firm Ownership and Investment Efficiency in China" (working paper 13103, National Bureau of Economic
Research, Cambridge, MA, May 2007), http://www.nber.org/papers/w13103.

49. "Public Procurement in China: European Business Experiences Competing for
Public Contracts in China" (report, European Chamber of Commerce, 2011),
http://www.publictendering.com/pdf/PPStudyENFinal.pdf.

50. Dewey and LeBoeuf, LLP, *China's Promotion of the Renewable Electric Power
Equipment Industry* (Washington, DC: National Foreign Trade Council, 2010),
i–vi, 27–29, http://www.nftc.org/default/Press%20Release/2010/China%20
Renewable%20Energy.pdf; U.S. Trade Representative staff, *2010 National Trade
Estimate Report on Foreign Trade Barriers* (Washington, DC: Office of the USTR,
2010), 1, 6, http://www.ustr.gov/sites/default/files/uploads/reports/2010/NTE
/NTE_COMPLETE_WITH_APPENDnonameack.pdf.

51. Hout and Ghemawat, "China vs. the World," 7.

52. Information Technology Industry Council, "China Policy," http://www.itic.org
/index.php?src=gendocs&ref=china_policy&category=trade (accessed February
25, 2012).

53. U.S.-China Business Council, "Issue Brief: New Developments in China's Domestic Innovation and Procurement Policies," January 2010, http://www.us
china.org/public/documents/2010/domestic_innovation_policies.pdf.

54. Stanley Lubman, "Changes to China's 'Indigenous Innovation' Policy: Don't
Get Too Excited," *Wall Street Journal*, July 22, 2011, http://blogs.wsj.com/china
realtime/2011/07/22/changes-to-chinas-indigenous-innovation-policy-dont-get
-too-excited/.

55. Hout and Ghemawat, "China vs. the World," 3.

56. For example, the European Chamber of Commerce issued a report stating that
it's concerned that local governments will continue to use the catalogs to guide
procurement. See European Chamber of Commerce, "Public Procurement in
China."

57. World Trade Organization, *Trade Policy Review: China* (Geneva: WTO, 2008),
http://www.wto.org/english/tratop_e/tpr_e/tp299_e.htm.

58. Richard Suttmeier, Ziangkui Yao, and Alex Zixiang Tan, *Standards of Power?
Technology, Institutions, and Politics in the Development of China's National Standards Strategy* (Seattle, WA: National Bureau of Asian Research, 2006), 13–14.

59. Hedlund and Atkinson, "Rise of the New Mercantilists," 25.

60. Institute of Electrical and Electronics Engineers "WAPI Position Paper," Doc. IEEE 802.11–05/0967r9, November 15, 2005.

61. Hedlund and Atkinson, "Rise of the New Mercantilists," 26.

62. Ezell and Atkinson, *Good, Bad, Ugly*, 87.

63. Jason Dean, Andrew Browne, and Shai Oster, "China's 'State Capitalism' Sparks a Global Backlash," *Wall Street Journal*, November 16, 2010, http://online.wsj.com /article/SB10001424052748703514904575602731006315198.html.

64. Terence Stewart, Elizabeth Argenti, and Philip Butler, *The Crisis in Intellectual Property Protection and China's Role in That Crisis* (Washington, DC: U.S.-China Economic and Security Review Commission, 2007), http://www.uscc .gov/researchpapers/2008/TLAG%20Report%20-%20Crisis%20in%20IP %20Protection%20and%20China%27s%20Role.pdf.

65. U.S. Chamber of Commerce Global Intellectual Property Center, "Why Are Intellectual Property Rights Important?" http://gipcdev.blackbarn.net/sites /default/files/documents/iparguments.pdf (accessed November 21, 2011).

66. Nam D. Pham, *The Impact of Innovation and the Role of Intellectual Property Rights on U.S. Productivity, Competitiveness, Jobs, Wages, and Exports* (Washington, DC: NPD Consulting, April 2010), 3, http://www.theglobalipcenter .com/sites/default/files/reports/documents/IP_Jobs_Study_Exec_Summary .pdf.

67. Stanton Sloane, "The U.S. Needs a Cybersecurity Czar Now," *BusinessWeek*, August 13, 2009, http://www.businessweek.com/technology/content/aug2009 /tc20090813_393090.htm.

68. Michael Ryan, "Useful Knowledge and the Development Agenda Debate at the World Intellectual Property Organization" (working paper, Creative and Innovative Economy Center, George Washington University, 2006), 2–3.

69. Marcia Hamilton, "The TRIPS Agreement: Imperialistic, Outdated, and Overprotective," *Vanderbilt Journal of Transnational Law* 29 (1996): 613; A. Samuel Oddi, "The International Patent System and Third World Development: Reality or Myth?" *Duke Law Journal*, no. 5 (1987): 831–878; A. Samuel Oddi, "TRIPS: Natural Rights and a Polite Form of Economic Imperialism," *Vanderbilt Journal of Transnational Law* 29 (1996): 415.

70. Carlos Correa, *Intellectual Property Rights, the WTO, and Developing Countries: The TRIPS Agreement and Policy Options* (New York: Zed Books, 2000).

71. John Barton et al., *Integrating Intellectual Property Rights and Development Policy* (London: Commission on Intellectual Property Rights, 2002), 8, http://www .iprcommission.org/papers/pdfs/final_report/CIPRfullfinal.pdf.

72. Lord Sydney Templeman, "Intellectual Property," *Journal of International Economic Law* 1, no. 4 (1998): 604.

73. Gene Grossman and Elhanan Helpman, *Innovation and Growth in the Global Economy* (Cambridge, MA: MIT Press, 1991).

74. Robert Shapiro, *Futurecast: How Superpowers, Populations, and Globalization Will Change Your World by the Year 2020* (New York: St. Martin's Griffin, 2009).

75. Zachary Karabell, "Obama and Chinese President Meeting Should Cover New Topics," *Washington Post*, November 8, 2009, http://www.washingtonpost.com /wp-dyn/content/article/2009/11/06/AR2009110601904.html.

76. Xiolan Fu, "Foreign Direct Investment, Absorptive Capacity and Regional Innovation Capabilities: Evidence from China" (working paper, Department of International Development, University of Oxford), http://www.oecd.org/data oecd/44/23/40306798.pdf.

77. "Generic Drugs in Brazil Are a Hard Pill for Big Pharma to Swallow," Knowledge@Wharton, January 16, 2006, http://www.wharton.universia.net/index .cfm?fa=viewArticle&id=1086&language=english.

78. Ibid.

79. Robert D. Atkinson and Scott Andes, *The Atlantic Century: Benchmarking EU and U.S. Innovation and Competitiveness* (Washington, DC: ITIF, February, 2009), 12, http://www.itif.org/files/2009-atlantic-century.pdf.

80. "W.T.O. Rules against European Union on Tariffs for Electronics," *New York Times*, August 16, 2010, http://www.nytimes.com/2010/08/17/business/global /17wto.html?_r=1&partner=rss&emc=rss.

81. World Trade Organization, "Tariff Download Facility," http://tariffdata.wto .org/ReportersAndProducts.aspx (accessed February 25, 2012).

82. Hedlund and Atkinson, "Rise of the New Mercantilists," 23.

83. Keith Maskus, Tsunehiro Otsuki, and John Wilson, "The Costs of Complying with Foreign Product Standards for Firms in Developing Countries: An Econometric Study" (working paper, Research Program on Political and Economic Change, University of Colorado at Boulder, 2004), http://www.colorado.edu/ibs /pubs/pec/pec2004-0004.pdf.

84. Ed Gerwin and Anne Kim, *Why We Need Fairer Trade: How Export Barriers Cost America Jobs* (Washington, DC: Third Way, July 2010), http://content.thirdway .org/publications/318/Third_Way_Report_-_Why_We_Need_Fairer_Trade -How_Export_Barriers_Cost_America_Jobs_.pdf.

85. Alberto Pera, "Changing View of Competition, Economic Analysis and EC Antitrust Law," *European Competition Journal* 4, no. 1 (2008): 142. See also Robert D. Atkinson and David Audretsch, *Economic Doctrines and Approaches to Antitrust* (Washington, DC: ITIF, January 2010), http://www.itif.org/files/2011-antitrust .pdf.

86. Phil Levy, "Global Imbalance Redux," *Foreign Policy*, August 25, 2010, http:// shadow.foreignpolicy.com/posts/2010/08/25/global_imbalance_redux/.

87. Census Bureau, Foreign Trade Statistics (Trade in Goods with China), http:// www.census.gov/foreign-trade/balance/c5700.html (accessed February 25, 2012).

88. Hout and Ghemawat, "China vs. the World."

89. Robert D. Atkinson, "Why China Needs to End Its Economic Mercantilism," *Huffington Post* (blog), January 30, 2008, http://www.huffingtonpost.com/robert -d-atkinson-phd/why-china-needs-to-end-it_b_84028.html.

90. Tom Miles and Ben Blanchard, "China 2010 Rare Earth Exports Slip but Value Rockets," *Reuters,* January 19, 2011, http://www.reuters.com/article/2011/01/19/us-china-rareearths-idUSTRE70I11T20110119/.

91. Robert Samuelson, "A Trade War With China?" *RealClearPolitics.com,* September 27, 2010, http://www.realclearpolitics.com/articles/2010/09/27/a_trade_war_with_china_107310.html.

92. Atkinson, "Why China Needs to End Its Economic Mercantilism."

93. Michael W. Klein, Scott Schuh, and Robert K. Triest, "Job Creation, Job Destruction, and International Competition: A Literature Review" (working paper, Federal Reserve Bank of Boston, December 2002), http://www.bos.frb.org/economic/wp/wp2002/wp027.pdf.

94. Robert D. Atkinson, "Response: How Can We Boost Productivity?" *Economy* (blog), *National Journal,* August 9, 2010, http://economy.nationaljournal.com/2010/08/how-can-we-boost-productivity.php.

95. James Manyika et al., *How to Compete and Grow: A Sector Guide to Policy* (New York: McKinsey, 2010), http://www.mckinsey.com/Insights/MGI/Research/Productivity_Competitiveness_and_Growth/How_to_compete_and_grow.

96. Robert D. Atkinson, *The Past and Future of America's Economy: Long Waves of Innovation That Power Cycles of Growth* (Northampton, MA: Edward Elgar, 2004).

97. P. D. Kaushik and Nirvikar Singh, "Information Technology and Broad-Based Development: Preliminary Lessons from North India," *World Development* 32, no. 4 (2004), http://people.ucsc.edu/~boxjenk/kaushik_singh.pdf.

98. Saul Lach, Gil Shiff, and Manuel Trajtenberg, "Together but Apart: ICT and Productivity Growth in Israel," (London: Centre for Economic Policy Research, February 2008), 3, http://papers.ssrn.com/sol3/papers.cfm?abstract_id=1094469.

99. Manyika et al., *How to Compete and Grow,* 35.

100. Gabriel Sanchez, "Understanding Productivity Levels, Growth and Dispersion in Argentina: The Case of Supermarkets" (conference paper, Fifth Conference on Micro Evidence on Innovation in Developing Economies, San José, Costa Rica, 2009), http://www.merit.unu.edu/MEIDE/papers/2009/1236010806_GS.pdf.

101. Manyika et al., *How to Compete and Grow,* 36.

102. Atkinson, "Time to End Rampant Mercantilism."

103. Atkinson, "Globalisation, New Technology."

Chapter 8: Winning the Race for Innovation Advantage
with the Eight "I's" of Innovation Policy

1. Dana Priest and William Arkin, "A Hidden World, Growing beyond Control," *Washington Post,* July 19, 2010, http://projects.washingtonpost.com/top-secret-america/articles/a-hidden-world-growing-beyond-control/1/.

2. John F. Kennedy, "Inaugural Address," January 20, 1961, http://www.bartleby.com/124/pres56.html.

3. These included things like fiscal discipline, openness to trade, and moderate interest rates.

4. Irving Janis, *Groupthink: Psychological Studies of Policy Decisions and Fiascoes* (Boston: Houghton Mifflin, 1982), 9.

5. Andy Grove, "How America Can Create Jobs," *BusinessWeek*, July 1, 2010, http://www.businessweek.com/magazine/content/10_28/b4186048358596.htm.

6. Paul Samuelson, interview by Tom Ashbrook, *On Point*, National Public Radio (NPR), September 27, 2004, http://onpoint.wbur.org/2004/09/27/paul-samuelson-rethinking-free-trade/.

7. Andrew Reamer, "The Role of Statistics in U.S. Economic Policy: Assessment and Agenda for Action" (presentation, Committee on National Statistics, Washington, DC, May 6, 2010), http://www.brookings.edu/~/media/Files/rc/speeches/2010/0506_economy_reamer/0506_economy_reamer.pdf.

8. This proposal was based on an Information Technology and Innovation Foundation (ITIF) proposal along similar lines. See Robert D. Atkinson, *Eight Ideas for Improving the America COMPETES Act* (Washington, DC: ITIF, March 2010), http://www.itif.org/files/2010-america-competes.pdf. See: U.S. Department of Commerce, *The Competitiveness and Innovative Capacity of the United States*, January 2012, http://www.commerce.gov/sites/default/files/documents/2012/january/competes_010511_0.pdf.

9. The U.S. lead may not last long. Other nations and regions are targeting medical devices as key sectors they want to lead in. As part of their effort, the European Union has streamlined its process by which to get medical devices approved, in order to attract more global medical device firms to set up operations in Europe.

10. Kimberly Clausing, "The Role of U.S. Tax Policy in Offshoring," *Brookings Trade Forum* (2005): 457–490, http://citeseerx.ist.psu.edu/viewdoc/summary?doi=10.1.1.128.8648.

11. Douglass North, *Poverty in the Midst of Plenty* (Palo Alto, CA: Hoover Institution, October 2, 2000), http://www.hoover.org/news/daily-report/24745/.

12. Patrick Temple-West and Kim Dixon, "U.S. Displacing Japan as No. 1 for Highest Corp Taxes," *Reuters*, March 30, 2012, http://www.reuters.com/article/2012/03/30/us-usa-tax-japan-idUSBRE82T17R20120330.

13. Michael Maibach, "An Atlantic Century? Will the West Remain Globally Competitive?" (presentation, European American Business Council, January 2011).

14. Robert D. Atkinson and Scott Andes, *The Atlantic Century: Benchmarking EU and U.S. Innovation and Competitiveness* (Washington, DC: ITIF, February, 2009), 20, http://www.itif.org/files/2009-atlantic-century.pdf.

15. Kevin S. Markle and Douglas A. Shackelford, "Cross-Country Comparisons of Corporate Income Taxes" (working paper No. 16839, National Bureau of Economic Research, February 2011), http://www.nber.org/papers/w16839.

16. Rosanna Altshuler, Harry Grubert, and T. Scott Newlon, "Has U.S. Investment Abroad Become More Sensitive to Tax Rates?" in *International Taxation and Multinational Activity*, ed. James Hines (Chicago: University of Chicago Press, 2004).

17. Simeon Djankov et al., "The Effect of Corporate Taxes on Investment and Entrepreneurship," *American Economic Journal: Macroeconomics* 2, no. 3 (2010): 31–64.

18. Stephen Shay, the deputy assistant secretary for international tax affairs at the U.S. Treasury Department for the Obama administration, argued that the large size of the U.S. domestic market makes it unique and justifies America's higher corporate tax rate. Cited in Markle and Shackelford, "Cross-Country Comparisons of Corporate Income Taxes," 4.

19. Robert D. Atkinson, *Corporate Tax Reform: Groupthink or Rational Analysis?* (Washington, DC: ITIF, July 2011), http://www.itif.org/files/2011-corporate-tax-reform.pdf.

20. For a review of this literature, see Robert D. Atkinson, *Effective Corporate Tax Reform in the Global Innovation Economy* (Washington, DC: ITIF, July 2009), http://www.itif.org/files/090723_CorpTax.pdf.

21. Robert D. Atkinson, "Expanding the R&E Tax Credit to Drive Innovation, Competitiveness and Prosperity," *Journal of Technology Transfer* 32, no. 6 (2007): 617–628, http://www.itif.org/files/AtkinsonRETaxCreditJTT.pdf.

22. Andrew Paradise, "2008 State of the Industry Report," American Society for Training and Development, Washington, DC.

23. To ensure that companies use this credit to focus on the skills of the majority of their workers, and not just managers, firms taking advantage of the credit would need to abide by rules similar to those for pension program distribution, which limit any focus on highly compensated employees.

24. See Robert D. Atkinson, *Supply-Side Follies: Why Conservative Economics Fails, Liberal Economics Falters, and Innovation Economics Is the Answer* (Lanham, MD: Rowman and Littlefield, 2006).

25. Robert D. Atkinson, *Create Jobs by Expanding the R&D Tax Credit* (Washington, DC: ITIF, January 26, 2010), http://www.itif.org/files/2010-01-26-RandD.pdf.

26. Gary Hufbauer and Paul Grieco, *Reforming the U.S. Corporate Tax* (Washington, DC: Peterson Institute, 2005).

27. Charles H. Blum and Donna Tung, "Fundamental Tax Reform: The Key to American Competitiveness," July 30, 2009, http://www.iasworldtrade.com/tax%20reform%20final.ppt.

28. Matthew Stepp and Robert D. Atkinson, *An Innovation Carbon Price: Spurring Clean Energy Innovation while Advancing U.S. Competitiveness* (Washington, DC: ITIF, February 2011), http://www.itif.org/files/2011-innovation-carbon-price.pdf.

29. George Will, "Rev the Scientific Engine," *Washington Post,* January 2, 2011, http://www.washingtonpost.com/wp-dyn/content/article/2010/12/31/AR2010123102007.html.

30. Jane Gravelle, "Equity Effects of the Tax Reform Act of 1986," *Journal of Economic Perspectives* 6, no. 1 (1992): 27–44. As Gravelle notes, from 1987 to 1992, corporate tax revenues increased by $120 billion, while individual tax revenues were expected to decrease by $122 billion.

31. Alan Auerbach and Lawrence Summers, "The Investment Tax Credit: An Evaluation" (working paper, National Bureau of Economic Research, 1979), http://www.nber.org/papers/w0404.pdf.

32. National Science Board, *Science and Engineering Indicators: 2010* (Arlington, VA: National Science Foundation, 2010), http://www.nsf.gov/statistics/seind10/pdf/seind10.pdf.

33. National Science Foundation (NSF), *FY 2009 Budget Request to Congress* (Arlington, VA: NSF, 2008), http://www.nsf.gov/about/budget/fy2009/pdf/entire_fy2009.pdf.

34. "Focus Center Research Program," Semiconductor Research Corporation, 2011, http://www.src.org/program/fcrp/.

35. The White House, Office of the Press Secretary, "President Obama to Announce New Efforts to Support Manufacturing Innovation, Encourage Insourcing," news release, March 19, 2012, http://www.whitehouse.gov/the-press-office/2012/03/09/president-obama-announce-new-efforts-support-manufacturing-innovation-en.

36. "ARPA-e PSRP," Department of Energy, June 24, 2010, http://www.recovery.gov/Transparency/agency/Recovery%20Plans/Revised%20DOE%20Recovery%20Act%20Plan%20-%20June%202010.pdf.

37. Douglass North, *Institutions, Institutional Change and Economic Performance* (New York: Cambridge University Press, 1990).

38. "About Olin: Overview," Franklin W. Olin College of Engineering, http://www.olin.edu/about_olin/default.aspx (accessed May 10, 2011).

39. Robert D. Atkinson et al., *Addressing the STEM Challenge by Expanding Specialty Math and Science High Schools* (Washington, DC: ITIF, March 2007), http://www.itif.org/files/STEM.pdf.

40. Battelle Technology Partnership Practice, *Gone Tomorrow? A Call to Promote Medical Innovation, Create Jobs, and Find Cures in America* (Columbus, OH: Battelle, 2010), http://www.americanmedicalinnovation.org/sites/default/files/Gone_Tomorrow.pdf.

41. Stuart Benjamin and Arti Rai, *Structuring U.S. Innovation Policy: Creating a White House Office of Innovation Policy* (Washington, DC: ITIF, June 2009), http://www.itif.org/files/WhiteHouse_Innovation.pdf.

42. Saul Kaplan, "Government as Innovation Catalyst," *BusinessWeek*, May 19, 2010, http://www.businessweek.com/print/innovate/content/may2010/id20100517_512312.htm.

43. Robert D. Atkinson, *The Past and Future of America's Economy: Long Waves of Innovation That Power Cycles of Growth* (Northampton, MA: Edward Elgar, 2004).

44. Daniel Castro, *Explaining International Health IT Leadership* (Washington, DC: ITIF, December 2009), http://www.itif.org/files/2009-leadership-healthit.pdf.

45. Julie Hedlund and Robert D. Atkinson, "The Rise of the New Mercantilists: Unfair Trade Practices in the Innovation Economy," (Washington, DC: ITIF, June 2007), http://www.itif.org/files/ITMercantilism.pdf.

46. Trade Enforcement Act of 2009, S. 1466, 111th Cong. (2009); see also *Combating Unfair Trade Practices in the Innovation Economy, before the Committee on Finance, United States Senate*, 110th Cong. (2008), statement of Robert D. Atkinson, president, ITIF, http://www.itif.org/files/atkinsonfinancecommittee testimony.pdf.

47. Stephen Ezell, *Understanding the Importance of Export Credit Financing to U.S. Competitiveness* (Washington, DC: ITIF, June 2011), http://www.itif.org/files/2011 -export-credit-financing.pdf.

48. David Hart, *Global Flows of Talent: Benchmarking the United States* (Washington, DC: ITIF, November 17, 2006), http://www.itif.org/files/Hart-GlobalFlowsof Talent.pdf.

49. Shel Israel, "Immigrants Launched over Half of Silicon Valley Startups," *Global Neighbourhoods* (blog), January 5, 2007, http://redcouch.typepad.com/weblog /2007/01/immigrants_laun.html.

50. Surendra Gera and Thitima Songsakul, "Benchmarking Canada's Performance in the Global Competition for Mobile Talent," *Canadian Public Policy* 33, no. 1 (2007): 63–84, http://www.jstor.org/pss/30032513.

51. EnglishForums.com, http://www.englishforums.com/English/SirWinston ChurchillAmericansAlways/llnnb/post.htm (accessed February 25, 2012).

Chapter 9: Why Don't We Have More Innovation and Innovation Policy?

1. Niccoló Machiavelli, *The Prince* (New York: Dover Publications, 1992).

2. Joseph Schumpeter, *Capitalism, Socialism and Democracy* (New York: Harper, 1975).

3. Ibid., 82–85.

4. Mancur Olson, *The Logic of Collective Action: Public Goods and the Theory of Groups* (Boston, MA: Harvard University Press, 1971).

5. Mancur Olson, *The Rise and Decline of Nations: Economic Growth, Stagflation, and Social Rigidities* (New Haven, CT: Yale University Press, 1982), 41.

6. Heather Smith, "French Unions Lead May Day Protests, Europe Marches," *Bloomberg*, May 1, 2009, http://www.bloomberg.com/apps/news?pid=newsar chive&sid=alspwvle_qXA.

7. Steve Berberich, "Grocers Turn to Handheld Personal Scanners for Shoppers," *Maryland Gazette*, August 10, 2007, http://ww2.gazette.net/stories/081607/bu siplo140957_32357.shtml.

8. Alcoholic Beverage Licenses: Self-Service Checkouts, A.B. 1060, California State Legislature (2009), http://www.leginfo.ca.gov/pub/09-10/bill/asm/ab _1051-1100/ab_1060_bill_20100830_enrolled.html.

9. Daniel Castro, Robert D. Atkinson, and Stephen Ezell, *Embracing the Self-Service Economy* (Washington, DC: ITIF, 2010), 43, http://www.itif.org/files /2010-self-service-economy.pdf.

10. David Noble, *Progress without People: New Technology, Unemployment and the Message of Resistance* (Toronto: Between the Lines, 1995), 151.

11. Robert D. Atkinson and Mark Cooper, "A Cure by Way of the Consumer," *Washington Times*, December 17, 2008, http://www.washingtontimes.com/news /2008/dec/17/ailing-auto-industry/.

12. "New Jersey Home Buyers Now to Receive a Rebate from ZipRealty," *ZipRealty Blog*, January 19, 2010, http://ziprealty.typepad.com/blog/2010/01/new-jersey -home-buyers-now-to-receive-a-rebate-from-ziprealty.html.

13. Robert D. Atkinson, *Public versus Private Restraints on the Online Distribution of Contact Lenses* (Washington, DC: ITIF, July 10, 2006), http://www.itif.org/files /contactlens.pdf.

14. Elizabeth Wasserman, "Stuck in the Middle," *Industry Standard*, March 6, 2000, http://www.dlc.org/ppi/ppi_ci.cfm?knlgAreaID=140&subsecID=900055 &contentID=251531.

15. Charles Lane, "Justices Reject Curbs on Wine Sales," *Washington Post*, May 17, 2005, http://www.washingtonpost.com/wp-dyn/content/article/2005/05/16/AR 2005051600441.html.

16. Greg Greeley, "Brussels' Attack on Online Shopping," *Wall Street Journal*, February 1, 2010, http://online.wsj.com/article/SB10001424052748704107204575 039071694275514.html.

17. Charles Smith, "Wall Street's 'Recovery' vs. Main Street's," *Seeking Alpha* (blog), November 18, 2010, http://seekingalpha.com/article/237531-wall-street-s -recovery-vs-main-street-s/.

18. Arnold King, "Main Street vs. Wall Street" (Washington, DC: Cato Institute, June 3, 2008), http://www.cato.org/pub_display.php?pub_id=9691.

19. Don McNay, "Bernanke: The Main Street versus Wall Street Litmus Test," *Huffington Post* (blog), January 24, 2010, http://www.huffingtonpost.com/don-mcnay /bernanke-the-main-street-b_434848.html.

20. Art Levine, "Wall Street vs. Main Street: Final Showdown Threatens Reform," *Working in These Times* (blog), June 24, 2010, http://inthesetimes.com/working /entry/6136/wall_street_vs._main_street_final_showdown_threatens_reform/.

21. *CBS News*, "Newton, Iowa: Anger in the Heartland," November 1, 2010, http:// www.cbsnews.com/stories/2010/10/28/60minutes/main6999868.shtml ?tag=contentMain]sCarousel.

22. John Cassidy, "What Good Is Wall Street?" *New Yorker*, November 29, 2010, http://www.newyorker.com/reporting/2010/11/29/101129fa_fact_cassidy.

23. Erik Hurst and Benjamin W. Pugsley, "What Do Small Businesses Do?" (working paper, National Bureau of Economic Research, May 2011), http://papers .ssrn.com/sol3/papers.cfm?abstract_id=1841278.

24. Charles Kenny, "Rethinking the Boosterism about Small Business," *Business-Week*, September 28, 2011, http://www.businessweek.com/magazine/rethinking -the-boosterism-about-small-business-09282011.html.

25. Census Bureau, "Profile of U.S. Exporting Companies: 2007–2008," news release, April 13, 2010, http://www.census.gov/foreign-trade/Press-Release/edb/2008/.

26. Lawrence Rausch, *Indicators of U.S. Small Business's Role in R&D* (Washington, DC: National Science Foundation, March 2010), http://www.nsf.gov/statistics /infbrief/nsf10304/nsf10304.pdf.

27. Bureau of Labor Statistics, "Employer Costs for Employee Compensation," news release, December 8, 2010, http://www.bls.gov/news.release/ecec.nro.htm.

28. Ibid.

29. Martin Baily, Matthew Slaughter, and Laura D'Andrea Tyson, "The Global Jobs Competition Heats Up," *Wall Street Journal,* July 1, 2010, http://online.wsj.com /article/SB10001424052748703426004575338553459934636.html.

30. Atkinson, *Supply Side Follies.*

31. "Issues—Labor," National Federation of Independent Businesses, http://www .nfib.com/issues-elections/labor (accessed May 23, 2011).

32. "About the Citizens for Tax Justice," Citizens for Tax Justice, http://www.ctj .org/about/background.php (accessed May 24, 2011).

33. "Tell Congress: Don't Choose Tax Cuts for the Rich over Help for the Unemployed," *Tax Justice Digest* (blog), Citizens for Tax Justice, November 19, 2010, http://ctj.org/taxjusticedigest/archive/2010/11/tell_congress_dont_choose_tax .php.

34. Democratic National Convention Committee, *Strong at Home, Respected in the World: The 2004 Democratic National Platform for America* (Washington, DC: Democratic National Convention, 2004).

35. Office of House Democratic Leader Nancy Pelosi, "Democrat's Fight for America's Small Businesses," news release, October 6, 2004, www.house.gov/smbiz /democrats/SMALL%20BUSINESS%20FACT%20SHEET%20FINAL%20(2) %20(2).doc.

36. Martin Ford, "Your Job in 2020," *Forbes,* April 8, 2010, http://www.forbes.com /2010/04/08/unemployment-google-2020-technology-data-companies-10 -economy.html.

37. Erik Brynjolfsson and Andrew McAfee, *Race against the Machine* (Digital Frontier Press, 2011), Kindle edition, chap. 5, location 1060.

38. *NBC Today Show,* "Ann Curry One-on-One Interview with President Obama," June 14, 2011, http://video.today.msnbc.msn.com/today/43391550.

39. Stephen Ezell, "Technology and Automation Create, Not Destroy Jobs," *The Innovation Files* (blog), June 15, 2011, http://www.innovationfiles.org/technology -and-automation-create-not-destroy-jobs/.

40. Castro, Atkinson, and Ezell, *Embracing the Self-Service Economy.*

41. Bharat Trehan, "Productivity Shocks and the Unemployment Rate," *Federal Reserve Bank of San Francisco Economic Review* (2003): 13–27, http://www.frbsf .org/publications/economics/review/2003/article2.pdf.

42. Pu Chen, Armon Rezai, and Willi Semmler, "Productivity and Unemployment in the Short and Long Run" (working paper, Schwartz Center for Economic Policy Analysis, New School, September 2007), http://www.newschool.edu /scepa/publications/workingpapers/SCEPA%20Working%20Paper%202007-8 .pdf.

43. Organization for Economic Cooperation and Development (OECD), *The OECD Jobs Study: Facts, Analysis, Strategies,* 1994, http://www.oecd.org/dataoecd/42 /51/1941679.pdf.

44. Susanto Basu, John Fernald, and Miles Kimball, "Are Technology Improvements Contractionary?" *American Economic Review* 96, no. 5 (2006): 1418–1448, http://www.jstor.org/pss/30034981; Chen, Rezai, and Semmler, "Productivity and Unemployment."

45. For firms, see Erik Brynjolfsson, "The Digital Organization" (presentation, "Where IT's @," Federal Reserve Bank of Dallas, September 10, 2004), http:// www.dallasfed.org/news/research/2004/04it_brynj.pdf; For the economy, see Robert D. Atkinson and Andrew McKay, *Digital Prosperity: Understanding the Economic Benefits of the Information Technology Revolution* (Washington, DC: ITIF, 2007), http://www.itif.org/files/digital_prosperity.pdf.

46. Clay Shirky, *Cognitive Surplus: Creativity and Generosity in a Connected Age* (New York: Penguin Press, 2010).

47. Stefan Theil, "What Lurks Beneath," *Newsweek,* July 18, 2009, http://www .newsweek.com/2009/07/17/what-lurks-beneath.html.

48. Ibid.

49. Bill McKibben, *Deep Economy* (New York: Holt and Company, 2008), 221.

50. Statement by Deven McGraw during debate. See "The Cost of Privacy: A Debate on the Impact of Privacy Laws on Health IT Adoption," June 22, 2009, http:// www.itif.org/media/cost-privacy-debate-impact-privacy-laws-health-it-adoption.

51. Avi Goldfarb and Catherine Tucker, "Privacy Regulation and Online Advertising" (working paper, 2010), http://papers.ssrn.com/sol3/papers.cfm?abstract _id=1600259.

52. Shane Ham and Robert D. Atkinson, "Does Digital Politics Still Matter?" *New Atlantis,* no. 3 (Fall 2003): 77–87, http://www.thenewatlantis.com/publications /does-digital-politics-still-matter.

53. Amy Sue Bix, *Inventing Ourselves Out of Jobs? America's Debate over Technological Unemployment, 1929–1981* (Baltimore, MD: Johns Hopkins University Press, 2000).

54. Eugene Robinson, "Toyota's Payback for Stealing Fire from the Gods," *Washington Post,* February 5, 2010, http://www.washingtonpost.com/wp-dyn/content /article/2010/02/04/AR2010020403936.html.

55. Michael Kompf, "The Legacy of Neil Postman," *College Quarterly* 7, no. 1 (2004), http://www.senecac.on.ca/quarterly/2004-vol07-num01-winter/kompf.html.

56. Bob Thompson, "History for Sale," *Washington Post,* May 8, 2001.

57. World Values Survey, "Values Change the World," 2008, http://www.worldvalues survey.org/wvs/articles/folder_published/article_base_110/files/WVS brochure4.pdf.

58. All values are expressed as a percent of those stating an opinion.

59. David Vogel, "Why Businessmen Distrust Their State: The Political Consciousness of American Corporate Executives," *British Journal of Political Science* 8, no. 1 (1978): 45–78.

60. Ibid.

61. "TDEP-02 Economic Policy," National Association of Manufacturers, http://www
.nam.org/Issues/Official-Policy-Positions/Tax-Technology-Domestic-Economic
-Policy/TTDEP-02-Economic-Policy.aspx (accessed September 14, 2011).

62. Ylan Mui and David Cho, "Small Businesses Leery of Obama's Jobs Plan,"
Washington Post, January 29, 2010, http://www.washingtonpost.com/wp-dyn
/content/article/2010/01/28/AR2010012803818.html.

63. *Supporting Innovation in the 21st Century Economy, before the House of Representatives Subcommittee on Technology and Innovation, House Committee on Science
and Technology,* 111th Cong. (2010), testimony of Paul Holland, general partner,
Foundation Capital, http://www.gpo.gov/fdsys/pkg/CHRG-111hhrg55847/pdf
/CHRG-111hhrg55847.pdf.

64. Phil Britt, "Federal Deficits Will Damage Tech Sector, CEA Chief Warns,"
Heartlander.org, March 13, 2010, http://news.heartland.org/newspaper-article
/2010/03/13/federal-deficits-will-damage-tech-sector-cea-chief-warns.

65. Michael Arrington, "Here's How the Government Can Fix Silicon Valley: Leave
It Alone," *TechCrunch*, June 7, 2010, http://techcrunch.com/2010/06/07/heres
-how-the-government-can-fix-silicon-valley-leave-it-alone/.

66. Guy Dinmore and Geoff Dyer, "Immelt Hits Out at China and Obama," *Financial Times*, July 1, 2010, http://www.ft.com/intl/cms/s/0/ed654fac-8518-11df-adfa
-00144feabdco.html.

67. Andy Grove, "How America Can Create Jobs," *BusinessWeek*, July 1, 2010, http://
www.businessweek.com/magazine/content/10_28/b4186048358596.htm.

68. Bill Gates, "Why We Need Innovation, Not Just Insulation," *The Gates Notes*
(blog), January 24, 2010, http://www.thegatesnotes.com/Thinking/article.aspx
?ID=47.

69. Andrew N. Liveris, *Make It in America* (Hoboken, NJ: Wiley, 2011).

70. Stephen LeRoy, "Is the 'Invisible Hand' Still Relevant?" Federal Reserve Bank
of San Francisco, May 3, 2010, http://www.frbsf.org/publications/economics
/letter/2010/el2010-14.html.

71. Schumpeter, *Capitalism, Socialism and Democracy.*

72. Alan Blinder, *Hard Heads Soft Hearts: Tough-Minded Economics for a Just Society*
(New York: Basic Books, 2000).

73. N. Gregory Mankiw, "Remarks" (speech, National Association of Business
Economists, Atlanta, GA, September 15, 2003), http://www.economics.harvard
.edu/files/faculty/40_nabe.pdf.

74. Elhanan Helpman, *The Mystery of Economic Growth* (Cambridge, MA: Belknap
Press, 2004).

75. Blinder, *Hard Heads Soft Hearts,* 31.

76. Larry Summers, "Innovation and Economic Growth," interview by Judy Wood-
ruff, transcript, Innovation Economy Conference, Washington, DC, November
30, 2009, http://www.theinnovationeconomy.org/_layouts/IEC/PDF/Transcripts
/Innovation_And_Economic_Growth.pdf.

77. To find your economic type, visit: www.innovationeconomics.org/type/.

78. Peter Klenow and Andrés Rodríguez-Clare, "The Neoclassical Revival in Growth Economics: Has It Gone Too Far?" *NBER Macroeconomics Annual* 12 (1997): 73–103, http://klenow.com/NBERMA.pdf.

79. Jonathan Temple, "The New Growth Evidence," *Journal of Economic Literature* 37, no. 1 (1999): 112–156.

80. Phillipe Aghion, Paul A. David, and Dominique Foray, "Linking Policy Research and Practice in STIG Systems: Many Obstacles, but Some Ways Forward" (CEMI Working Papers, Working Paper 2007–002, Ecole Polytechnique Federale De Lausanne, Chaire en Economie et Management de l'Innovation, June 2007), 13.

Chapter 10: Can Nations Overcome the Barriers to Innovation?

1. Vinny Catalano, "The Greater Good," *Vinny Catalano* (blog), April 29, 2010, http://vinnycatalano.blogspot.com/2010/04/greater-good.html.

2. Steven Johnson, *Where Good Ideas Come From: The Natural History of Innovation* (New York: Riverhead Books, 2011).

3. Eric Beinhocker, *The Origin of Wealth* (Boston, MA: Harvard Business School Press, 2006), 427. Emphasis in original.

4. World Values Survey, "Values Change the World," 2008, http://www.world valuessurvey.org/wvs/articles/folder_published/article_base_110/files/WVS brochure4.pdf.

5. Meaning that fewer than 3 percent of people answered with an 8, 9, or 10 answer, with 10 being the strongest position in favor of government ownership and with 1 being the strongest for more private ownership.

6. Adam Smith, *An Inquiry into the Natures and Causes of the Wealth of Nations* (New York: Modern Library, 1937), 32.

7. Robert D. Atkinson et al., *Taking on the Three Deficits: An Investment Guide to American Renewal* (Washington, DC: Information Technology and Innovation Foundation [ITIF] and the Breakthrough Institute, November 2011), http://www .itif.org/files/2011-taking-three-deficits.pdf.

8. Klaus Schwab, Xavier Sala-i-Martin, and Robert Greenhill, *The Global Competitiveness Report 2010–2011* (Geneva: World Economic Forum, 2010), 388.

9. American Society of Civil Engineers, "Report Card for America's Infrastructure," http://www.infrastructurereportcard.org/ (accessed December 2, 2011).

10. Robert D. Atkinson et al., *Paying Our Way: A New Framework for Transportation Finance* (Washington, DC: National Surface Transportation Infrastructure Financing Commission, 2009), http://financecommission.dot.gov/Documents /NSTIF_Commission_Final_Report_Mar09FNL.pdf.

11. Bureau of Economic Analysis, Fixed Assets Accounts Tables (Table 3.9ES; current-cost average age at year end of private fixed assets by industry), http:// www.bea.gov/national/FA2004/index.asp (accessed January 31, 2011); Mike Mandel, "Our Aging Capital Stock," *Mandel on Innovation and Growth* (blog), December 14, 2010, http://innovationandgrowth.wordpress.com/2010/12/14/our-aging -capital-stock/.

12. Keith Richburg, "China's Stimulus Spending Created Infrastructure Projects That May Not Be Needed," *Washington Post,* June 18, 2010, http://www.washing tonpost.com/wp-dyn/content/article/2010/06/17/AR2010061705794.html.

13. Marc Chandler, "China Ramps Up Infrastructure Spending," *The Street,* July 6, 2010, http://www.thestreet.com/story/10799388/china-ramps-up-infrastructure -spending.html.

14. Andrew Peaple, "China's Infrastructure Spending Still on Rails," *Wall Street Journal,* March 3, 2010, http://online.wsj.com/article/SB100014240527487038 62704575098921097436494.html.

15. Richburg, "China's Stimulus Spending."

16. Han Jingjing, "China Invests 4.3 Trillion Yuan in Internet Infrastructure Construction over Past 13 Years," *Xinhua,* June 8, 2010, http://news.xinhuanet.com /english2010/china/2010-06/08/c_13339080.htm.

17. Jane Macartney, "Progress Anything but Smooth on China's Ambitious, and Costly, Water Plan," *Australian,* September 20, 2010, http://www.theaustralian .com.au/news/world/progress-anything-but-smooth-on-chinas-ambitious-and -costly-water-plan/story-e6frg6so-1225926385461/.http://webcache.googleuser content.com/search?q=cache:jgH7zkOOSiIJ:kn.theiet.org/magazine/issues /0904/taming-the-yangtze-0904.cfm+%22taming+the+yangtze%22&cd=1 &hl=en&ct=clnk&gl=us.

18. Pew Charitable Trusts, *Trillion Dollar Gap* (Washington, DC: Pew, 2010), http:// www.pewcenteronthestates.org/trends_detail.aspx?id=58297.

19. James Lincoln Collier, *The Rise of Selfishness in America* (New York: Oxford University Press, 1991), 259.

20. "Labour Pains," *Economist,* November 6, 2010, http://www.economist.com /node/17421434/.

21. Gabriel Sanchez, "Understanding Productivity Levels, Growth and Dispersion in Argentina: The Case of Supermarkets" (conference paper, Fifth Conference on Micro Evidence on Innovation in Developing Economies, San José, Costa Rica, 2009), http://www.merit.unu.edu/MEIDE/papers/2009/1236010806_GS .pdf.

22. European Expert Group, "Flexicurity Pathways: Turning Hurdles into Stepping Stones," European Centre for the Development of Vocational Training, June 2007, http://zope298.itcilo.org/delta/hld2008/hld/en/thematical-papers/session-2/ec -flexicurity-pathways-turning-hurdles-into-stepping-stones.pdf.

23. "Mission for Flexicurity: Mission Report," Finnish Ministry of Economy and Employment, June 26, 2008, http://ec.europa.eu/social/BlobServlet?docId=522 &langId=en.

24. Mark Goldman, *High Hopes: The Rise and Decline of Buffalo, New York* (Albany: State University of New York Press, 1983).

25. Robert D. Atkinson, Stephen Ezell, and Scott Andes, *One from Column A, B, and C: Finding a New Bipartisan Consensus on U.S. Competitiveness and Innovation Policy* (Washington, DC: ITIF, March 2011), http://www.itif.org/files/2011 -column-abc.pdf.

26. Paolo Ramazzotti, "Industrial Districts and Economic Decline in Italy" (working paper, University of Macerata, 2008), http://www.unimc.it/dief/wpaper/wpaper00045/filePaper/.

27. Coleen Berry, "Decline of Artisan Exports Italy," *Boston Globe,* December 20, 2010, http://www.boston.com/news/education/k_12/articles/2010/12/20/decline_of_artisan_exports_afflicts_italy_economy/.

28. "No Italian Jobs," *Economist,* January 6, 2011, http://www.economist.com/node/17862256/.

29. Organization for Economic Cooperation and Development (OECD) Tax Database (Table II.1; basic corporate income tax rates).

30. Robert D. Atkinson and Scott Andes, *The Atlantic Century II: Benchmarking EU and U.S. Innovation and Competitiveness* (Washington, DC: ITIF, July 2011), 3–4, http://www.itif.org/files/2011-atlantic-century.pdf.

31. Ibid.

32. European Commission, "More than Half of EU27 Enterprises Are Innovative," November 10, 2010, http://ec.europa.eu/enterprise/newsroom/cf/itemlongdetail.cfm?item_id=4691&lang=en&tpa_id=135&ref=newsbytheme.cfm%3Flang%3Den%26displayType%3Dnews%26fosubtype%3D%26tpa%3D135%26tpa_id%3D135%26period%3D2010%26month%3D%26page%3D1.

33. Mark Boroush, "NSF Releases New Statistics on Business Innovation," National Science Foundation, October 2010, http://www.nsf.gov/statistics/infbrief/nsf11300/nsf11300.pdf. What accounts for this difference in reported innovation activity between U.S. and European firms is unclear. Since the survey instruments are similar, the differences either reflect a different industrial composition in the United States, the inexperience of U.S. firms in responding to the survey, or the less sanguine possibility that European firms as a whole may actually be more innovative than American ones. So important is the question that in February 2011, the U.S. National Academies of Science commissioned a new study that will seek to ascertain the reasons for the different reported rates of innovation between U.S. and EU enterprises.

34. Eric Bartelsman, Stefano Scarpetta, and Fabiano Schivardi, "Comparative Analysis of Firm Demographics and Survival: Evidence from Micro-Level Sources in OECD Countries," *Industrial and Corporate Change* 14, no. 3 (2005): 365, http://digilander.libero.it/fschivardi/images/demographics.pdf.

35. "Europe 2020," European Commission, http://ec.europa.eu/europe2020/index_en.htm (accessed December 2, 2011).

36. FORA, *New Nature of Innovation* (Copenhagen: OECD, 2009), 87, http://www.newnatureofinnovation.org/full_report.pdf.

37. Paul Giacobbi, "The Attraction of France for Foreign Investors," April 15, 2010, 17, http://www.paul-giacobbi.org/attachment/219867/.

38. "Japan's Technology Champions: Invisible but Indispensable," *Economist,* November 5, 2009, http://www.economist.com/node/14793432.

39. Atkinson and Andes, *Atlantic Century II,* 3–4.

40. "Japan's Economy: Whose Lost Decade?" *Economist,* November 19, 2011, http://www.economist.com/node/21538745; Atkinson and Andes, *Atlantic Century,* 24.

41. William H. Lewis, "The Power of Productivity: Wealth, Poverty, and the Threat to Global Stability" (presentation, ITIF, Washington, DC, May 6, 2008), 7, http://www.itif.org/files/LewisPresentation.pdf.

42. Kim Jung Woo, "International Comparison of the Korean Service Industries' Productivity," Samsung Economic Research Institute, *Weekly Insight,* April 14, 2008, 10–15, http://www.seriworld.org/01/wldContV.html?&mn=A&mncd=0301&key=20080415000003&pubkey=20080415000003&seq=20080415000003&kdy=E5JjH5a6=&sectno=3.

43. Robert D. Atkinson, "Time to End Rampant Mercantilism," *G8/G20 Summit 2010,* http://www.itif.org/files/G8G20_RAtkinson.pdf.

44. Kyoji Fukao and Tsutomu Miyagawa, "Productivity in Japan, the U.S., and the Major EU Economies: Is Japan Falling Behind?" (discussion paper, Research Institute of Economy, Trade and Industry, 2007), http://www.rieti.go.jp/jp/publications/dp/07e046.pdf.

45. Robert D. Atkinson and Andrew McKay, *Digital Prosperity: Understanding the Economic Benefits of the Information Technology Revolution* (Washington, DC: ITIF, 2007), 38, http://www.itif.org/files/digital_prosperity.pdf.

46. Jong-Won Yoon, "Beyond the Crisis: Toward a New Horizon," *SERI Quarterly,* October 2009, 40, 54.

47. "Dancing Elephants" *Economist,* January 29, 2011, http://www.economist.com/node/18010749/.

48. Vikas Bajaj, "India to Ease Retail Rules for Foreign Companies," *New York Times,* November 24, 2011, http://www.nytimes.com/2011/11/25/business/global/india-to-allow-foreign-retailers-to-own-stores.html?_r=1.

49. Stephan Haggard, *Pathways from the Periphery: The Politics of Growth in the Newly Industrialized Countries* (Ithaca, NY: Cornell University Press, 1990).

50. Rudiger Dornbusch and F. Leslie Helmers, eds., *The Open Economy: Tools for Policymakers in Developing Countries* (New York: Oxford University Press, 1988).

51. Matt Moffett, "Taxes Put Chill on Electronics," *Wall Street Journal,* February 27, 2012, http://online.wsj.com/article/SB1000142405297020477860457723936154994060808.html?KEYWORDS=Argentina#printMode.

52. An inspiring video about the Colombia 2025 vision is available at: http://www.youtube.com/watch?v=rl2nD5AcRow&playnext=1&list=PL9BAD510BC296FE8E (accessed March 17, 2011).

Chapter 11: Creating a Robust Global Innovation System

1. We are not dismissive of concerns about growing income inequality, but believe that in the United States at least, while inequality has increased, much of the gains from productivity have still flowed to workers. One reason workers have not seen greater gains is that productivity and competitiveness have not been

stronger. See Stephen Rose, *Does Productivity Growth Still Benefit Working Americans?* (Washington, DC: Information Technology and Innovation Foundation [ITIF], June 2007), http://www.itif.org/files/DoesProductivityGrowthStillBenefit WorkingAmericans.pdf.

2. International Monetary Fund (IMF), "About the IMF: Cooperation and Reconstruction," http://www.imf.org/external/about/histcoop.htm (accessed June 14, 2011).

3. IMF, "IMF Executive Board Concludes 2010 Article IV Consultation with China," news release, July 27, 2010, http://www.imf.org/external/np/sec/pn/2010 /pn10100.htm.

4. IMF, *Annual Report 2010: Supporting a Balanced Global Recovery* (Washington, DC: IMF, 2010), http://www.imf.org/external/pubs/ft/ar/2010/eng/pdf/ar10 _eng.pdf.

5. Vivek Arora and Athanasios Vamvakidis, "China's Economic Growth: International Spillovers" (working paper, IMF, 2010), http://www.imf.org/external/pubs /ft/wp/2010/wp10165.pdf.

6. "Min Zhu on Asia's Economy and More," *Finance & Development,* June 2010, http://www.imf.org/external/pubs/ft/fandd/2010/06/pdf/zhu.pdf.

7. World Bank, "Implementation Completion and Results Report on a Loan in the Amount of 4.16 Million U.S. Dollars and a Credit of SDR 25.7 Million to the People's Republic of China for a Fourth Technical Cooperation Project," June 15, 2010, http://www-wds.worldbank.org/external/default/WDSContentServer /WDSP/IB/2010/08/10/000356161_20100810013916/Rendered/PDF/ICR 13660P042291ICodisclosed08161101.pdf.

8. Ibid., 23.

9. Geoff Dyer, "China's Lending Hits New Heights," *Financial Times,* January 17, 2011, http://www.ft.com/intl/cms/s/0/488c60f4-2281-11e0-b6a2-00144feab49a .html.

10. World Bank, "Implementation Completion and Results Report," vi.

11. World Bank, "China Economic Reform Implementation Project: Subproject Procurement Plan," March 26, 2008, http://www-wds.worldbank.org/external /default/WDSContentServer/WDSP/IB/2008/12/02/000333037_200812 02233449/Rendered/PDF/467050PROP0P081C10Nov020080TCC0V008.pdf.

12. World Bank, "Implementation Project of Chinese Economic Reforms: Fifth Technique Aid: Purchase Plan for Sub-project Consultation Service," November 27, 2007, 52–58, http://www-wds.worldbank.org/external/default/WDSCon tentServer/WDSP/IB/2007/11/27/000020953_20071127145624/Rendered/PDF /41638.pdf.

13. Ibid. (ODA is overseas development assistance that rich countries provide nations such as China.)

14. Export-Import Bank of China, *2009 Annual Report* (Beijing: Export-Import Bank of China, 2009), http://english.eximbank.gov.cn/annual/2009/2009nb34 .shtml.

15. The World Bank, *China 2030: Building a Modern, Harmonious, and Creative High-Income Society* (Washington, DC: The World Bank, 2012), http://www.worldbank .org/content/dam/Worldbank/document/China-2030-complete.pdf.

16. World Trade Organization (WTO), "Comparative Advantage Is Dead? Not at All, Lamy Tells Paris Economists," news release, April 12, 2010, http://www.wto.org /english/news_e/sppl_e/sppl152_e.htm.

17. Ibid.

18. Paul Krugman, *Rethinking International Trade* (Boston, MA: MIT Press, 1994).

19. Josh Bivens, *Marketing the Gains from Trade* (Washington, DC: Economic Policy Institute, June 19, 2007), http://www.epi.org/publications/entry/ib233/.

20. International Bank for Reconstruction and Development, World Bank, *Information and Communications for Development 2009* (Washington, DC: World Bank, 2009), http://web.worldbank.org/WBSITE/EXTERNAL/TOPICS/EXTI NFORMATIONANDCOMMUNICATIONANDTECHNOLOGIES/EXTIC4D/o ,,contentMDK:22229759~menuPK:5870649~pagePK:64168445~piPK: 64168309~theSitePK:5870636,00.html. See also Asheeta Bhavnani et al., *The Role of Mobile Phones Is Sustainable Rural Poverty Reduction* (Washington, DC: World Bank, July 15, 2008), http://siteresources.worldbank.org/EXTINFORMA TIONANDCOMMUNICATIONANDTECHNOLOGIES/Resources/The_Role _of_Mobile_Phones_in_Sustainable_Rural_Poverty_Reduction_June_2008 .pdf.

21. Ibid.

22. Mohsen Khalil and Charles Kenny, "The Next Decade of ICT Development: Access, Applications and the Forces of Convergence" (working paper, World Bank, 2006), http://www-wds.worldbank.org/servlet/main?menuPK=64187510 &pagePK=64193027&piPK=64187937&theSitePK=523679&entityID= 000090341_20061219144328.

23. Christine Qiang, Zhen-Wei, and Alexander Pitt, "Contribution of Information and Communication Technologies to Growth" (working paper, World Bank, 2004), http://www-wds.worldbank.org/servlet/WDSContentServer/WDSP/IB/ 2004/02/02/000090341_20040202135005/Rendered/PDF/277160PAPER 0wbwp024.pdf.

24. Terence Stewart, "Opening Up the World Trade Organization," *Trade Flows from Stewart and Stewart* (blog), May 12, 2010, http://www.stewartlaw.com/stewart andstewart/TradeFlows/tabid/127/language/en-US/Default.aspx?udt_583 _param_detail=504. Under the WTO classification system, documents that are given a "JOB" number do not become part of the "official WTO documents" and hence escape categorization, listing, or derestriction to the public.

25. Thomas Lum, "U.S. Foreign Aid to East and South Asia: Selected Recipients," Congressional Research Service, October 8, 2008, http://www.fas.org/sgp/crs /row/RL31362.pdf.

26. "Germany Plans to Stop Giving Foreign Aid to China," *The Local*, October 30, 2009, http://www.thelocal.de/politics/20091030-22929.html.

27. Lum, "U.S. Foreign Aid to East and South Asia."
28. Jack Chow, "China's Billion Dollar Aid Appetite," *Foreign Policy*, July 19, 2010, http://www.foreignpolicy.com/articles/2010/07/19/chinas_billion_dollar_aid _appetite.
29. Ibid.
30. John Heilprin, "Global Fund for World Health Halts New Programs," *Guardian*, November 24, 2011, http://www.guardian.co.uk/world/feedarticle/9963924.
31. Overseas Private Investment Corporation, "India Private Equity Fund," http:// www.opic.gov/node/1140/ (accessed September 9, 2010).
32. Robert D. Atkinson, *Meeting the Offshoring Challenge* (Washington, DC: Progressive Policy Institute, July 2004), 10, http://www.dlc.org/documents/offshor ing2_0704.pdf.
33. Ibid.
34. Clyde Prestowitz, "The $64 Trillion Question (Part I)" *New Republic*, June 22, 2010, http://www.tnr.com/article/economy/75733/the-64-trillion-question-part-1/.
35. Office of the United States Trade Representative, "USTR Fact Sheet: The United States in the Trans-Pacific Partnership," http://www.ustr.gov/about-us/press -office/fact-sheets/2011/november/united-states-trans-pacific-partnership (accessed February 25, 2012).
36. Stephen Ezell and Robert D. Atkinson, *Gold Standard or WTO-Lite? Why the Trans-Pacific Partnership Must Be a True 21st Century Trade Agreement* (Washington, DC: ITIF, May 2011), http://www.itif.org/files/2011-trans-pacific-partnership .pdf.
37. Robert D. Atkinson, *Policies to Increase Broadband Adoption at Home* (Washington, DC: ITIF, November 2009), http://www.itif.org/files/2009-demand-side -policies.pdf.
38. Robert D. Atkinson, *Apocalypse Soon? Why Alan Blinder Gets It Wrong on Offshoring* (Washington, DC: ITIF, July 6, 2006), http://www.itif.org/files/blinder 1final.pdf.
39. *Globalization That Works for Working Americans, before the Committee on Ways and Means, U.S. House of Representatives*, 110th Cong. (January 30, 2007), testimony of Lawrence Mishel, president, Economic Policy Institute, http://www.epi .org/publications/entry/webfeatures_viewpoints_globalization_works_4all/.
40. Russell Shaw, "Mr. Outsourcing CEO, You're Evil," *Huffington Post* (blog), November 22, 2005, http://www.huffingtonpost.com/russell-shaw/mr-outsourcing -ceo-youre-_b_11095.html.
41. Thomas Donohue, "Accessing New Markets: New Opportunities" (presentation, Forum on Global Leadership, IBM Corporation, Washington, DC, July 25, 2007), http://www.ibm.com/ibm/globalleadership/event_presentations.shtml.
42. Dianna Farrell, "Who Wins in Offshoring?" *International Herald Tribune*, February 7, 2004.
43. Martin Carnoy and Derek Schearer, *Economic Democracy: The Challenge of the 1980s* (New York: Random House, 1980).

44. Harold Meyerson, "Corporate America, Paving a Downward Economic Slide," *Washington Post,* January 5, 2011, http://www.washingtonpost.com/wp-dyn/con tent/article/2011/01/04/AR2011010403742.html.

45. Alan Tonelson, "After the Bailout, Congress Must Get Down to the Real Economic Policy Work," AmericanEconomicAlert.org, September 29, 2008, http:// americaneconomicalert.org/view_art.asp?Prod_ID=3056.

46. Kevin Hechtkopf, "Rick Perry Fails to Remember What Agency He'd Get Rid of in GOP Debate," *CBS News,* November 9, 2011, http://www.cbsnews.com/8301 -503544_162-57321982-503544/rick-perry-fails-to-remember-what-agency-hed -get-rid-of-in-gop-debate/?tag=contentMain;contentBody.

47. Linda Cohen and Roger Noll, *The Technology Pork Bell* (Washington, DC: Brookings Institution Press, 1991).

INDEX

global economic institutions: failure of, 339–348; in global innovation system, 350–352, 358–359

Global Fund to Fight AIDS, Tuberculosis, and Malaria, 353–354

global innovation advantage: competitiveness in, 5–8; decline and growth in, 4–5; governments' roles in, 14–15

Global Innovation Index, 89

global innovation system, creating: and failure of global innovation institutions, 339–348; international innovation policy framework for, 348–359; and U.S. innovation policy leadership, 359–366; vision for, 338–339

Global Science and Innovation Foundation (GSIF), 358–359

goals, in crafting innovation policy, 163–166, 228–229

Goldman, Mark, 318–319

Gompers, Samuel, 70

Google, 139

government-owned enterprises, 204–205, 304–305, 306

government(s): business attitudes toward, 289–292; and free market, 142; as global competitors, 91–101, 159–161; growth of U.S., 39–40; and institutional innovation, 180–181; intervention of, in markets, 98–99, 102–103; and investment-deterring economic policies, 74–75; neoclassical economists' view on, 295–296; and prioritizing innovation, 297–300; and private-sector regulation, 360–361; as R&D investor, 145–146; role of, in global innovation, 14–15, 27, 62–63; role of, in industrial development, 69, 72–74; role of, in innovation, 135–141, 361–362, 365

Great Britain. *See* United Kingdom

Great Recession: effects of, 1–2; and long-term U.S. structural decline, 33–34; nature and causes of, 17–32; and U.S. corporate R&D investment, 51–52

Green, Kenneth, 115–116

green energy products manufacturing. *See* clean technology

Greenspan, Alan, 29

groupthink, 231

Grove, Andy, 291–292

GSIF (Global Science and Innovation Foundation), 358–359

Guangzhou Wuyang Steel Structure Corporation, 204

Gurria, Angel, 130

Hancock, Russell, 54

"hardware" of innovation, 110

"Harrison Bergeron" (Vonnegut), 223–224

Hassett, Kevin, 82, 92, 116

health assistance, international, 353–354

health IT, 187, 257, 258

HEEAP (Higher Engineering Education Alliance Program), 105

Helpman, Elhanan, 295

Higher Engineering Education Alliance Program (HEEAP), 105

high school completion, in United States, 54

high-skills immigration, 262–263

high-speed rail market, 199–200

high-value-added sectors, 92–94, 115–121, 216–217, 220, 236–237

Himmelberg, Charles, 28, 29–30

Horie, Takfumi, 332

Horizon 2020, 324

Houseman, Susan, 39, 120

housing market collapse, 18–21, 24–31

Hout, Thomas, 206

Hu Jintao, 107